TextGraphs-17: Graph-based Methods for Natural Language Processing

Bangkok, Thailand
15 August 2024

ISBN: 979-8-3313-0180-4

Printed from e-media with permission by:

Curran Associates, Inc.
57 Morehouse Lane
Red Hook, NY 12571

Some format issues inherent in the e-media version may also appear in this print version.

Association for Computational Linguistics
209 N. Eighth Street
Stroudsburg, Pennsylvania 18360

Phone: 1-570-476-8006
Fax: 1-570-476-0860

acl@aclweb.org

Additional copies of this publication are available from:

Curran Associates, Inc.
57 Morehouse Lane
Red Hook, NY 12571 USA
Phone: 845-758-0400
Fax: 845-758-2633
Email: curran@proceedings.com
Web: www.proceedings.com

TextGraphs @ ACL 2024

Proceedings of TextGraphs-17: Graph-based Methods for Natural Language Processing

The 62nd Annual Meeting of the Association of Computational Linguistics

August 15, 2024

The TextGraphs @ ACL organizers gratefully acknowledge the support from the following sponsors.

Shared Task

JETBRAINS

Association for Computational Linguistics (ACL)
317 Sidney Baker St. S
Suite 400 - 134
Kerrville, TX 78028
USA
Tel: +1-855-225-1962
acl@aclweb.org

Preface

Welcome to the seventeenth edition of TextGraphs, the workshop on graph-based methods for natural language processing. This edition was organized on August 15, 2024, in Bangkok, Thailand, co-located with the 62nd Annual Meeting of the Association for Computational Linguistics (ACL 2024). **TextGraphs-17 commemorates Prof. Dragomir Radev (1968–2023) and his seminal contributions to the TextGraphs community and the natural language processing field.**

Recent years have witnessed remarkable advances in natural language processing (NLP) and graph theory domains that mostly develop independently with rare intersections. The seventeenth edition of the TextGraphs workshop surpassed its boundaries, widening the workshop topic coverage to capture not only a well-studied graph domain but a more general yet underexplored structured data domain as well. Besides, we strongly encouraged novel research efforts that aim to explore the hot topic of the large language model (LLM) prompting from the unique perspective of graph theory. Thus, our workshop sought to establish more mutually beneficial relationships between NLP and structured data to address the pivotal limitations of each domain.

Toward this end, the key topic for TextGraphs-17 was **Knowledge Graphs meet LLMs**. A proper utilization of graph-based methods for reasoning over a Knowledge Graph (KG) is a prospective way to overcome critical limitations of the existing LLMs which lack interpretability and factual knowledge and are prone to the hallucination problem. Vice versa, the incorporation of LLM knowledge discovered from large textual collections may help many graph-related tasks, such as KG completion and graph representation learning. This topic calls for research on the joint use of KG and LLM for improved processing of either the NLP or graph domain. In line with this topic, a shared task on KGQA was organized and co-located with the workshop.

We highlight three more topics relevant to the TextGraphs workshop:

- **Chain Prompting of LLMs.** Recent studies show that prompting strategies like Chain-of-Thought and Graph-of-Thought enhance language understanding and generation tasks compared to the traditional few-shot methods. This topic calls for research on advanced prompting schemes and software for LLMs and other pre-trained machine learning models.
- **Learning from Structured Data.** This topic calls for research that bridges textual and structured data formats, including relational and non-relational databases, as well as standardized data formats (such as XML, JSON, RDF, etc.)
- **Interpretability of NLP Systems.** This topic calls for research which adopts structured data and employs graph-based methods to shed light on decision-making and logic behind modern LLMs. This includes work on applying a KG to explore and evaluate factual awareness, treating the interpretability problem from the GT perspective, or other applications of graphs to make LLMs more understandable.

Besides the main paper presentations, we ran a shared task on Knowledge Graph Question Answering (KGQA). In this task, given a textual question and a list of entities with the corresponding KG subgraphs, the participating system should choose the entity that correctly answers the question. Our competition attracted thirty teams, four of which outperformed our strong ChatGPT-based zero-shot baseline.

Overall, this year, we received 25 submissions, out of which 8 submissions were accepted, 7 submissions were accepted as shared task papers (including a report by shared task organizers), 8 submissions were rejected by the reviewers, and 2 submissions were desk rejected.

We want to thank our keynote speaker, Rada Mihalcea, and we are also thankful to the members of the program committee for their valuable and high-quality reviews. Their expert feedback has benefited all submissions. Their timely contribution was the basis for accepting an excellent list of papers and making the seventeenth edition of TextGraphs a success. Also, we are grateful to JetBrains, which provided prizes for the competition participants.

Dmitry Ustalov, Yanjun Gao, Alexander Panchenko, Elena Tutubalina, Irina Nikishina, Arti Ramesh, Andrey Sakhovskiy, Ricardo Usbeck, Gerald Penn, Marco Valentino

TextGraphs-17 Organizers

August 2024

Organizing Committee

General Chair

Dmitry Ustalov, JetBrains, Serbia

Program Chairs

Alexander Panchenko, Artificial Intelligence Research Institute, Russia
Elena Tutubalina, Artificial Intelligence Research Institute, Russia
Irina Nikishina, University of Hamburg, Germany
Arti Ramesh, Binghamton University, USA
Andrey Sakhovskiy, Kazan Federal University, Russia
Ricardo Usbeck, University of Hamburg, Germany
Gerald Penn, University of Toronto, Canada
Marco Valentino, Idiap Research Institute, Switzerland

Publication Chair

Yanjun Gao, University of Wisconsin-Madison, USA

Keynote Talk

A Legacy of Graphs: Celebrating Dragomir Radev's Contributions to Graph-Based Natural Language Processing

Rada Mihalcea
University of Michigan

2024-08-15 14:00:00 – Room: **Centara Grand and Bangkok Convention Centre, Thailand**

Bio: Rada Mihalcea is the Janice M. Jenkins Professor of Computer Science and Engineering at the University of Michigan and the Director of the Michigan Artificial Intelligence Lab. Her research interests are in natural language processing, with a focus on multimodal processing and computational social sciences. She is an ACM Fellow, a AAAI Fellow, and served as ACL President (2018–2022 Vice/Past). She is the recipient of a Sarah Goddard Power award (2019) for her contributions to diversity in science, and the recipient of a Presidential Early Career Award for Scientists and Engineers awarded by President Obama (2009).

Table of Contents

Program

Thursday, August 15, 2024

09:00 - 09:10	*Opening Remarks*
09:10 - 09:30	*Learning Human Action Representations from Temporal Context in Lifestyle Vlogs*
09:30 - 09:50	*ConGraT: Self-Supervised Contrastive Pretraining for Joint Graph and Text Embeddings*
09:50 - 10:10	*A Pipeline Approach for Parsing Documents into Uniform Meaning Representation Graphs*
10:10 - 10:30	*Financial Product Ontology Population with Large Language Models*
10:30 - 11:00	*Break 1*
11:00 - 11:20	*Prompt Me One More Time: A Two-Step Knowledge Extraction Pipeline with Ontology-Based Verification*
11:20 - 11:40	*Towards Understanding Attention-based Reasoning through Graph Structures in Medical Codes Classification*
11:40 - 12:00	*Leveraging Graph Structures to Detect Hallucinations in Large Language Models*
12:00 - 12:20	*Semantic Graphs for Syntactic Simplification: A Revisit from the Age of LLM*
12:30 - 14:00	*Lunch Break*
14:00 - 15:00	*Invited Talk: A Legacy of Graphs: Celebrating Dragomir Radev's Contributions to Graph-Based Natural Language Processing*
15:00 - 15:30	*TextGraphs 2024 Shared Task on Text-Graph Representations for Knowledge Graph Question Answering.*
15:30 - 16:00	*Break 2*
16:00 - 17:30	*Poster Session*

Learning Human Action Representations from Temporal Context in Lifestyle Vlogs

Oana Ignat Santiago Castro Weiji Li Rada Mihalcea
University of Michigan - Ann Arbor, USA
oignat@umich.edu

Abstract

We address the task of human action representation and show how the approach of generating word representations based on co-occurrence can be adapted to generate human action representations by analyzing their co-occurrence in videos. To this end, we formalize the new task of human action co-occurrence identification in online videos, i.e., determine whether two human actions are likely to co-occur in the same interval of time. We create and make publicly available the CO-ACT (Action Co-occurrence) dataset, consisting of a large graph of $\sim$12k co-occurring pairs of visual actions and their corresponding video clips. We describe graph link prediction models that leverage visual and textual information to automatically infer if two actions are co-occurring. We show that graphs are particularly well suited to capture relations between human actions, and the learned graph representations are effective for our task and capture novel and relevant information across different data domains.

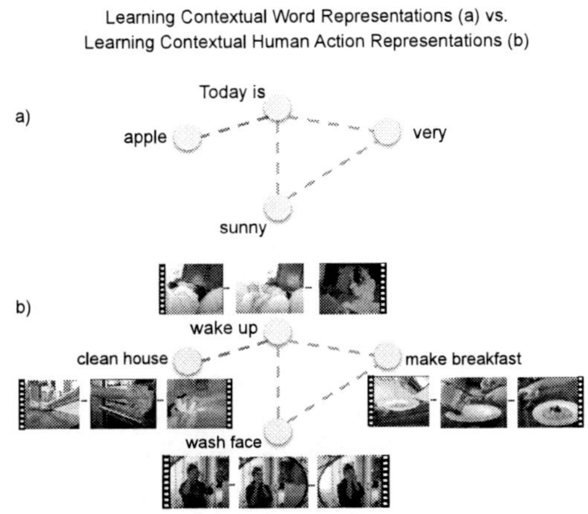

Figure 1: We draw inspiration from contextual word representations to create novel action representations based on video temporal context. Specifically, when predicting the next word in a sentence, it is more expected to see certain words, for instance, after "Today is" an expected word is "sunny" and not "apple". Similarly, human actions also follow a certain pattern, for instance, after "waking up", an expected next action is to "wash the face" and not to "clean the house".

1 Introduction

Action understanding is a long-standing goal in the development of intelligent systems that can meaningfully interact with humans, with recent progress made in several fields including natural language processing (Fast et al., 2016; Wilson and Mihalcea, 2017, 2019), computer vision (Carreira and Zisserman, 2017; Shou et al., 2017; Tran et al., 2018; Chao et al., 2018; Girdhar et al., 2019; Feichtenhofer et al., 2019), data mining (Kato et al., 2018; Xu et al., 2019), and others. Many of the action understanding systems developed to date, however, rely mostly on pattern memorization and do not effectively understand the action, which makes them fragile and unable to adapt to new settings (Sigurdsson et al., 2017; Kong and Fu, 2018).

Effective action understanding requires reliable action representations. In this paper, we introduce a strategy to generate contextual representations for human actions by adopting an approach for creating word representations based on co-occurrence information. In linguistics, co-occurrence is defined as an above-chance frequency of ordered occurrence of two adjacent terms in a text corpus. For example, if the concepts "peanut butter", "jelly", and "sandwich" appear more often together than apart, they would be grouped into a concept co-occurrence rule. Co-occurrence is a building block concept for word representations and language models. We adapt this approach to human actions, which also have their own co-occurrence relations, expressed as temporal context. Most human actions are interconnected, as an action that ends is usually followed by the start of a related action and not a random one (e.g., after "waking up", one would "wash face" or "make breakfast" and not "sell books" or "go to bed"). We model this information through co-occurrence relations: in general, we expect that the

Proceedings of TextGraphs-17: Graph-based Methods for Natural Language Processing, pages 1–18
August 15, 2024

actions 'wake up", "wash face" and "make breakfast" co-occur in a short interval of time, while "wake up", "clean house" or "go to bed" do not. A natural way to model the connections between human actions is through a graph representation, where actions are represented as nodes, and their co-occurrences are represented as edges (Fig. 1).

The interconnection of human actions is well captured in lifestyle vlogs, where vloggers visually record their everyday routine consisting of the activities they perform during a regular day (Fouhey et al., 2018; Ignat et al., 2019, 2021). We collect a dataset of lifestyle vlogs from YouTube that are currently very challenging for systems to solve.

Contributions. Our paper makes four main contributions. First, we show how the approach to generating word representations based on co-occurrence can be adapted to generating representations for human actions by analyzing their co-occurrence in videos. To this end, **we formalize the new human action co-occurrence identification task** in online videos. Second, **we introduce a new dataset**, CO-ACT, consisting of a large graph of co-occurring actions in online vlogs. Third, **we propose several models to solve the task of human action co-occurrence**, by using textual, visual, multi-modal, and graph-based action representations. Finally, **we show that our action representations based on co-occurrence capture novel and relevant information across different data domains**, which leads to rich avenues for future work for improving action representation and making progress toward the broader goal of action understanding.

2 Related Work

There are three areas of research related to our work: human action co-occurrence, graph link prediction and webly-supervised learning

Human Action Co-occurrence. Recent work shows that action co-occurrence priors (Kim et al., 2020, 2021) increase the performance of human-object interaction models and lead to more effective training, especially in long-tail classes. Unlike our work, they assume that the action co-occurrence information is provided and do not attempt to learn it. To the best of our knowledge, we are the first to propose the task of learning human action co-occurrence in videos.

Human action co-occurrence identification is also related to learning action temporal order in videos which is used to construct the co-occurring action pairs. Misra et al. (2016) propose the task of temporal order verification, i.e., to determine whether a sequence of frames from a video is in the correct temporal order. Using this simple task and no semantic labels, they learn visual representation. In our work, we learn action representations using the information extracted from the action co-occurrence graph, a more general relation reflecting a shared context among the actions.

Link Prediction. Link prediction is a key problem for graph-structured data and is relevant for our graph formulation of action co-occurrence. The objective of link prediction is to predict whether two nodes in a graph are likely to be linked (Liben-Nowell and Kleinberg, 2007).

Link prediction approaches can be categorized into three main categories (Kumar et al., 2020): similarity-based/heuristic (Newman, 2001; Jaccard, 1901; Salton and McGill, 1983; Adamic and Adar, 2003; Ravasz et al., 2002; Zhou et al., 2009; Liben-Nowell and Kleinberg, 2007); probabilistic-based (Kashima and Abe, 2006); and dimensionality reduction-based (e.g., embedding-based or other learning approaches; Grover and Leskovec, 2016; Kipf and Welling, 2017).

For our task, we apply the similarity-based, embedding-based, and learning-based models. Similarity-based methods are the simplest and measure similarity between every pair of nodes using topology properties of the graph (e.g., common neighbors). The embedding-based link prediction models map the embedding of nodes to a lower dimension such that similar nodes have similar embeddings. The learning-based link prediction models can be cast using supervised classification models where a point corresponds to a node pair in the graph, and the point label represents the presence or absence of an edge/link between the pair.

Webly-Supervised Learning. In our work, we identify human action co-occurrence in the context of rich, virtually unlimited, constantly evolving online videos from YouTube, using the video transcripts as a web supervision signal. Large-scale video datasets on instructional videos (Miech et al., 2019) and lifestyle vlogs (Fouhey et al., 2018; Ignat et al., 2019, 2021, 2022) are other examples of web supervision. The latter is similar to our work as they analyze online vlogs, but unlike ours, their focus is on action detection or the reasons behind actions and not on action co-occurrence.

3 Dataset

To develop and test models for determining if two actions co-occur, we compile a novel dataset, which we refer to as CO-ACT (Action Co-occurrencE).

3.1 Data Collection

We start by compiling a set of lifestyle videos from YouTube, consisting of people performing their daily routine activities, such as cleaning, cooking, studying, relaxing, etc. We build a data-gathering pipeline to automatically extract and filter videos and their transcripts.

We select 20 YouTube channels and download all the videos and their transcripts. The channels are selected to have good-quality videos with automatically generated transcripts containing detailed verbal descriptions of the actions depicted.

An analysis of the videos indicates that both the textual and visual information are rich sources for describing not only the actions but also in what order the actions are performed, making them a great source of data for developing action co-occurrence models. The routine nature of the videos means that the vloggers record and describe their actions in the order they normally occur in a day: e.g., "wake up", "make bed", "wash face", "make breakfast", "drive to work", and so on. They can also choose to focus on certain activities (e.g., often cooking) and enumerate more fine-grained actions related to those activities (e.g., "cut apple", "add peanut butter"). Therefore, our dataset contains both general and fine-grained actions. We present data analyses in Appendix A.2.

Action extraction. Having a comprehensive list of actions is necessary for creating graphs that contain most of the actions in the videos. At the same time, not all the actions from the transcripts are useful, as many of them are not visible in the video or hard to detect by computer vision systems (e.g., "feel", "talk", "thank", "hope", "need", "see').

Therefore, we first ensure that the actions we collect are mostly visible in the videos. Our strategy is to extract all the verbs from the transcripts and then filter them using a list of "visual verbs" collected from imSitu (Yatskar et al., 2016), COCO-a (Ronchi and Perona, 2015) and Levin (Levin, 1993).[1] Verbs from imSitu and COCO-a are considered visual as the dataset collection pipelines include an explicit annotation step to determine if verbs are visual. We manually filter and check the verbs collected from Levin.

Next, we extract all actions from the video transcripts using the dependency parser from spaCy (Honnibal et al., 2020) by extracting all the verbs and their corresponding verb phrase direct objects, prepositions, and objects of prepositions. We find that extracting only verbs and their corresponding direct objects does not always return comprehensive actions (e.g., "add teaspoon" versus "add a teaspoon of salt"). We also find that many verbs do not have informative direct objects (e.g., "write it", "clean them"), which makes the actions harder to differentiate and visually recognize. To address this, we apply co-reference resolution on the video transcripts using spaCy (Honnibal et al., 2020) NeuralCoref[2] model and re-extract the actions from the processed transcripts.

Finally, we obtain our visible actions by filtering all the transcript-extracted actions that contain visual verbs.

Video extraction. As transcripts are temporally aligned with videos, we can obtain meaningful video clips related to the narration. We extract clips corresponding to the visual actions based on transcript timestamps. From 2,571 videos, we obtain 19,685 unique video clips and 25,057 (action, video-clip) pairs. Note that an action can be present in multiple video clips, and conversely, a video clip can contain multiple actions. To control the number of clips per action, we randomly sample up to 10 random video clips for each action and finally obtain 12,994 (action, video-clip) sampled pairs.

Quality Assurance. As described above, we perform multiple steps to ensure the actions appear in the videos. First, we manually select 20 YouTube channels from vloggers with high-quality filming styles, who usually provide detailed visual and textual descriptions of their actions. Second, we automatically extract actions that contain visual verbs. We manually check around 100 extracted actions to see if they are parsed well and if they correctly match their corresponding video and transcript context. Third, we automatically filter out videos that do not contain any transcripts or no significant motion. We filter out the motionless videos by following the procedure from Ignat et al. (2019): we sample one out of every one hundred frames of the videos and compute the 2D correlation coefficient between these sampled frames. We filter out all the videos with a median of the values greater than a threshold (0.8). We manually check around 100 (action, video) pairs to see if they correctly match and find around 18 complete misalignments. Finally, to mediate the misalignment and obtain diverse filming perspectives, we randomly sample up

[1] Levin's taxonomy provides a classification of 3,024 verbs (4,186 senses) into 48 broad and 192 fine-grained classes. We leave analyzing the Levin verb taxonomy impact on human action model performance as a future work direction.

[2] https://spacy.io/universe/project/neuralcoref

	#Verbs	#Actions	#Action pairs
Initial	608	20,718	-
Co-occurrence	439	18,939	80,776
Clustering	172	2,513	48,934
Graph	164	2,262	11,711

Table 1: Statistics for the collected number of unique verbs, actions, and co-occurring action pairs at each stage of data pre-processing.

to 10 video clips for each action, which increases the chances that the action is present in at least one video. Random examples of actions and their video-frames are found in sample-frames.

3.2 Data Pre-processing

After collecting videos, transcripts, and actions, the following data pre-processing steps are applied.

Action Co-occurrence Selection. From all the extracted visual actions, we automatically select all the action pairs that are co-occurring. We define two actions as co-occurring if they are less than 10 seconds away from each other. The 10 seconds is an *intermediate value threshold* we set after experimenting with other values. This threshold controls the scale of time we choose to focus on when collecting co-occurring actions: e.g., mostly short actions (e.g., "open fridge", "get milk") are captured in a small interval of time (1-5 sec), while longer intervals allow for longer and more diverse actions to co-occur (e.g., "prepare meal"). We choose an intermediate value that allows for both shorter and longer actions to co-occur[3]. Our intuition is that modeling the relations between both shorter and longer actions would result in learning more comprehensive information about human actions. We also consider the in-depth analysis of this threshold and its downstream effects as an interesting future work direction and our framework allows for effortless threshold tune.

For computing the distance in time between two actions, we use the transcript time stamps. This allows scaling data with no constraints from the annotation budget. The transcript time stamps do not always match the time the action appears in the video. However, this hardly impacts our task because the actions mentioned in the transcript usually follow the order from the video. Furthermore, we mediate misalignments by collecting multiple videos per action and filtering steps described in the previous section.

[3]The captured actions also depend on the filming style (e.g., vloggers could increase the filming time of normally short actions).

Action Clustering. We find that many actions are often very similar in meaning. This leads to many action repetitions: e.g., "use iron", "iron shirt", "iron cloth". To avoid such repetitions, we group similar actions by clustering all actions. We represent each action using the pre-trained model Sentence-BERT (Reimers and Gurevych, 2019) and apply Agglomerative Clustering (Murtagh and Legendre, 2014). We filter out the clusters of actions with less than two actions, as they are likely to be outliers that were not well extracted. The actions in each cluster are then renamed to the most common action in the cluster: e.g., "iron shirt" and "iron cloth" are renamed to "use iron".

We observe that the clustering model is introducing some noise level as it does not perfectly cluster all actions. We tried to mitigate this with different Sentence-BERT pre-trained models for sentence similarity[4] and fine-tuning our clustering model hyper-parameters[5] based on automatic evaluation metrics for measuring the quality of clusters[6].

Action Graph Filtering. After we rename the actions based on clustering, we create a graph where the nodes represent the actions, and the edges represent the relations between two actions. Specifically, we create an undirected graph for each video, where the graph nodes are represented by the actions in the video and the co-occurring actions are connected by an edge. Each edge has a weight equal to the number of times the corresponding actions co-occur in the video.

We combine all the video graphs to obtain a single large graph that contains all the co-occurring actions in our data. We filter out the action pairs that co-occur only once in the graph (their edge weight equals one), as their co-occurrence relation is not strong and might be random. We show the statistics before and after all the action filtering steps in Table 1. More information (e.g., action frequency distributions, action pairs) can be found in Appendix A.

3.3 ACE vs. current Human Action Datasets

Many publicly available visual action datasets (Carreira and Zisserman, 2017; Soomro et al., 2012; Kuehne et al., 2011) do not have video transcripts and do not have videos with multiple actions presented in their natural order, therefore we cannot leverage the textual information and the relations

[4]sbert.net/docs/pretrained_models.html

[5]linkage distance threshold (1.5), linkage criterion (ward)

[6]Silhouette Coefficient (Rousseeuw, 1987), Calinski-Harabasz Score (Caliński and Harabasz, 1974), and Davies-Bouldin Index (Davies and Bouldin, 1979)

between actions, as we can do in our dataset.

The majority of human actions datasets with transcripts are restricted to one or few domains (e.g., cooking (Zhou et al., 2018) or instructional videos (Miech et al., 2019; Tang et al., 2019)). The main difference between lifestyle vlogs and instructional videos is the domain of the actions. Instructional videos are usually from just one domain (e.g., either cooking, repairing, or construction) and tend to have a specialized vocabulary (e.g., car repair). Lifestyle vlogs contain various everyday actions from multiple domains in the same video (cleaning, cooking, DIY, entertainment, personal care). Due to the diversity of domains in our data, our model learns not only the co-occurrence between in-domain actions (e.g., cooking: "cut potato" & "add onion") but also the relations from different domains (e.g., personal care and cooking: "wash face" & "make breakfast").

4 Action Co-occurrence in Vlogs

We formulate our action co-occurrence identification task as a link prediction task. Link prediction aims to predict the existence of a link between two nodes in a graph. In our setup, nodes are represented by actions, and every two co-occurring actions are connected by a weighted edge, where the weight represents the number of times the two actions co-occur. Our goal is to determine if an edge exists between two given actions.[7]

4.1 Data Representation

Textual Representations. To represent the textual data – actions and their transcript context, we use Sentence Embeddings computed using the pre-trained model Sentence-BERT embeddings (Reimers and Gurevych, 2019) calculated using the graph topology and the textual embeddings obtained from CLIP (Radford et al., 2021). When computing CLIP textual action embeddings, we concatenate the action with given prompts (e.g., "This is a photo of a person"), as described in the original paper (Radford et al., 2021).

Video Representations. We use the CLIP model (Radford et al., 2021) to represent all the actions and their corresponding video clips. One action can have multiple video clips: an action has at most 10 corresponding videos. From each video clip, we extract four equally spaced frames and preprocess them as done before (Radford et al., 2021). We use the pre-trained Vision Transformer model ViT-B/16 (Dosovitskiy et al., 2021) to encode the video frames and the textual information. We apply the model to each of the four frames and average their representations (Luo et al., 2021).

Graph Representations. We also use the training graph topology information (node neighbors and edge weights) to compute action embeddings as the weighted average of all of their neighbor node embeddings, where the weights are edge weights (i.e., how many times the two nodes co-occur). The neighbor node embeddings are represented using either textual embeddings (Sentence-BERT; Reimers and Gurevych, 2019) or visual embeddings (CLIP; Radford et al., 2021). All the graph-based models described in the next section use graph topology information from the validation graph (see Section 5.1).

We use the representations described above as input to different action co-occurrence models.

4.2 Action Co-occurrence Models

We explore many models with various input representations. We group the models as described in the related work link prediction section: random baseline, heuristic-based models (graph topology models), embedding-based models (cosine similarity and graph neural networks), and learning-based models (SVM models). As described in Section 4.1, we run experiments with various types of data representations: Textual: Action and Action Transcript; Visual: Action, Video, and Multi-modal (Action&Videos; the average between action and video visual embeddings); Graph: Action and Multi-modal (Action&Videos) using graph topology.

4.2.1 Random Baseline

The action pairs to be predicted as co-occurring or not are split into equal amounts, therefore a random baseline would have an accuracy score of 50%.

4.2.2 Heuristic-based Graph Topology Models

We apply several popular node similarity methods that only use graph topology information in the prediction process: Common Neighbours (Newman, 2001), Salton Index (Salton and McGill, 1983), Adamic-Adar Index (Adamic and Adar, 2003), Hub Promoted Index (Ravasz et al., 2002), and Shortest Path (Liben-Nowell and Kleinberg, 2007). Note that the heuristic-based methods do not use any data representations described in Section 4.1. We describe each of the methods above:

Notation. Let s_{xy} be the similarity between nodes x and y, $\Gamma(x)$ be the set of nodes connected to node x and k_x be the degree of node x.

[7] At this point, we do not aim to also identify the strength of the link.

Common Neighbours. Two nodes are more likely to be connected if they have more common neighbors.

$$s_{xy} = |\Gamma(x) \cap \Gamma(y)| \quad (1)$$

Salton Index. Measures the cosine of the angle between columns of the adjacency matrix corresponding to given nodes.

$$s_{xy} = \frac{|\Gamma(x) \cap \Gamma(y)|}{\sqrt{k_x k_y}} \quad (2)$$

Hub Promoted Index. This measure assigns higher scores to edges adjacent to hubs (high-degree nodes), as the denominator depends on the minimum degree of the nodes of interest.

$$s_{xy} = \frac{|\Gamma(x) \cap \Gamma(y)|}{\min\{k_x, k_y\}} \quad (3)$$

Adamic-Adar Index. This measure counts common neighbors by assigning weights to nodes inversely proportional to their degrees. That means that a common neighbor, which is unique for a few nodes only, is more important than a hub.

$$s_{xy} = \sum_{z \in \Gamma(x) \cap \Gamma(y)} \frac{1}{\log k_z} \quad (4)$$

Shortest Path. The similarity score is inversely proportional to the length of the shortest path between two nodes.

$$s_{xy} = \frac{1}{min\{l : path_{xy}^{<l>} exists\}} \quad (5)$$

Weighted Graph Models. Our graph is weighted, therefore we also apply weighted graph models. We modify some of the above models (Common Neighbours, Adamic-Adar Index) to use the link weight information, as proposed in Zhu and Xia (2016). We find that using link weights achieves similar results as without them.

4.2.3 Embedding-based Models

Cosine Similarity. We compute the cosine similarity between their embeddings to determine if two given actions co-occur. If the similarity score is greater than a threshold fine-tuned on validation data, we predict the actions as co-occurring.

Graph Neural Networks. We also use Graph Neural Network (GNN) models. We choose four diverse and popular models (Kumar et al., 2020): attri2vec (Zhang et al., 2019), GraphSAGE (Hamilton et al., 2017), GCN (Kipf and Welling, 2017). GNN models can also be classified as learning-based models: they learn a new heuristic from a given network, as opposed to Graph Topology models, which use predefined heuristics, i.e., score functions. We create our graph based on a known heuristic: co-occurring actions are closely connected in the graph. Therefore, we hypothesize that heuristic models will perform better. Indeed, we observe that for our graph, the GNN methods do not perform better than the heuristic models: the best-performing model is GraphSAGE with 77.2% accuracy, while the best-performing topology model has an 82.9% accuracy (see Table 2). Therefore, we conclude that our task does not benefit from these neural models.

4.2.4 Learning-based Model

We run a support vector machine (SVM) (Cortes and Vapnik, 1995) classifier on each action pair to be classified as co-occurring. We concatenate all the input representations and the heuristic scores, and we standardize the features by removing the mean and scaling to unit variance. We fine-tune the model hyper-parameters (kernel, C, gamma) on the validation data using a grid search.

5 Evaluation

We conduct extensive experiments to evaluate the action pairs co-occurrence identification task. The task can be represented as a graph link prediction task. Therefore, we adopt the link prediction evaluation process.

5.1 Evaluation Data Split

We split the original graph into train, validation, and test graphs. In link prediction, the goal is to predict which links will appear in the future of an evolving graph. Therefore, while keeping the same number of nodes as the original graph, the number of edges is changed as some of the edges are removed during each split and used as the positive samples for training, fine-tuning, and testing the link prediction models. The edges are split into the train, validation, and test sets using a transductive split, which is considered the default evaluation splitting technique for link prediction models (Xu et al., 2018). Specifically, we randomly sample 10% of all existing edges from the original graph as positive testing data and the same number of nonexistent edges (unconnected node pairs) as negative testing data. The reduced graph becomes the test graph and, together with the set of sampled edges, is used for testing the models. We repeat the same procedure to create the validation and the train data for the models. The validation graph is created by reducing the test graph, and the training graph is created by reducing the validation graph.

Model	Accuracy
BASELINE	
Random	50.0
HEURISTIC-BASED	
Common Neighbours	82.9
Salton Index	71.2
Hub Promoted Index	78.3
Adamic-Adar Index	82.9
Shortest Path	82.9
EMBEDDING-BASED	
Cosine similarity	82.8
attri2vec	65.7
GCN	77.2
GraphSAGE	78.1
LEARNING-BASED	
SVM	**91.1**

Table 2: Accuracy results for all the models.

5.2 Results and Ablations

Table 2 contains the results, measured by accuracy, for each model type. The learning-based model, SVM, using all input representations (textual, visual, graph) and all graph heuristic scores obtains the highest accuracy score. Therefore, using both graph topology information and textual embeddings leads to the best performance for our task. The results for each of the heuristic-based graph-topology models are shown in Table 2. Simple heuristics (common neighbors or shortest path) are enough to perform well.

Modality Ablation. The ablation results, split by input representation are shown in Table 3. We analyze how different input representations influence the model's performance: textual (Sentence-BERT and CLIP textual) vs. visual (CLIP visual) vs. multi-modal (CLIP textual and visual) vs. graph (Sentence-BERT and CLIP textual and visual). The input representations are described in Section 4.1. The textual embeddings are a strong signal for our task, even when not using any graph information: SVM with only Action Sentence-BERT embeddings has a 76.3% accuracy. Using graph representations or graph heuristic information leads to significantly better performance (80.9% and 91.1% accuracy, respectively). The visual and multi-modal embeddings are also valuable but perform worse than the textual embeddings. We hypothesize that CLIP embeddings might be affected by the time misalignment between the transcript and the video. However, the visual modality offers important information about human actions and can be used in future work with more robust visual models.

5.3 Downstream Task: Action Retrieval

Similar to how word embeddings have been used for word similarity and for retrieving similar words and documents (Mikolov et al., 2013; Devlin et al., 2019), our graph dataset enables *action similarity* and *similar action retrieval* leveraging action-specific properties in the multi-modal space.

To show the usefulness of our graph-based action embeddings, we test them on the *similar action retrieval* downstream task. Specifically, we compare two action representations: textual (Action Sentence-BERT embeddings) and graph-based (graph weighted average of neighbor nodes Action Sentence-BERT embeddings). In Fig. 2, we show the top three nearest neighbor actions from each of the representations for three random action queries from our dataset. We observe that *each representation captures different types of information*. The actions obtained with textual representations are more syntactically similar to the action query, sharing either the verb or the object. This can be undesirable, as many retrieved actions are too repetitive and not always relevant to the action query: e.g., "build desk": "build bookshelf", "build house". In contrast, the actions obtained with graph representations are more *diverse* and capture *location information*, i.e., actions expected to be temporally close in a video: e.g., "build desk": "use knife", "add storage", "put piece of wood".

Novelty vs. Relevance in Action Retrieval. A major focus in the field of Information Retrieval has been the development of retrieval models that maximize both the relevance and the novelty among higher-ranked documents (Carbonell and Goldstein-Stewart, 1998). For the task of action retrieval, we can approximate *relevance* through the *location* relevance of an action, and *novelty* through the *diversity* of the actions retrieved.

Diversity in Action Representations. Similar to word or document retrieval, diversity in action retrieval reflects novel results. To measure the *diversity* captured by the action representations, we compute the *overlap score* as the number of overlapping words between the action query and the retrieved top k action nearest neighbors, divided by the total number of words in the retrieved actions. For example, in Fig. 2, the action query "chop potato", for $k = 3$, the action kNNs using textual representations (in blue) have 3 overlapping words ("chop", "potato", "potato"), from a total

Model	Input Representations						
	Textual		Visual			Graph	
	Action	Transcript	Action	Video	Action&Video	Action	Action&Video
Cosine Similarity	60.6	65.2	62.7	57.0	65.4	**82.8**	50.6
SVM	76.3	71.1	73.1	76.2	76.1	80.9	74.6

Table 3: Ablations and accuracy results on test data. We compute the ablations for each input representation: textual, visual, and graph, for an embedding-based model (cosine similarity) and a learning-based model (SVM); the heuristic-based models do not depend on input representation type, therefore we do not ablate them.

k	Input Representations	
	Textual	Graph
	Diversity/ Overlap Score ↓	
3	0.35	**0.12**
5	0.31	**0.11**
10	0.26	**0.10**
Dataset	Location / Recall Score ↑	
Breakfast	0.16	**0.22**
COIN	0.23	**0.60**
EPIC-KITCHENS	0.14	**0.26**

Table 4: Scores measuring the difference of information, diversity, and location, between the action kNNs using different types of embeddings: textual and graph-based.

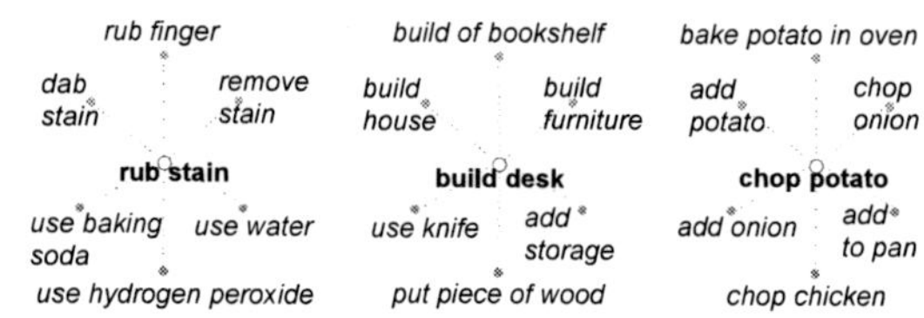

Figure 2: Top three action neighbors, obtained from textual (blue) and graph-based (purple) representations, for three random action queries from our dataset: "rub stain", "build desk", "chop potato".

of 8 words, resulting in an overlap score of 3/8. We average the overlap scores across all the action queries in our dataset (2,262 unique actions) for $k \in 3, 5, 10$. Table 4 shows that the actions retrieved using our graph representations have around three times fewer overlapping words with the action query; i.e., they are more diverse than those retrieved using the textual representation.

Location in Action Representations. To quantify how much *location* information an action representation holds, we use three annotated action localization datasets: COIN (Tang et al., 2019), which includes instructional videos; EPIC-KITCHENS (Damen et al., 2018); and Breakfast (Kuehne et al., 2014, 2016). We use the training data to create an action co-occurrence graph and learn action graph representations and the testing data to test our action representations. For each action query in the test set, we obtain the actions localized before and after as the gold standard action neighbors. We also calculate the predicted action kNNs ($k = 3$) of the action query using textual and graph-based representations. To measure the location information, we compute the recall score between the gold standard action temporal neighbors and the predicted action kNNs. Table 4 shows that graph-based representations hold more location information than textual representations.

Action representations that capture location information would likely benefit models in many computer vision applications, such as action localization, segmentation, or detection.[8] This leads to future research directions for effectively utilizing graph-based representations and co-occurring actions.

6 Conclusion

In this paper, we addressed the task of learning human action representations from co-occurring human actions in videos. We explored the genre of lifestyle vlogs and constructed Co-Act, a new dataset of ~12k pairs of visual actions and their corresponding clips. We evaluated models that leverage textual, visual, multi-modal, and graph information. We built Co-Act and action co-occurrence identification models to capture human action relations, which leads to progress towards the goal of action understanding. We are the first to address this problem and to use graph representations in this setting. We showed that graph representations are useful for our task, capture information about human actions across diverse domains, and complement the representations learned from current language and visual models. The Co-Act dataset and code are available at `https://github.com/MichiganNLP/vlog_action_co-occurrence`.

[8]For more on how our graph can be used in other downstream tasks, see Appendix A.1.

Ethics and Broad Impact Statement

Our dataset contains public YouTube vlogs, in which vloggers choose to share episodes of their daily life routine. We use the videos to detect co-occurring actions without relying on information about the person's identity, such as gender, age, or location.

The data can be used to better understand people's lives by looking at their daily routines and in which order they choose to perform their actions. The data contains videos of men and women and sometimes children, but most videos come from women. The routine videos present mostly ideal routines and are not comprehensive about all people's daily lives. Most of the people represented in the videos are middle-class Americans, and the language spoken is English.

In our data release, we only provide the YouTube URLs of the videos, so the creator of the videos can always have the option to remove them. YouTube videos are a frequent source of data in research papers (Miech et al., 2019; Fouhey et al., 2018; Abu-El-Haija et al., 2016), and we followed the typical process used by all this previous work of compiling the data through the official YouTube API and only sharing the URLs of the videos. We have the right to use our dataset how we use it, and we bear responsibility in case of a violation of rights or terms of service.

Limitations

Weak supervision from video transcripts. We use the weakly supervised time signal from automatically generated video transcripts without manual annotations. This allows for no limits in scale at the cost of some noise. To reduce the noise, we use multiple (up to 10) videos to obtain the temporal action information and perform various filtering steps described in the Quality Assurance subsection. Furthermore, the time information is used only to find the co-occurrence information between actions, not the actual time location of the actions; therefore, it is not necessary to be clear-cut.

Directed vs. Undirected graph representations. A directed graph also captures the order between the actions, which can be used in a future work direction for action prediction applications. However, an undirected graph is sufficient to obtain co-occurrence information, which suits our goal for our paper. We looked into transforming our graph into a directed one. However, we could not do this reliably because the transcripts do not preserve the exact order of the actions. This is due to how vloggers choose to verbally describe their routines: e.g. from "during washing my face, I will wake up" - it is not trivial to automatically extract the correct/natural order of the actions, as in this case, the result would be incorrect (wash face, then wake up). We tried modeling this using time keywords (e.g., "during", "after", "before") but due to the complexity of natural language, we found exceptions and other complex scenarios that could not be modeled automatically.

More advanced multimodal fusion techniques. More advanced multimodal fusion techniques might improve the performance, and we also include this direction in future work. However, in this paper, we focused on data collection and providing a set of comprehensive link prediction baselines: heuristic-based, embedding-based, and learning-based. These baselines are challenging, as demonstrated by the high accuracy results from Table 2.

Acknowledgements

We thank the anonymous reviewers for their constructive feedback. We are also grateful to the members of the Language and Information Technologies lab at the University of Michigan for the helpful discussions and paper feedback. This project was partially funded by a grant from the Michigan Automotive Research Center ("ARC"). Any opinions, findings, and conclusions or recommendations expressed in this material are those of the authors and do not necessarily reflect the views of the ARC.

References

Sami Abu-El-Haija, Nisarg Kothari, Joonseok Lee, A. Natsev, G. Toderici, Balakrishnan Varadarajan, and Sudheendra Vijayanarasimhan. 2016. Youtube-8m: A large-scale video classification benchmark. *ArXiv*, abs/1609.08675.

Lada A. Adamic and Eytan Adar. 2003. Friends and neighbors on the web. *Soc. Networks*, 25:211–230.

Tadeusz Caliński and Joachim Harabasz. 1974. A dendrite method for cluster analysis. *Communications in Statistics-theory and Methods*, 3:1–27.

Jaime G. Carbonell and Jade Goldstein-Stewart. 1998. The use of mmr, diversity-based reranking for reordering documents and producing summaries. In *Annual International ACM SIGIR Conference on Research and Development in Information Retrieval*.

João Carreira and Andrew Zisserman. 2017. Quo vadis, action recognition? a new model and the kinetics dataset. *2017 IEEE Conference on Computer Vision and Pattern Recognition (CVPR)*, pages 4724–4733.

Yu-Wei Chao, Sudheendra Vijayanarasimhan, Bryan Seybold, David A. Ross, Jia Deng, and R. Sukthankar. 2018. Rethinking the faster r-cnn architecture for temporal action localization. *2018 IEEE/CVF Conference on Computer Vision and Pattern Recognition*, pages 1130–1139.

Kenneth Ward Church and Patrick Hanks. 1989. Word association norms, mutual information and lexicography. In *ACL*.

Corinna Cortes and Vladimir Vapnik. 1995. Support-vector networks. *Machine learning*, 20(3):273–297.

Dima Damen, Hazel Doughty, Giovanni Maria Farinella, Sanja Fidler, Antonino Furnari, Evangelos Kazakos, Davide Moltisanti, Jonathan Munro, Toby Perrett, Will Price, and Michael Wray. 2018. Scaling egocentric vision: The epic-kitchens dataset. In *European Conference on Computer Vision (ECCV)*.

David L. Davies and Donald W. Bouldin. 1979. A cluster separation measure. *IEEE Transactions on Pattern Analysis and Machine Intelligence*, PAMI-1:224–227.

Jacob Devlin, Ming-Wei Chang, Kenton Lee, and Kristina Toutanova. 2019. Bert: Pre-training of deep bidirectional transformers for language understanding. *ArXiv*, abs/1810.04805.

Alexey Dosovitskiy, Lucas Beyer, Alexander Kolesnikov, Dirk Weissenborn, Xiaohua Zhai, Thomas Unterthiner, Mostafa Dehghani, Matthias Minderer, Georg Heigold, Sylvain Gelly, Jakob Uszkoreit, and Neil Houlsby. 2021. An image is worth 16x16 words: Transformers for image recognition at scale. *ICLR*.

Ethan Fast, William McGrath, Pranav Rajpurkar, and Michael S. Bernstein. 2016. Augur: Mining human behaviors from fiction to power interactive systems. *Proceedings of the 2016 CHI Conference on Human Factors in Computing Systems*.

Christoph Feichtenhofer, Haoqi Fan, Jitendra Malik, and Kaiming He. 2019. Slowfast networks for video recognition. *2019 IEEE/CVF International Conference on Computer Vision (ICCV)*, pages 6201–6210.

David F. Fouhey, Weicheng Kuo, Alexei A. Efros, and Jitendra Malik. 2018. From lifestyle vlogs to everyday interactions. *2018 IEEE/CVF Conference on Computer Vision and Pattern Recognition*, pages 4991–5000.

Rohit Girdhar, João Carreira, Carl Doersch, and Andrew Zisserman. 2019. Video action transformer network. *2019 IEEE/CVF Conference on Computer Vision and Pattern Recognition (CVPR)*, pages 244–253.

Aditya Grover and Jure Leskovec. 2016. node2vec: Scalable feature learning for networks. *Proceedings of the 22nd ACM SIGKDD International Conference on Knowledge Discovery and Data Mining*.

William L. Hamilton, Zhitao Ying, and Jure Leskovec. 2017. Inductive representation learning on large graphs. In *NIPS*.

Matthew Honnibal, Ines Montani, Sofie Van Landeghem, and Adriane Boyd. 2020. spaCy: Industrial-strength Natural Language Processing in Python.

Oana Ignat, Laura Burdick, Jia Deng, and Rada Mihalcea. 2019. Identifying visible actions in lifestyle vlogs. In *Proceedings of the 57th Annual Meeting of the Association for Computational Linguistics*, pages 6406–6417, Florence, Italy. Association for Computational Linguistics.

Oana Ignat, Santiago Castro, Hanwen Miao, Weijia Li, and Rada Mihalcea. 2021. Whyact: Identifying action reasons in lifestyle vlogs. In *EMNLP*.

Oana Ignat, Santiago Castro, Yuhang Zhou, Jiajun Bao, Dandan Shan, and Rada Mihalcea. 2022. When did it happen? duration-informed temporal localization of narrated actions in vlogs. *ACM Transactions on Multimedia Computing, Communications, and Applications*, 18:1 – 18.

Paul Jaccard. 1901. Etude de la distribution florale dans une portion des alpes et du jura. *Bulletin de la Societe Vaudoise des Sciences Naturelles*, 37:547–579.

Hisashi Kashima and Naoki Abe. 2006. A parameterized probabilistic model of network evolution for supervised link prediction. *Sixth International Conference on Data Mining (ICDM'06)*, pages 340–349.

Keizo Kato, Yin Li, and Abhinav Kumar Gupta. 2018. Compositional learning for human object interaction. In *ECCV*.

Dong-Jin Kim, Xiao Sun, Jinsoo Choi, Stephen Lin, and In So Kweon. 2020. Detecting human-object interactions with action co-occurrence priors. In *ECCV*.

Dong-Jin Kim, Xiao Sun, Jinsoo Choi, Stephen Lin, and In-So Kweon. 2021. Acp++: Action co-occurrence priors for human-object interaction detection. *IEEE Transactions on Image Processing*, 30:9150–9163.

Thomas Kipf and Max Welling. 2017. Semi-supervised classification with graph convolutional networks. *ArXiv*, abs/1609.02907.

Yu Kong and Yun Fu. 2018. Human action recognition and prediction: A survey. *ArXiv*, abs/1806.11230.

H. Kuehne, A. B. Arslan, and T. Serre. 2014. The language of actions: Recovering the syntax and semantics of goal-directed human activities. In *Proceedings of Computer Vision and Pattern Recognition Conference (CVPR)*.

H. Kuehne, H. Jhuang, E. Garrote, T. Poggio, and T. Serre. 2011. HMDB: a large video database for human motion recognition. In *Proceedings of the International Conference on Computer Vision (ICCV)*.

Hilde Kuehne, Juergen Gall, and Thomas Serre. 2016. An end-to-end generative framework for video segmentation and recognition. In *Proc. IEEE Winter Applications of Computer Vision Conference (WACV 16)*, Lake Placid.

Ajay Kumar, Shashank Sheshar Singh, Kuldeep Singh, and Bhaskar Biswas. 2020. Link prediction techniques, applications, and performance: A survey. *Physica A-statistical Mechanics and Its Applications*, 553:124289.

Beth Levin. 1993. *English verb classes and alternations: A preliminary investigation.* University of Chicago press.

David Liben-Nowell and Jon M. Kleinberg. 2007. The link-prediction problem for social networks. *Journal of the Association for Information Science and Technology*, 58:1019–1031.

Huaishao Luo, Lei Ji, Ming Zhong, Yang Chen, Wen Lei, Nan Duan, and Tianrui Li. 2021. Clip4clip: An empirical study of clip for end to end video clip retrieval. *ArXiv*, abs/2104.08860.

Antoine Miech, D. Zhukov, Jean-Baptiste Alayrac, Makarand Tapaswi, I. Laptev, and Josef Sivic. 2019. Howto100m: Learning a text-video embedding by watching hundred million narrated video clips. *2019 IEEE/CVF International Conference on Computer Vision (ICCV)*, pages 2630–2640.

Tomas Mikolov, Kai Chen, Gregory S. Corrado, and Jeffrey Dean. 2013. Efficient estimation of word representations in vector space. In *ICLR*.

Ishan Misra, C. Lawrence Zitnick, and Martial Hebert. 2016. Shuffle and learn: Unsupervised learning using temporal order verification. In *ECCV*.

F. Murtagh and P. Legendre. 2014. Ward's hierarchical agglomerative clustering method: Which algorithms implement ward's criterion? *Journal of Classification*, 31:274–295.

Mark E. J. Newman. 2001. Clustering and preferential attachment in growing networks. *Physical review. E, Statistical, nonlinear, and soft matter physics*, 64 2 Pt 2:025102.

Alec Radford, Jong Wook Kim, Chris Hallacy, Aditya Ramesh, Gabriel Goh, Sandhini Agarwal, Girish Sastry, Amanda Askell, Pamela Mishkin, Jack Clark, Gretchen Krueger, and Ilya Sutskever. 2021. Learning transferable visual models from natural language supervision. In *ICML*.

Erzsébet Ravasz, Audrey Somera, D A Mongru, Zoltán N. Oltvai, and A.-L. Barabasi. 2002. Hierarchical organization of modularity in metabolic networks. *Science*, 297:1551 – 1555.

Nils Reimers and Iryna Gurevych. 2019. Sentence-BERT: Sentence embeddings using Siamese BERT-networks. In *Proceedings of the 2019 Conference on Empirical Methods in Natural Language Processing and the 9th International Joint Conference on Natural Language Processing (EMNLP-IJCNLP)*, pages 3982–3992, Hong Kong, China. Association for Computational Linguistics.

Matteo Ruggero Ronchi and Pietro Perona. 2015. Describing common human visual actions in images. *arXiv preprint arXiv:1506.02203*.

Peter J. Rousseeuw. 1987. Silhouettes: a graphical aid to the interpretation and validation of cluster analysis. *Journal of Computational and Applied Mathematics*, 20:53–65.

Gerard Salton and Michael J McGill. 1983. *Introduction to modern information retrieval.* mcgraw-hill.

Zheng Shou, J. Chan, Alireza Zareian, K. Miyazawa, and S. Chang. 2017. Cdc: Convolutional-deconvolutional networks for precise temporal action localization in untrimmed videos. *2017 IEEE Conference on Computer Vision and Pattern Recognition (CVPR)*, pages 1417–1426.

Gunnar A. Sigurdsson, Olga Russakovsky, and A. Gupta. 2017. What actions are needed for understanding human actions in videos? *2017 IEEE International Conference on Computer Vision (ICCV)*, pages 2156–2165.

Khurram Soomro, Amir Roshan Zamir, and Mubarak Shah. 2012. Ucf101: A dataset of 101 human actions classes from videos in the wild. *ArXiv*, abs/1212.0402.

Yansong Tang, Dajun Ding, Yongming Rao, Yu Zheng, Danyang Zhang, Lili Zhao, Jiwen Lu, and Jie Zhou. 2019. Coin: A large-scale dataset for comprehensive instructional video analysis. *2019 IEEE/CVF Conference on Computer Vision and Pattern Recognition (CVPR)*, pages 1207–1216.

Du Tran, Heng Wang, L. Torresani, Jamie Ray, Y. LeCun, and Manohar Paluri. 2018. A closer look at spatiotemporal convolutions for action recognition. *2018 IEEE/CVF Conference on Computer Vision and Pattern Recognition*, pages 6450–6459.

Laurens Van der Maaten and Geoffrey Hinton. 2008. Visualizing data using t-sne. *Journal of machine learning research*, 9(11).

Steven R. Wilson and Rada Mihalcea. 2017. Measuring semantic relations between human activities. In *IJCNLP*.

Steven R. Wilson and Rada Mihalcea. 2019. Predicting human activities from user-generated content. In *ACL*.

Bingjie Xu, Yongkang Wong, Junnan Li, Qi Zhao, and M. Kankanhalli. 2019. Learning to detect human-object interactions with knowledge. *2019 IEEE/CVF Conference on Computer Vision and Pattern Recognition (CVPR)*, pages 2019–2028.

Keyulu Xu, Weihua Hu, Jure Leskovec, and Stefanie Jegelka. 2018. How powerful are graph neural networks? *ArXiv*, abs/1810.00826.

Mark Yatskar, Luke Zettlemoyer, and Ali Farhadi. 2016. Situation recognition: Visual semantic role labeling for image understanding. In *Conference on Computer Vision and Pattern Recognition*.

Daokun Zhang, Jie Yin, Xingquan Zhu, and Chengqi Zhang. 2019. Attributed network embedding via subspace discovery. *Data Mining and Knowledge Discovery*, 33:1953–1980.

Luowei Zhou, Chenliang Xu, and Jason J. Corso. 2018. Towards automatic learning of procedures from web instructional videos. In *AAAI*.

Tao Zhou, Linyuan Lü, and Yicheng Zhang. 2009. Predicting missing links via local information. *The European Physical Journal B*, 71:623–630.

Boyao Zhu and Yongxiang Xia. 2016. Link prediction in weighted networks: A weighted mutual information model. *PLoS ONE*, 11.

A Appendix

A.1 How to use the graph in other datasets and downstream tasks

Our comprehensive graph can be extended to new data and new tasks. We intentionally included a large number of actions in our graph, making it comprehensive and exhaustive (see Table 1: 164 verbs/ 2,262 unique actions), precisely to increase the chance that actions from new data can be found in our graph.

We do not need to create a new graph for each new data or new task. Instead, we can directly use our provided learned action representations, which can also be fine-tuned on the new data. If there is a sufficiently similar (i.e., based on cosine similarity) class match between the actions we provide and the actions from the new data, then we can use our corresponding learned action representations. Otherwise, the new actions can be added to the graph, and new action representations can be computed. We provide code and guidelines on how to extend our graph and obtain new action representations.

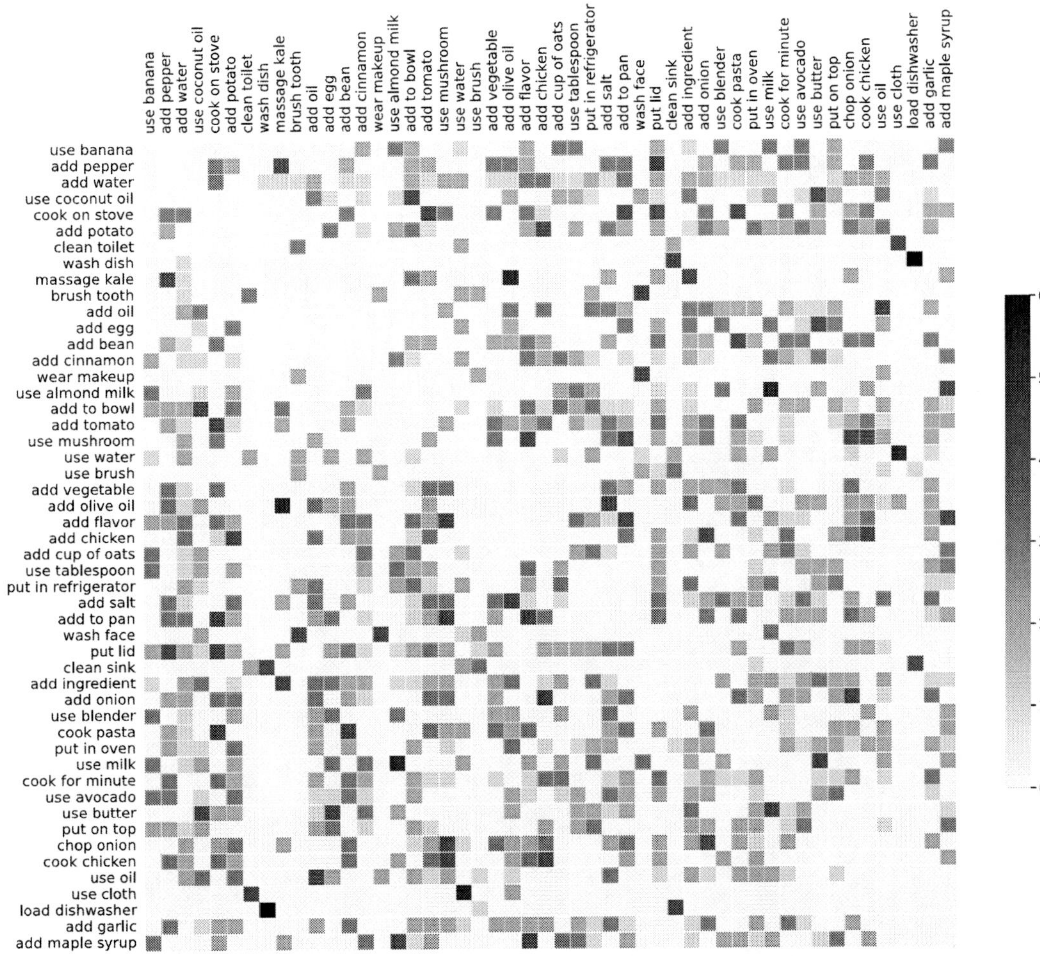

Figure 3: Co-occurrence matrix for the top 50 most frequent actions in our dataset, CO-ACT. The scores are computed using the PPMI measure: actions with higher scores have a stronger co-occurrence relation and vice-versa. For better visualization, we sort the matrix rows to highlight clusters. Best viewed in color.

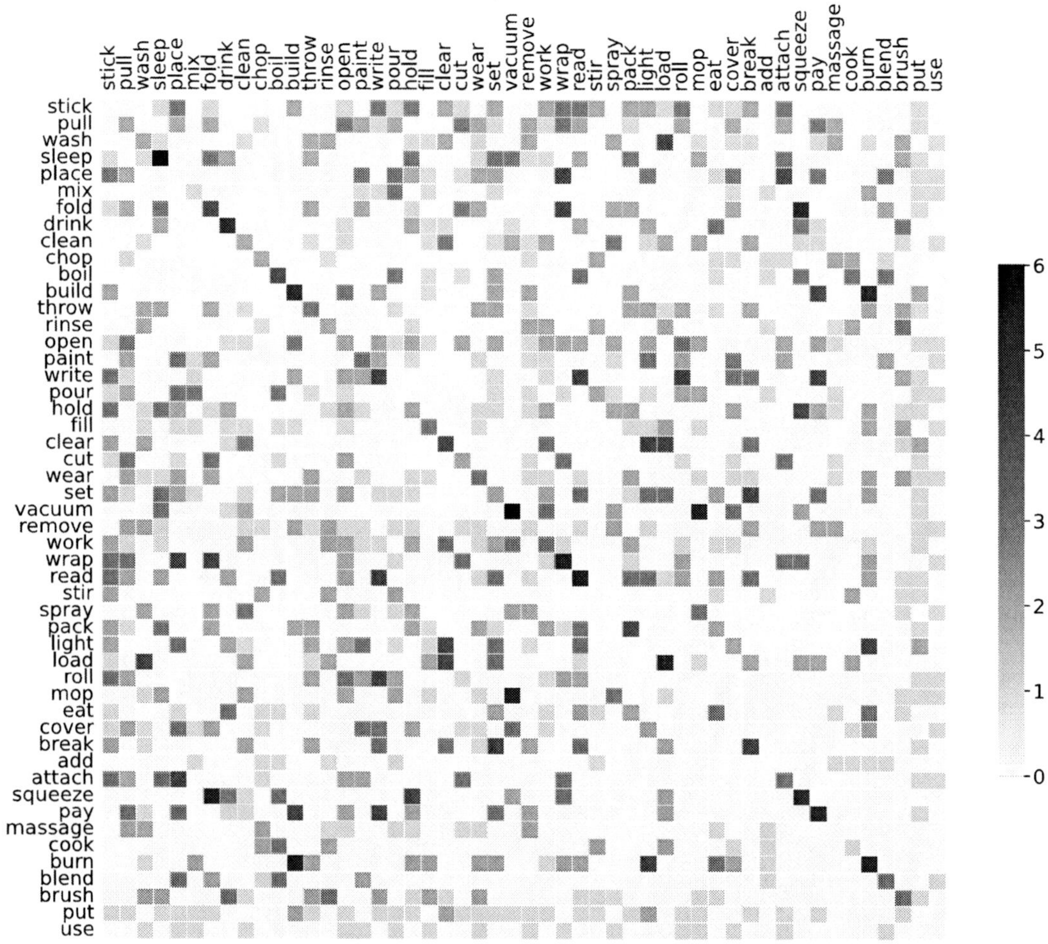

Figure 4: Co-occurrence matrix for the top 50 most frequent verbs in our dataset, CO-ACT. The scores are computed using the PPMI measure: actions with higher scores have a stronger co-occurrence relation and vice-versa. For better visualization, we sort the matrix rows to highlight clusters. Best viewed in color.

Action pair	Frequency
load dishwasher, wash dish	52
eat food, eat in day	29
use shampoo, wash hair	26
use cloth, use water	24
add sweetener, add teaspoon of maple syrup	23
use almond milk, use milk	22
use butter, use purpose flour	22
add olive oil, massage kale	22
load dishwasher, load dishwasher at night	22
clean steel appliance, use cloth	21
put dish, wash dish	19
clean toilet, spray toilet	19
clean sink, use dish soap	19
add cocoa powder, use purpose flour	17
squeeze lemon juice, use lemon	17
brush tooth, wash face	16
curl eyelash, use mascara	15
put in freezer, put in smoothie	15
add tomato, cook on stove	15
clean bathtub, use broom	15
...	...
pack makeup bag with, put in ziploc bag	2
put on skin, use for lip	2
put stuff, use on cuticle	2
put under eye, use on cuticle	2
put on eyelid, use on cuticle	2
fill brow, use on cuticle	2
read book, use business card	2
spray paint, use iron	2
use product, use vegetable peeler	2
teach responsibility, work in beauty industry	2
use charcoal scrub, use scrub	2
use charcoal scrub, use vegetable peeler	2
use charcoal scrub, use steamer	2
add tea to water, use charcoal scrub	2
open pore, use charcoal scrub	2
use charcoal scrub, use sheep mask from store	2
use on drugstore, use product	2
break surface of water, remove makeup	2
brush hair, spray with hairspray	2
fill brow, fill browser bed	2

Verb pair	Frequency
add, use	3864
use, use	2987
add, add	2895
put, use	1786
add, put	1060
add, cook	814
clean, use	724
put, put	620
use, wear	366
add, chop	355
clean, clean	330
cut, use	328
use, wash	317
add, eat	293
cook, use	284
add, cut	256
clean, put	246
eat, use	244
eat, eat	201
fill, use	191
...	...
bake, pull	2
bake, stick	2
pack, pull	2
empty, hold	2
brush, mix	2
attach, paint	2
pour, wrap	2
fight, wash	2
drink, massage	2
add, poke	2
stick, stir	2
fill, scrape	2
carve, cover	2
curl, open	2
curl, rinse	2
fill, pump	2
build, draw	2
teach, work	2
break, remove	2
brush, spray	2

Top 20 most and least frequent action pairs (left) and verb pairs (right) in our dataset.

A.2 Data Analysis

We want to determine which actions co-occur the most in our dataset, as it may be valuable knowledge for action recognition and action prediction systems. Systems enriched with this knowledge can make more informed decisions when predicting or recognizing actions. Specifically, action recognition systems can discard actions that are unlikely to happen given a previous action and assign a higher probability to actions known to co-occur with the previous action (e.g., given a previously recognized action "wake up", a likely next action could be "wash face", and not "clean house").

Given two actions, we compute their co-occurrence score using the Positive Pointwise Mutual Information (PPMI) (Church and Hanks, 1989). PMI is biased towards infrequent words, therefore we do not compute PMI for infrequent actions (that appear less than 10 times).

$$PPMI_{a_i,a_j} = \max(\log \frac{P_{a_i,a_j}}{P_{a_i}P_{a_j}}, 0) \quad (6)$$

$$P_{a_i,a_j} = \frac{\#(a_i, a_j)}{\#action\ pairs}, P_{a_k} = \frac{\#a_k}{\#actions} \quad (7)$$

Figure 5 shows the co-occurrence matrix for the top 20 most frequent actions. The most frequent actions are related to cooking. We can see how actions related to adding ingredients are co-occurring among themselves (e.g., "add potato" and "add avocado") or with actions related to adding something to a container (e.g., "add potato" and "add to bowl"). Appendix A includes additional information: co-occurrence matrices of the top 50 most frequent actions and verbs (Figs. 3 and 4), top 20 actions and verb pairs co-occurring the most/least (Appendix A.1), actions and verbs distributions (Figs. 6 and 7), top 10 most frequent clusters (Fig. 8).

A.3 Action and Verb Distribution

A.4 Action Clustering

Recall that all the raw actions extracted from the transcript are clustered as described in Section 3.2. To analyze the content of the clusters, we show the 10 most frequent clusters using t-distributed Stochastic Neighbor Embedding (t-SNE) (Van der Maaten and Hinton, 2008) (see Fig. 8)

By examining the clusters, we can distinguish some open challenges or future work directions. First, there are multiple ways of expressing the same action, which can be seen when looking at the actions inside each cluster (e.g., "add to bowl',

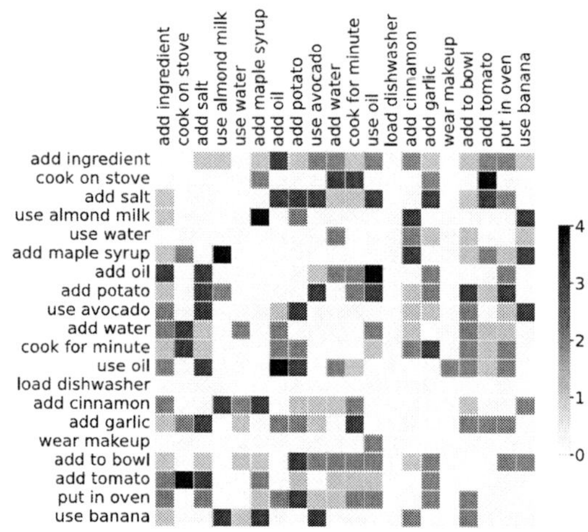

Figure 5: Co-occurrence matrix for the top 20 most frequent actions in our dataset, CO-ACT. The scores are computed using the PPMI measure: actions with higher scores have a stronger co-occurrence relation and vice-versa. For better visualization, we sort the matrix rows to highlight clusters. Best viewed in color.

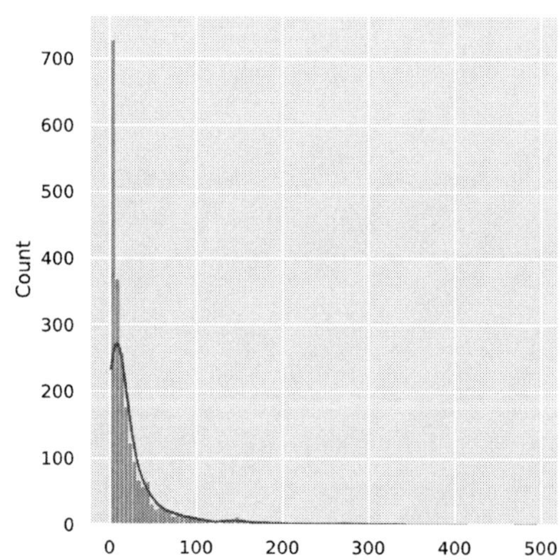

Figure 6: Action distribution in our dataset, CO-ACT: count of actions frequencies.

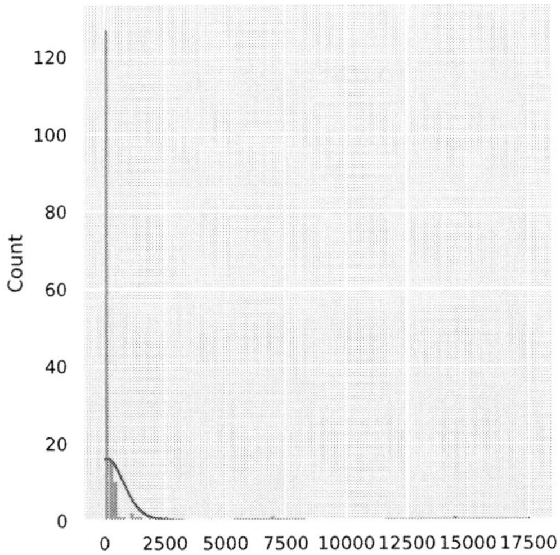

Figure 7: Verb distribution in our dataset, CO-ACT: count of verb frequencies.

"add into bowl", "place in bowl", "use measuring bowl"). This showcases the complexity of language. Second, the cluster algorithms are not perfect and some clusters could be merged (e.g., "add water" and "use water") or some actions should not belong in some of the clusters (e.g., "put engine oil" and "paint with oil"). Third, actions can be too ambiguous ("use water") or too broad (e.g., "add ingredient").

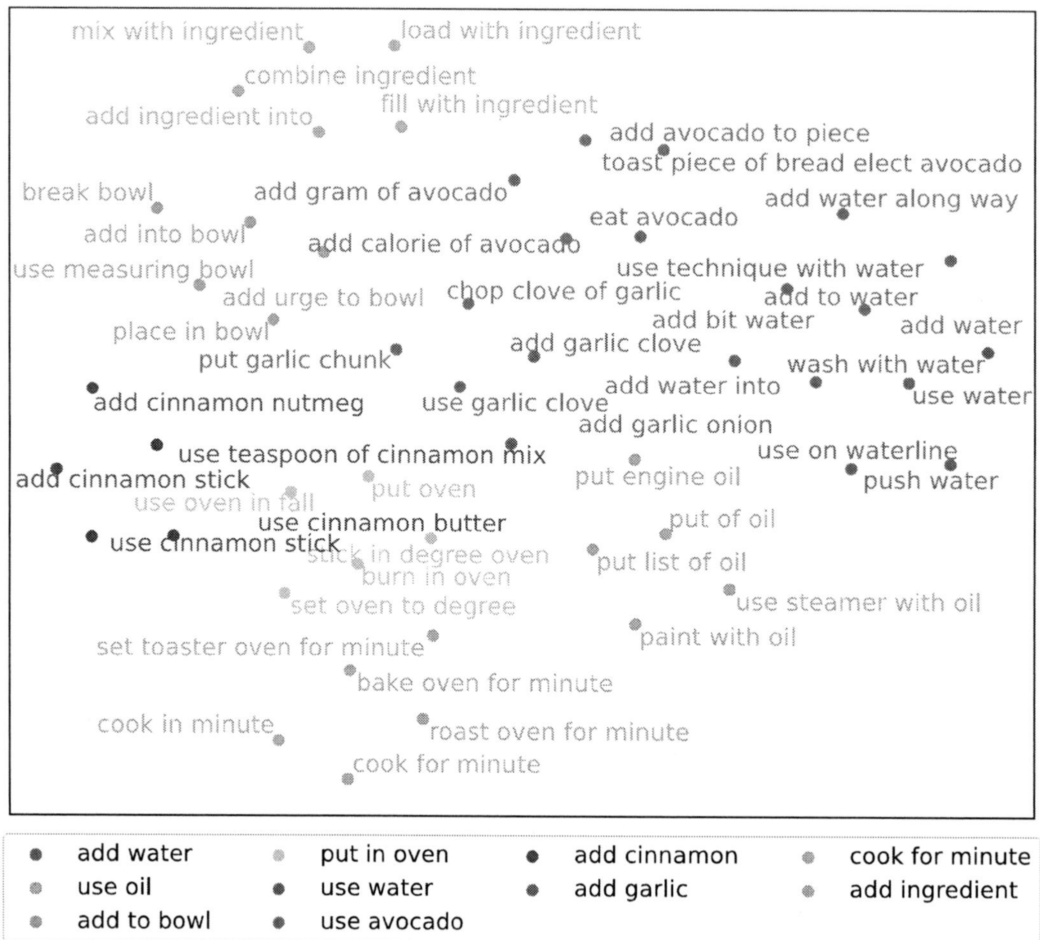

Figure 8: The t-SNE representation (Van der Maaten and Hinton, 2008) of the ten most frequent action clusters in our dataset. Each color represents a different action cluster. Best viewed in color.

ConGraT: Self-Supervised Contrastive Pretraining for Joint Graph and Text Embeddings

William Brannon* **Wonjune Kang**

Suyash Fulay **Hang Jiang** **Brandon Roy** **Deb Roy** **Jad Kabbara**

MIT Center for Constructive Communication
{wbrannon, wjkang, sfulay, hjian42, bcroy, dkroy, jkabbara}@mit.edu

Abstract

Learning on text-attributed graphs (TAGs), in which nodes are associated with one or more texts, has been the subject of much recent work. However, most approaches tend to make strong assumptions about the downstream task of interest, are reliant on hand-labeled data, or fail to equally balance the importance of both text and graph representations. In this work, we propose **Con**trastive **Gra**ph-**T**ext pretraining (ConGraT), a general, self-supervised approach for jointly learning separate representations of texts and nodes in a TAG. Our method trains a language model (LM) and a graph neural network (GNN) to align their representations in a common latent space using a batch-wise contrastive learning objective inspired by CLIP. We further propose an extension to the CLIP objective that leverages graph structure to incorporate information about inter-node similarity. Extensive experiments demonstrate that ConGraT outperforms baselines on various downstream tasks, including node and text category classification, link prediction, and language modeling. Finally, we present an application of our method to community detection in social graphs, which enables finding more *textually grounded* communities, rather than purely graph-based ones.

1 Introduction

Recent advances in multimodal representation learning have shown the benefits of simultaneously modeling language with other modalities, which allows for more efficient training and improved downstream performance of both sets of learned representations. These benefits have been especially clear in text/vision or text/audio applications, which often see large improvements in predictive performance or generative modeling ability (Radford et al., 2021; Li et al., 2022; Mu et al., 2022; Elizalde et al., 2023). In this work, we address another modality that frequently co-occurs with text: network- or graph-structured data.

We consider in particular the scenario of a text-attributed graph (TAG); that is, a graph over entities (i.e., nodes) associated with one or more texts. Such graphs occur frequently in the real world; examples include social media graphs of users and their posts, link graphs over web pages and their content, and citation networks of articles or authors and the texts of academic articles. In this setting, rather than modeling each source of data separately, graph information may be used to improve performance on language tasks and text information may be leveraged for graph tasks such as link prediction or node classification.

Prior work has approached the problem of combining these two modalities in several ways. Some approaches have used textual data to inform or supervise training of graph neural networks (GNNs) (Yang et al., 2015; Zhang et al., 2017; Liu et al., 2018; Zhang and Zhang, 2020), but these methods do not produce graph-informed text representations. This is more parameter-efficient for graph-only tasks, but means that separate modeling is needed to solve text-based tasks while leveraging graph data. Other works have considered the converse case of employing a TAG structure to fine-tune pretrained language models (PLMs) (Cohan et al., 2020; Yasunaga et al., 2022; Ostendorff et al., 2022). Although these approaches allow for the extraction of graph-informed text embeddings, they have the opposite limitation to the above of not learning node representations. While there have been attempts to learn joint representations of nodes and texts, they all have certain limitations, such as requiring a supervised objective and labeled data (Li and Goldwasser, 2019; Chandra et al., 2020), freezing either the text or graph embeddings/encoders (Gourru et al., 2020; Karpov and Kartashev, 2022), or relying on the particu-

* Corresponding author.

Proceedings of TextGraphs-17: Graph-based Methods for Natural Language Processing, pages 19–39
August 15, 2024 ©2024 Association for Computational Linguistics

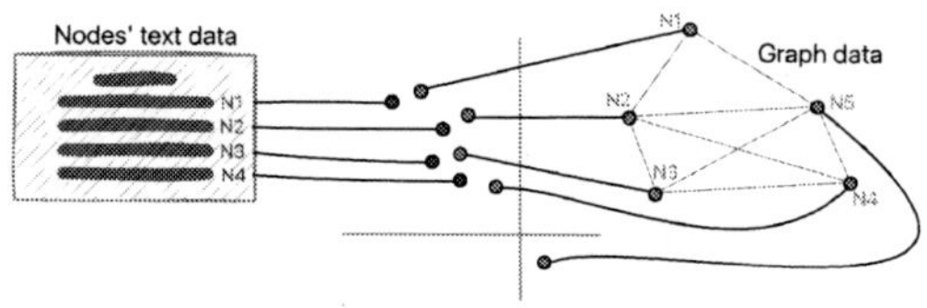

Figure 1: Embeddings of graph nodes in red (e.g., Twitter users), and their associated texts in blue (e.g., tweets). They are placed into a common embedding space, with nodes near their associated texts. Node-text pairs are labeled N1 to N5. Note that not every node must have an associated text (here, N5 does not).

lar structure of one application (Li et al., 2017). Several recent works have leveraged joint training of PLMs with GNNs to integrate both text and graph information for representation learning in each modality (Yang et al., 2021; Chien et al., 2022; Zhao et al., 2023). These methods, however, make specific modeling assumptions based on the tasks that they aim to solve, employ complex training procedures that alternately optimize the PLM and GNN modules, or need human-annotated knowledge distillation, which in general go against the goal of self-supervised learning.

In this work, we propose ConGraT (**Con**trastive **Gra**ph-**T**ext pretraining), a general approach to self-supervised joint graph-text learning based on a batch-wise contrastive learning objective inspired by CLIP (Radford et al., 2021). The idea is to have separate encoders for texts and graph nodes (more specifically, a PLM and a GNN, respectively) that are trained to align their representations within a common latent space, as shown in Figure 1. Taking advantage of the fact that graphs have greater structure than images, we propose an extension to the CLIP objective that incorporates information about plausible "next guesses" based on graph similarity. Our objective also admits an interpretation as a continuous relaxation of the contrastive CLIP objective over each node's two-hop neighborhood.

ConGraT provides flexibility in the choice of text and graph encoders and does not make assumptions on the structure of the TAG or any downstream task. As illustrated in our experiments, it is also inductive (Hamilton et al., 2017), with the encoders being able to generalize to previously unseen graphs as well as previously unseen texts. Experiments on various datasets show that ConGraT models consistently outperform strong baselines on various downstream tasks such as node and text category classification and link prediction. Additionally, we analyze how joint training affects language modeling performance, finding that ConGraT also results in improvements on this task on all datasets.

The contributions of this work are threefold: 1) We propose ConGraT, a general self-supervised pretraining method for jointly learning graph node and text representations on TAGs, such as citation, link, or social graphs. 2) We demonstrate that our joint pretraining method improves performance over strong unimodal and cross-modal baselines on various downstream tasks. 3) We release our code and datasets, including in particular a version of the Pubmed (Sen et al., 2008) graph learning dataset fully rebuilt from ground-truth Pubmed APIs, which includes the text of titles and abstracts as well as network data.

2 Related Work

2.1 Text-Augmented GNNs

Text data can be incorporated into the learning of GNN representations in various ways. For example, Yang et al. (2015) extend the DeepWalk algorithm to incorporate text features into node representations. Liu et al. (2018) develop a seq2seq framework which learns node embeddings with inputs based on texts associated with the nodes. Tu et al. (2017) use a selective attention mechanism to generate text-informed node embeddings for particular social contexts. Zhang et al. (2017) leverage kernel methods to construct node representations from user profile information in a way that incorporates network structure. Other methods include extracting graphs from entity co-occurrence in texts and modeling them (Zhang and Zhang, 2020; Waller and Anderson, 2021). However, these approaches are limited in that, while they learn to represent nodes, they do not also learn graph-informed text representations.

2.2 Graph-Augmented PLMs

Another line of work uses information from graph structures to inform finetuning or further training of PLMs. SPECTER (Cohan et al., 2020) contrastively finetunes a language model by augmenting it with a measure of inter-node relatedness, with positive and negative examples for a triplet loss selected according to citation graph edges. LinkBERT (Yasunaga et al., 2022) uses a graph structure to assemble training samples for a masked language model, pairing anchor texts with texts from contiguous, linked, or random documents, and uses an auxiliary document relation prediction (DRP) objective. SciNCL (Ostendorff et al., 2022) relaxes a discrete citation graph into a continuous domain with nearest-neighbor sampling. Social-BERT (Karpov and Kartashev, 2022) and LMSOC (Kulkarni et al., 2021) condition or augment the inputs to PLMs with frozen node representations that the model can attend over. The models these methods learn produce text embeddings for documents, but do not also generate text-informed node representations.

2.3 Joint Learning of PLMs and GNNs on TAGs

More recently, representation learning on TAGs that jointly leverages graph and text information has been growing in popularity. Prefix tuning (Li and Liang, 2021) is a lightweight way of learning node-specific linguistic information and generates dense node representations in the process; however, it takes no advantage of the graph structure over the nodes. For fixed text and graph encoders, one can learn mappings from their separate embedding spaces to a common one, such as by canonical correlation analysis (Gupta and Varma, 2017). Other methods jointly train text and graph encoders using an externally supervised objective (Chandra et al., 2020) or tailored for certain tasks (Li and Goldwasser, 2019; Gourru et al., 2020). However, these methods all address specific settings that are not generalizable to more diverse tasks.

GraphFormers (Yang et al., 2021) jointly train a GNN with a PLM so as to learn text-informed node representations. However, they require a complex progressive learning strategy that iteratively utilizes manipulated and raw data. GIANT (Chien et al., 2022) predicts graph structure using PLMs to provide better initial embeddings for GNNs. However, the language model embeddings cannot be jointly optimized during the GNN training phase. GLEM (Zhao et al., 2023) uses a variational expectation-maximization (EM) framework that alternately updates a PLM and GNN separately using pseudo-labels predicted by the other module. While it enables improved scalability, the training procedure is complex and relies on the availability of task-specific target labels. In contrast, ConGraT is a general representation learning method for both graph nodes and texts, applicable to any inductive or transductive setting without such assumptions or complex training paradigms.

3 Methodology

We consider a directed or undirected TAG, each node of which is associated with a set of one or more texts. The goal is to learn a shared latent space that allows us to place the embeddings of nodes and texts in semantically meaningful locations within that space. Formally, let $G = (V, E)$ be a graph, with V the set of nodes and $E \subseteq V \times V$ the set of edges. Also, let $T^{(v)} = \{t_i^{(v)}\}_{i=1}^{N_v}$, for $v \in V$, be the set of node v's texts, with N_v the number of texts corresponding to node v. We model $t_i^{(v)}$, the i-th text of node v, as a finite sequence of tokens over a vocabulary W, where $L_i^{(v)}$ is the length of $t_i^{(v)}$: $t_i^{(v)} = (S_0, S_1, S_2, ..., S_{L_v^{(i)}})$. The first and last tokens are always special start and end tokens.

Our training framework involves a *text encoder*, a function $F_T : \cup_{i=1}^{\infty} \otimes_i W \rightarrow \mathbb{R}^d$ from the set of all token sequences to a d-dimensional Euclidean embedding space. Similarly, we have a *node encoder*, a function $F_G : V \rightarrow \mathbb{R}^d$ from nodes to an embedding space of the same dimension. (Note that while its domain is nodes, not edges, F_G also depends on the edge set E.) We aim to train the two encoders such that they learn a joint latent space between the text and graph node embeddings. This will allow us to use geometric properties of a common space to relate nodes and texts to each other for downstream inferential purposes.

3.1 Approach

The text and node encoders in ConGraT (a PLM and GNN, respectively) are connected at the output layers by a batch-wise contrastive training objective inspired by CLIP (Radford et al., 2021). The encoders are trained to align their representations in a joint latent embedding space. As in CLIP, each encoder is set behind an adapter module which generates embeddings of the same dimension. Each adapter consists of two fully connected layers with a GeLU activation (Hendrycks and Gimpel, 2020) in between, followed by layer normalization (Ba et al., 2016), and dropout (Srivastava et al., 2014). This approach is flexible and allows use of many different kinds of both text and node encoders. On the text side, we illustrate this flexibility with experiments employing both causal and masked PLMs.

Training objective. We augment the standard InfoNCE loss (Oord et al., 2019) in CLIP with additional graph-specific elements. Unlike the vision-language case, in graphs, there are easily com-

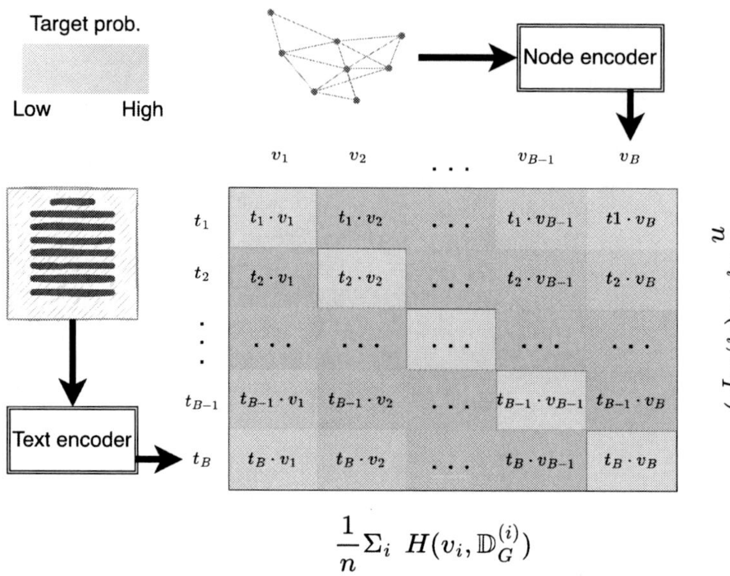

Figure 2: The overall architecture of our model. Given a minibatch of (text, origin node) pairs, node and text embeddings are generated by their respective encoders, then used to compute pairwise cosine similarities. The final loss is the average of cross entropies along each row and column of the similarity matrix, with each row i's target probabilities (labeled $\mathbb{D}_T^{(i)}$ and $\mathbb{D}_G^{(i)}$) a mixture of the true targets (on the diagonal) and a (row- or column-specific) distribution proportional to a graph-based similarity measure.

putable measures of how similar pairs of nodes are, such as their SimRank (Jeh and Widom, 2002) or their number of mutual in- and out-edges. We use these measures to incorporate information about the most likely second, third, and further choices for the nodes a text may originate from as well as the texts that may be associated with a node. The method is visualized in Figure 2.

More formally, let $X = \cup_{v \in V} \{(v, t_i^{(v)})\}_{i=1}^{|T^{(v)}|}$ be a dataset of (node, text) pairs, and let $B = \{(v_i, t_i^{(v_i)})\}_{i=1}^{N_B} \subseteq X$ be a minibatch of size N_B sampled from X. Now, fix an ordering of nodes, with v_j the j-th node. Then, in terms of the text and node encoders F_T and F_G, the matrix C given by

$$C_{ij} \triangleq e^{\tau} \frac{F_T(t_i^{(v_i)}) \cdot F_G(v_j)}{\|F_T(t_i^{(v_i)})\| \cdot \|F_G(v_j)\|}$$

is the $N_B \times N_B$ matrix of cosine similarities between texts and nodes in the batch. (Note that C is square but not symmetric: rows are texts and columns are nodes.) The matrix is multiplied by a scalar factor e^{τ}, where τ is a log-temperature parameter that allowing some learnable control over the learning rate, reducing sensitivity to the choice of learning rate. We empirically initialize $\tau = 3.5$ based on our experiments (see Appendix F).

Further, let $S_T(\cdot, \cdot)$ and $S_G(\cdot, \cdot)$ be graph-based *similarity functions* for texts and nodes, respectively, assigning non-negative continuous similarity scores. Then, we define graph-based similarity distributions for texts and nodes. Where $K_T(i) = \sum_{k=1}^{N_B} S_T(t_i^{(v_i)}, t_k^{(v_k)})$ and $K_G(i) = \sum_{k=1}^{N_B} S_G(v_i, v_k)$, then $\forall i, j$, we have

$$s_T^{(i)}(j) = \frac{S_T(t_i^{(v_i)}, t_j^{(v_j)})}{K_T(i)}, s_G^{(i)}(j) = \frac{S_G(v_i, v_j)}{K_G(i)}.$$

The target distributions are mixtures of these distributions and indicator variables for the true source node of a text and matching text of a node. For each example $X_j = (v_j, t_j^{(v_j)})$ in the minibatch, fixing some hyperparameter $\alpha \in [0, 1]$, we define the target distribution in the text case by $\mathbb{D}_T^{(j)}(\alpha) = (1 - \alpha)\mathbb{1}_i\{v_i = v_j\} + \alpha s_T(j)$, where $s_T(j)$ is the vector of $s_T^{(i)}(j)$ values for all i. In the graph case, where $s_G(j)$ is defined analogously, we have $\mathbb{D}_G^{(j)}(\alpha) = (1 - \alpha)\mathbb{1}_i\{t_i = t_j\} + \alpha s_G(j)$. Then where H is the cross-entropy and $C_{i,:}$, $C_{:,i}$ are the i-th row and i-th column of C, our loss is

$$\mathcal{L}(B; \alpha) = \frac{1}{2N_B} \sum_{i=1}^{N_B} \begin{matrix} H(C_{i,:}, \mathbb{D}_T^{(i)}(\alpha)) \\ + H(C_{:,i}, \mathbb{D}_G^{(i)}(\alpha)). \end{matrix}$$

With $\alpha = 0$, this loss is equivalent to the average of cross-entropies for predictions of which node in the minibatch goes with which text and which text goes with which node. With higher values of α, the target distributions are mixtures of indicators for the true source node and text and the distribution of other nodes and texts by graph similarity. If similar nodes produce similar texts, as suggested by the homophily principle (De Choudhury et al., 2010), positive α values should allow the model to learn more efficiently. Even if not all graph nodes are closely related to their texts, this objective should be able to learn from those that are.

Similarity function. For undirected graphs, we base our similarity function on a node pair's number of mutual neighbors. If A is the graph adjacency matrix, we compute AA^T to find the number of mutual in- or out-neighbors of each node pair, and find the cosine similarity of each row i and column j of AA^T to measure the similarity of nodes i and j. A benefit of this function over alternatives like SimRank (Jeh and Widom, 2002) is its lower computational cost and faster runtime for large graphs. On the text side, because we are interested in leveraging graph information, we approximate the similarity of a pair of texts as that of the associated nodes. The digraph case is more complicated, as it requires a directed similarity function that can distinguish between edges (i, j) and (j, i). We defer choosing and validating such a function to future work; thus, all experiments with $\alpha > 0$ in Section 4 discard edge directions.

3.2 Theoretical View

From a theoretical perspective, the above similarity function allows our training objective to be viewed as a continuous relaxation of the contrastive CLIP objective across a node's two-hop neighborhood. (Only nodes with shared neighbors, which are in each other's two-hop neighborhoods, will have positive similarity.) Different choices of similarity correspond to different choices of how to relax the contrastive objective across the graph; in particular, restricting to the one-hop neighborhood amounts to using a coarse, binary indicator of similarity, with $S_G(u, v)$ the indicator function for edge (u, v).

This view indicates a connection to label smoothing (Szegedy et al., 2015), but with the smoothing distribution based on graph similarity rather than being uniformly random. It also casts our model as an extension to a graph setting of prior work on similarity-based smoothing in non-graph contexts (Liu and JaJa, 2021). Note that this is a different sense of "smoothing" than the aggregation over neighbor representations that the term refers to in the context of message-passing GNNs.

4 Experimental Setup

We evaluate our approach on three tasks: node category classification, link prediction, and language modeling. Link prediction and language modeling are fundamental modality-specific metrics that measure how well our node and text encoders retain the ability to model their individual modalities. We perform node classification using each encoder's embeddings in order to measure how effective the learned representations are for downstream tasks. Further details are provided in Appendix F.

4.1 Datasets

We evaluate on three datasets, comprising one each of citation, link, and social graphs: (1) the Pubmed dataset (Sen et al., 2008), (2) a dataset of Wikipedia articles represented by their introductory paragraphs and the hyperlinks between the articles in those paragraphs, selected from the broader T-REx Corpus (Elsahar et al., 2018), and (3) a novel Twitter dataset comprising high-profile public figures, which includes the tweets, the follow graph over the associated users, and some demographic information about them (age, gender, United States political party, etc.). We include the last Twitter dataset to demonstrate the performance of our method on social network TAGs, which is a setting that has been less explored in prior work on joint graph and language learning. Table 1 shows descriptive statistics of the datasets. Because we use entirely separate train, validation, and test splits, without shared graph structure, our results below are in an inductive (rather than transductive) setting. More information about the datasets and our collection procedures for Twitter data and the other datasets' raw text are provided in Appendix E.

4.2 Models

For each dataset, we train two ConGraT variants with masked and causal PLMs, initializing with weights from MPNet (Song et al., 2020) and DistilGPT-2 (Sanh et al., 2019), respectively. Specifically, we use the pretrained `all-mpnet-base-v2` and `distilgpt2` models from the `sentence-transformers` toolkit (Reimers and Gurevych, 2019). For the graph node

	Pubmed	T-REx	Twitter
# Nodes	19,716	9,214	8,721
# Edges	61,110	22,689	2,373,956
# Texts	59,381	18,422	167,558
# Classes	3	5	13 (5 tasks)

Table 1: Statistics for the Pubmed, T-REx, and Twitter datasets used in our experiments.

encoder, we use a graph attention network (GAT) (Veličković et al., 2018) with 3 layers of 2 attention heads each, randomly initialized and trained from scratch. All text and graph embeddings have dimension 768, and we obtain text-level representations from the PLM text encoder by mean pooling.

We examine models with ($\alpha = 0.1$) and without ($\alpha = 0.0$) graph similarity information included in the loss. We also examine models which consider edge directions (and thus have $\alpha = 0.0$).[1] In all, between these three factors (masked or causal PLM, $\alpha = 0.0$ or $\alpha = 0.1$, directed or undirected edges), and without experiments with $\alpha = 0.1$ for directed edges, there are 6 possible model combinations on each dataset, for a total of 18 combinations.

4.3 Baselines

For node representations, we compare against embeddings from a GNN-only baseline: a unimodal GAT autoencoder with the same architecture as the ConGraT node encoder, trained as usual to reconstruct the adjacency matrix without added similarity information. For text representations, in addition to unimodal masked and causal PLM baselines finetuned on each dataset, we also compare against two models leveraging both modalities: LinkBERT (Yasunaga et al., 2022) and Social-LM, a modified implementation of SocialBERT (Karpov and Kartashev, 2022) and LMSOC (Kulkarni et al., 2021). Because LinkBERT uses a masked language modeling objective, it is used as a baseline only for the masked versions of ConGraT. Initial node representations for all GNN models are sentence embeddings of text associated with each node: for Pubmed, the concatenated text of the title and abstract sections; for Twitter, user bios; for T-REx, the Wikipedia article text. Further implementation details are given in Appendix F.

[1]Recall that because we defined a similarity function with $\alpha > 0$ only for undirected graphs, there are no experiments with directed edges where $\alpha = 0.1$.

		Pubmed		T-REx	
		C	M	C	M
Graph	ConGraT ($\alpha = 0$)	0.967	**0.964**	**0.951**	0.937
Graph	ConGraT ($\alpha = 0.1$)	**0.973**	0.963	0.949	**0.946**
Graph	GAT	0.956	0.956	0.939	0.939
Text	ConGraT ($\alpha = 0$)	0.962	0.958	0.920	0.911
Text	ConGraT ($\alpha = 0.1$)	**0.969**	**0.966**	**0.931**	**0.928**
Text	LinkBERT	–	0.954	–	0.906
Text	Social-LM	0.858	0.878	0.890	0.851
Text	Unimodal LM	0.931	0.943	0.908	0.892

Table 2: Node classification performance (test-set AUC) on article labels of the Pubmed and T-REx datasets. For T-REx, we show the average AUC over the category labels because the dataset is multilabel rather than multiclass. **Bold** values mark best-performing models. C = causal, M = masked.

5 Results

5.1 Node Classification

We train logistic regression models to perform node classification on the Pubmed, Twitter, and T-REx datasets using the embeddings generated from each ConGraT model or baseline. Overall, ConGraT models achieve high performance on this set of tasks relative to baselines on all three datasets.

Table 2 shows AUCs for article label classification on Pubmed and T-REx, and Table 3 shows AUCs for demographic classification tasks on age, gender, occupation, party, and region on users in our Twitter dataset. (At the text level, the dependent variable is that of the corresponding node.) The best ConGraT model achieves the highest node classification performance on all datasets, and the differences from the nearest baseline are statistically significant by a bootstrap test ($p < 10^{-4}$) in all cases. Even the less performant ConGraT model outperforms all baselines in 26 of 28 experiments.

Notably, we see some of ConGraT's largest improvements when one modality has less signal than the other. For example, tweet text is less useful than graph data in predicting users' geographic region. Many Twitter edges are geographically nearby (Takhteyev et al., 2012), and our method is more effective than baselines at infusing this information into an encoder which at inference time sees only text.

The more discriminative nature of representations learned by ConGraT can also be seen visually; Figure 3 shows a 2D UMAP plot comparing ConGraT and GAT embeddings on the Twitter data

		Age		Gender		Occupation		Party		Region	
		C	M	C	M	C	M	C	M	C	M
Graph	ConGraT ($\alpha = 0$)	0.646	0.665	**0.811**	**0.802**	**0.993**	0.989	**0.966**	0.959	**0.755**	**0.780**
	ConGraT ($\alpha = 0.1$)	**0.650**	**0.682**	0.803	0.801	0.992	**0.993**	0.960	**0.986**	0.742	0.774
	GAT	0.631	0.631	0.713	0.713	0.967	0.967	0.757	0.757	0.678	0.678
Text	ConGraT ($\alpha = 0$)	**0.622**	**0.628**	0.663	**0.668**	**0.961**	**0.959**	**0.771**	0.787	**0.693**	0.679
	ConGraT ($\alpha = 0.1$)	0.620	0.624	**0.668**	0.661	0.960	0.958	0.771	**0.796**	0.686	**0.680**
	LinkBERT	–	0.617	–	0.661	–	0.954	–	0.762	–	0.606
	Social-LM	0.566	0.567	0.602	0.608	0.921	0.909	0.628	0.676	0.582	0.572
	Unimodal LM	0.610	0.613	0.649	0.655	0.948	0.945	0.742	0.769	0.587	0.598

Table 3: Node classification performance (test-set AUC) on user traits from the Twitter dataset. **Bold** values mark best-performing models. C = causal, M = masked.

(a) GAT (b) ConGraT

Figure 3: 2D UMAP visualizations of GAT and ConGraT ($\alpha = 0.0$) embeddings on the Twitter data subset with U.S. political party labels (blue = Democrat, orange = Republican).

subset with U.S. political party labels, which validates that ConGraT embeddings have a much more clearly separated class boundary.

5.2 Link Prediction

We evaluate link prediction performance using inner product decoding (Kipf and Welling, 2016) to derive edge existence probabilities from embeddings. As a baseline, we use the same GAT architecture as in our jointly trained ConGraT models and train it directly on link prediction using the same inner product decoding.

Results are shown in Table 4. All ConGraT models outperform the baselines, despite those baselines being specifically trained for link prediction. In some cases, these improvements are quite large, with the best-performing model on the Twitter dataset recording an AUC of 0.806 vs. 0.723 for the best-performing baseline, a relative increase of 11.5%. Training with graph-based similarity information ($\alpha = 0.1$) often also leads to further improvements. Performance is similar for directed and undirected models, demonstrating our approach's adaptability to different types of graphs. Notably, our model's high performance is zero-shot, with no additional training on link prediction.

			Pubmed	T-REx	Twitter
Masked	$\alpha = 0$	U	0.953	0.899	0.791
		D	0.952	0.902	0.797
	$\alpha = 0.1$	U	**0.980**	**0.951**	**0.802**
Causal	$\alpha = 0$	U	0.956	0.908	**0.806**
		D	0.950	0.897	0.799
	$\alpha = 0.1$	U	**0.979**	**0.957**	0.799
GAT	–	U	0.943	0.927	0.713
		D	0.940	0.925	0.723

Table 4: Link prediction performance (test-set AUC) by dataset. **Bold** values mark best-performing models. U = undirected edges, D = directed.

5.3 Language Modeling

Previous works that jointly trained LMs with GNNs on TAGs (Yang et al., 2021; Chien et al., 2022; Zhao et al., 2023) evaluated on node classification tasks using the representations learned by each module, but did not study in depth how joint training affected the LM component's capabilities. We perform this analysis, evaluating joint pretraining's impact on downstream language-modeling performance. To do this, we attach a randomly initialized LM head to the ConGraT text encoder and further train both the encoder and head on causal language modeling. We evaluate with perplexity, and thus limit evaluation to causal-LM variants of our model (those initialized from DistilGPT-2). As a baseline, we finetune the baseline DistilGPT-2 LM on each dataset's texts.

	Pubmed	T-REx	Twitter
$\alpha = 0$	6.95	**15.99**	16.08
$\alpha = 0.1$	**6.94**	16.07	**16.07**
LM	6.98	16.84	16.44

Table 5: Language modeling performance (mean perplexity) of the causal ConGraT models vs. a unimodal LM baseline. **Bold** marks each dataset's best model.

Table 5 shows the mean perplexity of causal LMs trained using ConGraT with $\alpha = 0$ and $\alpha = 0.1$ compared against the causal LM baseline. For all datasets, LMs trained using ConGraT achieve consistently lower average perplexity, and these differences are statistically significant by a paired t-test at the 5σ level ($p < 5.7 \times 10^{-7}$).

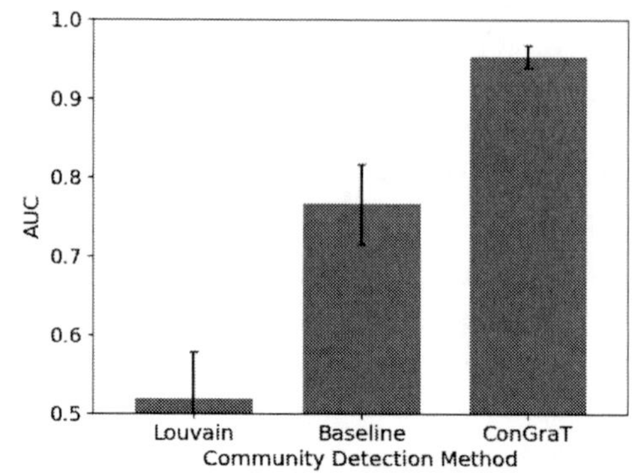

Figure 4: Test-set AUCs for predictions of community labels from text embeddings on the Twitter dataset. "Louvain" denotes Louvain communities detected in the follow graph, "Baseline" the GAT baseline model, and "ConGraT" our model with $\alpha = 0.0$.

5.4 Application: Community Detection

To illustrate ConGraT's broad usability in applications, we compare it to other methods of detecting communities in the Twitter data. As baselines, we use Louvain community detection (Blondel et al., 2008) on the follow graph, and a clustering-based approach on the GAT baseline's embeddings using UMAP (McInnes et al., 2020) and HDBSCAN (McInnes et al., 2017). For ConGraT, we use the same clustering approach with embeddings from the $\alpha = 0.0$ variant. We expect these methods will find different kinds of communities: while Louvain communities are entirely determined by graph structure, and the GAT baseline can take some advantage of text via use of sentence embeddings as initial node vectors, we expect ConGraT to be most able to infuse textual information into network communities.

Because we want to determine how informed each set of communities is by the text associated with the graph, we evaluate by predicting community labels from text embeddings. For each of the above community detection methods, we first compute the centroid of each node's text embeddings and label it with the user's community. Then, we fit a logistic regression model on the training split and predict the test set community label from these centroid text features.

The results, in Figure 4, demonstrate exactly the expected pattern: graph-based Louvain communities are poorly predictable from text, while communities clustered from baseline GAT embeddings are more predictable. The closest relationship to textual content occurs for communities detected with ConGraT embeddings. This pattern highlights a potential application of our method: detecting more *discursively* or *textually grounded* communities in social graphs, rather than ones based only on graph information (e.g., communities informed by discussion among political figures on Twitter).

6 Conclusion

We propose ConGraT (**Con**trastive **Gra**ph-**T**ext pretraining), a self-supervised pretraining framework for jointly learning text and graph node representations using pretrained language models (PLMs) and graph neural networks (GNNs) on a text-attributed graph (TAG). ConGraT uses a batch-wise contrastive learning objective to train text and graph encoders to align their representations within a common latent space. The framework is inductive, generalizable to any text or graph encoder architecture, and does not depend on the structure of the TAG or a particular downstream task. In experiments on citation, link, and social graphs, our method outperforms baselines on various downstream tasks, including node classification, link prediction, and language modeling. Our results also highlight the value of incorporating graph structure into our contrastive learning objective, with nonzero values of the α parameter often improving performance. Finally, an application to community detection, in which our method finds more textually grounded communities than alternative methods, highlights the broad applicability of this form of representation learning to many domains.

References

Jimmy Lei Ba, Jamie Ryan Kiros, and Geoffrey E. Hinton. 2016. Layer Normalization. *arXiv preprint*. ArXiv:1607.06450 [cs, stat].

Pablo Barberá. 2015. Birds of the Same Feather Tweet Together: Bayesian Ideal Point Estimation Using Twitter Data. *Political Analysis*, 23(1):76–91.

Vincent D. Blondel, Jean-Loup Guillaume, Renaud Lambiotte, and Etienne Lefebvre. 2008. Fast unfolding of communities in large networks. *Journal of Statistical Mechanics: Theory and Experiment*, 2008(10):P10008. ArXiv:0803.0476 [physics.soc-ph].

Shantanu Chandra, Pushkar Mishra, Helen Yannakoudakis, Madhav Nimishakavi, Marzieh Saeidi, and Ekaterina Shutova. 2020. Graph-based Modeling of Online Communities for Fake News Detection. *arXiv preprint*. ArXiv:2008.06274 [cs].

Eli Chien, Wei-Cheng Chang, Cho-Jui Hsieh, Hsiang-Fu Yu, Jiong Zhang, Olgica Milenkovic, and Inderjit S. Dhillon. 2022. Node Feature Extraction by Self-Supervised Multi-scale Neighborhood Prediction. In *Proceedings of the 10th International Conference on Learning Representations*.

Arman Cohan, Sergey Feldman, Iz Beltagy, Doug Downey, and Daniel Weld. 2020. SPECTER: Document-level Representation Learning using Citation-informed Transformers. In *Proceedings of the 58th Annual Meeting of the Association for Computational Linguistics*, pages 2270–2282, Online. Association for Computational Linguistics.

Munmun De Choudhury, Hari Sundaram, Ajita John, Doree Duncan Seligmann, and Aisling Kelliher. 2010. "Birds of a Feather": Does User Homophily Impact Information Diffusion in Social Media? *arXiv preprint*. ArXiv:1006.1702 [physics].

Benjamin Elizalde, Soham Deshmukh, Mahmoud Al Ismail, and Huaming Wang. 2023. CLAP: Learning Audio Concepts from Natural Language Supervision. In *ICASSP 2023 - 2023 IEEE International Conference on Acoustics, Speech and Signal Processing (ICASSP)*, pages 1–5, Rhodes Island, Greece. IEEE.

Hady Elsahar, Pavlos Vougiouklis, Arslen Remaci, Christophe Gravier, Jonathon Hare, Frederique Laforest, and Elena Simperl. 2018. T-REx: A Large Scale Alignment of Natural Language with Knowledge Base Triples. In *Proceedings of the Eleventh International Conference on Language Resources and Evaluation (LREC 2018)*, Miyazaki, Japan. European Language Resources Association (ELRA).

William Falcon, Jirka Borovec, Adrian Wälchli, Nic Eggert, Justus Schock, Jeremy Jordan, Nicki Skafte, Ir1dXD, Vadim Bereznyuk, Ethan Harris, Tullie Murrell, Peter Yu, Sebastian Præsius, Travis Addair, Jacob Zhong, Dmitry Lipin, So Uchida, Shreyas Bapat, Hendrik Schröter, Boris Dayma, Alexey Karnachev, Akshay Kulkarni, Shunta Komatsu, Martin.B, Jean-Baptiste SCHIRATTI, Hadrien Mary, Donal Byrne, Cristobal Eyzaguirre, Cinjon, and Anton Bakhtin. 2020. PyTorchLightning/pytorch-lightning: 0.7.6 release.

Matthias Fey and Jan Eric Lenssen. 2019. Fast Graph Representation Learning with PyTorch Geometric. In *Proceedings of the ICLR Workshop on Representation Learning on Graphs and Manifolds*.

Antoine Gourru, Julien Velcin, and Julien Jacques. 2020. Gaussian Embedding of Linked Documents from a Pretrained Semantic Space. In *Proceedings of the Twenty-Ninth International Joint Conference on Artificial Intelligence*, pages 3912–3918, Yokohama, Japan. International Joint Conferences on Artificial Intelligence Organization.

Shashank Gupta and Vasudeva Varma. 2017. Scientific Article Recommendation by using Distributed Representations of Text and Graph. In *Proceedings of the 26th International Conference on World Wide Web Companion - WWW '17 Companion*, pages 1267–1268, Perth, Australia. ACM Press.

William L. Hamilton, Rex Ying, and Jure Leskovec. 2017. Inductive Representation Learning on Large Graphs. In *Advances in Neural Information Processing Systems*, volume 30. Curran Associates, Inc.

Dan Hendrycks and Kevin Gimpel. 2020. Gaussian Error Linear Units (GELUs). *arXiv preprint*. ArXiv:1606.08415 [cs].

Aidan Hogan, Eva Blomqvist, Michael Cochez, Claudia D'amato, Gerard De Melo, Claudio Gutierrez, Sabrina Kirrane, José Emilio Labra Gayo, Roberto Navigli, Sebastian Neumaier, Axel-Cyrille Ngonga Ngomo, Axel Polleres, Sabbir M. Rashid, Anisa Rula, Lukas Schmelzeisen, Juan Sequeda, Steffen Staab, and Antoine Zimmermann. 2022. Knowledge Graphs. *ACM Computing Surveys*, 54(4):1–37.

Glen Jeh and Jennifer Widom. 2002. SimRank: a measure of structural-context similarity. In *Proceedings of the eighth ACM SIGKDD international conference on Knowledge discovery and data mining - KDD '02*, page 538, Edmonton, Alberta, Canada. ACM Press.

Ilia Karpov and Nick Kartashev. 2022. SocialBERT – Transformers for Online Social Network Language Modelling. In Evgeny Burnaev, Dmitry I. Ignatov, Sergei Ivanov, Michael Khachay, Olessia Koltsova, Andrei Kutuzov, Sergei O. Kuznetsov, Natalia Loukachevitch, Amedeo Napoli, Alexander Panchenko, Panos M. Pardalos, Jari Saramäki, Andrey V. Savchenko, Evgenii Tsymbalov, and Elena Tutubalina, editors, *Analysis of Images, Social Networks and Texts*, volume 13217, pages 56–70. Springer International Publishing, Cham. Series Title: Lecture Notes in Computer Science.

Pei Ke, Haozhe Ji, Yu Ran, Xin Cui, Liwei Wang, Linfeng Song, Xiaoyan Zhu, and Minlie Huang. 2021. JointGT: Graph-Text Joint Representation Learning for Text Generation from Knowledge Graphs. In *Findings of the Association for Computational Linguistics: ACL-IJCNLP 2021*, pages 2526–2538, Online. Association for Computational Linguistics.

Yoon Kim, Chris Dyer, and Alexander Rush. 2019. Compound Probabilistic Context-Free Grammars for Grammar Induction. In *Proceedings of the 57th Annual Meeting of the Association for Computational Linguistics*, pages 2369–2385, Florence, Italy. Association for Computational Linguistics.

Thomas N. Kipf and Max Welling. 2016. Variational Graph Auto-Encoders. In *Bayesian Deep Learning Workshop (NeurIPS 2016)*.

Dan Klein and Christopher D. Manning. 2001. A generative constituent-context model for improved grammar induction. In *Proceedings of the 40th Annual Meeting on Association for Computational Linguistics - ACL '02*, page 128, Philadelphia, Pennsylvania. Association for Computational Linguistics.

Vivek Kulkarni, Shubhanshu Mishra, and Aria Haghighi. 2021. LMSOC: An Approach for Socially Sensitive Pretraining. In *Findings of the Association for Computational Linguistics: EMNLP 2021*, pages 2967–2975, Punta Cana, Dominican Republic. Association for Computational Linguistics.

Sandra Kübler, Ryan McDonald, and Joakim Nivre. 2009. *Dependency Parsing*. Springer International Publishing, Cham.

Chang Li and Dan Goldwasser. 2019. Encoding Social Information with Graph Convolutional Networks for-Political Perspective Detection in News Media. In *Proceedings of the 57th Annual Meeting of the Association for Computational Linguistics*, pages 2594–2604, Florence, Italy. Association for Computational Linguistics.

Chang Li, Yi-Yu Lai, Jennifer Neville, and Dan Goldwasser. 2017. Joint Embedding Models for Textual and Social Analysis. In *Proceedings of the 34th International Conference on Machine Learning*, Sydney, Australia.

Xiang Lisa Li and Percy Liang. 2021. Prefix-Tuning: Optimizing Continuous Prompts for Generation. In *Proceedings of the 59th Annual Meeting of the Association for Computational Linguistics and the 11th International Joint Conference on Natural Language Processing (Volume 1: Long Papers)*, pages 4582–4597, Online. Association for Computational Linguistics.

Yangguang Li, Feng Liang, Lichen Zhao, Yufeng Cui, Wanli Ouyang, Jing Shao, Fengwei Yu, and Junjie Yan. 2022. Supervision Exists Everywhere: A Data Efficient Contrastive Language-Image Pre-training Paradigm. In *Proceedings of the International Conference on Learning Representations*. ArXiv:2110.05208 [cs].

Chihuang Liu and Joseph JaJa. 2021. Class-similarity based label smoothing for confidence calibration. *Preprint*, arXiv:2006.14028.

Jie Liu, Zhicheng He, Lai Wei, and Yalou Huang. 2018. Content to Node: Self-Translation Network Embedding. In *Proceedings of the 24th ACM SIGKDD International Conference on Knowledge Discovery & Data Mining*, pages 1794–1802, London United Kingdom. ACM.

Ilya Loshchilov and Frank Hutter. 2019. Decoupled Weight Decay Regularization. In *Proceedings of the Seventh International Conference on Learning Representations (ICLR 2019)*, New Orleans, LA, USA.

Hanjia Lyu and Jiebo Luo. 2022. Understanding Political Polarization via Jointly Modeling Users, Connections and Multimodal Contents on Heterogeneous Graphs. In *Proceedings of the 30th ACM International Conference on Multimedia*. ArXiv:2201.05946 [cs].

Trevor Martin. 2017. community2vec: Vector representations of online communities encode semantic relationships. In *Proceedings of the Second Workshop on NLP and Computational Social Science*, pages 27–31, Vancouver, Canada. Association for Computational Linguistics.

Leland McInnes, John Healy, and Steve Astels. 2017. hdbscan: Hierarchical density based clustering. *Journal of Open Source Software*, 2(11):205.

Leland McInnes, John Healy, and James Melville. 2020. Umap: Uniform manifold approximation and projection for dimension reduction. *Preprint*, arXiv:1802.03426.

Paulius Micikevicius, Sharan Narang, Jonah Alben, Gregory Diamos, Erich Elsen, David Garcia, Boris Ginsburg, Michael Houston, Oleksii Kuchaiev, Ganesh Venkatesh, and Hao Wu. 2018. Mixed Precision Training. In *Proceedings of the 2018 International Conference on Learning Representations*.

Jeremiah Milbauer, Adarsh Mathew, and James Evans. 2021. Aligning Multidimensional Worldviews and Discovering Ideological Differences. In *Proceedings of the 2021 Conference on Empirical Methods in Natural Language Processing*, pages 4832–4845, Online and Punta Cana, Dominican Republic. Association for Computational Linguistics.

Norman Mu, Alexander Kirillov, David Wagner, and Saining Xie. 2022. SLIP: Self-supervision Meets Language-Image Pre-training. In Shai Avidan, Gabriel Brostow, Moustapha Cissé, Giovanni Maria Farinella, and Tal Hassner, editors, *Computer Vision – ECCV 2022*, volume 13686, pages 529–544. Springer Nature Switzerland, Cham. Series Title: Lecture Notes in Computer Science.

Aaron van den Oord, Yazhe Li, and Oriol Vinyals. 2019. Representation Learning with Contrastive Predictive Coding. *arXiv preprint*. ArXiv:1807.03748 [cs, stat].

Malte Ostendorff, Nils Rethmeier, Isabelle Augenstein, Bela Gipp, and Georg Rehm. 2022. Neighborhood Contrastive Learning for Scientific Document Representations with Citation Embeddings. In *Proceedings of the 2022 Conference on Empirical Methods in Natural Language Processing (EMNLP 2022)*, Abu Dhabi. Association for Computational Linguistics.

Adam Paszke, Sam Gross, Francisco Massa, Adam Lerer, James Bradbury, Gregory Chanan, Trevor Killeen, Zeming Lin, Natalia Gimelshein, Luca Antiga, Alban Desmaison, Andreas Kopf, Edward Yang, Zachary DeVito, Martin Raison, Alykhan Tejani, Sasank Chilamkurthy, Benoit Steiner, Lu Fang, Junjie Bai, and Soumith Chintala. 2019. PyTorch: An imperative style, high-performance deep learning library. In *Advances in Neural Information Processing Systems 32*, pages 8024–8035. Curran Associates, Inc.

Fabian Pedregosa, Gaël Varoquaux, Alexandre Gramfort, Vincent Michel, Bertrand Thirion, Olivier Grisel, Mathieu Blondel, Peter Prettenhofer, Ron Weiss, Vincent Dubourg, Jake Vanderplas, Alexandre Passos, David Cournapeau, Matthieu Brucher, Matthieu Perrot, and Édouard Duchesnay. 2011. Scikit-learn: Machine Learning in Python. *Journal of Machine Learning Research*, 12(85):2825–2830.

Alec Radford, Jong Wook Kim, Chris Hallacy, Aditya Ramesh, Gabriel Goh, Sandhini Agarwal, Girish Sastry, Amanda Askell, Pamela Mishkin, Jack Clark, Gretchen Krueger, and Ilya Sutskever. 2021. Learning Transferable Visual Models From Natural Language Supervision. In *Advances in Neural Information Processing Systems 32*, volume 139 of *Proceedings of Machine Learning Research*, pages 8748–8763. Curran Associates, Inc.

Alec Radford, Jeffrey Wu, Rewon Child, David Luan, Dario Amodei, and Ilya Sutskever. 2019. Language Models are Unsupervised Multitask Learners.

Colin Raffel, Noam Shazeer, Adam Roberts, Katherine Lee, Sharan Narang, Michael Matena, Yanqi Zhou, Wei Li, and Peter J. Liu. 2020. Exploring the Limits of Transfer Learning with a Unified Text-to-Text Transformer. *Journal of Machine Learning Research*, 21(140):1–67.

Nils Reimers and Iryna Gurevych. 2019. Sentence-BERT: Sentence Embeddings using Siamese BERT-Networks. In *Proceedings of the 2019 Conference on Empirical Methods in Natural Language Processing and the 9th International Joint Conference on Natural Language Processing (EMNLP-IJCNLP)*, pages 3980–3990, Hong Kong, China. Association for Computational Linguistics.

Victor Sanh, Lysandre Debut, Julien Chaumond, and Thomas Wolf. 2019. DistilBERT, a distilled version of BERT: smaller, faster, cheaper and lighter. In *5th Workshop on Energy Efficient Machine Learning and Cognitive Computing - NeurIPS 2019*. Curran Associates, Inc.

Prithviraj Sen, Galileo Namata, Mustafa Bilgic, Lise Getoor, Brian Galligher, and Tina Eliassi-Rad. 2008. Collective Classification in Network Data. *AI Magazine*, 29(3):93.

Kaitao Song, Xu Tan, Tao Qin, Jianfeng Lu, and Tie-Yan Liu. 2020. MPNet: Masked and Permuted Pre-training for Language Understanding. In *Advances in Neural Information Processing Systems*, volume 33, pages 16857–16867. Curran Associates, Inc.

Nitish Srivastava, Geoffrey Hinton, Alex Krizhevsky, Ilya Sutskever, and Ruslan Salakhutdinov. 2014. Dropout: A Simple Way to Prevent Neural Networks from Overfitting. *Journal of Machine Learning Research*, 15(56):1929–1958.

Tianxiang Sun, Yunfan Shao, Xipeng Qiu, Qipeng Guo, Yaru Hu, Xuanjing Huang, and Zheng Zhang. 2020. CoLAKE: Contextualized Language and Knowledge Embedding. In *Proceedings of the 28th International Conference on Computational Linguistics*, pages 3660–3670, Barcelona, Spain (Online). International Committee on Computational Linguistics.

Christian Szegedy, Vincent Vanhoucke, Sergey Ioffe, Jonathon Shlens, and Zbigniew Wojna. 2015. Rethinking the inception architecture for computer vision. *Preprint*, arXiv:1512.00567.

Yuri Takhteyev, Anatoliy Gruzd, and Barry Wellman. 2012. Geography of Twitter networks. *Social Networks*, 34(1):73–81.

Kristina Toutanova, Danqi Chen, Patrick Pantel, Hoifung Poon, Pallavi Choudhury, and Michael Gamon. 2015. Representing Text for Joint Embedding of Text and Knowledge Bases. In *Proceedings of the 2015 Conference on Empirical Methods in Natural Language Processing*, pages 1499–1509, Lisbon, Portugal. Association for Computational Linguistics.

Cunchao Tu, Han Liu, Zhiyuan Liu, and Maosong Sun. 2017. CANE: Context-Aware Network Embedding for Relation Modeling. In *Proceedings of the 55th Annual Meeting of the Association for Computational Linguistics (Volume 1: Long Papers)*, pages 1722–1731, Vancouver, Canada. Association for Computational Linguistics.

Petar Veličković, Guillem Cucurull, Arantxa Casanova, Adriana Romero, Pietro Liò, and Yoshua Bengio. 2018. Graph Attention Networks. In *International Conference on Learning Representations (ICLR)*.

Prashanth Vijayaraghavan, Hugo Larochelle, and Deb Roy. 2019. Interpretable Multi-Modal Hate Speech Detection. In *AI for Social Good Workshop, International Conference on Machine Learning (ICML)*. ArXiv:2103.01616 [cs].

Isaac Waller and Ashton Anderson. 2021. Quantifying social organization and political polarization in online platforms. *Nature*, 600(7888):264–268. Number: 7888 Publisher: Nature Publishing Group.

Cheng Yang, Zhiyuan Liu, Deli Zhao, Maosong Sun, and Edward Y. Chang. 2015. Network representation learning with rich text information. In *Proceedings of the 24th International Conference on Artificial Intelligence*, IJCAI'15, pages 2111–2117, Buenos Aires, Argentina. AAAI Press.

Junhan Yang, Zheng Liu, Shitao Xiao, Chaozhuo Li, Defu Lian, Sanjay Agrawal, Amit Singh, Guangzhong Sun, and Xing Xie. 2021. GraphFormers: GNN-nested Transformers for Representation Learning on Textual Graph. In *Advances in Neural Information Processing Systems*, volume 34, pages 28798–28810. Curran Associates, Inc.

Michihiro Yasunaga, Jure Leskovec, and Percy Liang. 2022. LinkBERT: Pretraining Language Models with Document Links. In *Proceedings of the 60th Annual Meeting of the Association for Computational Linguistics (Volume 1: Long Papers)*, pages 8003–8016, Dublin, Ireland. Association for Computational Linguistics.

Michihiro Yasunaga, Hongyu Ren, Antoine Bosselut, Percy Liang, and Jure Leskovec. 2021. QA-GNN: Reasoning with Language Models and Knowledge Graphs for Question Answering. In *Proceedings of the 2021 Conference of the North American Chapter of the Association for Computational Linguistics: Human Language Technologies*, pages 535–546, Online. Association for Computational Linguistics.

Daokun Zhang, Jie Yin, Xingquan Zhu, and Chengqi Zhang. 2017. User Profile Preserving Social Network Embedding. In *Proceedings of the Twenty-Sixth International Joint Conference on Artificial Intelligence*, pages 3378–3384, Melbourne, Australia. International Joint Conferences on Artificial Intelligence Organization.

Haopeng Zhang and Jiawei Zhang. 2020. Text Graph Transformer for Document Classification. In *Proceedings of the 2020 Conference on Empirical Methods in Natural Language Processing (EMNLP)*, pages 8322–8327, Online. Association for Computational Linguistics.

Xikun Zhang, Antoine Bosselut, Michihiro Yasunaga, Hongyu Ren, Percy Liang, Christopher D. Manning, and Jure Leskovec. 2021. GreaseLM: Graph REASoning Enhanced Language Models for Question Answering. In *Proceedings of the 2021 International Conference on Learning Representations.*

Jianan Zhao, Meng Qu, Chaozhuo Li, Hao Yan, Qian Liu, Rui Li, Xing Xie, and Jian Tang. 2023. Learning on Large-scale Text-attributed Graphs via Variational Inference. In *Proceedings of the 11th International Conference on Learning Representations.*

A Sensitivity Analysis on α

To examine the hyperparameter α's impact on downstream performance, we conduct a sensitivity analysis on all three evaluation tasks, using the Pubmed dataset, with $\alpha = 0, 0.1, 0.5,$ and 1.0. We use only the causal model variant for the LM task.

	NCG	NCT	LP	LM
$\alpha = 0.0$	0.967	0.962	0.956	6.95
$\alpha = 0.1$	**0.973**	**0.969**	**0.979**	6.94
$\alpha = 0.5$	0.962	0.958	0.977	6.98
$\alpha = 1.0$	0.941	0.900	0.897	**6.88**
Baseline	0.956	0.931	0.943	6.98

Table 6: Results of sensitivity analysis. NCG = node classification, graph; NCT = node classification, text; LP = link prediction; LM = language modeling. Values are AUC for the first three columns and perplexity for language modeling.

We find that α's impact varies by task. For link prediction and node classification, we see an intuitive pattern: Performance is best for α between 0 and 1, especially compared to $\alpha = 1$. That is, both components of our objective—matching nodes to texts, and matching nodes and texts to similar nodes and texts—add value. This pattern is not universal, however; while $\alpha > 0$, particularly $\alpha = 0.1$, consistently outperforms $\alpha = 0$, LM performance is best with $\alpha = 1.0$. We conjecture this pattern may be due to inter-document similarity in language use, which $\alpha = 1.0$ more effectively trains into the PLM. Overall, our results suggest both that $\alpha = 0.1$ is a reasonable default and that it may be worth tuning this parameter in practice.

B Embedding Space Geometry Analysis

To complement evaluation on downstream applications like node classification, link prediction and language modeling, this section pursues certain analyses of the geometry of the joint embedding space. We compare these jointly learned embedding spaces to the null model of separate spaces, as learned by the unimodal LM and GAT baselines.

We expect in particular that ConGraT's joint pretraining should align the two embedding spaces with each other, as well as with non-embedded distance metrics based entirely on the graph. We focus on examining how these distances (in the embedding spaces and the graph) relate to each other, because the geometric properties of a metric space are chiefly determined by the underlying metric. A finding of significantly increased alignment between distance metrics would indicate the models are effectively integrating information across language and graph modalities. As discussed below and shown in Table 7, this is in fact exactly what we do see.

Inter-Embedding Distance Correlation. First, we examine the correlation of the distance between pairs of texts with the distance between the corresponding pairs of nodes. That is, we sample text pairs $(t_1^{(u)}, t_2^{(v)})$ from nodes u and v, and examine over many such samples the correlation between the text-embedding distance $d_T(t_1^{(u)}, t_2^{(v)})$ and the graph-embedding distance $d_G(u, v)$. We operationalize both in practice as the cosine distance.

With ConGraT pretraining, the cosine distance between text embeddings is substantially more correlated than in the separately trained case with the distance between the parent nodes. We see this effect for all model variants against the separate-spaces baseline on all datasets, and the increases are significant by a bootstrap test ($p < 10^{-6}$). Supporting our hypothesis, the two spaces have become systematically more aligned geometrically.

Embedding-Graph Distance Correlation. Next, we relate the cosine distance in the text embedding space to a purely graph-based distance — SimRank (Jeh and Widom, 2002) in our case. This extends the previous analysis by grounding the text-embedding distance more directly in the graph. In 34 out of 36 cases, we observe a significant increase over the separate-spaces baseline in the correlation between the text embedding distance and graph SimRank (at the $p = 10^{-6}$ level, using a similar bootstrap test).

B.1 Retrieval

Finally, as an additional test of geometric alignment and cross-modal data integration, we consider a simple retrieval task: identifying the node associated with a given text. For each text, we select the node whose embedding has the highest cosine similarity to the text's embedding, and report the top-k accuracy for k from 1 to 10. This task might itself be an important downstream measure in a retrieval setting, but for purposes of geometric analysis we consider only the comparison to separate embedding spaces here. Note that as with CLIP, this use

Dataset	Directed	LM Type	Sim.	Inter-Embedding		Text Emb.-Graph	
				Joint	Separate	Joint	Separate
Pubmed	Directed	Causal	$\alpha = 0.0$	**0.682**	0.100	**0.118**	0.019
		Masked	$\alpha = 0.0$	**0.604**	0.248	**0.120**	0.059
	Undirected	Causal	$\alpha = 0.0$	**0.670**	0.109	**0.157**	0.026
			$\alpha = 0.1$	**0.679**	0.109	**0.171**	0.026
		Masked	$\alpha = 0.0$	**0.603**	0.260	**0.155**	0.080
			$\alpha = 0.1$	**0.647**	0.260	**0.173**	0.080
TRex	Directed	Causal	$\alpha = 0.0$	**0.650**	0.038	**0.131**	0.022
		Masked	$\alpha = 0.0$	**0.564**	0.248	**0.179**	0.078
	Undirected	Causal	$\alpha = 0.0$	**0.647**	0.040	**0.215**	0.027
			$\alpha = 0.1$	**0.704**	0.040	**0.302**	0.027
		Masked	$\alpha = 0.0$	**0.600**	0.248	**0.220**	0.142
			$\alpha = 0.1$	**0.666**	0.248	**0.272**	0.142
Twitter	Directed	Causal	$\alpha = 0.0$	**0.319**	0.035	**0.048**	0.019
		Masked	$\alpha = 0.0$	**0.270**	0.084	**0.049†**	0.047
	Undirected	Causal	$\alpha = 0.0$	**0.317**	0.036	**0.041**	0.018
			$\alpha = 0.1$	**0.301**	0.036	**0.048**	0.018
		Masked	$\alpha = 0.0$	**0.300**	0.083	0.037	**0.044†**
			$\alpha = 0.1$	**0.226**	0.083	**0.052**	0.044

Table 7: Correlations between pairs of distances as discussed in Appendix B: those of the text and graph embedding spaces ("Inter-Embedding"), on the one hand, and the text embedding space and the graph-based SimRank distance ("Text Emb.-Graph"), on the other. The "Joint" column indicates the jointly trained embedding spaces from our ConGraT models, and the "Separate" column indicates the separately trained embedding spaces of the GAT and LM baselines. The most closely aligned pair of distances in each comparison, joint or baseline, is shown in **bold**. Differences marked with a † are not significant at the $p = 10^{-6}$ level by a bootstrap test.

of our representations can be thought of as zero shot transfer for text or node classification (where objects in the other modality are the classes).

Results are shown in Figure 5. Top-k accuracy is substantially higher than the separately-trained baseline for all models at all values of k. All differences are significant at the $p = 10^{-6}$ level according to a bootstrap test. Moreover, the top-k accuracies achieved are often high relative to the size of the datasets. With 1,996 articles (i.e., nodes) in the Pubmed test set, the best-performing model includes the correct article for a text snippet in its top 10 most similar articles (0.5% of the test set) 94.3% of the time.

C Robustness Check: SVD-Based Initial Vectors

In this section, we replicate the analysis described in Section 4, with a twist: instead of the sentence embeddings used there as initial node representations for those models which rely on them, we use vectors from the truncated SVD of the graph adjacency matrix. We train and evaluate entirely new models, in which all other properties of training, inference and datasets besides the choice of initial node vectors are the same as in the main text. Doing so provides an additional check on the soundness of our approach and gives evidence of its adaptability to various kinds of attributed graphs.

We truncate the SVD embeddings produced by scikit-learn's implementation (Pedregosa et al., 2011) to 768 dimensions, so that the embedding dimensionality is the same as for the sentence embeddings. To avoid leakage between train and test, we use the V^* matrix from the train set to generate test-set embeddings (thus relying only on test-set nodes' connections to nodes in the training set).

C.1 Node Classification

Node classification performance is similar to that reported in the main text, with the best-performing

		Age		Gender		Occupation		Region	
		C	M	C	M	C	M	C	M
Graph	ConGraT ($\alpha = 0$)	0.769	0.782	0.803	**0.832**	0.993	**0.994**	0.765	0.769
	ConGraT ($\alpha = 0.1$)	**0.776**	**0.801**	**0.811**	0.826	**0.993**	0.993	**0.773**	**0.774**
	GAT	0.767	0.767	0.791	0.791	0.991	0.991	0.706	0.706
Text	ConGraT ($\alpha = 0$)	**0.620**	0.631	0.658	**0.667**	**0.961**	**0.962**	**0.692**	**0.689**
	ConGraT ($\alpha = 0.1$)	0.619	**0.635**	**0.661**	0.666	0.959	0.960	0.684	0.684
	LinkBERT	–	0.617	–	0.661	–	0.954	–	0.606
	Social-LM	0.566	0.567	0.602	0.608	0.921	0.909	0.582	0.572
	Unimodal LM	0.610	0.613	0.649	0.655	0.948	0.945	0.587	0.598

Table 8: Node classification performance on user traits from the Twitter dataset. (C = causal, M = masked.) Values are test-set AUCs. **Bold** values denote the best models in each experiment. All differences between the best ConGraT model and the closest baseline are statistically significant ($p < 10^{-4}$) by a bootstrap test. These results are from models which use initial node representations (where applicable) based on the truncated SVD of the graph adjacency matrix rather than sentence embeddings.

ConGraT model outperforming all of our baseline models in all tested cases.

Twitter. Table 8 shows AUCs for the demographic classification tasks. Results are similar to what we observe with sentence embeddings as initial node representations: the best-performing ConGraT model beats all baselines in evaluation with both graph and text embeddings.

Unlike in the maint text, however, we do not present results for the political-party outcome variable. This is because the SVD-based embeddings are too predictive: all graph models (and thus also all joint models) are able to perfectly separate the two classes. This phenomenon is a good example of the Twitter follow graph's powerful organizing principle of homophily: Users tend to be connected to other users who are similar to them (Barberá, 2015), in this case politically.

Pubmed and T-REx. AUCs for article category classification are shown in Table 9. As with the models using sentence embeddings, the best ConGraT model outperforms our baselines in all experiments, using both graph and text embeddings.

C.2 Link Prediction

Link prediction results, given in Table 10, are broadly similar to those in the main text and its Table 4. On all three datasets, we see ConGraT node encoders deliver much better than chance performance as zero-shot link predictors.

Performance is often very similar to the levels achieved with sentence embeddings, as on the Pubmed and undirected T-REx datasets. The most notable difference in relative performance vs baseline is on the Twitter dataset, where in fact ConGraT performance is quite close to that in Table 4 — the GAT baseline, however, performs much better with SVD-based embeddings.

		Pubmed		T-Rex	
		C	M	C	M
Graph	ConGraT ($\alpha = 0$)	**0.877**	0.870	0.835	0.799
	ConGraT ($\alpha = 0.1$)	0.868	**0.878**	**0.854**	**0.833**
	GAT	0.600	0.600	0.720	0.720
Text	ConGraT ($\alpha = 0$)	0.955	0.954	**0.926**	0.902
	ConGraT ($\alpha = 0.1$)	**0.961**	**0.955**	0.923	**0.910**
	LinkBERT	–	0.954	–	0.906
	Social-LM	0.858	0.878	0.890	0.851
	Unimodal LM	0.931	0.943	0.908	0.892

Table 9: Node classification performance on article labels of the Pubmed and T-REx datasets. Values are test-set AUCs. (C = causal, M = masked.) For T-REx, we show the average AUC over the category labels because the dataset is multilabel rather than multiclass. **Bold** values denote the best model in each experiment. All differences between the best ConGraT model and the closest baseline are statistically significant ($p < 10^{-4}$) by a bootstrap test. These results are from models which use initial node representations (where applicable) based on the truncated SVD of the graph adjacency matrix rather than sentence embeddings.

C.3 Language Modeling

Results here are similar to those presented in the main text, though ConGraT model performance

			Pubmed	TRex	Twitter
Masked	$\alpha = 0$	Undir.	0.985	0.816	0.805
		Dir.	0.955	0.663	0.826
	$\alpha = 0.1$	Undir.	**0.990**	**0.882**	0.790
Causal	$\alpha = 0$	Undir.	0.976	0.886	0.793
		Dir.	0.952	0.758	0.819
	$\alpha = 0.1$	Undir.	**0.984**	**0.925**	0.785
Baseline	GAT	Undir.	0.866	0.839	**0.875**
		Dir.	0.864	0.719	0.838

Table 10: Link prediction performance on each dataset. Values are test-set AUCs. **Bold** values denote the best model in each experiment. These results are from models which use initial node representations (where applicable) based on the truncated SVD of the graph adjacency matrix rather than sentence embeddings.

declines slightly on the Pubmed dataset.

	Pubmed	T-REx	Twitter
ConGraT (Causal, $\alpha = 0$)	7.03	17.42	16.05
ConGraT (Causal, $\alpha = 0.1$)	7.03	**15.62**	**16.05**
Unimodal LM (Baseline)	**6.98**	16.84	16.44

Table 11: Language modeling performance of the ConGraT models with causal text encoders, vs. a unimodal LM baseline. Values are mean perplexity (lower is better). **Bold** values are the best models on each dataset. All differences from the unimodal baseline are significant by a paired t-test at the 5σ level ($p < 5.7 \times 10^{-7}$). These results are from models which use initial node representations (where applicable) based on the truncated SVD of the graph adjacency matrix rather than sentence embeddings.

D Additional Related Work

Many traditional NLP tasks focus on learning graph structures that exist within a text, such as dependency parsing (Kübler et al., 2009) or grammar induction (Klein and Manning, 2001; Kim et al., 2019). More recent lines of work have extended this focus on graph structures to knowledge graphs, where the graph structure is over knowledge-base entities which may appear in the text, and citation or social networks, where the relevant graph is the one between the entities which write or contain the texts. Social science applications have also frequently motivated approaches to learning from joint graph/text data.

Knowledge graphs. Work on knowledge graphs (KGs) uses graph representations to encode facts about the world (Hogan et al., 2022), with real-world entities as nodes and edges used to encode inter-entity relationships. Previous works have presented models for jointly representing texts and KG entities, or entire graphs associated with each text (Toutanova et al., 2015), often focusing on question answering or reasoning (Zhang et al., 2021; Sun et al., 2020; Yasunaga et al., 2021) or text generation (Ke et al., 2021). Our work differs in the architecture employed (a contrastive text/graph matching objective) and in the setting it is specialized for: text-attributed graphs, where the graph is over entities which produce (e.g., Twitter users) or contain (e.g., academic articles) their associated texts.

Applications. Many studies in the joint graph/text domain have focused on social-science questions in addition to machine-learning ones. Learning the community structure of social networks is a common application (Martin, 2017; Waller and Anderson, 2021), as is detecting hate speech, misinformation or fake news (Vijayaraghavan et al., 2019; Chandra et al., 2020). Some work has also focused on understanding political polarization or ideological differences between groups (Milbauer et al., 2021; Lyu and Luo, 2022).

E Dataset Details

Twitter. We created a Twitter dataset of 167,558 tweets posted by a set of 8,721 influential users in media, politics, and entertainment, and the follow graph among these users, which consists of 2,373,956 edges. We included up to 20 tweets per user in the dataset, sampled from each user's most recent 3,200 tweets as of May 9, 2021. We also collected certain demographic data about these users (region of residence, age, gender, politician vs. entertainer occupation, and political party) by matching them to Wikipedia and Ballotpedia[2].

To obtain the age and gender of Twitter users, we connected the accounts to their corresponding Wikipedia pages and used Wikidata to infer those two features. Users also self-report locations in their Twitter bios; from these locations, we created four regional categories. Finally, we used data from Ballotpedia to label whether a user is a politician or not and to identify their political party. Note that politician status and party are derived in different ways, from different data fields, with politician status being defined more strictly. These variables,

[2]https://ballotpedia.org/

used as targets in node classification tasks, are broken down in Table 12.

Pubmed. We built from scratch a version of the popular Pubmed graph learning benchmark (Sen et al., 2008) that includes the titles and abstracts of each article; widely available versions of the dataset do not include any text. We began with the standard list of PMIDs for the articles in the dataset and fetched the title, abstract, and list of references using the Pubmed API. We kept directed citation edges only to other articles in the dataset. One PMID was not found in the Pubmed database and was thus left out. The final dataset includes 19,716 nodes, 61,110 edges, and 59,381 texts, including both titles and abstracts. The included articles are about diabetes and the standard node categories are from the Pubmed database: type-1 diabetes, type-2 diabetes, or experimental evidence.

T-REx. We used the articles in the T-REx corpus (Elsahar et al., 2018) of Wikipedia articles that were labeled with the "Robots" category or any of its descendant categories. From these categories, we constructed several binary target label sets for the T-REx prediction task. However, since the most commonly occurring category was only associated with 526 (roughly 5.7%) of the articles, we expanded each article's labels to include both first and second level ancestors in the category hierarchy to obtain better class label balance. From the initial set of 1,433 unique categories, this expansion yielded a total of 6,643 unique categories, with the most frequent ("Spacecraft") occurring on 1,342 articles. We then selected five categories to use as labels for separate binary prediction tasks, choosing frequent categories that generally had small overlap with each other (i.e. were associated with mostly disjoint document sets.) Note that not every data point in the dataset, then, received a label. The resultant categories we selected are listed in Table 12.

Splitting. We divide the datasets into a 70% train set, 10% validation set, and 20% test set, splitting at the node level so that every text associated with a given node is in the same split. Because evaluation is inductive, any graph edges which cross split boundaries are dropped.

Dataset	Feature	Category	# Nodes
Twitter	Region	Midwest	64
		Northeast	1207
		South	1411
		West	1100
	Age	19-39	575
		40-49	2216
		>=65	844
	Gender	Female	1586
		Male	2495
	Occupation	Non-politician	8271
		Politician	434
	Party	Democrat	241
		Republican	193
Pubmed	Article Type	Experimental	4103
		Type I	7875
		Type II	7738
T-REx	Wiki Category	Robots	666
		Rockets	843
		Sci-Fi	712
		Spacecraft	1342
		Space Telescopes	701

Table 12: Breakdowns of the dependent variables for node classification experiments on the three datasets.

F Model Architectures and Training Details

We estimate that training all of our joint and baseline models together used 263 hours of GPU time. Because the assumptions made for this value are conservative, the actual value is likely slightly less.

F.1 ConGraT Models

We trained all ConGraT models on either a single NVIDIA RTX A6000 GPU or a single NVIDIA A100 GPU. For masked LM experiments, we used the pretrained `all-mpnet-base-v2` model (Song et al., 2020) from the sentence-transformers toolkit (Reimers and Gurevych, 2019), which has 12 layers of 12 heads each, producing 768-dimensional embeddings. It was pretrained constrastively on several corpora from similar domains to those we consider here,[3] making it a good match for our work. Our causal LM experiments used the pretrained `distilgpt2` model (Sanh et al., 2019), distilled from the larger GPT-2 model (Radford et al., 2019), with 6 layers of 12 heads each, producing 768-dimensional embeddings.[4] For the graph node encoder, all models used a graph attention network

[3]See the model card for details: `https://huggingface.co/sentence-transformers/all-mpnet-base-v2`.

[4]Again see the model card for more details: `https://huggingface.co/distilgpt2`.

(GAT) (Veličković et al., 2018) with 3 layers and 2 attention heads in each layer. As in a standard transformer, each graph convolutional layer is separated from the next by a linear layer, with layer normalization (Ba et al., 2016) applied afterwards. Hidden representations are 64-dimensional, and the final output vectors are 768-dimensional so that baseline model outputs have the same shape as language model outputs.

Parameter counts are as follows: `distilgpt2`, 81.9 million; `all-mpnet-base-v2`, 109.4 million; our GAT encoder, 199.7 thousand. The jointly trained models, including the adapter layers after the text and graph encoders, have 83.9 million parameters (causal / `distilgpt2`) and 110.9 million parameters (masked / `all-mpnet-base-v2`).

Training is sensitive to the learning rate; we found that a good compromise between speed of training and instability was a value of `1e-4`. At a variety of learning rates, there were also intermittent large spikes in the norm of the gradient, which derailed training unless the gradients were clipped. We clipped the gradient at each step to a norm of 1. In order to reduce memory consumption and fit larger batches onto a single GPU, we used 16-bit mixed precision training (Micikevicius et al., 2018). We encountered numerical overflow problems with FP16, however, related to large gradient values at certain layers, and found it necessary to reduce the init-scale parameter of the gradient scaler from its default value of 2^{16} to 256 in order to avoid overflow. We initialized the log-temperature parameter τ to 3.5 and constrained it to be within $(-\log 100, +\log 100)$ in order to avoid training instability. We trained all models with PyTorch (Paszke et al., 2019) and pytorch-lightning (Falcon et al., 2020), also using pytorch-geometric (Fey and Lenssen, 2019) for graph encoders and GAT baselines, and Huggingface Transformers (Raffel et al., 2020) for textual baselines and text encoders.

We also found that performance suffers if each batch is not unique on nodes (i.e., if each node has multiple texts, only one text per node can be in any given batch). We experimented with simply dropping duplicates from uniformly sampled batches, but this discarded too much data. Instead, we randomly sorted the texts on each epoch so as to minimize the number of within-batch duplicates (assuming minibatches are taken consecutively from the sorted dataset), and dropped any remaining duplicates.

Finally, because the objective is batch-wise contrastive, the problem becomes quadratically more difficult as the batch size increases. We used the largest batch size we could consistently fit into available hardware, but future work should explore the question of returns to scale.

All models used the AdamW optimizer (Loshchilov and Hutter, 2019) with β values of (0.9, 0.999) and without weight decay. All joint models used a probability of 0.3 for dropout applied to text and node embeddings. Learning rates and batch sizes for our various models are shown in Table 13.

F.2 Unimodal Baselines

To better understand the effects of multi-modal pretraining, we also trained unimodal models, either language models or graph attention transformers, and evaluated these unimodal models on the downstream tasks. For textual models, we fine-tuned pretrained `all-mpnet-base-v2` and `distilgpt2` on the training splits of the evaluation datasets. Language models were fine-tuned for 3 epochs. For graph models, we trained graph attention network (GAT) models to do non-variational graph autoencoding (Kipf and Welling, 2016), also known as link prediction, on the network structure of the evaluation datasets. GAT models were trained from between 30 to 100 epochs with early stopping based on validation AUC, with patience of 3 epochs and minimum delta of 0.01. We compare these unimodal baselines against ConGraT. Parameter counts for the text and graph baselines are the same as reported for the appropriate modality's joint encoder in Subsection F.1. Batch sizes and learning rates, as for joint models, are reported in Table 13. Our unimodal baselines were trained on NVIDIA RTX A6000 GPUs, or on up to four NVIDIA GTX 1080 Ti GPUs.

F.3 Social-LM

We implemented a baseline Social-LM, as a modified version of SocialBERT[5] (Karpov and Kartashev, 2022) (also very closely related to LM-SOC (Kulkarni et al., 2021)), which uses pretrained, frozen node embeddings to prime language model pretraining. Specifically, we added a special node token [G] at the beginning of texts and used the pretrained GAT model to obtain the corresponding node embedding paired with each tweet or article, which was used to replace the token embedding

[5]The SocialBERT authors did not publish their code.

Model or Model Family	Batch Size	Base LR	LR Schedule
ConGraT	36	1.0e-4	Constant LR
LM Baseline	36	5.0e-5	Linear 10% warmup
SocialLM	36	5.0e-5	Linear 10% warmup
LinkBERT	36	5.0e-5	Linear 10% warmup
GNN AE (Baseline), Twitter, Dir.	n/a	1.0e-2	Constant LR
GNN AE (Baseline), Twitter, Undir.	n/a	1.0e-2	Constant LR
GNN AE (Baseline), T-REx, Dir.	n/a	1.0e-2	Constant LR
GNN AE (Baseline), T-REx, Undir.	n/a	1.0e-2	Constant LR
GNN AE (Baseline), Pubmed, Dir.	n/a	1.0e-2	Constant LR
GNN AE (Baseline), Pubmed, Undir.	n/a	1.0e-2	Constant LR
GNN AE (SVD), Twitter, Dir.	n/a	1.0e-2	Constant LR
GNN AE (SVD), Twitter, Undir.	n/a	1.0e-2	Constant LR
GNN AE (SVD), T-REx, Dir.	n/a	1.0e-3	Constant LR
GNN AE (SVD), T-REx, Undir.	n/a	1.0e-3	Constant LR
GNN AE (SVD), Pubmed, Dir.	n/a	1.0e-3	Constant LR
GNN AE (SVD), Pubmed, Undir.	n/a	1.0e-3	Constant LR

Table 13: Batch sizes and learning rates for all models. (AE = autoencoder.) Except for the GNN baseline's learning rate, where we tried both 1.0e-2 and 1.0e-3 and found large dataset-specific effects on performance, all models listed in the same model family use the same parameter settings for all datasets. In particular, all ConGraT models, whether directed or undirected, with $\alpha = 0$ or $\alpha = 0.1$, and causal or masked encoders, used the same batch size and learning rate. GNN baselines do not list a batch size because the entire graph is processed at once.

for [G]. During the language model pretraining, we froze the node embeddings and only fine-tuned the language model to generate texts conditioned on the node embeddings. Our Social-LM implementation has some key differences from SocialBERT and LMSOC: (1) for masked LM experiments, we used `all-mpnet-base-v2` to replace BERT, to be consistent with other experiments for a fair comparison; (2) we also experimented with a causal language model `distilgpt2` under the Social-LM baseline, whereas LMSOC and SocialBERT only used the masked language model BERT; (3) we injected the node embedding as the zero token embedding of texts as SocialBERT suggests, whereas LMSOC appends the node embedding at the end. We adopted the zero token injection approach because the same strategy is adaptable for both causal and masked language modeling, while last token injection does not work for causal LMs like `distilgpt2`; (4) we used our unimodal GAT model trained on the graph autoencoding task to generate node embeddings for each tweet or article, whereas LMSOC uses node2vec and SocialBERT uses vectors from SVD and Deep Walk. We used the GAT in order to be consistent with ConGraT and the unimodal baseline, to ensure that the comparisons were fair, and because it was likely to be a stronger baseline than using SVD. Social-LM models were fine-tuned for 3 epochs with the same hyperparameters used for the language modeling baseline, and have the same number of parameters as `all-mpnet-base-v2`, our masked LM baselines and the joint masked text encoders.

F.4 LinkBERT

We implemented and trained LinkBERT (Yasunaga et al., 2022) as described in the original paper, with the only difference being that we used the same `all-mpnet-base-v2` architecture as the other baseline models (instead of BERT-Base) in order to maintain consistency across experiments. We initialized weights from the pretrained `all-mpnet-base-v2` model from sentence-transformers, and fine-tuned it on the masked language modeling (MLM) and document relation prediction (DRP) tasks for 3 epochs. Hyperparameters used for training are listed in Table 13. Note that because of its MLM training objective, we used LinkBERT as a baseline for masked language model variants of ConGraT only. All LinkBERT models have the same number of parameters as `all-mpnet-base-v2`, as the DRP head is dropped at inference time.

We created training instances for LinkBERT by sampling contiguous, linked, or random text segment pairs for the DRP training objective from each dataset, with the three options appearing uniformly (1/3, 1/3, 1/3). For the Pubmed and Twitter datasets, we sampled 100,000 text pairs for each category, for a total of 300,000 pairs. For T-REx, which is a substantially smaller dataset, we sampled 10,000 text pairs for each category, for a total of 30,000 pairs. Text pairs consisted of anchor text segment X_A and paired text segment X_B: (X_A, X_B). The specific methods we used to sample pairs for each dataset were as follows:

Pubmed. Text segments in each pair consisted of individual sentences from the abstracts of each article in the dataset. Anchor segments X_A were taken by sampling a random abstract, then sampling a random sentence from that abstract. For contiguous pairs, X_B was chosen as the sentence immediately following X_A in the abstract (X_A could not be the last sentence of the abstract). For linked pairs, X_B was chosen as a random sentence from the abstract of one of the articles that was connected to X_A's corresponding article in the citation graph. For random pairs, X_B was chosen as a random sentence from an abstract whose article was not connected to X_A's corresponding article in the citation graph.

T-REx. Text segments in each pair consisted of individual sentences from the introductory paragraphs of each article in the dataset. Anchor segments X_A were taken by sampling a random article, then sampling a random sentence from that article's introductory paragraphs. For continuous pairs, X_B was chosen as the sentence immediately following X_A, with the same restriction as in Pubmed that X_A could not be the last sentence. For linked pairs, X_B was chosen as a random sentence from the introductory paragraphs of one of the articles connected to X_A's corresponding article in the link graph. For random pairs, X_B was chosen as a random sentence from an article not connected to X_A's corresponding article in the link graph.

Twitter. Twitter has a different graph-text structure than Pubmed and T-REx; rather than the nodes consisting of texts themselves, the nodes are users who can each produce multiple tweets. Therefore, the notion of what constitutes continuous or linked text segments (tweets) is less clearly defined. We defined these relationships as follows. For contiguous pairs, we sampled a random tweet as X_A, and chose X_B as a different tweet from the same user as X_A. For linked pairs, we sampled X_A from the set of tweets that *mentioned* other users that were present in our dataset. Then, X_B was chosen as a random tweet from the mentioned user. Random pairs were taken by randomly sampling two tweets from different users to use as X_A and X_B.

F.5 Node Classification Methodology

We use the standard scikit-learn (Pedregosa et al., 2011) implementation of logistic/softmax regression with the default L2 regularization, balancing our sometimes very imbalanced classification problems by downsampling before fitting. For performance reasons we use the `liblinear` solver for problems with no more than 5000 training data points and the `saga` solver otherwise. To ensure convergence, we increase the maximum iterations for the solvers from the default of 100 to 10000.

G Licenses and Terms of Use

All software and pretrained models we used were available under open-source licenses which permit our use for research purposes. Our non-Twitter datasets were available under Creative Commons or other licenses allowing research use. We have access to Twitter data pursuant to an agreement with Twitter permitting use of data for research and publication. The agreement permits releasing the tweet IDs, which can be used to get the corresponding tweets from the public Twitter API. Along with the tweet IDs, we plan to release the demographic data collected from Wikipedia and Ballotpedia. Our code and datasets, when released upon publication, will be subject to an open-source license allowing use for research purposes.

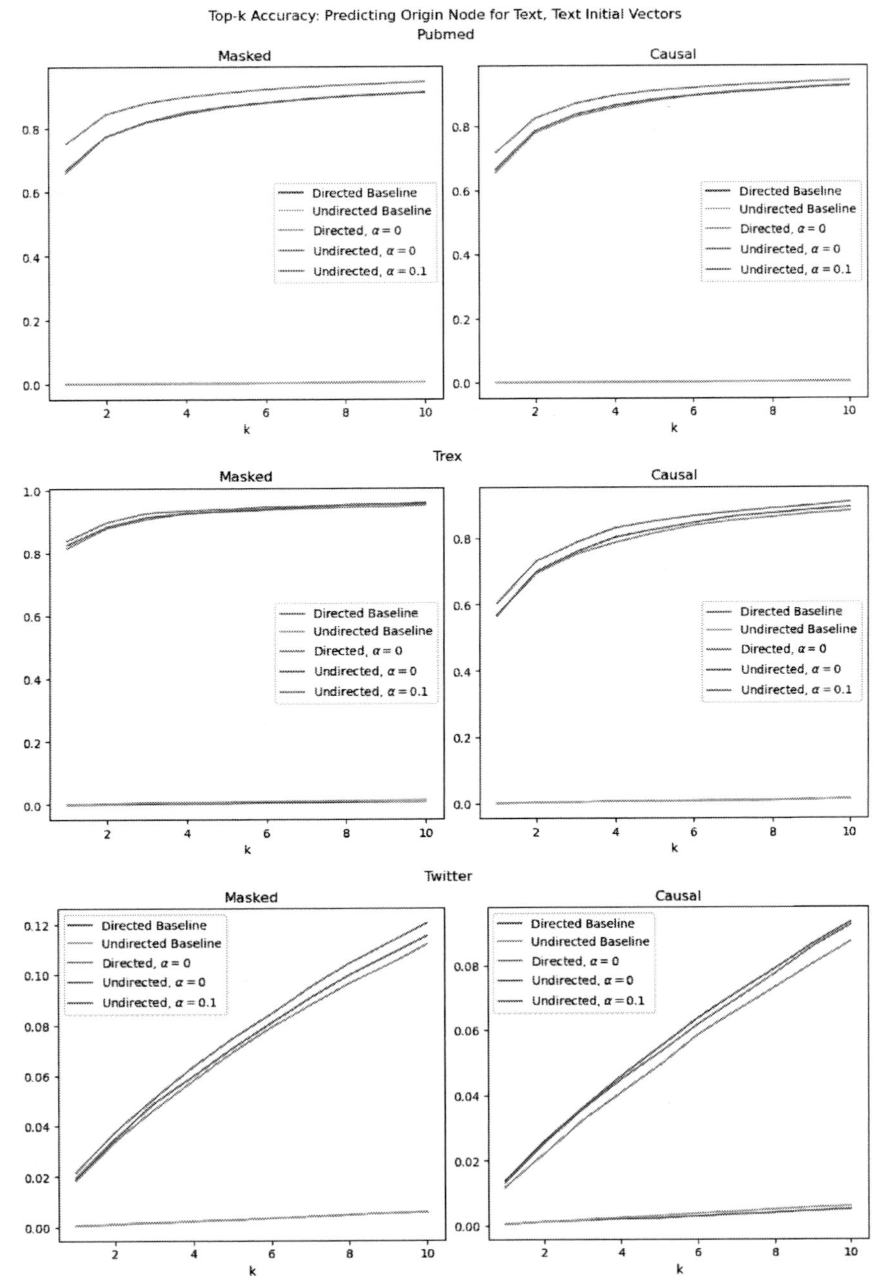

Figure 5: Top-k accuracy on selection of the node which produced a text, for various values of k, as discussed in Subsection B.1. “Baseline” indicates the use of separately pretrained embeddings, and other results are for models with various combinations of edge-direction use and graph-similarity information.

Uniform Meaning Representation Parsing as a Pipelined Approach

Jayeol Chun
Brandeis University
415 South Street, Waltham, MA 02453
jchun@brandeis.edu

Nianwen Xue
Brandeis University
415 South Street, Waltham, MA 02453
xuen@brandeis.edu

Abstract

Uniform Meaning Representation (UMR) is the next phase of semantic formalism following Abstract Meaning Representation (AMR), with added focus on inter-sentential relations allowing the representational scope of UMR to cover a full document. This, in turn, greatly increases the complexity of its parsing task with the additional requirement of capturing document-level linguistic phenomena such as coreference, modal and temporal dependencies. In order to establish a strong baseline despite the small size of recently released UMR v1.0 corpus, we introduce a pipeline model that does not require any training. At the core of our method is a two-track strategy of obtaining UMR's sentence and document graphs separately, with the document-level triples being compiled at the token level and the sentence graph being converted from AMR graphs. By leveraging alignment between AMR and its sentence, we are able to generate the first automatic English UMR parses.

1 Introduction

While the end-to-end deep learning methods based on transformers (Vaswani et al., 2017; Devlin et al., 2019; Radford et al., 2019) helped usher in an era of Large Language Models (LLM) with outstanding results especially in the practical domains of Natural Language Processing (NLP), they also brought about significant advances in the performance of Abstract Meaning Representation (AMR) parsing. Once thought extremely challenging due to its inherently multi-tasking nature, AMR parsing with its adoption of transformer architecture (Bevilacqua et al., 2021; Lee et al., 2022a; Vasylenko et al., 2023) has since matured to a point where its automatic parses feature in various downstream applications (Bonial et al., 2020; Mansouri et al., 2023; Wang et al., 2023), often as a meaningful companion to the Pre-trained Language Models (PLM) llke T5 (Raffel et al., 2019) or BART (Lewis et al., 2020). This trend serves to highlight the enduring interest of the community in leveraging symbolic meaning representations not only for the computational benefit in boosting the model performance but also as a way to better understand how a model seems to 'understand' language.

However, AMR by design is limited to the representational scope of a single sentence. Although efforts have been made to bring together multiple AMRs into a single unified structure (O'Gorman et al., 2018; Naseem et al., 2022), additional annotations across different sentences remain largely confined to coreference and implicit role labeling.

Uniform Meaning Representation

In contrast, Uniform Meaning Representation (UMR) (Van Gysel et al., 2021) begins by inheriting AMR's focus on predicate-argument structure in its sentence-level representation and further adds semantic coverage for aspect, scope, person and number for cross-lingual compatibility (Flanigan et al., 2022; Bonn et al., 2023b). In addition, UMR introduces new document-level triples which cover linguistic phenomena such as coreference, modal and temporal dependencies (Vigus et al., 2019; Zhang and Xue, 2018a; Yao et al., 2022) that potentially go beyond sentence boundaries.

Figure 1 provides an example of UMR annotation for a sample document of two sentences:

1. Kim left to join the others.
2. "They are probably eating," she said.

At the top is an abstract `ROOT` node, whose immediate children `AUTHOR` (author of the text) and `DCT` (document creation time) serve as sub-roots of modal and temporal dependencies respectively. These abstract nodes are highlighted in lightblue.

A modal dependency graph (MDG), shown as a series of red edges in the figure, captures the epistemic certainty and polarity with which

Proceedings of TextGraphs-17: Graph-based Methods for Natural Language Processing, pages 40–52
August 15, 2024 ©2024 Association for Computational Linguistics

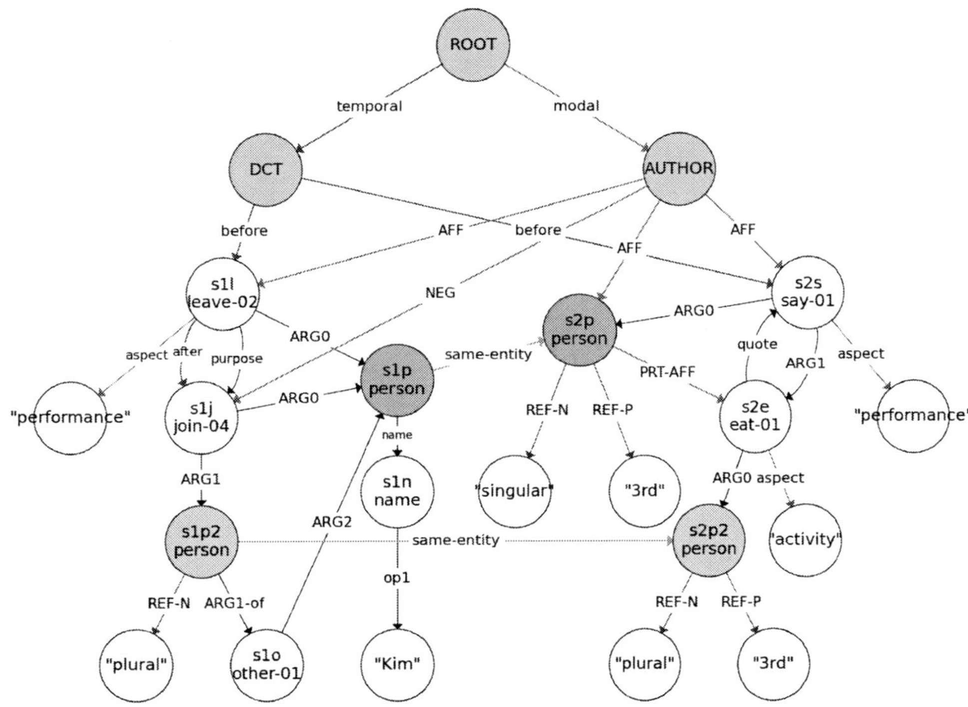

Figure 1: Example of UMR for "Kim left to join the others. 'They are probably eating,' she said." Lightblue nodes indicate special semantic nodes `ROOT`, `AUTHOR` and `DCT` (Document Creation Time) that are implied in every document. Modal relations are shown in red edges, temporal relations in green edges, and the clusters of coreferent entities are highlighted in the same color such as orange and green. `AFF` stands for `full-affirmative`, `NEG` for `full-negative`, `PRT-AFF` for `partial-affirmative`, `REF-N` for `refer-number`, and `REF-P` for `refer-person`.

the sources (formally known as *conceivers*) view another conceivers or events (Yao et al., 2021; Van Gysel et al., 2021). In the example, the `Author` knows with full certainty that *Kim* already *left* (`:full-affirmative` edge from the `Author` to `s1l:leave-02`), while *Kim* expresses uncertainty in her belief that *They* are *eating* at the moment (`:partial-affirmative` edge from `s2p:person` to `s2e:eat-01`). Since the `Author` presumably knew about *Kim*'s state of mind, a `:full-affirmative` modal relation between these two sources is finally established.

On the other hand, a temporal dependency graph (TDG) represents the temporal relations between events and time expressions such as `DCT` (Zhang and Xue, 2018b). The past tense of the main predicates *left* and *said* in the above example provides a strong indication of the actions having taken place before `DCT`, hence its two `:before` outgoing edges to `s1l:leave-02` and `s2e:eat-01`. Furthermore, the chain of events dictates that *Kim* could not have possibly *joined* the others without having first *left*. This is annotated with the `:after` edge from `s1l:leave-2` to `s1j:join-04`, which adds the temporal aspect to the `:purpose` relation that already exists between the two. Following the green edges in the figure reveals the temporal graph in its entirety.

Finally, the two sentences are further linked via the participation of same entities: *Kim* and *the others*. Their presence in the second sentence solely as pronouns, *she* and *they*, requires the context from the first sentence for anaphora resolution. These clusters of coreferent entities are highlighted as the same colored nodes in the figure connected by `:same-entity` edges between (1) `s1p:person` and `s2p:person`, and (2) `s1p2:person` and `s2p2:person`.

It is also worth noting the core differences between UMR sentence graphs and AMRs despite

Document ID	Sentences	Doc. Level	Tokens	AMR R3 Overlaps
english_umr-0001	28	28	700	NW_AFP_ENG_0024_2006_0217.[1~28]
english_umr-0002	2	28	18	-
english_umr-0003	9	9	140	NW_PRI_ENG_0153_2000_1214.[1~9]
english_umr-0004	141	135	1,165	-
english_umr-0005	29	29	566	NW_PRI_ENG_0152_2000_1208.[1~29]
Total	209	203	2,589	66

Table 1: UMR v1.0 English dataset statistics. *Doc. Level* refers to the number of non-empty document-level graphs. *R3 Overlaps*, if any, displays the AMR ids from AMR R3 corpus that share the same source sentence with UMRs.

their striking similarities. One of the notable discrepancies is the addition of `:aspect` annotations in UMR, visualized as purple edges in Figure 1, representing the internal state of an eventive concept as it relates to its status as an on-going, finished or habitual event, or simply a state with no changes over the course of action, or something else[1] (Donatelli et al., 2018, 2019). In the figure, *Kim* having *left* and *said* had already come to an end ("`performance`"), whereas *eating* is presumably still an on-going process at the time of writing ("`activity`").

Finally, pronouns in AMRs are replaced with generic `person` nodes with `:refer-person` edges denoting first, second or third point of view. Generic, non-named entities, including pronouns, are further annotated for their plurality with `:refer-number` relations, as seen with the blue outgoing edges from variables `s1p2:person`, `s2p:person` and `s2p2:person` in Figure 1.

UMR Parsing

While these new features help expand the representational scope of UMR to include a full document, they come at a great cost to the parsing complexity. In addition to the sentence graph generation, a parser would have to produce an additional document-level structure whose scope generally encompasses multiple sentences. Since the triples in the document graph need to be grounded in the context of the sentence graphs (Figure 1), the parsing task effectively revolves around a series of pairwise relation classifications between sentence graph nodes that have been abstracted away from their source tokens, much like AMRs. This is further complicated by the limited number of publicly available annotations in the recently released UMR v1.0 corpus[2] (Bonn et al., 2023a, 2024) .

[1]See umr-guidelines for the full lattice of aspectual values.

In light of these challenges, we propose to settle for a more tractable version of the problem that does not require any training. Our approach adopts a two-track strategy of obtaining sentence and document graphs separately. This is possible if we obtain the document-level triples at the token level, i.e., between the source tokens, *not* between the sentence graph nodes. By leveraging models individually trained for each of the document-level parsing tasks, we can set up a pipeline that compiles a list of document-level triples without any training on the limited UMR corpus. At the same time, we rely on off-the-shelf AMR parsers to first generate AMR, which is then subsequently converted into the UMR sentence graph using linguistically motivated heuristics. The final step involves the alignment of source tokens in the document-level triples to their corresponding nodes in the sentence graph, resulting in the final UMR structure.

The performance of our pipelined model is evaluated against the entire English section of the UMR v1.0 corpus, using a recently introduced AnCast++[3] whose details are provided in Section 5. We report the highest comprehensive macro F1 score at **61.5**, establishing a strong baseline for future improvement. The code is available at `https://github.com/umr4nlp/umrlib`.

2 UMR-v1.0 Corpus

UMR v1.0 corpus consists of documents annotated in 6 languages: Arapaho, Chinese, Cocama-Cocamilla, English, Navajo, and Sanapaná[4]. This work focuses only on 5 English documents, whose summary statistics are

[2]`https://lindat.mff.cuni.cz/repository/xmlui/handle/11234/1-5198`

[3]`https://github.com/sxndqc/ancast`

[4]`https://umr4nlp.github.io/web/data.html` shows the number of annotations for all 6 languages.

given in Table 1. The entire newsire domain (english_umr-0001, english_umr-0003, and english_umr-0005) overlaps with the LDC's latest release of AMR R3 corpus LDC2020T02[5] (Knight et al., 2021). Each sentence receives 2 core layers of annotations: (1) sentence graph and (2) document-level triples involving at least one local variable from its sentence graph.

Corpus Preprocessing

The corpus exhibits a few labeling inconsistencies. For instance, there are 12 occurrences of :AFF abbreviated modal relation label in addition to the more established :full-affirmative at 324. We attribute these and other similar occurrences to be simple errors and apply a cleanup to ensure labeling consistency across all of the annotations, e.g., :AFF replaced with :full-affirmative.

In addition, the :modal-strength relation (sometimes abbreviated as :modstr) is used as a shorthand to annotate a modal triple *within* a UMR sentence graph, although modal triples typically belong to a document-level annotation. In order to facilitate correct evaluation in our parsing experiments as required by AnCast++, these embedded modal triples are relocated from the sentence graph to its document-level annotation. It should be noted that this operation does not modify the content of the original annotation. We report parsing performance results with and without these procedures.

3 Model Description

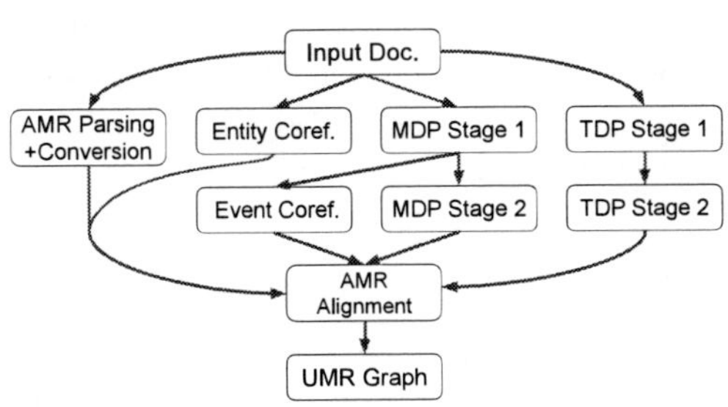

Figure 2: Flowchart for the proposed pipelined parser. MDP stands for Modal Dependency Parsing and TDP stands for Temporal Dependency Parsing.

In this section, we provide a detailed description of each of the models that makes up our pipeline. The entire flowchart is depicted in Figure 2.

[5]https://catalog.ldc.upenn.edu/LDC2020T02

3.1 AMR Parsing

AMR parsing aims to transform text into AMR where the meaning of a sentence is encoded in a single-rooted, directed and acyclic graph, as partially seen with the two sentence graphs in Figure 1 rooted by variables s1l and s2s whose black edges reveal the predicate-argument structure of each sentence. Due to its graphical nature, previous parsing methods often adopted graph methods such as finding the maximum spanning AMR graph (Flanigan et al., 2014, 2016), while others exploited the structural similarity between AMR and a dependency graph by applying a series of actions to transform the dependency graph into AMR in a transition-based framework (Wang et al., 2015, 2016; Wang and Xue, 2017). These approaches were largely superseded by larger models that began to pivot around various deep learning-based approaches (Foland and Martin, 2017; Lyu and Titov, 2018; Cai and Lam, 2020), culminating in the adoption of transformers (Bevilacqua et al., 2021). The subsequent advancements in AMR parsing relied on pretrained language models to consume and predict linearized AMRs (Chen et al., 2022; Bai et al., 2022; Yu and Gildea, 2022; Vasylenko et al., 2023), and the linearized representation of AMRs further opened up the possibility of a transition-based approach where a sequence of transductions are interpreted graphically to incrementally build towards the final AMR graph (Zhou et al., 2021b,a; Drozdov et al., 2022).

Given the efficacy of transformers-based AMR parsers, along with the unmistakable similarity of AMR to the UMR sentence graph, it is only natural to choose AMR parsing as a starting point of the pipeline. We experiment with four AMR parsers: LeakDistill (Vasylenko et al., 2023), SPRING (Bevilacqua et al., 2021), AMRBART (Bai et al., 2022) and IBM Transition Parser (Zhou et al., 2021b,a; Lee et al., 2022b; Drozdov et al., 2022). Maximum Bayes Smatch Ensemble (MBSE) (Lee et al., 2022b) is additionally used to ensemble best performing parsers for further improvement. Experiments using BLINK (Ledell Wu, 2020) entity linker for Wikification did not improve the model performance and is thus omitted in our experimental setup. Finally, we run LEAMR (Blodgett and Schneider, 2021) to produce sentence-AMR alignment for subsequent use in AMR-to-UMR conversion. Appendix A provides more details on the setup used in our experiments.

AMR Parser	Before Conversion		After Conversion	
	AnCast	Smatch	AnCast	Smatch
LeakDistill (Vasylenko et al., 2023)	51.3	56.7	63.2	71.3
SPRING (Bevilacqua et al., 2021)	51.1	56.4	62.9	71.2
Struct-BART (Zhou et al., 2021b)	49.3	56.0	60.9	70.6
AMRBART (Bai et al., 2022)	51.4	57.0	63.0	71.7
3-way MBSE* (Lee et al., 2022b)	51.3	57.2	63.1	71.8
4-way MBSE†	**52.6**	**57.5**	**64.2**	**72.2**
5-way MBSE‡	52.1	57.4	64.1	71.9

Table 2: Results on AMR-to-UMR Sentence Graph Conversion. *3-way MBSE includes LeakDistill + SPRING + AMRBART. †4-way MBSE includes LeakDistill + SPRING + AMRBART + Struct-BART. ‡5-way MBSE includes LeakDistill + SPRING + AMRBART (2 checkpoints) + Struct-BART.

3.2 AMR-to-UMR Conversion

Once an AMR parse is obtained, we apply heuristics for in-place conversion to the UMR sentence graph based on the mapping methodology described in Bonn et al. (2023b) and UMR guidelines[6]. We notice a few minor discrepancies between the methodology and some of the annotations in UMR v1.0; for instance, the guidelines advocates for `:ref-person` label whereas the corpus prefers `:refer-person`. In cases like this, we choose to follow the corpus for consistent parsing evaluation. A more recent work on AMR-to-UMR conversion provides fine-grained, nondeterministic mapping strategies based on the graph context (Post et al., 2024) but was not consulted for this work.

One of the practical challenges in AMR-to-UMR conversion is the `:aspect` edge creation task for events. Its heavily context-dependent nature makes it difficult to reliably determine its child node label—i.e., aspectual value—via heuristics. For this reason, we seek the help of Universal Dependency-style syntactic analysis from UDPipe v2 (Straka, 2018) whose UD features such as `Tense` and `Verbform` provide limited but helpful insights. The distribution of the aspect labels from the corpus is shown in Table 3.

Another important aspect of conversion is handling of the non-named entities including the pronouns. Their ubiquitous presence makes it a high-priority sub-task, and here again we rely on UD features from which we are able to infer the plurality of any generic entity.

Table 2 provides the overall results with AMR parsers and subsequent in-place conversion to UMR sentence graph, using Smatch (Cai and Knight, 2013) and AnCast[7] (Sun and Xue, 2024). AnCast is a recently introduced metric for evaluating graph-based meaning representations whose alignment strategy differs from the hill-climbing heuristics of Smatch by first identifying anchor nodes based on content similarity, and then iteratively propagating alignment throughout the neighborhood. It finally computes the labeled relation F1 score which measures the degree of matching for concepts and relations. This value represents the overall metric of AnCast and is reported in Table 2.

Aspect	Count
Performance	184
State	146
Activity	55
Endeavor	17
Process	16
Habitual	8
Total	426

Table 3: Distribution of the aspectual values in UMR v1.0 English dataset.

3.3 Modal Dependency Parsing

Modal dependency parsing (MDP) aims to construct a hierarchical structure representing the epistemic strength (`full`, `neutral` and `partial`) and polarity (`affirmative` and `negative`) of conceivers as related to other conceivers or events (Yao et al., 2021; Van Gysel et al., 2019). Largely based on FactBank (Saurí and Pustejovsky, 2009), UMR modal dependency sub-structure combines 3 modal strengths with 2 polarities as shown in Table 4. As

[6]https://github.com/umr4nlp/umr-guidelines/blob/master/guidelines.md

[7]not to be confused with AnCast++ whose details are provided in Section 5.

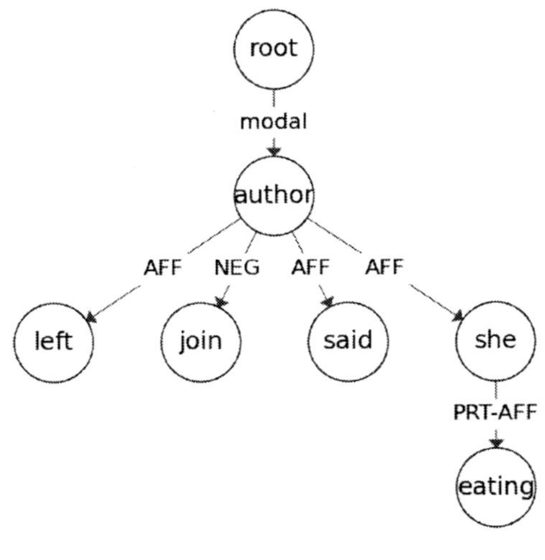

Figure 3: Example of Modal Dependency Graph for "Kim **left** to **join** the others. 'They are *probably* **eating**,' she **said**." `AFF` stands for `full-affirmative`, `NEG` for `full-negative`, and `PRT-AFF` for `partial-affirmative`.

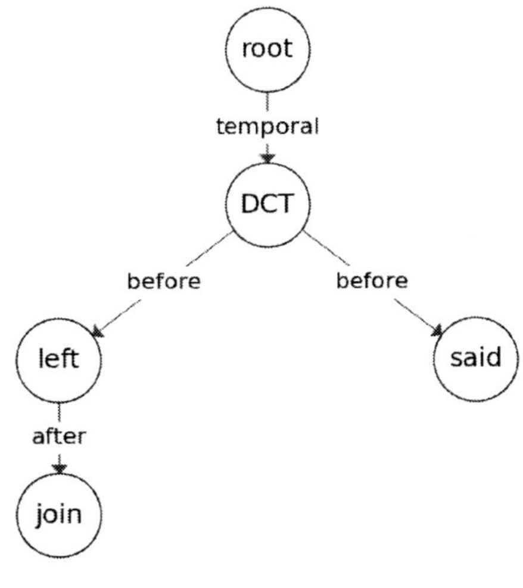

Figure 4: Example of Temporal Dependency Graph for "Kim **left** to **join** the others. 'They are probably eating,' she **said**."

seen with Figure 3, the resulting graph typically involves heavy traffic through the `Author` who displays confidence or doubt in various statements s/he commits to in writing.

Modal Label	Count
`:full-affirmative`	408
`:neutral-affirmative`	24
`:partial-affirmative`	14
`:full-negative`	23
`:neutral-negative`	3
`:partial-negative`	3
`:unspecified*`	10
Total	486

Table 4: Distribution of modal labels in UMR v1.0 English dataset. *UMR v1.0 corpus contains `:unspecified` which is not part of the target modal labels in MDP.

In practice, MDP consists of two different stages. First, the conceivers and events must be identified; then, each event or conceiver must be paired with the most appropriate parent in the text in a newly-created modal triple whose label needs to be predicted. In our experiments, we use a prompt-based model described in Yao et al. (2022), where the two tasks are trained end-to-end in a joint manner based on language model priming. Table 4 shows the distribution of modal labels in the UMR English corpus.

3.4 Temporal Dependency Parsing

In a similar vein to MDP, temporal dependency parsing (TDP) is the task of identifying a document-level graph whose nodes are time expressions (timex) and events, and edges represent the temporal relations between them. Specifically, an event first searches for its referent timex that is the most specific (i.e., closest) temporal anchor (Pustejovsky and Stubbs, 2011) in whose absence it settles for another event that can provide the most specific temporal context (Zhang and Xue, 2018b; Yao et al., 2020). Figure 4 depicts a temporal dependency graph for the sample document of two sentences.

TDP also consists of 2 stages. The timex and event identification is performed first, followed by edge generation between the identified nodes. For stage 1 we use the neural ranking model described in Yao et al. (2020) based on Zhang and Xue (2018a) and Ross et al. (2020) that extracts timex and events by labeling the appropriate span in the text[8]. Then we turn to the parser from Yao et al. (2023) which interprets TDP as a textual entailment (NLI) task in which the temporal relation is verbalized into text, requiring the model to infer entailment probability. Table 5 shows the distribu-

[8]We observed higher performance when TDP stage 1 output is augmented with events from MDP stage 1.

tion of temporal labels in the corpus.

Temporal Label	Count
overlap	143
after	106
before	54
contained	24
depends-on	7
Total	334

Table 5: Distribution of temporal labels in UMR v1.0 English dataset.

3.5 Coreference

UMR supports two types of coreference—event and entity—which form disjoint clusters. Both may additionally participate in the :subset-of relationship. Table 6 provides the number of coreference labels in the corpus.

Event Coreference

For cross-sentence event clustering, our pipeline relies on Cross-Document Coreference Resolution (CDLM) described in Cattan et al. (2021), which is pre-trained to include multiple documents by leveraging global attention. Although the model is designed with cross-document context in mind, we limit the global range to a single document. Since it requires event candidates be provided as input, we re-use the events identified in MDP stage 1.

Entity Coreference

For entities we use wl-coref (Dobrovolskii, 2021) and caw-coref (D'Oosterlinck et al., 2023) which attempt to build a coreference link between individual words.

Coref. Label	Count
same-entity	317
same-event	62
subset-of	55
Total	434

Table 6: Distribution of coreference labels in UMR v1.0 English dataset.

3.6 Context Grounding via Alignment

So far, the pipeline has produced two distinct structures—a sentence graph as a result of AMR-to-UMR conversion, and document-level triples from MDP, TDP and coreference—that are seemingly independent from each other. This is because the sentence graph is generated by transforming an AMR parse whose nodes have been abstracted away from their source tokens, whereas the document-level triples obtained from MDP, TDP and coreference are expressed as between these source tokens.

In order to bring these structures together, the final step of our pipelined approach involves the use of the alignment between the sentence graph and the source sentence provided by LEAMR[9] to map the tokens in document-level triples to the corresponding nodes in the UMR sentence graph. This effectively means transferring the context of the document-level triples from the source sentence to the UMR sentence graph, and only after this stage do these structures demonstrate cohesion as required for UMR.

4 Experiments

We follow the flowchart in Figure 2 to generate UMR parses. Appendix A provides details on the experimental setup. Our model is evaluated against all of the English section of UMR v1.0 corpus. In order to cope with the input length limitation of some of the pipeline models, english_umr-0004 is split into smaller fragments each of which is treated as a separate document. The intermediate results for the split data are pieced together at the end into a single document for evaluation. Table 7 shows the experimental results using AnCast++ evaluation which we introduce in the next section.

5 Evaluation

Currently, there is no published work that can evaluate the performance of a UMR parser. To this end, we first provide Smatch scores for the sentence graphs evaluation in Table 2. Since the UMR sentence graphs resemble AMRs, Smatch can continue to provide a meaningful and comparable evaluation score during the transition towards UMR.

For the full UMR evaluation we adopt AnCast++[10], a recently introduced open-source evaluation toolkit for UMR that provides an aggregated metric of Sentence, Modal, Temporal and Coreference scores. The Sentence graph evaluation is based on AnCast and is claimed to be highly correlated with Smatch despite differences in the align-

[9]LEAMR provides AMR-to-sentence alignment, which is preserved during the in-place conversion.

[10]https://github.com/sxndqc/ancast

Document ID	AnCast++ F1 Scores				
	Sentence Graph	Modal	Temporal	Coref.	Comprehensive
english_umr-0001	69.2 (66.2)	51.4 (40.2)	15.6 (16.2)	8.2 (8.2)	57.9 (55.5)
english_umr-0002	90.0 (90.0)	60.0 (60.0)	100.0 (100.0)	0.0* (0.0)	86.2 (86.2)
english_umr-0003	75.3 (71.8)	70.0 (53.9)	16.9 (18.2)	58.3 (40.0)	68.6 (63.4)
english_umr-0004	61.2 (60.7)	64.5 (65.3)	22.8 (22.8)	26.7 (26.7)	52.1 (51.9)
english_umr-0005	55.3 (55.0)	13.8 (12.3)	6.3 (7.3)	19.5 (20.4)	42.8 (42.9)
Macro F1	70.2 (68.8)	52.0 (46.3)	32.3 (32.9)	22.5 (19.1)	**61.5** (60.0)

Table 7: Parsing Evaluation Results on UMR v1.0 English corpus using AnCast++. Scores within the parenthesis are from evaluating against the UMR corpus without any preprocessing. *english_umr-0002 contains no coreference.

ment strategy (Sun and Xue, 2024). While the Modal score is based on the number of overlaps in the modal triples owing to its inherently tree structure, Temporal and Coreference scores require finding the transitive closures via Depth-First Search (DFS) in order to identify clusters of nodes and relations, from which precision and recall measures are computed in terms of closed sets as follows:

$$p = \frac{\sum_{r_i \in R}(|r_i| \times \sum_{k_j \in K} \frac{rel(r_i \cap k_j)}{rel(r_i)})}{\sum_{r_z \in R} |r_z|}$$

$$r = \frac{\sum_{k_i \in K}(|k_i| \times \sum_{r_j \in R} \frac{rel(k_i \cap r_j)}{rel(k_i)})}{\sum_{k_z \in K} |k_z|}$$

where k_i and r_i are node clusters in key (gold) and response (prediction) graphs, and $rel(k_i)$ and $rel(r_i)$ are the reference and deducted links respectively. This approach builds on Setzer et al. (2005) and Link-based Entity-Aware (LEA) metric (Moosavi and Strube, 2016; Moosavi, 2020).

6 Error Analysis

As a pipeline model, our parser is prone to error propagation when generating document-level triples. This is especially true with the event identification phase in MDP and TDP stage 1, where the identified event candidates are subsequently considered for the modal and temporal dependency edge generation as well as cross-sentence event coreference. Naturally, any event that goes undetected is non-recoverable in the subsequent pipeline. This is further compounded by the fact that the generated triples ultimately need to be aligned to the appropriate UMR sentence sub-graph but may be un-aligned or mis-aligned, resulting in low performance on the document-level parsing tasks. Nevertheless, MDP appears to show comparatively stronger performance because MDG is inherently a tree unlike TDG and coreference clusters, with most of traffic consolidated around the `Author`.

The parser is also unable to guarantee 100% coverage of UMR as it is unable produce certain labels such as "Habitual" aspectual value and "`:partial-negative`" modal label. Another prominent example is "`:subset-of`" coreference label which makes up a sizable portion of coreference labels (Table 6), and its lack thereof carries significant repercussions for overall parsing performance. This is to be expected as none of the models are directly trained on the UMR-style of annotations, and it remains a major source of error in our experiments.

The corpus itself shows highly varied annotation styles across different documents. For instance, English UMR documents 1, 2 and 4 consistently annotate `:modal` relation from `ROOT` to `AUTHOR`, although its presence is implied in every document and is not strictly necessary—a view taken in documents 3 and 5. `english_umr-0005` further stands out as what initially appears to be a news article abruptly turns into a dialogue, leading to subsequent sentence graphs being wrapped under `(s / say-01 :ARG0 (p / person) :ARG1 ...)` 'phantom' outer sub-graph. This explains the comparatively low score for the document.

7 Conclusions

This paper presents the first published UMR parsing model evaluated against UMR v1.0 English corpus using AnCast++. We describe our pipelined approach to cope with the shortage of publicly available UMR data so that no training on the UMR corpus is necessary. Our experimental results at 61.5 macro F1 establishes a strong baseline for future improvement. The proposed parser is suitable for modular upgrade by optimizing individual models, which we plan to visit in future work.

Limitations

Due to the small number of UMR data available for evaluation, current parsing result is not yet stable. UMR English dataset further shows highly skewed distribution of number of sentences per document—as small as 2 for `english_umr-0002` and over 140 for `english_umr-0004` which is not taken into account by AnCast++. Increased number of UMR annotations will partially mitigate this issue.

The proposed UMR parser uses sub-models trained in English and is unable to parse any other languages. To apply this model in a cross-lingual setting depends on the availability of models such as temporal dependency parser being trained either multi-lingually or on non-English datasets.

Since the pipeline consists of multiple models each of which may require a different set of dependencies, the parser is difficult to set up for use in practice. We therefore provide a WebUI version of our parser which serves as a one-stop interface to interact with every component in the pipeline.

Acknowledgments

This work is supported by grants from the CNS Division of National Science Foundation (Awards no: NSF_2213804) entitled "Building a Broad Infrastructure for Uniform Meaning Representations". Any opinions, findings and conclusions or recommendations expressed in this material do not necessarily reflect the views of NSF.

References

Xuefeng Bai, Yulong Chen, and Yue Zhang. 2022. Graph pre-training for AMR parsing and generation. In *Proceedings of the 60th Annual Meeting of the Association for Computational Linguistics (Volume 1: Long Papers)*, pages 6001–6015, Dublin, Ireland. Association for Computational Linguistics.

Michele Bevilacqua, Rexhina Blloshmi, and Roberto Navigli. 2021. One spring to rule them both: Symmetric amr semantic parsing and generation without a complex pipeline. *Proceedings of the AAAI Conference on Artificial Intelligence*, 35(14):12564–12573.

Austin Blodgett and Nathan Schneider. 2021. Probabilistic, structure-aware algorithms for improved variety, accuracy, and coverage of AMR alignments. In *Proceedings of the 59th Annual Meeting of the Association for Computational Linguistics and the 11th International Joint Conference on Natural Language Processing (Volume 1: Long Papers)*, pages 3310–3321, Online. Association for Computational Linguistics.

Claire Bonial, Lucia Donatelli, Mitchell Abrams, Stephanie M. Lukin, Stephen Tratz, Matthew Marge, Ron Artstein, David Traum, and Clare Voss. 2020. Dialogue-AMR: Abstract Meaning Representation for dialogue. In *Proceedings of the Twelfth Language Resources and Evaluation Conference*, pages 684–695, Marseille, France. European Language Resources Association.

Julia Bonn, Matthew J. Buchholz, Jayeol Chun, Andrew Cowell, William Croft, Lukas Denk, Sijia Ge, Jan Hajič, Kenneth Lai, James H. Martin, Skatje Myers, Alexis Palmer, Martha Palmer, Claire Benet Post, James Pustejovsky, Kristine Stenzel, Haibo Sun, Zdeňka Urešová, Rosa Vallejos, Jens E. L. Van Gysel, Meagan Vigus, Nianwen Xue, and Jin Zhao. 2024. Building a broad infrastructure for uniform meaning representations. In *Proceedings of the 2024 Joint International Conference on Computational Linguistics, Language Resources and Evaluation (LREC-COLING 2024)*, pages 2537–2547, Torino, Italia. ELRA and ICCL.

Julia Bonn, Chen Ching-wen, James Andrew Cowell, William Croft, Lukas Denk, Jan Hajič, Kenneth Lai, Martha Palmer, Alexis Palmer, James Pustejovsky, Haibo Sun, Rosa Vallejos Yopán, Jens Van Gysel, Meagan Vigus, Nianwen Xue, and Jin Zhao. 2023a. Uniform meaning representation. LINDAT/CLARIAH-CZ digital library at the Institute of Formal and Applied Linguistics (ÚFAL), Faculty of Mathematics and Physics, Charles University.

Julia Bonn, Skatje Myers, Jens E. L. Van Gysel, Lukas Denk, Meagan Vigus, Jin Zhao, Andrew Cowell, William Croft, Jan Hajič, James H. Martin, Alexis Palmer, Martha Palmer, James Pustejovsky, Zdenka Urešová, Rosa Vallejos, and Nianwen Xue. 2023b. Mapping AMR to UMR: Resources for adapting existing corpora for cross-lingual compatibility. In *Proceedings of the 21st International Workshop on Treebanks and Linguistic Theories (TLT, GURT/SyntaxFest 2023)*, pages 74–95, Washington, D.C. Association for Computational Linguistics.

Deng Cai and Wai Lam. 2020. AMR parsing via graph-sequence iterative inference. *CoRR*, abs/2004.05572.

Shu Cai and Kevin Knight. 2013. Smatch: an evaluation metric for semantic feature structures. In *Proceedings of the 51st Annual Meeting of the Association for Computational Linguistics (Volume 2: Short Papers)*, pages 748–752, Sofia, Bulgaria. Association for Computational Linguistics.

Arie Cattan, Alon Eirew, Gabriel Stanovsky, Mandar Joshi, and Ido Dagan. 2021. Cross-document coreference resolution over predicted mentions. In *Findings of the Association for Computational Linguistics: ACL-IJCNLP 2021*, pages 5100–5107, Online. Association for Computational Linguistics.

Liang Chen, Peiyi Wang, Runxin Xu, Tianyu Liu, Zhifang Sui, and Baobao Chang. 2022. ATP: AMRize then parse! enhancing AMR parsing with PseudoAMRs. In *Findings of the Association for Computational Linguistics: NAACL 2022*, pages 2482–2496, Seattle, United States. Association for Computational Linguistics.

Alexis Conneau, Kartikay Khandelwal, Naman Goyal, Vishrav Chaudhary, Guillaume Wenzek, Francisco Guzmán, Edouard Grave, Myle Ott, Luke Zettlemoyer, and Veselin Stoyanov. 2020. Unsupervised cross-lingual representation learning at scale. *Preprint*, arXiv:1911.02116.

Agata Cybulska and P. Vossen. 2014. Using a sledgehammer to crack a nut? lexical diversity and event coreference resolution. In *International Conference on Language Resources and Evaluation*.

Jacob Devlin, Ming-Wei Chang, Kenton Lee, and Kristina Toutanova. 2019. BERT: Pre-training of deep bidirectional transformers for language understanding. In *Proceedings of the 2019 Conference of the North American Chapter of the Association for Computational Linguistics: Human Language Technologies, Volume 1 (Long and Short Papers)*, pages 4171–4186, Minneapolis, Minnesota. Association for Computational Linguistics.

Vladimir Dobrovolskii. 2021. Word-level coreference resolution. In *Proceedings of the 2021 Conference on Empirical Methods in Natural Language Processing*, pages 7670–7675, Online and Punta Cana, Dominican Republic. Association for Computational Linguistics.

Lucia Donatelli, Michael Regan, William Croft, and Nathan Schneider. 2018. Annotation of tense and aspect semantics for sentential AMR. In *Proceedings of the Joint Workshop on Linguistic Annotation, Multiword Expressions and Constructions (LAW-MWE-CxG-2018)*, pages 96–108, Santa Fe, New Mexico, USA. Association for Computational Linguistics.

Lucia Donatelli, Nathan Schneider, William Croft, and Michael Regan. 2019. Tense and aspect semantics for sentential amr. pages 346–348.

Karel D'Oosterlinck, Semere Kiros Bitew, Brandon Papineau, Christopher Potts, Thomas Demeester, and Chris Develder. 2023. CAW-coref: Conjunction-aware word-level coreference resolution. In *Proceedings of The Sixth Workshop on Computational Models of Reference, Anaphora and Coreference (CRAC 2023)*, pages 8–14, Singapore. Association for Computational Linguistics.

Andrew Drozdov, Jiawei Zhou, Radu Florian, Andrew McCallum, Tahira Naseem, Yoon Kim, and Ramon Fernandez Astudillo. 2022. Inducing and using alignments for transition-based amr parsing. *Preprint*, arXiv:2205.01464.

Jeffrey Flanigan, Chris Dyer, Noah A. Smith, and Jaime Carbonell. 2016. Generation from Abstract Meaning Representation using tree transducers. In *Proceedings of the 2016 Conference of the North American Chapter of the Association for Computational Linguistics: Human Language Technologies*, pages 731–739, San Diego, California. Association for Computational Linguistics.

Jeffrey Flanigan, Ishan Jindal, Yunyao Li, Tim O'Gorman, Martha Palmer, and Nianwen Xue. 2022. Meaning representations for natural languages: Design, models and applications. In *Proceedings of the 2022 Conference on Empirical Methods in Natural Language Processing: Tutorial Abstracts*, pages 1–8, Abu Dubai, UAE. Association for Computational Linguistics.

Jeffrey Flanigan, Sam Thomson, Jaime Carbonell, Chris Dyer, and Noah A. Smith. 2014. A discriminative graph-based parser for the Abstract Meaning Representation. In *Proceedings of the 52nd Annual Meeting of the Association for Computational Linguistics (Volume 1: Long Papers)*, pages 1426–1436, Baltimore, Maryland. Association for Computational Linguistics.

William Foland and James H. Martin. 2017. Abstract Meaning Representation parsing using LSTM recurrent neural networks. In *Proceedings of the 55th Annual Meeting of the Association for Computational Linguistics (Volume 1: Long Papers)*, pages 463–472, Vancouver, Canada. Association for Computational Linguistics.

Kevin Knight, Bianca Badarau, Laura Baranescu, Claire Bonial, Madalina Bardocz, Kira Griffitt, Ulf Hermjakob, Daniel Marcu, Martha Palmer, Tim O'Gorman, and Nathan Schneider. 2021. Abstract meaning representation (amr) annotation release 3.0.

Martin Josifoski Sebastian Riedel Luke Zettlemoyer Ledell Wu, Fabio Petroni. 2020. Zero-shot entity linking with dense entity retrieval. In *EMNLP*.

Young-Suk Lee, Ramón Astudillo, Hoang Thanh Lam, Tahira Naseem, Radu Florian, and Salim Roukos. 2022a. Maximum Bayes Smatch ensemble distillation for AMR parsing. In *Proceedings of the 2022 Conference of the North American Chapter of the Association for Computational Linguistics: Human Language Technologies*, pages 5379–5392, Seattle, United States. Association for Computational Linguistics.

Young-Suk Lee, Ramon Fernandez Astudillo, Thanh Lam Hoang, Tahira Naseem, Radu Florian, and Salim Roukos. 2022b. Maximum bayes smatch ensemble distillation for amr parsing. *Preprint*, arXiv:2112.07790.

Mike Lewis, Yinhan Liu, Naman Goyal, Marjan Ghazvininejad, Abdelrahman Mohamed, Omer Levy, Veselin Stoyanov, and Luke Zettlemoyer. 2020. BART: Denoising sequence-to-sequence pre-training for natural language generation, translation, and comprehension. In *Proceedings of the 58th Annual Meeting of the Association for Computational Linguistics*, pages 7871–7880, Online. Association for Computational Linguistics.

Yinhan Liu, Myle Ott, Naman Goyal, Jingfei Du, Mandar Joshi, Danqi Chen, Omer Levy, Mike Lewis, Luke Zettlemoyer, and Veselin Stoyanov. 2019. Roberta: A robustly optimized bert pretraining approach. *Preprint*, arXiv:1907.11692.

Chunchuan Lyu and Ivan Titov. 2018. AMR parsing as graph prediction with latent alignment. In *Proceedings of the 56th Annual Meeting of the Association for Computational Linguistics (Volume 1: Long Papers)*, pages 397–407, Melbourne, Australia. Association for Computational Linguistics.

Behrooz Mansouri, Ricardo Campos, and Adam Jatowt. 2023. Towards timeline generation with abstract meaning representation. In *Companion Proceedings of the ACM Web Conference 2023*, WWW '23 Companion, page 1204–1207, New York, NY, USA. Association for Computing Machinery.

Nafise Sadat Moosavi. 2020. Robustness in coreference resolution.

Nafise Sadat Moosavi and Michael Strube. 2016. Which coreference evaluation metric do you trust? a proposal for a link-based entity aware metric. In *Proceedings of the 54th Annual Meeting of the Association for Computational Linguistics (Volume 1: Long Papers)*, pages 632–642, Berlin, Germany. Association for Computational Linguistics.

Tahira Naseem, Austin Blodgett, Sadhana Kumaravel, Tim O'Gorman, Young-Suk Lee, Jeffrey Flanigan, Ramón Astudillo, Radu Florian, Salim Roukos, and Nathan Schneider. 2022. DocAMR: Multi-sentence AMR representation and evaluation. In *Proceedings of the 2022 Conference of the North American Chapter of the Association for Computational Linguistics: Human Language Technologies*, pages 3496–3505, Seattle, United States. Association for Computational Linguistics.

Tim O'Gorman, Michael Regan, Kira Griffitt, Ulf Hermjakob, Kevin Knight, and Martha Palmer. 2018. AMR beyond the sentence: the multi-sentence AMR corpus. In *Proceedings of the 27th International Conference on Computational Linguistics*, pages 3693–3702, Santa Fe, New Mexico, USA. Association for Computational Linguistics.

Claire Benet Post, Marie C. McGregor, Maria Leonor Pacheco, and Alexis Palmer. 2024. Accelerating UMR adoption: Neuro-symbolic conversion from AMR-to-UMR with low supervision. In *Proceedings of the Fifth International Workshop on Designing Meaning Representations @ LREC-COLING 2024*, pages 140–150, Torino, Italia. ELRA and ICCL.

James Pustejovsky and Amber Stubbs. 2011. Increasing informativeness in temporal annotation. In *Proceedings of the 5th Linguistic Annotation Workshop*, pages 152–160, Portland, Oregon, USA. Association for Computational Linguistics.

Alec Radford, Jeff Wu, Rewon Child, David Luan, Dario Amodei, and Ilya Sutskever. 2019. Language models are unsupervised multitask learners.

Colin Raffel, Noam Shazeer, Adam Roberts, Katherine Lee, Sharan Narang, Michael Matena, Yanqi Zhou, Wei Li, and Peter J. Liu. 2019. Exploring the limits of transfer learning with a unified text-to-text transformer. *CoRR*, abs/1910.10683.

Hayley Ross, Jonathon Cai, and Bonan Min. 2020. Exploring Contextualized Neural Language Models for Temporal Dependency Parsing. In *Proceedings of the 2020 Conference on Empirical Methods in Natural Language Processing (EMNLP)*, pages 8548–8553, Online. Association for Computational Linguistics.

Roser Saurí and James Pustejovsky. 2009. Factbank: A corpus annotated with event factuality. *Language Resources and Evaluation*, 43:227–268.

Andrea Setzer, Robert Gaizauskas, and Mark Hepple. 2005. Using semantic inferences for temporal annotation comparison. In *The Language of Time: A Reader*, pages 575–584.

Milan Straka. 2018. UDPipe 2.0 prototype at CoNLL 2018 UD shared task. In *Proceedings of the CoNLL 2018 Shared Task: Multilingual Parsing from Raw Text to Universal Dependencies*, pages 197–207, Brussels, Belgium. Association for Computational Linguistics.

Haibo Sun and Nianwen Xue. 2024. Anchor and broadcast: An efficient concept alignment approach for evaluation of semantic graphs. In *Proceedings of the 2024 Joint International Conference on Computational Linguistics, Language Resources and Evaluation*.

Jens E. L. Van Gysel, Meagan Vigus, Jayeol Chun, Kenneth Lai, Sarah Moeller, Jiarui Yao, Tim O'Gorman, Andrew Cowell, William Croft, Chu-Ren Huang, Jan Hajič, James H. Martin, Stephan Oepen, Martha Palmer, James Pustejovsky, Rosa Vallejos, and Nianwen Xue. 2021. Designing a uniform meaning representation for natural language processing. *KI - Künstliche Intelligenz*, 35(3):343–360.

Jens E. L. Van Gysel, Meagan Vigus, Pavlina Kalm, Sook-kyung Lee, Michael Regan, and William Croft. 2019. Cross-linguistic semantic annotation: Reconciling the language-specific and the universal. In *Proceedings of the First International Workshop on Designing Meaning Representations*, pages 1–14, Florence, Italy. Association for Computational Linguistics.

Ashish Vaswani, Noam Shazeer, Niki Parmar, Jakob Uszkoreit, Llion Jones, Aidan N. Gomez, Lukasz Kaiser, and Illia Polosukhin. 2017. Attention is all you need. *CoRR*, abs/1706.03762.

Pavlo Vasylenko, Pere-Lluís Huguet Cabot, Abelardo Carlos Martínez Lorenzo, and Roberto Navigli. 2023. Incorporating graph information in transformer-based amr parsing. *Preprint*, arXiv:2306.13467.

Meagan Vigus, Jens E. L. Van Gysel, and William Croft. 2019. A dependency structure annotation for modality. In *Proceedings of the First International Workshop on Designing Meaning Representations*, pages 182–198, Florence, Italy. Association for Computational Linguistics.

Chuan Wang, Sameer Pradhan, Xiaoman Pan, Heng Ji, and Nianwen Xue. 2016. CAMR at SemEval-2016 task 8: An extended transition-based AMR parser. In *Proceedings of the 10th International Workshop on Semantic Evaluation (SemEval-2016)*, pages 1173–1178, San Diego, California. Association for Computational Linguistics.

Chuan Wang and Nianwen Xue. 2017. Getting the most out of AMR parsing. In *Proceedings of the 2017 Conference on Empirical Methods in Natural Language Processing*, pages 1257–1268, Copenhagen, Denmark. Association for Computational Linguistics.

Chuan Wang, Nianwen Xue, and Sameer Pradhan. 2015. A transition-based algorithm for AMR parsing. In *Proceedings of the 2015 Conference of the North American Chapter of the Association for Computational Linguistics: Human Language Technologies*, pages 366–375, Denver, Colorado. Association for Computational Linguistics.

Cunxiang Wang, Zhikun Xu, Qipeng Guo, Xiangkun Hu, Xuefeng Bai, Zheng Zhang, and Yue Zhang. 2023. Exploiting Abstract Meaning Representation for open-domain question answering. In *Findings of the Association for Computational Linguistics: ACL 2023*, pages 2083–2096, Toronto, Canada. Association for Computational Linguistics.

Jiarui Yao, Steven Bethard, Kristin Wright-Bettner, Eli Goldner, David Harris, and Guergana Savova. 2023. Textual entailment for temporal dependency graph parsing. In *Proceedings of the 5th Clinical Natural Language Processing Workshop*, pages 191–199, Toronto, Canada. Association for Computational Linguistics.

Jiarui Yao, Haoling Qiu, Bonan Min, and Nianwen Xue. 2020. Annotating Temporal Dependency Graphs via Crowdsourcing. In *Proceedings of the 2020 Conference on Empirical Methods in Natural Language Processing (EMNLP)*, pages 5368–5380, Online. Association for Computational Linguistics.

Jiarui Yao, Haoling Qiu, Jin Zhao, Bonan Min, and Nianwen Xue. 2021. Factuality assessment as modal dependency parsing. In *Proceedings of the 59th Annual Meeting of the Association for Computational Linguistics and the 11th International Joint Conference on Natural Language Processing (Volume 1: Long Papers)*, pages 1540–1550, Online. Association for Computational Linguistics.

Jiarui Yao, Nianwen Xue, and Bonan Min. 2022. Modal dependency parsing via language model priming. In *Proceedings of the 2022 Conference of the North American Chapter of the Association for Computational Linguistics: Human Language Technologies*, pages 2913–2919, Seattle, United States. Association for Computational Linguistics.

Chen Yu and Daniel Gildea. 2022. Sequence-to-sequence AMR parsing with ancestor information. In *Proceedings of the 60th Annual Meeting of the Association for Computational Linguistics (Volume 2: Short Papers)*, pages 571–577, Dublin, Ireland. Association for Computational Linguistics.

Yuchen Zhang and Nianwen Xue. 2018a. Neural ranking models for temporal dependency structure parsing. *CoRR*, abs/1809.00370.

Yuchen Zhang and Nianwen Xue. 2018b. Structured interpretation of temporal relations. In *Proceedings of the Eleventh International Conference on Language Resources and Evaluation (LREC 2018)*, Miyazaki, Japan. European Language Resources Association (ELRA).

Jiawei Zhou, Tahira Naseem, Ramón Fernandez Astudillo, and Radu Florian. 2021a. AMR parsing with action-pointer transformer. In *Proceedings of the 2021 Conference of the North American Chapter of the Association for Computational Linguistics: Human Language Technologies*, pages 5585–5598, Online. Association for Computational Linguistics.

Jiawei Zhou, Tahira Naseem, Ramón Fernandez Astudillo, Young-Suk Lee, Radu Florian, and Salim Roukos. 2021b. Structure-aware fine-tuning of sequence-to-sequence transformers for transition-based AMR parsing. In *Proceedings of the 2021 Conference on Empirical Methods in Natural Language Processing*, pages 6279–6290, Online and Punta Cana, Dominican Republic. Association for Computational Linguistics.

A Experimental Setup

Experiments were run on NVIDIA RTX 3090.

AMR Parser

We found 4-way and 5-way MBSE models to produce the highest Smatch and AnCast scores on UMR sentence graphs evaluation (Table 2). We were also able to obtain the highest AnCast++ scores on full UMR evaluation using 5-way MBSE (Table 7). These include:

1. LeakDistill trained on AMR R3[11].
2. SPRING trained on AMR R3.
3. Struct-BART trained on AMR R3 and parsed using ensemble of 3 seeds: 42, 43, and 44.

[11]Checkpoint 'best-smatch_checkpoint_12_0.8534' is available upon request to the authors

4. AMRBART 3.0 trained on AMR R3.

5. AMRBART 2.0 trained on AMR R2 (not part of 4-way MBSE).

We do not run the BLINK entity linking system in our pipeline.

Modal Dependency Parsing

mdp-prompt (Yao et al., 2022) is the prompt-based modal dependency parser trained on publicly available English modal dependency dataset[12] (Yao et al., 2021). We exactly follow the training configurations described in the paper for English.

Temporal Dependency Parsing

Unlike MDP where a single parser can perform stage 1 and stage 2 jointly, we train two separate models since the best stage 2 parser does not produce stage 1 outputs.

TDP Stage 1

To identify events and timex, we use the XLM-Roberta (Conneau et al., 2020) based ranking model (Yao et al., 2020) whose source code is not publicly available but is similar to that of mdp-prompt.

The model is trained on publicly available English temporal dependency dataset[13] for 30 epochs with learning rate of 2e-5 and max sequence length of 128. The model processes a long document by splitting it into smaller segments before encoding each with the language model. When doing so, we allow the model to apply segmentation by letting each overlap with one another. These procedures are in accordance with what is described in the paper.

In practice, the identified events are merged with those found by mdp-prompt, leading to better results. Finally, the merged events also serve as inputs to CDLM for event coreference.

TDP Stage 2

thyme-tdg (Yao et al., 2023) is trained following the model implementation details as specified for the general-domain experiments, but we allow training to last for 10 epochs rather than 3. We use seed 42 for data preparation as well as model training.

In practice, we find that the ranking model (Yao et al., 2020) should also be trained for stage 2 event-to-time and event-to-event edge generation task, whose outputs are then fed to thyme-tdg. In both scenarios the hyperparameters remain the same as described in the paper.

Coreference

CDLM for event coreference is trained on ECB+ corpus[14] (Cybulska and Vossen, 2014). For wl-coref and caw-coref, we use the Roberta (Liu et al., 2019) based pre-trained models publicly available at their respective Github repositories. In our experiments, using wl-coref led to higher AnCast++ scores.

[12] https://github.com/Jryao/modal_dependency/tree/main/data

[13] https://github.com/Jryao/temporal_dependency_graphs_crowdsourcing/tree/master/tdg_data

[14] https://www.newsreader-project.eu/results/data/the-ecb-corpus/

Financial Product Ontology Population with Large Language Models

Chanatip Saetia[1], Jiratha Phruetthiset[2], Tawunrat Chalothorn[1], Monchai Lertsutthiwong[1], Supawat Taerungruang[2], Pakpoom Buabthong[3,*]

[1]Kasikorn Labs, Kasikorn Business-Technology Group, Nonthaburi, Thailand
[2]Department of Thai, Faculty of Humanities, Chiangmai University, Chiangmai, Thailand
[3]Faculty of Science and Technology, Nakhon Ratchasima Rajabhat University, Nakhon Ratchasima, Thailand

Abstract

Ontology population, which aims to extract structured data to enrich domain-specific ontologies from unstructured text, typically faces challenges in terms of data scarcity and linguistic complexity, particularly in specialized fields such as retail banking. In this study, we investigate the application of large language models (LLMs) to populate domain-specific ontologies of retail banking products from Thai corporate documents. We compare traditional span-based approaches to LLMs-based generative methods, with different prompting techniques. Our findings reveal that while span-based methods struggle with data scarcity and the complex linguistic structure, LLMs-based generative approaches substantially outperform, achieving a 61.05% F1 score, with the most improvement coming from providing examples in the prompts. This improvement highlights the potential of LLMs for ontology population tasks, offering a scalable and efficient solution for structured information extraction, especially in low-resource language settings.

1 Introduction

With an increasing volume of text document repositories, the need for efficient and accurate information management systems has become inevitable. Ontology is one of the tools that facilitate structured representations of knowledge within specific domains, promoting interoperability and reasoning from unstructured data sources (Gruber, 1993). In addition, a specialized subset of ontologies, such as Schema markup, can also empower organizations to publish machine-readable web pages, thereby enhancing their visibility on search engines (Schema.org, 2008).

*Corresponding author: pakpoom.b@nrru.ac.th

However, the task of extracting and populating domain-specific ontologies from unstructured texts presents significant challenges due to the diversity of the source materials (Chasseray et al., 2023). Particularly in the banking sector, source documents, often authored by various internal units, lack a standardized format, frequently comprising only phrases or fragmented information rather than complete sentences (Petrova et al., 2017). In this domain, especially under low-resource language settings, structured storage can also be leveraged to construct a knowledge graph to facilitate downstream tasks such as recommendation systems (Guo et al., 2020) or question answering systems (Khongcharoen et al., 2022).

Recent advances in natural language processing (NLP), especially the development of large language models (LLMs), have led to new approaches to semantic annotation and ontology population (Babaei Giglou et al., 2023). These models, with their capacity for language comprehension, allow for automating the extraction of structured information, even in languages with limited training resources (Huang et al., 2023; Saetia et al., 2024). However, the effectiveness of LLMs for ontology populations in specific domains, such as banking, where the accuracy of extracted information is paramount, remains underexplored.

Tuning the prompts is one of the techniques to optimize LLMs for a specific task. A range of prompting techniques, including few-shot learning (Brown et al., 2020), chain-of-thought (CoT) prompting (Wei et al., 2022), and others, have been proposed to enhance the performance of LLMs across various NLP tasks, from named-entity recognition (NER) to complex question answering. These techniques aim to guide the model's attention and reasoning process, facilitat-

Proceedings of TextGraphs-17: Graph-based Methods for Natural Language Processing, pages 53–60
August 15, 2024 ©2024 Association for Computational Linguistics

ing a more accurate extraction and interpretation of the desired information. While the impact of these prompting strategies has been extensively studied in other NLP applications, their application in structured information extraction from unstructured text, particularly within the context of low-resource languages, has yet to be thoroughly investigated. This gap necessitates a study to understand the potential of various prompting methods in improving the efficiency and accuracy of ontology population tasks especially in low-resource language. Herein, we study the extraction of structured information from corporate banking documents, particularly credit card product descriptions, using both traditional span-based methods and innovative LLMs-based generative approaches.

The main contributions of our work are summarized as follows:

- We provide a comparative study between span-based and generative approaches for ontology population tasks within the banking sector.
- We present LLM-based generative approaches with different prompting techniques for extracting structured information from text in a low-resource language context.

Our proposed approach could offer benefits to organizations maintaining internal documents in low-resource languages, seeking to streamline their data warehousing and enhance data interoperability across departments, particularly when resources for comprehensive data annotation are limited.

2 Related Work

2.1 LLMs for Generative Information Extraction

The recent advancements in LLMs have attracted attention to investigate their role in generative structured information extraction (IE), such as Named Entity Recognition (NER) and Relation Extraction (RE). Early studies have pioneered the approaches to address the limitations of LLMs in NER, introducing methods that formulate NER into a generative task and employ self-verification strategies for accuracy enhancement (Xia et al., 2023; Wang et al., 2023). Particularly, (Xia et al., 2023) proposes a training-free framework that improves the LLM performance in zero-shot NER. Similarly, frameworks like QA4RE (Zhang et al., 2023) have been proposed to improve LLM accuracy for RE tasks by aligning the task with question-answering tasks. GPT-RE (Wang et al., 2023) develops further by incorporating task-aware representations and reasoning logic to mitigate the issues of low relevance between entity and relation. To address the issues on the large number of relation types, (Li et al., 2023a) integrates the LLM with a dedicated inference module to improve document-level relation extraction.

Another paradigm to tailor the models to specific tasks is through prompt tuning, which has been shown to improve the overall performance (Yin et al., 2023). Code4UIE utilizes prompts that align the input-output pair with the pre-training stage of LLM for code generation (Guo et al., 2023). Few-shot prompting has also been used to provide task-specific examples for the LLMs to learn from (Brown et al., 2020). Techniques like CoT also encourage logical inferences and reasoning from the models (Wei et al., 2022). Additionally, interactive prompt strategies, like multi-turn QA, facilitate iterative refinement and feedback on generated extractions (Zhang et al., 2023). In IE, explicitly stating the definition of the field in the prompt is also reported to have a substantial influence on the extraction accuracy (Sousa et al., 2023).

3 Methodology

3.1 Data Collection

In this study, we analyze internal corporate documents detailing 20 retail banking products, specifically credit cards. These documents were manually tagged by a Thai linguist and subsequently verified by two computational linguistics researchers, to follow banking product ontology. The ontology employed herein aligns closely with the Schema's PaymentCard concept. Namely, we consider four main properties from PaymentCard (floorLimit, monthlyMinimumRepaymentAmount), FinancialProduct (annualPercentageRate), and Service (availableChannel). Schema's structure is selected because of its relevancy to the original documents. Other ontologies are discussed in A.1.

The primary objective of the ontology population task is to extract these properties from the original, unstructured text. This objective is achieved through the use of either span-based approaches or variations of the LLMs-based generative approaches.

3.2 Span-based Approach

This approach adopts the widely utilized BIO extraction concept (B-named entity for the beginning; I-entity name for the inside; O; for non-entity tokens) (Ramshaw and Marcus, 1999), which effectively detects the beginning and intermediate tokens within spans or entities. As pre-trained language models have shown success in this task (Devlin et al., 2018; Brown et al., 2020), here, we finetune Wangchanberta, a Thai pre-trained language model (Lowphansirikul et al., 2021), on the dataset while incorporating the BIO concept. A few-shot setting is also applied using two-state prototypical networks similar to previous few-shot NER methods (Ding et al., 2021; Li et al., 2023b)

3.3 LLMs-based Generative Approach

In this approach, GPT-3.5 (Brown et al., 2020; OpenAI, 2023b) is employed to extract structured properties or entities from the provided text (The comparison between GPT-3.5 and GPT-4 is provided in A.2). The prompts are designed as a prefix-prompt (Liu et al., 2023) to generate JSON-formatted outputs, ensuring ease of parsing and storing.

The prompt initially consists solely of a task description to guide the model in a zero-shot setting. As illustrated in Figure A.1 in part A, the prompt comprises three sentences. The first sentence provides the instruction while specifying the output format. The second sentence includes the name of the primary field, and the final sentence lists the associated sub-properties.

To improve the conciseness in the context of extracting the structured properties, three prompt construction strategies are presented as follows.

3.3.1 Few-shot Prompting

We adhere to the original method outlined in the previous work (Brown et al., 2020), which involves the insertion of examples after the task description but before the expected input text. Specifically, we use "TEXT:" to mark the commencement of the input, and "ANSWER:" to indicate the beginning of the output for each example. The structure of this few-shot setting prompt is depicted in Figure A.1 part C.

In a positive example, the input text contains all sub-properties in the task description. Conversely, the negative example deliberately excludes all sub-properties.

3.3.2 CoT Prompting

To guide the reasoning capability of the model, we follow a similar CoT approach as presented in (Wei et al., 2022). We include a segment of the extracted text that mentions all sub-properties as the preceding reasoning before generating the sub-properties themselves. The initial step guides the model to extract this text as a preliminary step before extracting each sub-field. Consequently, the model can identify the relevant text within the primary field without necessarily comprehending the sub-field at the beginning. In the positive example, the extracted text is populated as the first field (labeled as "extracted_text") within the JSON-formatted output. The structure of the prompt, where "extract_text" is integrated into a few-shot setting, is shown in Figure A.1 part C.

3.3.3 Definition from schema.org

The definition of each primary field and its respective sub-properties are sourced from "schema.org" (Schema.org, 2008) and are provided explicitly in the prompts. Notably, only the meaning or description of each field is selected, with other details such as examples being excluded. The segment containing these definition within the prompt is after the task description but before the inclusion of example, as shown in Figure A.1 part B.

3.4 Evaluation Metrics

To evaluate the performance of both span-based approaches and the LLM-based generate approach, we employ F1 scores to compare the extracted entities and the annotated ones.

For the span-based approaches, evaluation entails the computation of a macro-averaged F1 score based on token prediction. In this work, macro-averaging is used to ensure equal consideration of all classes.

Meanwhile, the evaluation of the generative uses an F1 score based on exact matches. The evaluation involves determining the intersection between the predicted entities and the labeled entities within each sub-field.

4 Results and Discussion

4.1 Experiment - Span-based Approach

The results of the span-based approaches are shown in Table 1. When the Wangchanberta model is finetuned using the BIO extraction concept, the model yields only a 4.92% F1 score across all four main

Model	Precision (%)	Recall (%)	F1 score (%)
BIO extraction model (with classes)	13.89	2.99	4.92
Span detection (no classes)	**96.43**	11.79	21.01
Zero-shot	14.00	35.90	20.14
Few-shot (pos)	27.27	69.23	39.13
Few-shot (pos + neg)	55.81	61.54	58.54
Few-shot + Definition	47.79	69.23	56.54
Few-shot + CoT	49.54	69.23	57.75
Few-shot + CoT + Definition	51.79	**74.36**	**61.05**

Table 1: The results of span-based and LLMs-based generative approaches.

classes. This result confirms the limited efficiency of the fundamental span-based approach when employed with a restricted volume of training data.

In the subsequent experiment, conducted in a few-shot setting, span detection without considering specific classes yields a 21.01% F1 score. This result indicates that using traditional span-based approaches is still relatively limited even for just identifying the span without classifying the class.

4.2 Experiment - LLMs-based Generative Approach

The results, shown in Table 1, indicate that when utilizing a prompt containing solely a task description, the model achieved 20.14% F1 score. This poor performance likely arises from the model making assumptions on the definition of given fields.

To address this limitation, the incorporation of a positive example as a context, results in a notable improvement, yielding a 39.13% F1 score. This improvement is particularly significant in terms of recall, as it mimics the provided example, enhancing the models' ability to recognize relevant information. Subsequently, after introducing the negative example, the precision further increases (an F1 score of 58.54%). This enhancement suggests a better model comprehension, being able to identify what should be disregarded. Importantly, this outcome underscores that adopting even with only two labeled examples can yield substantial improvements.

To further improve performance, the inclusion of the proposed CoT and the field definition from schema.org provides a more comprehensive context for the model to understand each respective field. While there is a slight decrease in precision and the F1 score when utilizing CoT and definition separately, their combined integration results in approximately 2.5% increase in the F1 score compared to the prompt without these components, yielding the overall F1 score of 61.05%.

The results herein show the ability of LLMs to adapt to complex, domain-specific tasks using relatively simple prompt adjustments, even in a low-resource setting. Particularly, providing both positive and negative examples has the most influence on improving the performance in this information extraction task.

As these prompting techniques are not language specific, the prompting sequences proposed here can also be applied to other languages. However, the accuracy of the output depends on the proficiency of the selected LLM in the target language (Nguyen et al., 2023; Le Scao et al., 2023).

5 Conclusion

In this study, we conduct an evaluation of structured information extraction from unstructured Thai corporate documents describing retail banking products. We show that while LLM-based approaches allow for the extraction of relevant concepts without prior task-specific, the models face limitations in accurately interpreting unstructured text in low-resource language. This work demonstrates the efficiency of LLMs-based generative approaches enhanced by advanced prompting techniques, achieving an F1 score up to 61.05%. Our findings reveal that providing both positive and negative examples leads to the most improvement in the F1 score.

6 Future Work

This work can be extended outside of financial domain, leveraging Schema.org's extensive entities and properties. Additionally, the generated knowledge graph can be employed for question-answering or other information retrieval applications (Yang et al., 2015; Yani and Krisnadhi, 2021).

Integrating this graph into Large Language Models (LLMs) can potentially enhance their capabilities through graph neural networks and other reasoning methods (Kang et al., 2022; Liu et al., 2020).

7 Limitations

In this study, we note several limitations. First, GPT-3.5 was trained for general-purpose tasks and can be replaced with more robust, task-specific models. Specifically, Thai, as a low-resource language, tends to exhibit lower performance when compared to high-resource languages such as English. Second, the writing style can vary among different authors and languages, potentially making consistent annotation challenging. Also, identifying the span of the target entities within the document can sometimes be subjective. The span of the target entities can be a word or a phrase depending on the entity type. For example, "serviceLocation" can include a long phrase of an address but "value" in "floorLimit" can be only one number.

References

Hamed Babaei Giglou, Jennifer D'Souza, and Sören Auer. 2023. LLMs4OL: Large language models for ontology learning. In *The Semantic Web – ISWC 2023*, pages 408–427, Cham. Springer Nature Switzerland.

Bank-Ontology-Project. 1999. Bank ontology project. https://www.bankontology.com. Accessed on June 15, 2023.

Mike Bennett. 2013. The financial industry business ontology: Best practice for big data. *Journal of Banking Regulation*, 14(3-4):255–268.

Tim Berners-Lee, James Hendler, and Ora Lassila. 2001. The semantic web. *Scientific american*, 284(5):34–43.

Tom Brown, Benjamin Mann, Nick Ryder, Melanie Subbiah, Jared D Kaplan, Prafulla Dhariwal, Arvind Neelakantan, Pranav Shyam, Girish Sastry, Amanda Askell, et al. 2020. Language models are few-shot learners. *Advances in neural information processing systems*, 33:1877–1901.

Yohann Chasseray, Anne-Marie Barthe-Delanoë, Stéphane Négny, and Jean-Marc Le Lann. 2023. Knowledge extraction from textual data and performance evaluation in an unsupervised context. *Information Sciences*, 629:324–343.

Jacob Devlin, Ming-Wei Chang, Kenton Lee, and Kristina Toutanova. 2018. BERT: Pre-training of deep bidirectional transformers for language understanding. *arXiv preprint arXiv:1810.04805*.

Ning Ding, Guangwei Xu, Yulin Chen, Xiaobin Wang, Xu Han, Pengjun Xie, Haitao Zheng, and Zhiyuan Liu. 2021. Few-NERD: A few-shot named entity recognition dataset. In *Proceedings of the 59th Annual Meeting of the Association for Computational Linguistics and the 11th International Joint Conference on Natural Language Processing (Volume 1: Long Papers)*, pages 3198–3213.

Thomas R. Gruber. 1993. A translation approach to portable ontology specifications. *Knowledge Acquisition*, 5(2):199–220.

Ramanathan V Guha, Dan Brickley, and Steve Macbeth. 2016. Schema.org: evolution of structured data on the web. *Communications of the ACM*, 59(2):44–51.

Qingyu Guo, Fuzhen Zhuang, Chuan Qin, Hengshu Zhu, Xing Xie, Hui Xiong, and Qing He. 2020. A survey on knowledge graph-based recommender systems. *arXiv preprint arXiv:2003.00911*.

Yucan Guo, Zixuan Li, Xiaolong Jin, Yantao Liu, Yutao Zeng, Wenxuan Liu, Xiang Li, Pan Yang, Long Bai, Jiafeng Guo, and Xueqi Cheng. 2023. Retrieval-augmented code generation for universal information extraction. *arXiv preprint arXiv:2311.02962*.

Haoyang Huang, Tianyi Tang, Dongdong Zhang, Wayne Xin Zhao, Ting Song, Yan Xia, and Furu Wei. 2023. Not all languages are created equal in LLMs: Improving multilingual capability by cross-lingual-thought prompting. *arXiv preprint arXiv:2305.07004*.

Minki Kang, Jinheon Baek, and Sung Ju Hwang. 2022. KALA: Knowledge-augmented language model adaptation. In *Proceedings of the 2022 Conference of the North American Chapter of the Association for Computational Linguistics: Human Language Technologies*, pages 5144–5167.

Wirit Khongcharoen, Chanatip Saetia, Tawunrat Chalothorn, and Pakpoom Buabthong. 2022. Question answering over knowledge graphs for thai retail banking products. In *2022 17th International Joint Symposium on Artificial Intelligence and Natural Language Processing (iSAI-NLP)*, pages 1–5.

Teven Le Scao, Angela Fan, Christopher Akiki, Ellie Pavlick, Suzana Ilić, Daniel Hesslow, Roman Castagné, Alexandra Sasha Luccioni, François Yvon, Matthias Gallé, et al. 2023. Bloom: A 176b-parameter open-access multilingual language model.

Junpeng Li, Zixia Jia, and Zilong Zheng. 2023a. Semi-automatic data enhancement for document-level relation extraction with distant supervision from large language models. In *Proceedings of the 2023 Conference on Empirical Methods in Natural Language Processing*, pages 5495–5505, Singapore. Association for Computational Linguistics.

Yongqi Li, Yu Yu, and Tieyun Qian. 2023b. Type-aware decomposed framework for few-shot named entity recognition. *arXiv preprint arXiv:2302.06397*.

Pengfei Liu, Weizhe Yuan, Jinlan Fu, Zhengbao Jiang, Hiroaki Hayashi, and Graham Neubig. 2023. Pre-train, prompt, and predict: A systematic survey of prompting methods in natural language processing. *ACM Computing Surveys*, 55(9):1–35.

Weijie Liu, Peng Zhou, Zhe Zhao, Zhiruo Wang, Qi Ju, Haotang Deng, and Ping Wang. 2020. K-BERT: Enabling language representation with knowledge graph. In *Proceedings of the AAAI Conference on Artificial Intelligence*, volume 34, pages 2901–2908.

Lalita Lowphansirikul, Charin Polpanumas, Nawat Jantrakulchai, and Sarana Nutanong. 2021. Wangchanberta: Pretraining transformer-based thai language models. *arXiv preprint arXiv:2101.09635*.

Xuan-Phi Nguyen, Wenxuan Zhang, Xin Li, Mahani Aljunied, Qingyu Tan, Liying Cheng, Guanzheng Chen, Yue Deng, Sen Yang, Chaoqun Liu, et al. 2023. Seallms–large language models for southeast asia. *arXiv preprint arXiv:2312.00738*.

OpenAI. 2023a. GPT-4 technical report. *arXiv preprint arXiv:2303.08774*.

OpenAI. 2023b. Introducing ChatGPT. `https://openai.com/blog/chatgpt`. Accessed on February 5, 2024.

GG Petrova, Anatoly Tuzovsky, and Nataliya Valerievna Aksenova. 2017. Application of the financial industry business ontology (FIBO) for development of a financial organization ontology. In *Journal of Physics: Conference Series*, volume 803. 012116.

Lance A Ramshaw and Mitchell P Marcus. 1999. Text chunking using transformation-based learning. In *Natural language processing using very large corpora*, pages 157–176. Springer.

Chanatip Saetia, Areeya Thonglong, Thanpitcha Amornchaiteera, Tawunrat Chalothorn, Supawat Taerungruang, and Pakpoom Buabthong. 2024. Streamlining event extraction with a simplified annotation framework. *Frontiers in Artificial Intelligence*, 7:1361483.

Schema.org. 2008. Schema.org. `https://schema.org/`. Accessed on June 15, 2023.

Hugo Sousa, Nuno Guimarães, Alípio Jorge, and Ricardo Campos. 2023. GPT Struct Me: Probing gpt models on narrative entity extraction. In *2023 IEEE International Conference on Web Intelligence and Intelligent Agent Technology (WI-IAT)*, pages 383–387. IEEE.

Ana Tănăsescu. 2016. A financial reporting ontology design according to IFRS standards. *Economic Insights-Trends & Challenges*, 68(4):37–44.

Eileen Z Taylor and Ann C Dzuranin. 2010. Interactive financial reporting: an introduction to extensible business reporting language (XBRL). *Issues in Accounting Education*, 25(1):71–83.

Shuhe Wang, Xiaofei Sun, Xiaoya Li, Rongbin Ouyang, Fei Wu, Tianwei Zhang, Jiwei Li, and Guoyin Wang. 2023. GPT-NER: Named entity recognition via large language models. *arXiv preprint arXiv:2304.10428*.

Jason Wei, Xuezhi Wang, Dale Schuurmans, Maarten Bosma, Fei Xia, Ed Chi, Quoc V Le, Denny Zhou, et al. 2022. Chain-of-thought prompting elicits reasoning in large language models. *Advances in Neural Information Processing Systems*, 35:24824–24837.

Yu Xia, Yongwei Zhao, Wenhao Wu, and Sujian Li. 2023. Debiasing generative named entity recognition by calibrating sequence likelihood. In *Proceedings of the 61st Annual Meeting of the Association for Computational Linguistics (Volume 2: Short Papers)*, pages 1137–1148, Toronto, Canada. Association for Computational Linguistics.

Min-Chul Yang, Do-Gil Lee, So-Young Park, and Hae-Chang Rim. 2015. Knowledge-based question answering using the semantic embedding space. *Expert Systems with Applications*, 42(23):9086–9104.

Mohammad Yani and Adila Alfa Krisnadhi. 2021. Challenges, techniques, and trends of simple knowledge graph question answering: a survey. *Information*, 12(7):271.

Shukang Yin, Chaoyou Fu, Sirui Zhao, Ke Li, Xing Sun, Tong Xu, and Enhong Chen. 2023. A survey on multimodal large language models. *arXiv preprint arXiv:2306.13549*.

Kai Zhang, Bernal Jiménez Gutiérrez, and Yu Su. 2023. Aligning instruction tasks unlocks large language models as zero-shot relation extractors. *arXiv preprint arXiv:2305.11150*.

A Supplementary Information

A.1 Financial Ontology

Current ontologies in the financial and banking sectors are designed to provide a formal representation of financial knowledge. This often encompasses the categorization of financial entities and the definition of properties for each entity. In the early stages of ontology and knowledge engineering, the primary objective was to create a machine-readable Semantic Web to enhance information retrieval and enable reasoning with structured knowledge (Berners-Lee et al., 2001).

While various financial ontologies have been developed to represent concepts from both the customer perspective (such as transactions) and the organization perspective (like banking products), there is often a degree of conceptual overlap among these ontologies, each capable of representing information relevant to the financial and banking industries. The Financial Industry Business Ontology (FIBO), developed by the Enterprise Data Management (EDM) Council, stands out as one of the most comprehensive, encompassing loans, securities, and financial processes (Bennett, 2013). The eXtensible Business Reporting Language (XBRL) provides a global framework for exchanging business information, primarily focused on processing financial statements and regulatory filings (Taylor and Dzuranin, 2010).

Similarly, the International Financial Reporting Standards (IFRS) ontology is tailored to financial reporting standards (Tănăsescu, 2016). In contrast, the Bank Ontology offers a wider array of concepts covering products offered by banking institutions (Bank-Ontology-Project, 1999). Conversely, although not strictly adhering to the W3C Web Ontology Language (OWL) standards initially intended for the Semantic Web, the Schema.org markup provides centralized, extensible schemas for representing structured data vocabularies across various industries, including financial and banking products (Guha et al., 2016).

A.2 The comparison of GPT-3.5 and GPT-4

In the following comparative analysis, both GPT-3.5 and GPT-4 were subjected to identical prompts, with the results shown in Table A.1. Contrary to GPT-3.5, prompting GPT-4 under a zero-shot setting yields a better result, likely from broader general reasoning capability (OpenAI, 2023a). When positive and negative examples are provided, GPT-4 exhibits improvements similar to GPT-3.5. Nevertheless, GPT-3.5 demonstrates a slightly better F1 score, likely because the outputs from GPT-4 are paraphrased into more readable text, while those from GPT-3.5 maintain the exact text extracted from the input text. Moreover, the GPT-4 output may include additional information, in some cases, the start and end dates, or the special condition of the property. A similar comparison between GPT-3.5 and GPT-4 also be observed when prompting with CoT and definition. In summary, although GPT-4 may be employed for this task and may generatively extract accurate information, additional post-processing or restrictive prompting will need to be used to prevent the model from generating additional information. Other metrics that measure semantic similarity or human evaluation can be used to further investigate the comparative performance of the two models.

Model	Precision (%)	Recall (%)	F1 score (%)
Zero-shot	22.82	43.59	29.96
Few-shot (pos + neg)	53.41	60.26	56.63
Few-shot + CoT + Definition	50.49	66.67	57.46

Table A.1: The results of LLMs-based generative approach using GPT-4.

Your task is to extract structured data (JSON format) from the TEXT given the DEFINITION. The structured data has a field as availableChannel. In the field "availableChannel" includes three sub fields: "serviceLocation", "servicePhone", and "serviceUrl". A

DEFINITION:
serviceLocation: **{Definition from schema.org}**
... B

TEXT: **{NEGATIVE_EXAMPLE_TEXT}**
ANSWER: {'availableChannel': []}

TEXT: **{POSITIVE_EXAMPLE_TEXT}**
ANSWER: {'availableChannel': [{
'extracted_text': '**{EXTRACTED_TEXT}**',
'serviceLocation': '...',
'serviceUrl': '...',
'servicePhone': '...'
}]} C

TEXT: **{INPUT_TEXT}**
ANSWER:

Figure A.1: The prompt for extracting “availableChannel” integrating all construction strategies

Prompt Me One More Time: A Two-Step Knowledge Extraction Pipeline with Ontology-Based Verification

Alla Chepurova[1] **Yuri Kuratov**[2,1] **Aydar Bulatov**[1] **Mikhail Burtsev**[3]

[1]Neural Networks and Deep Learning Lab, MIPT, Dolgoprudny, Russia
[2]AIRI, Moscow, Russia
[3]London Institute for Mathematical Sciences, London, UK
chepurova@deeppavlov.ai, {bulatov.as,yurii.kuratov}@phystech.edu, mb@lims.ac.uk

Abstract

This study explores a method for extending real-world knowledge graphs (specifically, Wikidata) by extracting triplets from texts with the aid of Large Language Models (LLMs). We propose a two-step pipeline that includes the initial extraction of entity candidates, followed by their refinement and linkage to the canonical entities and relations of the knowledge graph. Finally, we utilize Wikidata relation constraints to select only verified triplets. We compare our approach to a model that was fine-tuned on a machine-generated dataset and demonstrate that it performs better on natural data. Our results suggest that LLM-based triplet extraction from texts, with subsequent verification, is a viable method for real-world applications.

1 Introduction

Today, a vast amount of knowledge exists in unstructured textual formats such as books, articles, news reports, blog posts, and social media. Knowledge graphs (KG), which organize data in a structured form, are crucial for making world knowledge accessible across various applications. One of the largest open real-world knowledge graphs, WikiData (Vrandečić, 2012), contains over 1.54 billion items and is maintained collaboratively by volunteers. Keeping such a resource up-to-date requires significant manual curation. Populating knowledge graphs with information extracted from texts presents a promising solution to this challenge, aiming to automate the process, keep these databases relevant and updated, and help the community support them.

Knowledge graphs (KGs) are directed multi-relational graphs that use entities as nodes and their relationships as edges. To represent KGs, a set of triplets referred to as (head entity, relation, tail entity) or (h, r, t) is used. KGs provide a structured representation of facts regarding both real-world objects and abstract concepts.

Knowledge Extraction, or Triplet Extraction is a crucial task towards automatically constructing large-scale KGs. Such methods are used to identify entity pairs and their relationships in unstructured texts. Three independent steps are usually involved in the KG construction: 1) entity discovery, 2) coreference resolution, and 3) relation extraction. Unfortunately, in this pipeline errors in entity discovery propagate to the subsequent stages limiting overall performance. To address this issue, approaches have recently been developed to jointly extract entities and relations from texts (Melnyk et al., 2021). Such methods tackle both tasks simultaneously as a sequence-to-sequence learning problem in an end-to-end manner using generative language models (LMs). End-to-end generative triple extraction eliminates the issue of error propagation and improves efficiency without requiring additional annotation. However, training a separate LM for a specific KG has several limitations, including 1) requiring labeled corpora of sufficient size for LM training; 2) the need for a re-training model as the KG may actively evolve or LM retraining for a different KG, e.g. KG with distinct ontology, entity, and relation set or a KG from other domain. The last limitation is mediated by the fact that during training LM was provided with only the entities and relations that were present in the previous version of KG or an entirely different KG with a predefined ontology and triplet set.

Large Language Models (LLMs), such as ChatGPT and GPT4, with billions of parameters, are empowering natural language processing with their universal language understanding and generation capabilities, thus creating possibilities for end-to-end KG construction. Although the most advanced methods for generative information extraction depend on fine-tuning sequence-to-sequence models, recent studies (Li et al., 2023) propose that triplet extraction may be possible with LLM by in-context learning (ICL) (Brown et al., 2020) and

Proceedings of TextGraphs-17: Graph-based Methods for Natural Language Processing, pages 61–77
August 15, 2024

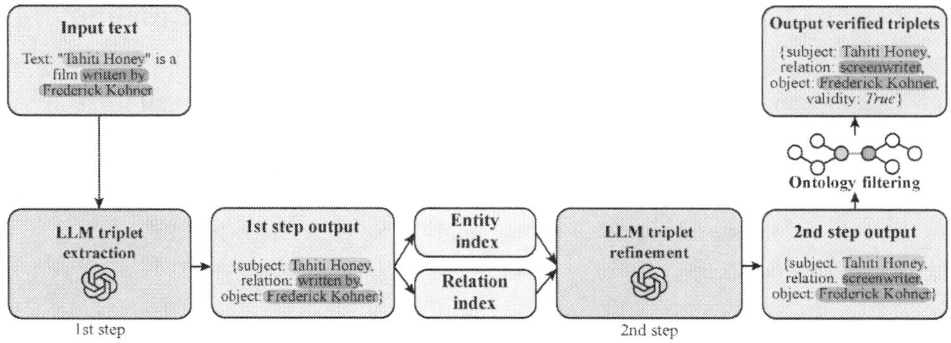

Figure 1: **Proposed pipeline for KG extension.** First, we perform a prompt-based triplet extraction from input text with LLM. The output from this step is a list of triplets in JSON format with possibly inaccurate entity and relation names. Then, we retrieve canonical names of entities and relations for extracted triplets and use them in an LLM prompt to refine triplets. Finally, the refined output is verified with KG ontology to ensure consistency.

instruction following (Ouyang et al., 2022). Using these methods can be advantageous because it eliminates the need for training or fine-tuning models. Thus, triplet extraction can be accomplished by LLMs with the provision of carefully crafted prompts (instructions and in-context examples) and mechanisms for linking names of generated entities and relations to the canonical names from KG.

In this study, we explore the ability of LLMs for tasks of knowledge extraction and KG extension for Wikidata. Despite previous works documenting the poor ability of LLMs to extract structured information from texts (Josifoski et al., 2023), we propose a novel two-step pipeline, which includes 1) LLM to extract entity candidates; 2) LLM to refine triplets by linking exact names of entities and relations based on similar entities and relations from KG; 3) ontology-based triplets verification to enhance the quality of LLM output. Furthermore, we evaluate our pipeline and model that was fine-tuned on the SynthIE dataset to assess their efficacy on real-world data.

2 Methods

To extract triplets from texts, we propose a multi-step pipeline (Figure 1). The first step (Section 2.2) is a candidate triplets extraction. Triplet candidates may include entities and relation names that do not directly match the formats used in the WikiData KG. Therefore, the second step (Section 2.3) refines these candidates based on similar entities and relations that are present in the KG. Finally, we verify the refined triplets and filter out those that are not consistent with the KG ontology (Section 2.4). This involves checking relation constraints and ensuring compatibility of entity types. We use the OpenAI `gpt-3.5-turbo` model to implement the first two steps of the pipeline by providing in-context examples and instructions.

2.1 Datasets

Gathering datasets for the triplet extraction task is both time-consuming and costly as annotators must be familiar with all the entities and relations from a KG to reason about every potential fact stated in the text. In the case of large real-world KGs such as Wikidata, it represents a substantial challenge. This leads to the lack of quality datasets for the KG construction task, while only sparse or noisy datasets are available. For instance, texts in the largest accessible dataset, REBEL (Huguet Cabot and Navigli, 2021), frequently lack extractable information about entities in the text, instead substituting pronouns for factual information about entities. Moreover, target triplets in REBEL also do not contain all the facts provided in the input or are partially inaccurate (Josifoski et al., 2023). Other popular datasets for this task have similar problems (Josifoski et al., 2021).

Evaluation on distantly supervised datasets like REBEL would therefore give an extremely erroneous assessment of the models' performance. Therefore, we used a higher quality SynthIE (Josifoski et al., 2023) dataset. Despite the fact that the dataset was synthetically generated, authors claimed LLMs' inability to solve the information extraction task. Therefore, the task was considered asymmetrical since LLMs can produce text from KG triplets but not KG from text.

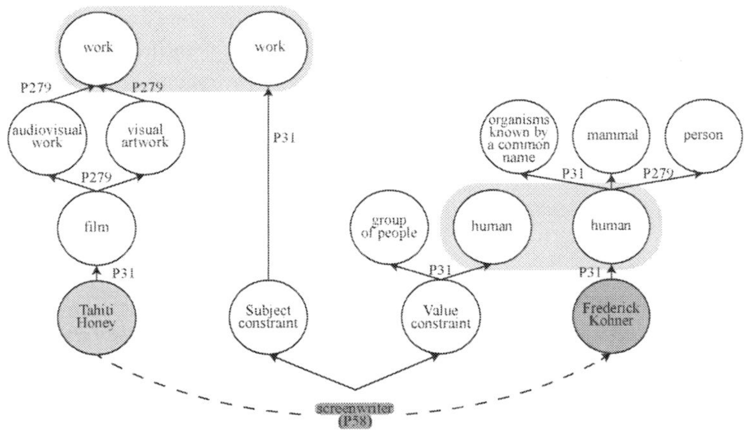

Figure 2: **Ontology-based verification.** Triplets generated in the proposed pipeline undergo ontology verification aimed at ensuring consistency between the output and KG ontology. Triplet claimed to be valid in case its subject's and object's hierarchy types intersect with the types from relation constraints. The ontology hierarchy is simplified for demonstration purposes. P31 and P279 stand for *"instance of"* and *"subclass of"* relations correspondingly.

2.2 Extraction of triplet candidates

In the first step, we extract triplet candidates from the provided text. We benchmarked OpenAI `gpt-3.5-turbo`[1] on triplet extraction with in-context examples. In the prompt, we described the essence of the task and used three examples from the train split from the Wiki-cIE Code dataset (Josifoski et al., 2023) for demonstration. We provide details on prompts construction in Appendix A. In this step, for example, one of the triplets extracted by LLM from the text *"Tahiti Honey" is a film written by Frederick Kohner* would be: *("Tahiti Honey", "written by", "Frederick Kohner").*

However, the subject, object, and relation in the extracted triplet are not necessarily normalized, i.e. they could be inconsistent with the name conventions used in the original KG.

2.3 Refinement of triplet candidates

The primary limitation of LLMs applied to KG construction is that, despite their ability to extract the essential information from a text, they are still unable to link extracted names with the canonical ones of Wikidata entities or relations. To address this limitation, we used a two-step LLM prompting strategy. After extracting information from the text on the first step, the FAISS (Johnson et al., 2019) index was used to retrieve canonical names from the Wikidata KG, ranked by cosine similarity to the entities and relations from identified triplets. The index was built using pre-trained Contriever embeddings (Izacard et al., 2021) that demonstrated robustness and strong performance across various retrieval scenarios. Based on the top-5 retrieved exact names of entities and relations similar to the ones extracted in the first step, we define the task of choosing the names that fit the context of a text and triplet itself. The full structure of the second step prompt is described in Appendix A. For example, for the above-mentioned triplet, there would be retrieved 5 canonical names ranked by similarity to the extracted one for both subject and object entities and relation:

"written by" : ["lyrics by", "adapted by", "produced by", "screenwriter", "author"],

"Tahiti Honey" : ["Tahiti Honey", "Honey", "Honey Chile", "Celtic Honey", "Tahitipresse"],

"Frederick Kohner" : ["Frederick Kohner", "Paul Kohner", "Adolf Kohner", "Susan Kohner", "Henry Rohner"].

As a result, after choosing the corresponding names that fit the context of the text, the refined triplet is *("Tahiti Honey", "screenwriter", "Frederick Kohner").*

2.4 Ontology-based verification

To increase the reliability of the pipeline outputs to possible LLM hallucinations, we proposed an automatic verification of generated triplets based on the KG ontology. An ontology is a semantical model for knowledge representation in a specific domain, which specifies types of entities represented in this

[1] `gpt-3.5-turbo-0125`: `https://platform.openai.com/docs/models/gpt-3-5`

domain as well as constraints regulating how the entities can interact through relations. To ensure the consistency between generated triplets and the WikiData KG ontology model, we used information about types of subjects and objects from generated triplets and relation constraints that specify which types of entities can be connected through the extracted relations.

After both stages of prompting, output triplets underwent an automated check on semantics and property constraints available in Wikidata KG. For this purpose, we used *subject* (Q21503250) and *value* (Q21510865) constraints of the extracted relation. These constraints are attributed to a specific relation and declare which type of head and tail entity correspondingly should be used in a triplet with this relation. Further, classes of both subject and value entities from generated triplet were extracted from Wikidata Query Service (WDQS) by querying *"instance of"* (P31) and *"subclass of"* (P279) properties of subject and object up to the root of their subclass hierarchy. The full SPARQL queries used to retrieve WDQS are described in Appendix B. A triplet is considered valid if the hierarchical types of both the subject and object align with the types specified in the relation constraints. In this way, the validity of the logical structure of extracted information was ensured. An example of the ontology verification process is schematically described in Figure 2.

3 Results and discussion

3.1 Proposed pipeline improves LLM KG extension performance

We suggest that triplet extraction can be accomplished by LLMs with the provision of carefully designed prompts and refining mechanisms for converting imprecise names of generated outputs to the canonical ones from KG. Table 1 shows performance metrics of the full and ablated method.

It is worth noting that the most crucial part of the pipeline is providing the LLM with representative examples of triplets. Using two-step prompting with example demonstration and triplet verification results in a five times better F1 score compared to the same pipeline without example demonstration.

Enhancing the pipeline with the triplet refinement step significantly improves the recall score compared to the single-prompt approach. In turn, the verification step is essential to retain the precision score after triplet refinement comparable to one obtained solely after the first step. In a single-prompt setup, verification does not provide significant improvement. The explanation for this is that after the first step, all triplets whose names KG lacks are automatically filtered out, thus leaving only those that have been referred to most accurately in the text, so LLM can identify them precisely. In the second step, however, LLM may lack knowledge of the specific KG ontology while composing new triplets with exact names of entities and relations that were originally inaccurately specified in the text. Providing ontologies in the second prompt would make it unreasonably large, so we used filtering in the post-processing step to retain a higher precision score, while not reducing the recall value.

3.2 Synthetic data is not a cure-all

Table 2 demonstrates the score of the entire proposed pipeline compared to SynthIE T5-large, the best-reported model trained on SynthIE dataset (Josifoski et al., 2023). Although the improved two-step pipeline with verification and in-context examples demonstrates the potential to improve the quality of KG construction with LLM, its performance on synthetic data compared to the pre-trained model appears rather modest.

In turn, by manually reviewing the synthetic dataset, we observed frequent inconsistencies between the texts and the target triplets, examples of which are provided in Appendix C. To demonstrate the shortcomings of the synthetically generated dataset, we chose a strategy different from utilized in (Josifoski et al., 2023) for REBEL. Instead of assessing the whole dataset itself, we selected 100 random samples from the WikicIE-test-small. Employing the reference entities used for the generation of each text, we manually added similar texts in natural language about these entities from Wikipedia paragraphs. In this way, we obtained a set of texts in natural language referring to the KG entities from the original dataset. Both LM trained on the synthetic data and our LLM-based pipeline generated triplets based on these texts. Then, LM's and LLM's outputs were subjected to human evaluation, described in detail in Appendix D. Results of human evaluation are presented in Table 2. LLM-based pipeline outperforms SynthIE T5-large by a wide margin in terms of human-evaluated precision. The pre-trained model tends to generate triplets that do not directly fit the context of the text, using learned triplets instead of extracting rel-

Table 1: The LLM-based two-stage strategy for triplet refinement and ontology verification increases performance in KG construction tasks. We report mean and std of three runs with different in-context examples.

Method	Metrics (SynthIE-text-small)			Conclusion
	F1	Precision	Recall	
Full pipeline	**0.55** $\pm$0.01	0.59 $\pm$0.03	**0.52** $\pm$0.005	
Full pipeline I no verification	0.53 $\pm$0.01	0.55$\pm$0.03	**0.52**$\pm$0.005	Verification helps
Full pipeline I no refinement	0.51$\pm$0.01	0.60 $\pm$0.03	0.44 $\pm$0.006	Refinement helps
Full pipeline I no refinement I no verification	0.50 $\pm$0.01	0.58$\pm$0.03	0.44 $\pm$0.006	Verification helps
Full pipeline I no in-context examples	0.16	**0.65**	0.09	In-context examples help

Table 2: Our proposed two-step approach outperforms the SynthIE model on a natural language set with human evaluation. While it does not outperform the SynthIE model tuned directly on the SynthIE-text-small dataset and learned its specifics, low IoU metric indicate that the two methods produce very different predictions. (*) results were obtained by the model fine-tuned on the dataset.

Model	SynthIE-text-small			Natural Language corpora		
	F1	Precision	Recall	Precision	# Correct	IoU
Prompt me one more time (Ours)	0.55 $\pm$0.01	0.59 $\pm$0.03	0.52 $\pm$0.005	0.74	187	0.08
SynthIE T5-large (Josifoski et al., 2023)	0.88*	0.87*	0.88*	0.55	201	

evant ones from the context. The reason for this is the quality of the dataset used for training and for in-context learning in our pipelines, due to the inconsistencies between triplets in the annotation and input text.

It is also worth noting that the correct triplets predicted by the two models exhibit notable differences from each other. The intersection over union (IoU) metric shows that only 8 percent of correct triplets are predicted by both models. This suggests that each model has a different area of specialization, excelling in different aspects of information extraction. Consequently, their predictions may be combined, yielding further improvements in the pipeline performance.

4 Conclusions and Future work

Our study identified that LLMs coupled with a two-stage strategy for triplet refinement and ontology verification are competitive in extracting triplets from texts. Furthermore, the proposed LLM-based pipeline shows better performance on non-synthetic data, compared to the model fine-tuned on the SynthIE dataset, making our approach a promising way to address the extraction of triplets from real-world data.

Exploration of possible improvement mechanisms for the triplet refinement step could be a focus of further studies to obtain quality comparable with methods fine-tuned for this task. Current entity and relation linking uses cosine similarity on pre-trained embeddings applied to canonical names from Wikidata. However, enhancing retrieval augmented part is crucial to increase the recall of the whole system. Hence further research may focus on fine-tuning embeddings for this task and the use of additional information from Wikidata, e.g. entities from node neighborhood (Kochsiek et al., 2023; Chepurova et al., 2023), entity or relation textual description.

We identified drawbacks in the synthetic dataset, which was established as one with superior quality in prior work (Josifoski et al., 2023). Considering the demonstrated potential of LLM applied to a triplet extraction task, the creation of smaller, yet higher quality benchmarks for LLM based on texts expressed in natural language could resolve challenges of dataset collection in terms of time and cost and eliminate a bias introduced by synthetic generation.

Limitations

Fine-tuning Overhead. Despite the significant performance improvement achieved by our two-stage pipeline with in-context examples, the models directly fine-tuned for specific graphs and datasets may still outperform our approach. This means that in cases where the text and information domain are sufficiently narrow and computational resources are available, specialized models may be preferred.

Domain Specifics. Furthermore, the effectiveness of the proposed pipeline may vary depending on the domain of source text and knowledge graph. Particularly challenging is dealing with texts that are significantly different from the pre-training domain. The domain adaptation may require manual intervention such as augmentation of in-context examples with domain-specific terms.

Prompt Sensitivity. Our experiments have revealed the considerable influence that prompt quality exerts on the overall performance of the pipeline. This underscores the significance of prompt selection, as it directly affects the pipeline performance, particularly when extending its applicability to new domains.

Acknowledgements

This work was supported by a grant for research centers, provided by the Analytical Center for the Government of the Russian Federation in accordance with the subsidy agreement (agreement identifier 000000D730324P540002) and the agreement with the Moscow Institute of Physics and Technology dated November 1, 2021 No. 70-2021-00138.

References

Tom Brown, Benjamin Mann, Nick Ryder, Melanie Subbiah, Jared D Kaplan, Prafulla Dhariwal, Arvind Neelakantan, Pranav Shyam, Girish Sastry, Amanda Askell, et al. 2020. Language models are few-shot learners. *Advances in neural information processing systems*, 33:1877–1901.

Alla Chepurova, Aydar Bulatov, Yuri Kuratov, and Mikhail Burtsev. 2023. Better together: Enhancing generative knowledge graph completion with language models and neighborhood information. In *Findings of the Association for Computational Linguistics: EMNLP 2023*, pages 5306–5316, Singapore. Association for Computational Linguistics.

Pere-Lluís Huguet Cabot and Roberto Navigli. 2021. Rebel: Relation extraction by end-to-end language generation. In *Findings of the Association for Computational Linguistics: EMNLP 2021*, Online and in the Barceló Bávaro Convention Centre, Punta Cana, Dominican Republic. Association for Computational Linguistics.

Gautier Izacard, Mathilde Caron, Lucas Hosseini, Sebastian Riedel, Piotr Bojanowski, Armand Joulin, and Edouard Grave. 2021. Unsupervised dense information retrieval with contrastive learning. *arXiv preprint arXiv:2112.09118*.

Jeff Johnson, Matthijs Douze, and Hervé Jégou. 2019. Billion-scale similarity search with GPUs. *IEEE Transactions on Big Data*, 7(3):535–547.

Martin Josifoski, Nicola De Cao, Maxime Peyrard, Fabio Petroni, and Robert West. 2021. Genie: Generative information extraction. *arXiv preprint arXiv:2112.08340*.

Martin Josifoski, Marija Sakota, Maxime Peyrard, and Robert West. 2023. Exploiting asymmetry for synthetic training data generation: SynthIE and the case of information extraction. In *Proceedings of the 2023 Conference on Empirical Methods in Natural Language Processing*, pages 1555–1574, Singapore. Association for Computational Linguistics.

Adrian Kochsiek, Apoorv Saxena, Inderjeet Nair, and Rainer Gemulla. 2023. Friendly neighbors: Contextualized sequence-to-sequence link prediction. In *Proceedings of the 8th Workshop on Representation Learning for NLP (RepL4NLP 2023)*, pages 131–138, Toronto, Canada. Association for Computational Linguistics.

Bo Li, Gexiang Fang, Yang Yang, Quansen Wang, Wei Ye, Wen Zhao, and Shikun Zhang. 2023. Evaluating chatgpt's information extraction capabilities: An assessment of performance, explainability, calibration, and faithfulness. *arXiv preprint arXiv:2304.11633*.

Igor Melnyk, Pierre Dognin, and Payel Das. 2021. Grapher: Multi-stage knowledge graph construction using pretrained language models. In *NeurIPS 2021 Workshop on Deep Generative Models and Downstream Applications*.

Long Ouyang, Jeffrey Wu, Xu Jiang, Diogo Almeida, Carroll Wainwright, Pamela Mishkin, Chong Zhang, Sandhini Agarwal, Katarina Slama, Alex Ray, et al. 2022. Training language models to follow instructions with human feedback. *Advances in neural information processing systems*, 35:27730–27744.

Denny Vrandečić. 2012. Wikidata: a new platform for collaborative data collection. In *Proceedings of the 21st International Conference on World Wide Web*, page 1063–1064, New York, NY, USA. Association for Computing Machinery.

A Prompts

We employed a two-step prompting strategy to 1) extract structural information in the form of triplets from a text, and 2) link imprecise names of entities and relations resulting in the first step to the canonical Wikidata names and ids. The output from the first step was parsed as a JSON object to obtain a list of extracted triplets. Then, relations and entities in those triplets were linked to the corresponding top-5 similar exact names from Wikidata using the FAISS index as it was described in 2.3. This resulted in the mapping of extracted triplets and the top-5 exact names were used to construct the second prompt.
For a few-shot prompting with in-context examples, we utilized several crafted examples from a training split of the Wiki-cIE Code dataset. We used different combinations of such examples in three launches, and 3 different sets of examples were taken for each launch of our pipeline.

A.1 System prompts

Triplet retrieval prompt

```
You are an algorithm designed for extracting facts from text in a structured format to build a knowledge graph.
Knowledge graphs consists of a set of triplets. Each triplet contains two entities (subject and object) and one relation
that connects these subject and object.
Entities represent nodes in the knowledge graph, while relation represents a link between these two nodes.
Subjects and objects could be named entities or concepts describing a group of people, events,or abstract objects
from the Wikidata knowledge graph.

You will be provided with the text entitled "Text:". You are expected to output only the list of identified triplets
in a JSON format. Each triplet should have fields "subject", "relation", and "object" for subject, relation, and object
correspondingly.

Here are a few examples of input texts and expected output for each of them:

<example>
...
</example>
```

Triplet refinement prompt

```
In the previous step, there were extracted triplets from the Wikidata knowledge graph.
Each triplet contains two entities (subject and object) and one relation that connects these subject and object.
However, some of the entities and relations extracted in the previous step may have not an exact name from Wikidata.
We linked each subject, relation, and object name with top similar exact names from the Wikidata by semantic similarity.

Your task is to choose appropriate names for entities and relations that correspond to the text's context and
triplet they were taken from.

The input format is following:
    Text: <Text from the previous step for triplets extraction>

    Triplets and corresponding entity and relation mappings:

        <triplet_1>
        {<extracted_subject_1>: <list of 5 exact names similar to subject_1>}
        {<extracted_relation_1>: <list of 5 exact names similar to relation_1>}
        {<extracted_object_1>: <list of 5 exact names similar to object_1>}

        ...

        <triplet_n>
        {<extracted_subject_n>: <list of 5 exact names similar to subject_n>}
        {<extracted_relation_n>: <list of 5 exact names similar to relation_n>}
        {<extracted_object_n>: <list of 5 exact names similar to object_n>}

For each triplet obtained in the previous step, you will be provided with the corresponding 5 exact names of similar
subjects, relations, and objects from the Wikidata knowledge graph.
For each subject, relation, and object from the extracted triplets, you should choose the most appropriate name only from
the corresponding list of 5 exact ones that better match each triplet and the context of the previously demonstrated text.
For each relation and entity in the triplets use chosen names only from the provided list of exact similar names.
You can keep the original name unchanged only in case it is already in the list and fits the context of the text
and extracted triplet better than other options.
In the output provide only the list of updated triplets in JSON format. Each triplet should have fields "subject",
"relation", and "object" for updated subject, relation, and object correspondingly.

Here are some examples of previously extracted triplets with imprecise names, a listsd of linked
exact names, and corresponding corrected outputs:

<example>
...
</example>
```

A.2 In-context examples for the first step prompting

Examples for the first step prompting

```
<example>
Input:
        Text: Józef Skrobiński was a Polish film director and member of the Association of Polish Artists and Designers,
    located in Warsaw, Poland.

Output:
        [
                {
                        "subject": "Józef Skrobiński",
                        "relation": "languages spoken, written or signed",
                        "object": "Polish language"
                },
                {
                        "subject": "Józef Skrobiński",
                        "relation": "occupation",
                        "object": "Film director"
                },
                {
                        "subject": "Józef Skrobiński",
                        "relation": "member of",
                        "object": "Association of Polish Artists and Designers"
                },
                {
                        "subject": "Józef Skrobiński",
                        "relation": "country of citizenship",
                        "object": "Poland"
                },
                {
                        "subject": "Józef Skrobiński",
                        "relation": "instance of",
                        "object": "Human"
                },
                {
                        "subject": "Association of Polish Artists and Designers",
                        "relation": "located in the administrative territorial entity",
                        "object": "Warsaw"
                },
                {
                        "subject": "Association of Polish Artists and Designers",
                        "relation": "country",
                        "object": "Poland"
                }
        ]
</example>

<example>
Input:
        Text: Jorge Merino is a Spanish footballer who plays as a midfielder for Marino de Luanco.

Output:
        [
                {
                        "subject": "Jorge Merino",
                        "relation": "languages spoken, written or signed",
                        "object": "Spanish language"
                },
                {
                        "subject": "Jorge Merino",
                        "relation": "sport",
                        "object": "Association football"
                },
                {
                        "subject": "Jorge Merino",
                        "relation": "occupation",
                        "object": "Football player"
                },
                {
                        "subject": "Jorge Merino",
                        "relation": "position played on team / speciality",
                        "object": "Midfielder"
                },
                {
                        "subject": "Jorge Merino",
                        "relation": "member of sports team",
                        "object": "Marino de Luanco"
                },
                {
                        "subject": "Jorge Merino",
                        "relation": "country of citizenship",
                        "object": "Spain"
                },
                {
                        "subject": "Midfielder",
                        "relation": "subclass of",
                        "object": "Football player"
                },
                {
                        "subject": "Midfielder",
                        "relation": "instance of",
                        "object": "Association football positions"
                }
        ]
</example>
```

Examples for the first step prompting

```
<example>
Input:
        Text: Mario Griguol is an Argentine football player born in Córdoba, Argentina. He speaks Spanish and plays for
    Club Atlético Atlanta.

Output:
        [
                {
                        "subject": "Mario Griguol",
                        "relation": "sport",
                        "object": "Association football"
                },
                {
                        "subject": "Mario Griguol",
                        "relation": "occupation",
                        "object": "Football player"
                },
                {
                        "subject": "Mario Griguol",
                        "relation": "place of birth",
                        "object": "Córdoba, Argentina"
                },
                {
                        "subject": "Mario Griguol",
                        "relation": "country of citizenship",
                        "object": "Argentina"
                },
                {
                        "subject": "Mario Griguol",
                        "relation": "languages spoken, written or signed",
                        "object": "Spanish language"
                },
                {
                        "subject": "Mario Griguol",
                        "relation": "member of sports team",
                        "object": "Club Atlético Atlanta"
                },
                {
                        "subject": "Mario Griguol",
                        "relation": "instance of",
                        "object": "Human"
                },
        ]
</example>

<example>
Input:
        Text: "Tahiti Honey" is an English-language film written by Frederick Kohner.

Output:
        [
                {
                        "subject": "Tahiti Honey",
                        "relation": "original language of film or TV show",
                        "object": "English language"
                },
                {
                        "subject": "Tahiti Honey",
                        "relation": "instance of",
                        "object": "Film"
                },
                {
                        "subject": "Tahiti Honey",
                        "relation": "screenwriter",
                        "object": "Frederick Kohner"
                }
        ]
</example>

<example>
Input:
        Text: Lexington Avenue is a thoroughfare in New York City, parallel to Park Avenue and Third Avenue.

Output:
        [
                {
                        "subject": "Lexington Avenue",
                        "relation": "instance of",
                        "object": "Thoroughfare"
                },
                {
                        "subject": "Lexington Avenue",
                        "relation": "parallel street",
                        "object": "Park Avenue"
                },
                {
                        "subject": "Lexington Avenue",
                        "relation": "parallel street",
                        "object": "Third Avenue"
                },
        ]
</example>
```

Examples for the first step prompting

```
<example>
Input:
        Text: ArXiv is funded by Los Alamos National Laboratory and Nagoya University.

Output:
        [
                {
                        "subject": "ArXiv",
                        "relation": "funder",
                        "object": "Los Alamos National Laboratory"
                },
                {
                        "subject": "ArXiv",
                        "relation": "funder",
                        "object": "Nagoya University"
                },
        ]
</example>
```

A.3 In-context examples for the second step prompting

Examples for the second step prompting

```
<example>
Input:
    Text: Mario Griguol is an Argentine football player born in Córdoba, Argentina. He speaks Spanish and plays for
    Club Atlético Atlanta.

    Triplets and corresponding entity and relation mappings:

        {"subject": "Mario Griguol", "relation": "sport", "object": "football"}
        {"Mario Griguol": ["Mario Griguol", "Carlos Timoteo Griguol", "Roberto Grigis", "M\u00e1rio Grman", "Mario Gromo"]}
        {"sport": ["sport", "sport number", "country for sport", "sports league level",
        "sports season of league or competition"]}
        {"football": ["Association football", "Football association", "The Football Association", "Football",
        "Association football positions"]}

        {"subject": "Mario Griguol", "relation": "occupation", "object": "footballer"}
        {"Mario Griguol": ["Mario Griguol", "Carlos Timoteo Griguol", "Roberto Grigis", "M\u00e1rio Grman", "Mario Gromo"]}
        {"occupation": ["occupation", "field of this occupation", "enclave within", "territory claimed by", "residence"]}
        {"footballer": ["Football player", "Football", "Football on 5", "Football at the Summer Olympics",
        "American football"]}

        {"subject": "Mario Griguol", "relation": "born in", "object": "Córdoba, Argentina"}
        {"Mario Griguol": ["Mario Griguol", "Carlos Timoteo Griguol", "Roberto Grigis", "M\u00e1rio Grman", "Mario Gromo"]}
        {"born in": ["place of birth", "family", "birth name", "family name", "presenter"]}
        {"Córdoba, Argentina": ["C\u00f3rdoba, Argentina", "C\u00f3rdoba F.C.", "C\u00f3rdoba, Spain",
        "C\u00f3rdoba Province, Argentina", "C\u00f3rdoba Department"]}

        {"subject": "Mario Griguol", "relation": "citizenship", "object": "Argentina"}
        {"Mario Griguol": ["Mario Griguol", "Carlos Timoteo Griguol", "Roberto Grigis", "M\u00e1rio Grman", "Mario Gromo"]}
        {"citizenship": ["country of citizenship", "allegiance", "diaspora", "country of origin", "flag"]}
        {"Argentina": ["Argentina", "Norma Argentina", "Argentine Northwest", "Argentina Classic", "Argentine Islands"]}

        {"subject": "Mario Griguol", "relation": "spoken language", "object": "Spanish language"}
        {"Mario Griguol": ["Mario Griguol", "Carlos Timoteo Griguol", "Roberto Grigis", "M\u00e1rio Grman", "Mario Gromo"]}
        {"spoken language": ["official language", "native language", "language used", "languages spoken, written or signed",
        "dialect of"]}
        {"Spanish language": ["Spanish language", "Standard Spanish", "Spanish language in the United States",
        "Mexican Spanish", "UN Spanish Language Day"]}

        {"subject": "Mario Griguol", "relation": "member of team", "object": "Club Atlético Atlanta"}
        {"Mario Griguol": ["Mario Griguol", "Carlos Timoteo Griguol", "Roberto Grigis", "M\u00e1rio Grman", "Mario Gromo"]}
        {"member of team": ["member of sports team", "member of the crew of", "member of military unit", "member of",
        "part of"]}
        {"Club Atlético Atlanta": ["Club Atl\u00e9tico Atlanta", "Club Atl\u00e9tico Palermo",
        "Club Atl\u00e9tico Nueva Chicago", "Atl\u00e9tico Boca del R\u00edo", "Club Atl\u00e9tico Del Plata"]}

        {"subject": "Mario Griguol", "relation": "is", "object": "Human"}
        {"Mario Griguol": ["Mario Griguol", "Carlos Timoteo Griguol", "Roberto Grigis", "M\u00e1rio Grman", "Mario Gromo"]}
        {"is": ["represents", "instance of", "replaces", "contains", "is a list of"]}
        {"Human": ["Human", "Humanos", "Human Is", "Human Entertainment", "Humanin"]}


Output:
        [
                {
                        "subject": "Mario Griguol",
                        "relation": "sport",
                        "object": "Association football"
                },
                {
                        "subject": "Mario Griguol",
                        "relation": "occupation",
                        "object": "Football player"
                },
                {
                        "subject": "Mario Griguol",
                        "relation": "place of birth",
                        "object": "Córdoba, Argentina"
                },
                {
                        "subject": "Mario Griguol",
                        "relation": "country of citizenship",
                        "object": "Argentina"
                },
                {
                        "subject": "Mario Griguol",
                        "relation": "languages spoken, written or signed",
                        "object": "Spanish language"
                },
                {
                        "subject": "Mario Griguol",
                        "relation": "member of sports team",
                        "object": "Club Atlético Atlanta"
                },
                {
                        "subject": "Mario Griguol",
                        "relation": "instance of",
                        "object": "Human"
                },
        ]
</example>
```

Examples for the second step prompting

```
<example>
Input:
    Text: Józef Skrobiński was a Polish film director and member of the Association of Polish Artists and Designers, located in Warsaw, Poland.

    Triplets and corresponding entity and relation mappings:

        {"subject": "Józef Skrobiński", "relation": "spoken language", "object": "Polish"}
        {"Józef Skrobiński": ["Józef Skrobiński", "Józef Żabiński", "Antoni Czubiński", "Jan Żabiński", "Bezek Dębiński"]}
        {"spoken language": ["official language", "native language", "language used", "languages spoken", "written or signed", "dialect of"]}
        {"Polish": ["Polish language", "Dialects of Polish", "Polish alphabet", "Warsaw dialect", "Polish manual alphabet"]}

        {"subject": "Józef Skrobiński", "relation": "occupation", "object": "film director"}
        {"Józef Skrobiński": ["Józef Skrobiński", "Józef Żabiński", "Jan Żabiński", "Bezek Dębiński"]}
        {occupation: ["occupation", "field of this occupation", "enclave within", "territory claimed by", "residence"]}
        {"film director": ["Film director", "Film producer", "Bi Gan (film director)", "Madan (film director)", "Television director"]}

        {"subject": "Józef Skrobiński", "relation": "member", "object": "Association of Polish Artists and Designers"}
        {"Józef Skrobiński": ["Józef Skrobiński", "Józef Żabiński", "Antoni Czubiński", "Jan Żabiński", "Bezek Dębiński"]}
        {"member": ["member of", "member of sports team", "member of military unit", "member count", "member of the crew of"]}
        {"Association of Polish Artists and Designers": ["Association of Polish Artists and Designers", "Association of Polish Architects",
        "Polish Association of Artists - 'The Capitol'", "Polish pavilion", "Polish Social and Cultural Association"]}

        {"subject": "Józef Skrobiński", "relation": "citizenship", "object": "Poland"}
        {"Józef Skrobiński": ["Józef Skrobiński", "Józef Żabiński", "Antoni Czubiński", "Jan Żabiński", "Bezek Dębiński"]}
        {"citizenship": ["country of citizenship", "country of origin", "country of registry", "place of birth", "place of origin"]}
        {"Poland": ["Poland", "Ł", "Polesia", "Poland Together", "Poland Railroad Station"]}

        {"subject": "Józef Skrobiński", "relation": "is", "object": "human"}
        {"Józef Skrobiński": ["Józef Skrobiński", "Józef Żabiński", "Antoni Czubiński", "Jan Żabiński", "Bezek Dębiński"]}
        {"is": ["represents", "instance of", "replaces", "contains", "is a list of"]}
        {"human": ["Human", "Humanos", "Human Is", "Human Entertainment", "Humanin"]}

        {"subject": "Association of Polish Artists and Designers", "relation": "location", "object": "Warsaw"}
        {"Association of Polish Artists and Designers": ["Association of Polish Artists and Designers", "Association of Polish Architects",
        "Polish Association of Artists - 'The Capitol'", "Polish pavilion", "Polish Social and Cultural Association"]}
        {"location": ["location", "work location", "coordinate location", "located in the administrative territorial entity",
        "terminus location"]}
        {"Warsaw": ["Warsaw", "Warsaw Confederation", "Tiger Warsaw", "Warsaw Derby", "Warsaw Arsenal"]}

        {"subject": "Association of Polish Artists and Designers", "relation": "country", "object": "Poland"}
        {"Association of Polish Artists and Designers": ["Association of Polish Artists and Designers", "Association of Polish Architects",
        "Polish Association of Artists - 'The Capitol'", "Polish pavilion", "Polish Social and Cultural Association"]}
        {"country": ["country", "country for sport", "basin country", "country of citizenship", "head of state"]}
        {"Poland": ["Poland", "Ł", "Polesia", "Poland Together", "Poland Railroad Station"]}

Output:
    [
        {
            "subject": "Józef Skrobiński",
            "relation": "languages spoken, written or signed",
            "object": "Polish language"
        },
        {
            "subject": "Józef Skrobiński",
            "relation": "occupation",
            "object": "Film director"
        },
        {
            "subject": "Józef Skrobiński",
            "relation": "member of",
            "object": "Association of Polish Artists and Designers"
        },
        {
            "subject": "Józef Skrobiński",
            "relation": "country of citizenship",
            "object": "Poland"
        },
        {
            "subject": "Józef Skrobiński",
            "relation": "instance of",
            "object": "Human"
        },
        {
            "subject": "Association of Polish Artists and Designers",
            "relation": "located in the administrative territorial entity",
            "object": "Warsaw"
        },
        {
            "subject": "Association of Polish Artists and Designers",
            "relation": "country",
            "object": "Poland"
        },
    ]
</example>
```

Examples for the second step prompting

```
<example>
Input
    Text: Jorge Merino is a Spanish footballer who plays as a midfielder for Marino de Luanco.

    Triplets and corresponding entity and relation mappings:

        {"subject": "Jorge Merino", "relation": "spoken language", "object": "Spanish"}
        {"Jorge Merino": ["Jorge Merino", "Luis Merino", "Juan Merino", "Roberto Merino", "Pedro Merino"]}
        {"spoken language": ["official language", "native language", "language used", "languages spoken", "written or signed", "dialect of"]}
        {"Spanish": ["Spanish language", "Standard Spanish", "Spanish language in the United States", "Mexican Spanish",
        "UN Spanish Language Day"]}

        {"subject": "Jorge Merino", "relation": "sport", "object": "football"}
        {"Jorge Merino": ["Jorge Merino", "Luis Merino", "Juan Merino", "Roberto Merino", "Pedro Merino"]}
        {"sport": ["sport", "sport number", "country for sport", "sports league level", "sports season of league or competition"]}
        {"football": ["Association football", "Football association", "The Football Association", "Football", "Association football positions"]}

        {"subject": "Jorge Merino", "relation": "occupation", "object": "footballer"}
        {"Jorge Merino": ["Jorge Merino", "Luis Merino", "Juan Merino", "Roberto Merino", "Pedro Merino"]}
        {"occupation": ["occupation", "field of this occupation", "enclave within", "territory claimed by", "residence"]}
        {"footballer": ["Football player", "Football", "Football on 5", "Football at the Summer Olympics", "American football"]}

        {"subject": "Jorge Merino", "relation": "position", "object": "midfielder"}
        {"Jorge Merino": ["Jorge Merino", "Luis Merino", "Juan Merino", "Roberto Merino", "Pedro Merino"]}
        {"position": ["position held", "position played on team / speciality", "direction", "academic appointment", "military rank"]}
        {"midfielder": ["Midfielder", "Liga Forward", "Tó (footballer)", "FC Copa", "Defender 2000"]}

        {"subject": "Jorge Merino", "relation": "member of team", "object": "Marino de Luanco"}
        {"Jorge Merino": ["Jorge Merino", "Luis Merino", "Juan Merino", "Roberto Merino", "Pedro Merino"]}
        {"member of team": ["member of sports team", "member of the crew of", "member of military unit", "member of", "part of"]}
        {"Marino de Luanco": ["Marino de Luanco", "Luanco", "Luan Cândido", "Luan Gabriel", "Luan Sérgio"]}

        {"subject": "Jorge Merino", "relation": "citizenship", "object": "Spain"}
        {"Jorge Merino": ["Jorge Merino", "Luis Merino", "Juan Merino", "Roberto Merino", "Pedro Merino"]}
        {"citizenship": ["country of citizenship", "member of military unit", "official residence", "place of birth", "member of the crew of"]}
        {"Spain": ["Spain", "Spain Rodriguez", "Spanish City", "Madrid", "María", "Spain"]}

        {"subject": "midfielder", "relation": "subclass", "object": "footballer"}
        {"midfielder": ["Midfielder", "Liga Forward", "Tó (footballer)", "FC Copa", "Defender 2000"]}
        {"subclass": ["subclass of", "is metaclass for", "has parts of the class", "social classification", "competition class"]}
        {"footballer": ["Football player", "Football", "Football on 5", "Football at the Summer Olympics", "American football"]}

        {"subject": "midfielder", "relation": "instance of", "object": "football position"}
        {"midfielder": ["Midfielder", "Liga Forward", "Tó (footballer)", "FC Copa", "Defender 2000"]}
        {"instance of": ["instance of", "part of", "follower of", "part of the series", "member of"]}
        {"football position": ["Association football positions", "American football positions", "Australian rules football positions",
        "Basketball positions", "Baseball positions"]}

Output:
    [
        {
            "subject": "Jorge Merino",
            "relation": "languages spoken, written or signed",
            "object": "Spanish language"
        },
        {
            "subject": "Jorge Merino",
            "relation": "sport",
            "object": "Association football"
        },
        {
            "subject": "Jorge Merino",
            "relation": "occupation",
            "object": "Football player"
        },
        {
            "subject": "Jorge Merino",
            "relation": "position played on team / speciality",
            "object": "Midfielder"
        },
        {
            "subject": "Jorge Merino",
            "relation": "member of sports team",
            "object": "Marino de Luanco"
        },
        {
            "subject": "Jorge Merino",
            "relation": "country of citizenship",
            "object": "Spain"
        },
        {
            "subject": "Midfielder",
            "relation": "subclass of",
            "object": "Football player"
        },
        {
            "subject": "Midfielder",
            "relation": "instance of",
            "object": "Association football positions"
        },
    ]
</example>
```

Examples for the second step prompting

```
<example>
Input:
    Text: "Tahiti Honey" is an English-language film written by Frederick Kohner.

    Triplets and corresponding entity and relation mappings:

        {"subject": "Tahiti Honey", "relation": "language of film", "object": "English language"}
        {"Tahiti Honey": ["Tahiti Honey", "Honey", "Honey Chile", "Celtic Honey", "Tahitipresse"]}
        {"language of film": ["original language of film or TV show", "language regulatory body", "language used",
        "native language", "dialect of"]}
        {"English language": ["English language", "English Hours", "English International School", "British English",
        "Business English"]}

        {"subject": "Tahiti Honey", "relation": "is", "object": "film"}
        {"Tahiti Honey": ["Tahiti Honey", "Honey", "Honey Chile", "Celtic Honey", "Tahitipresse"]}
        {"is": ["represents", "instance of", "replaces", "contains", "is a list of"]}
        {"film": ["Film", "The Film", "Dance film", "Film award", "Romance Film"]}

        {"subject": "Tahiti Honey", "relation": "written by", "object": "Frederick Kohner"}
        {"Tahiti Honey": ["Tahiti Honey", "Honey", "Honey Chile", "Celtic Honey", "Tahitipresse"]}
        {"written by": ["lyrics by", "has lyrics", "produced by", "adapted by", "screenwriter"]}
        {"Frederick Kohner": ["Frederick Kohner", "Paul Kohner", "Adolf Kohner", "Susan Kohner", "Henry Rohner"]}


Output:
        [
                {
                        "subject": "Tahiti Honey",
                        "relation": "original language of film or TV show",
                        "object": "English language"
                },
                {
                        "subject": "Tahiti Honey",
                        "relation": "instance of",
                        "object": "Film"
                },
                {
                        "subject": "Tahiti Honey",
                        "relation": "screenwriter",
                        "object": "Frederick Kohner"
                }
        ]
</example>

<example>
Input:
    Text: ArXiv is funded by Los Alamos National Laboratory and Nagoya University.

    Triplets and corresponding entity and relation mappings:
        {"subject": "ArXiv", "relation": "funded by", "object": "Los Alamos National Laboratory"}
        {"ArXiv": ["ArXiv", "EngrXiv", "Physics arXiv Blog", "SocArXiv", "PsyArXiv"]}
        {"funded by": ["supervised by", "grants", "donated by", "endorsed by", "funder"]}
        {"Los Alamos National Laboratory": ["Los Alamos National Laboratory", "Los \u00c1lamos",
        "Los Alamos Technical Associates", "Los Alamos, California", "Los Alamos Neutron Science Center"]}

        {"subject": "ArXiv", "relation": "funded by", "object": "Nagoya University"}
        {"ArXiv": ["ArXiv", "EngrXiv", "Physics arXiv Blog", "SocArXiv", "PsyArXiv"]}
        {"funded by": ["supervised by", "grants", "donated by", "endorsed by", "funder"]}
        {"Nagoya University": ["Nagoya University", "Nagoya City University", "Nagoya Gakuin University",
        "Nagoya Institute of Technology", "Nagoya International School"]}

Output:
        [
                {
                        "subject": "ArXiv",
                        "relation": "funder",
                        "object": "Los Alamos National Laboratory"
                },
                {
                        "subject": "ArXiv",
                        "relation": "funder",
                        "object": "Nagoya University"
                },
        ]
</example>
```

Examples for the second step prompting

```
<example>
Input:
        Text: Lexington Avenue is a thoroughfare in New York City, parallel to Park Avenue and Third Avenue.

    Triplets and corresponding entity and relation mappings:

        {"subject": "Lexington Avenue", "relation": "is", "object": "thoroughfare"}
        {"Lexington Avenue": ["Lexington Avenue", "450 Lexington Avenue", "599 Lexington Avenue", "731 Lexington Avenue", "Lexington Park"]}
        {"is": ["represents", "instance of", "replaces", "contains", "is a list of"]}
        {"thoroughfare": ["Thoroughfare", "No Thoroughfare", "Thoroughfare Gap", "Parisian Thoroughfare", "Central Arc Thoroughfare"]}

        {"subject": "Lexington Avenue", "relation": "parallel to", "object": "Park Avenue"}
        {"Lexington Avenue": ["Lexington Avenue", "450 Lexington Avenue", "599 Lexington Avenue", "731 Lexington Avenue", "Lexington Park"]}
        {"parallel to": ["parallel street", "direction", "crosses", "adjacent station", "relative"]}
        {"Park Avenue": ["Park Avenue", "79 Park Avenue", "7 Park Avenue", "Park Avenue Plaza", "245 Park Avenue"]}

        {"subject": "Lexington Avenue", "relation": "parallel to", "object": "Third Avenue"}
        {"Lexington Avenue": ["Lexington Avenue", "450 Lexington Avenue", "599 Lexington Avenue", "731 Lexington Avenue", "Lexington Park"]}
        {"parallel to": ["parallel street", "direction", "crosses", "adjacent station", "relative"]}
        {"Third Avenue": ["Third Avenue", "Third Avenue Railway", "T Third Street", "Third Street Promenade", "1111 Third Avenue"]}


Output:
        [
                {
                        "subject": "Lexington Avenue",
                        "relation": "instance of",
                        "object": "Thoroughfare"
                },
                {
                        "subject": "Lexington Avenue",
                        "relation": "parallel street",
                        "object": "Park Avenue"
                },
                {
                        "subject": "Lexington Avenue",
                        "relation": "parallel street",
                        "object": "Third Avenue"
                },
        ]
</example>
```

B Ontology queries

As the number of relations in the Wikidata is relatively small compared to the number of entities (in order of a thousand) we scraped relation constraints (constraint classes from Q21503250 and Q21510865) in advance. Therefore, we decreased the number of calls to WDQS and increased the throughput of the pipeline.

In turn, to retrieve the subclass hierarchy of a specific entity, the following SPARQL query was used:

```sparql
SELECT DISTINCT ?subclass ?subclassLabel WHERE {
            {
                wd:{entity_id} p:P31/ps:P31/wdt:P279* ?subclass.
            }
              UNION
            {
                wd:{entity_id} p:P279/ps:P279/wdt:P279* ?subclass.
            }
            SERVICE wikibase:label
            {bd:serviceParam wikibase:language "[AUTO_LANGUAGE],en".}
```

Listing 1: SPARQL query for retrieving entity subclass hierarchy

The query identifies 'subclass' and 'instance of' values for a specific entity and goes up to the root of its hierarchy collecting all names representing the classes of entity of interest.

C Examples inconsistencies in synthetic dataset

SynthIE dataset contains frequent cases of discrepancy between generated text (aimed as input text for KG construction methods) and triplets (aimed as target outputs expected in KG construction. Such samples introduce bias through LLM training and LLM in-context demonstration, resulting in skewed quality estimation for both methods.

Examples of mismatches between text and annotation in SynthIE

```
{
    "text": "Medan Marelan is in the same time zone as Krasnoyarsk.",
     "triplets": [
          ('Medan Marelan', "located in time zone",   "UTC+07:00'),
          ('UTC+07:00", "said to be the same as",
          "Krasnoyarsk Time')
    ]
}


{
    "text": "Dr. Babasaheb Ambedkar College of Arts, Commerce and Science is an academic
    institution in India.",

        "triplets": [
          ("Dr. Babasaheb Ambedkar College of Arts, Commerce and Science", "instance of",
          "Academic institution"),
          ("Dr. Babasaheb Ambedkar College of Arts Commerce and Science", "country",
          "India"),
          ("Academic institution", "subclass of", "Educational institution"),
          ("Academic institution", "subclass of", "Research institute"),
          ("India", "language used", "Brokskat"),
          ("India", "public holiday", "Independency Day (India)")
        ]
}
```

D Natural language dataset

We aimed to evaluate the performance across multiple domains, including those different from SynthIE-text-small. For this purpose, we manually sampled 100 paragraphs from Wikipedia that were relevant to WikicIE-test-small. We applied both our approach and SynthIE to the obtained text and compared the conformance of the resulting triplets with the input text. This sampling strategy ensures a fair comparison of models on a distribution that diverges from their pre-training data but remains within the same knowledge graph area.

For all model outputs, we selected the triplets that were consistent with the input text. These were either explicitly mentioned, implied, or readily derivable from the text without additional knowledge. This methodology aimed to evaluate the quality of triplet extraction in contexts closely resembling real-world applications, where the model meets unknown text mentioning known entities.

Each triplet was independently labeled by the three authors of this paper. A predicted triplet was deemed correct (i.e., consistent with the input text) if at least two of the three authors reached a consensus on its correctness. Precision was computed as the total number of valid triplets divided by the total number of predicted triplets across all samples.

The evaluation results show that both models perform well, but the proposed approach demonstrates much higher precision, though the number of generated triplets is close. It is worth noting that the predicted triplets of the two models differ from each other significantly, with the IoU metric less than 9%, meaning that less than 9 percent of correct triplets were predicted by both models.

Below we provide example pairs of original and natural language texts, each of both are about the same entity. Outputs of SynthIE T5-large and our method are highlighted with green color in case they are consistent with the input text and with red color otherwise:

Examples from the composed natural language dataset

Original text from the SynthIE dataset:
Elvira Barbey was the partner of Louis Barbey in business and sport. She competed in pair skating and participated in figure skating at the 1928 Winter Olympics - Pairs.

Natural language text from Wikipedia paragraph:
Elvira Barbey was a Swiss figure skater. She competed at the 1928 Winter Olympics and finished 19th in singles and 11th in pairs, together with her husband Louis Barbey.

SynthIE T5-large generated triplets:
(Elvira Barbey, sport, Figure skating)
(Elvira Barbey, country for sport, Switzerland)
(Elvira Barbey, participant in, 1928 Winter Olympics)
(Elvira Barbey, spouse, Louis Barbey)

GPT generated triplets:
(Elvira Barbey, country of citizenship, Switzerland)
(Elvira Barbey, participant in, 1928 Winter Olympics)
(1928 Winter Olympics, instance of, Olympic Games)
(Elvira Barbey, partner in business or sport, Louis Barbey)
(Louis Barbey, partner in business or sport, Elvira Barbey)

Original text from the SynthIE dataset:
Ilya Shatrov was a military personnel who served during the Russo-Japanese War. He was also a trumpet player.

Natural language text from Wikipedia paragraph:
Ilya Alekseevich Shatrov was a Russian military musician, conductor and composer, known for composing the waltz On the Hills of Manchuria in 1906, recounting his experiences at the Battle of Mukden during the Russo-Japanese War, which he dedicated to one of his comrades fallen at the battle.

SynthIE T5-large generated triplets:
(On the Hills of Manchuria, form of creative work, Waltz (music))
(On the Hills of Manchuria, language of work or name, Russian language)
(On the Hills of Manchuria, copyright status, Public domain)
(On the Hills of Manchuria, composer, Ilya Averbakh)
(Ilya Averbakh, conflict, Battle of Mukden)
(Ilya Averbakh, genre, Opera)
(Ilya Averbakh, conflict, Russo-Japanese War)
(Ilya Averbakh, notable work, On the Hills of Manchuria)

GPT generated triplets:
(On the Hills of Manchuria, publication date, 1906)
(Battle of Mukden, described by source, On the Hills of Manchuria)
(Battle of Mukden, part of, Russo-Japanese War)

Original text from the SynthIE dataset:
Srđan Radosavljev is a member of the Serbian League Vojvodina team FK Palić, where he plays as a midfielder.

Natural language text from Wikipedia paragraph:
Srđan Radosavljev is a Serbian professional footballer who plays mainly as midfielder for FK Bačka 1901. Born in Vršac, SR Serbia, he represented several clubs during his career, spending most of the time with Mladost Apatin and Banat Zrenjanin.

SynthIE T5-large generated triplets:
(UTC+01:00, said to be the same as, Central European Time)
(Ankara, located in time zone, Central European Time)
(Ankara, located in time zone, UTC+02:00)
(Ankara, located in time zone, UTC+01:00)

GPT generated triplets:
(Srđan Radosavljev, position played on team / speciality, Midfielder)
(Srđan Radosavljev, member of sports team, FK Bačka 1901)
(Srđan Radosavljev, sport, Association football)
(Srđan Radosavljev, place of birth Vršac)
(Srđan Radosavljev, country of citizenship, Serbia)
(Srđan Radosavljev, languages spoken, written or signed, Serbian language)

Towards Understanding Attention-based Reasoning through Graph Structures in Medical Codes Classification

Noon Pokaratsiri Goldstein[1] **Saadullah Amin**[2] **Günter Neumann**[1]

[1]German Research Center for Artificial Intelligence (DFKI), D3.2
[2]Department of Language Science and Technology, A2.2
[1,2]Saarland Informatics Campus, Saarland University, Saarbrücken, Germany
{noon.pokaratsiri, guenter.neumann}@dfki.de, saam00002@stud.uni-saarland.de

Abstract

A common approach to automatically assigning diagnostic and procedural clinical codes to health records is to solve the task as a multi-label classification problem. Difficulties associated with this task stem from domain knowledge requirements, long document texts, large and imbalanced label space, reflecting the breadth and dependencies between medical diagnoses and procedures. Decisions in the healthcare domain also need to demonstrate sound reasoning, both when they are correct and when they are erroneous. Existing works address some of these challenges by incorporating external knowledge, which can be encoded into a graph-structured format. Incorporating graph structures on the output label space or between the input document and output label spaces have shown promising results in medical codes classification. Limited focus has been put on utilizing graph-based representation on the input document space. To partially bridge this gap, we represent clinical texts as graph-structured data through the UMLS Metathesaurus; we explore implicit graph representation through pre-trained knowledge graph embeddings and explicit domain-knowledge guided encoding of document concepts and relational information through graph neural networks. Our findings highlight the benefits of pre-trained knowledge graph embeddings in understanding model's attention-based reasoning. In contrast, transparent domain knowledge guidance in graph encoder approaches is overshadowed by performance loss. Our qualitative analysis identifies limitations that contribute to prediction errors.

1 Introduction

The codification of clinical texts by assigning the International Classification of Diseases (ICD) codes for the purpose of streamlining research, insurance billing, and other workflow standardization is a necessary task in healthcare settings. To assign an accurate and complete set of ICD codes to a clinical text, both a knowledge of institutional guidelines and understanding of medical terminology are crucial. Consequently, it is time and cost intensive. Solving the task as a multi-label classification (MLC) problem is one of the common top-performing deep learning approaches to automating this task.

In addition to challenges stemming from the extensive domain knowledge requirements, clinical notes are often over 3,000 words long; due to computational time and memory limitations, models often have to truncate these documents to a smaller size (Moons et al., 2020; Kaur et al., 2021), risking information loss that could be helpful in predictions. Many pre-trained language models such as BERT (Devlin et al., 2019) and its variants, for instance, can only take inputs up to 512 tokens.

External knowledge resources such as the UMLS Metathesaurus (Bodenreider, 2004) for medical concepts and relational information have shown promising results in named entity recognition (NER) (Liang et al., 2023) and automatic ICD coding (Yuan et al., 2022). While attention mechanism (Bahdanau et al., 2015) in combination with knowledge graphs (KG) and graph neural networks (GNN) have been shown to be beneficial when applied to relational information from the output (label) space in this task, the effects of graph representation on the input (document) space are not yet extensively studied.

We are motivated by the applications of this work in modeling other clinical tasks that can also be set up as an MLC problem, e.g. inpatient documentation from multi-modal or non-text input data[1]. It is crucial in critical and highly-regulated fields that human domain experts can understand what con-

[1]Real-time charting in electronic health records (EHR) for clinicians in some settings involves selecting corresponding options from a fixed menu with optional unstructured texts, similar to data entries in a spreadsheet.

Proceedings of TextGraphs-17: Graph-based Methods for Natural Language Processing, pages 78–92
August 15, 2024

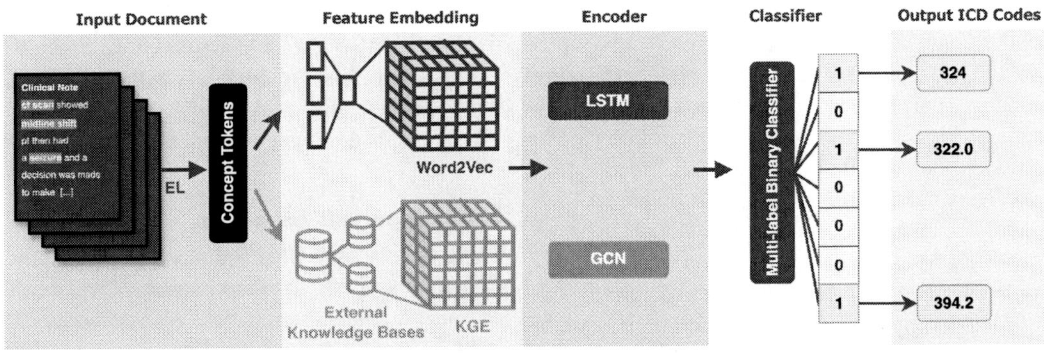

Figure 1: Overview of MLC pipeline: a) concept-based tokens are extracted to represent the input documents, b) tokens are represented by pre-trained feature embeddings (Word2Vec or KGE), c) encoding step transforms input features into latent representations (LSTM or GCN output) and d) binary classifiers determine whether the output representations belong to specific labels.

tribute to correct and incorrect predictions when incorporating automated systems' outputs in their workflow. These considerations influence our decision to investigate concept-based features and verify model's attention-based interpretability through qualitative analysis.

We investigate the impact of implicit graph structures in the form of knowledge graph embeddings (KGE) concept features representation and explicit domain-knowledge guided encoding of input document concepts and their relational information using GNN. Our contributions can be summarized as follows: 1) we highlight the benefits of domain knowledge injection through KGE over traditional contextualized embeddings in representing concept-based features and facilitating clinically intuitive attention-based reasoning, 2) we demonstrate the limitations of GNN encoding architecture, and 3) we identify challenges that contribute to attention-based reasoning errors.

2 Related Works

Knowledge Graph Embeddings: Teng et al. (2020) incorporate knowledge graph embeddings (KGE) as a supplement to text representations to simulate the human reasoning process of deriving ICD codes from a medical knowledge base and to make results more interpretable when combined with the attention mechanism. Chang et al. (2020) demonstrate that KGE are effective at leveraging relational information and representing biomedical domain knowledge; e.g. TransE (Bordes et al., 2013) and RotatE (Sun et al., 2018) are able to retain semantic group and type information inherent in the source knowledge base ontology e.g. SNOMED CT in the UMLS. Combining KG represented entities with input document representations also shows promising improvements in relation extractions (Matsubara et al., 2023). Beyond these works in the biomedical domain, to date, methods involving KGE in automatic ICD coding have been limited.

Graph Neural Networks: EHR data often contain information regarding diagnoses, lab values, encounters, and the patients organized in a graph-like structure to reflect clinical decisions process (Choi et al., 2020). These observations suggest that the features in an EHR encounter and clinical notes have structural relationships. GNN architectures are known to be effective at representing relational information, making them suitable for capturing dependencies among ICD codes and medical concepts. Choi et al. (2020) posit that Graph Convolutional Networks (GCN) represent a special case of Transformer (Vaswani et al., 2017) and propose Graph Convolutional Transformer (GCT) to structurally represent key components in an EHR document. Qiu et al. (2019), Zong and Sun (2020), and Cao et al. (2020) use GCN to model ICD code and/or concept co-occurrence to address the class imbalance problem in the output (label) space.

Attention Mechanism: To provide human-interpretable results, Mullenbach et al. (2018) and Teng et al. (2020) utilize attention mechanism (Bahdanau et al., 2015; Luong et al., 2015) to verify that relevant text spans are clinically informative. Teng et al. (2020), Vu et al. (2020), Saini et al. (2021), and Yuan et al. (2022) use the *softmax* operation to calculate label-wise attention weights from the encoder's output to create label-specific vectors representing the input document. Many high-performing models incorporate variations of the attention mechanism. In combination with domain knowledge implicitly represented through KGE, the attention mechanism helps the model focus on parts of the input document relevant to the predicted labels, resembling how a human medical coder concentrates on relevant parts of the document to determine the corresponding ICD codes based on their domain knowledge expertise. We refer to this process as attention-based reasoning in this work.

3 Methodology

When ICD coding is set up as an MLC task, as shown in Figure 1, a document D is represented as a sequence $\mathcal{X} = [x_1, x_2, x_3, ...x_n]$, where n represents the number of words or extracted concepts in $\mathcal{X}$. The classification model's learning task is to output a label vector $\mathcal{Y} = [y_1, y_2, ..., y_L]$, where L is the total number of codes from a label set L and each $y_i \in \{0, 1\}$. 1 denotes the document contains code i and 0 otherwise. A common training objective is to minimize the binary cross entropy (BCE) loss function between the predicted labels $\tilde{y}_i$ and the true labels y_i.

All experiments are conducted on the Multi-parameter Intelligent Monitoring in Intensive Care-III (**MIMIC-III**) dataset (Johnson et al., 2016). We focus on the discharge summaries and their assigned International Classification of Diseases, 9th Edition, (ICD-9) codes[2]. We follow pre-processing steps and measure results using the same evaluation metrics in Mullenbach et al. (2018) and Vu et al. (2020).

3.1 Concept Features Tokenization

Using text input as a baseline reference, we represent a document as a sequence of medical concepts. Exploiting mapping between medical terms and their textual descriptions in large ontological databases, e.g. the Unified Medical Language System (UMLS) (Bodenreider, 2004), identifying concepts in the input documents can be viewed as an entity linking (EL) task. Within the UMLS, terms across vocabularies are assigned Concept Unique Identifiers (CUIs). Additional attributes such as semantic types, relations, and hierarchical information are also available across CUIs. Since ICD codes are a subset of concepts within the UMLS, using concept (CUI) tokens also provides a way to incorporate additional external knowledge into the model.

3.1.1 Concepts Extraction

We use ScispaCy UMLS entity linking (EL) tool (Neumann et al., 2019) to extract CUIs from the original discharge summaries. We select only CUIs with at least 0.7 confidence scores. Choosing a higher score of 0.8 does not empirically improve results in our experiments (see Appendix A.4). Analogous to the pruning steps in a text pre-processing pipeline, we also prune out rare and frequent CUIs. Using analogous thresholds as in Mullenbach et al. (2018) and Vu et al. (2020), we determine the minimum and maximum frequency thresholds for CUI tokens as follows:

- **frequent**: normalized frequencies exceeding 1500 times per million tokens.
- **rare**: normalized frequencies less than 0.1 times per million tokens.

We also discard CUIs that do not belong to the semantic types of the MIMIC-III dataset ICD-9 codes as well as zero-shot CUIs.[3]

The resultant vocabulary size of the dataset is 26,485 unique CUI tokens. As seen in Table 1, the average input sequence lengths across partitions are well within the typical truncated input lengths of existing state-of-the-art models.

Version	Partition	Min	Mean	Max
Full	Train	9 (55)	696 (1,731)	4,560 (11,940)
	Validation	103 (244)	819 (2,049)	3,038 (7,247)
	Test	90 (252)	825 (2,057)	4,725 (8,209)
Top-50	Train	62 (117)	715 (1,782)	3,665 (8,387)
	Validation	102 (244)	826 (2,066)	3,036 (7,247)
	Test	108 (259)	841 (2,095)	3,061 (7,128)

Table 1: Minimum, mean, and maximum CUI and text tokens (in parentheses) per document for the Full and Top-50 MIMIC-III dataset partitions after pre-processing.

3.2 Feature Representation

Contextualized Representation: Word2Vec (W2V) embeddings for CUIs serve as a comparative baseline against KGE in our experiments due

[2]Multiple editions of ICD codes exist; for simplification, ICD and ICD-9 codes are used interchangeably in this work unless otherwise indicated.

[3]Zero-shot CUIs are defined as CUIs in the validation or test partition not seen in the train set.

EHR Feature	UMLS Semantic Group (SG) or Type (TUI)
Diagnosis	DISO - Disorders
	ANAT - Anatomy
	PHYS - Physiology
	PHEN - Phenomena
	LIVB - Living Beings
Procedure	PROC - Procedures
	DEVI - Devices
	ACTI - Activities & Behaviors
Lab Result	CHEM - Chemicals & Drugs
	T034 - Laboratory or Test Result
	T059 - Laboratory Procedure
Concept	CONC - Concepts & Ideas

Table 2: UMLS Semantic Groups (SG) and Semantic Type Information (TUI) and their corresponding EHR structural features: Diagnosis, Procedure, Lab Result, and Concept; features are identified based on our observations and findings in Choi et al. (2020).

to its usage in existing top-performing models for the text input type. The reference results with text features in Table 3 also use W2V embeddings. Using the same parameters as in Mullenbach et al. (2018) and Vu et al. (2020), we train W2V embeddings for CUI tokens with CBOW (Mikolov et al., 2013) algorithm. We use Gensim (Řehůřek and Sojka, 2010) W2V implementation.[4]

Knowledge Representation: We use TransE Bordes et al. (2013) KGE trained on pre-processed data of the UMLS 2019AB released publicly by Chang et al. (2020)[5]. Since both TransE (Bordes et al., 2013) and RotatE (Sun et al., 2018) achieve comparable results on semantic classification tasks and capture similar semantic information as investigated in Chang et al. (2020), experiments comparing performance between different types of KGE are beyond the focus of this works and are left for future works. We use DGL-KE (Zheng et al., 2020) implementation of TransE for training according to steps described in Chang et al. (2020).[6]

3.3 Encoders

Label Attention Encoder (LAAT): The LAAT model introduced by Vu et al. (2020) follows an MLC pipeline as shown in Figure 1. It consists of an embedding layer where pre-trained W2V embeddings are used to represent document input tokens. The encoder is a bidirectional Long Short Term Memory (LSTM) network whose output provides latent feature representations for the input tokens up to a specified number; this is represented as a vector $\mathbf{H}$ where $\mathbf{H} \in \mathbb{R}^{2u \times n}$. n refers to the number of input tokens and u is the LSTM hidden size. The attention layer $\mathbf{A} \in \mathbb{R}^{|L| \times n}$ transforms the feature representations $\mathbf{H}$ into label-specific vectors as shown in Eq. 1 to 3. $\mathbf{W} \in \mathbb{R}^{d_a \times 2u}$ and $\mathbf{U} \in \mathbb{R}^{|L| \times d_a}$ matrices are learnable parameters. u and d_a are tunable hyper-parameters. The output of the label-specific layer $\mathbf{V} \in \mathbb{R}^{2u \times |L|}$ is the representation of the input document where each ith column in $\mathbf{V}$ corresponds to the ith label in L. The last layer is a feed-forward neural network followed by a sigmoid activation function, which predicts whether a specific ICD code is assigned to the input document or not.

$$\mathbf{Z} = \tanh(\mathbf{WH}) \quad (1)$$

$$\mathbf{A} = \text{softmax}(\mathbf{UZ}) \quad (2)$$

$$\mathbf{V} = \mathbf{HA}^{\text{T}} \quad (3)$$

We re-implement the model to accommodate concept-based tokens using PyTorch (Paszke et al., 2017). We follow implementation details such as optimal hyper-parameters, learning rate, batch size, number of epochs, dropout probability, AdamW (Loshchilov and Hutter, 2018) optimization, and learning rate scheduler as implemented by Vu et al. (2020). In lieu of early stopping, we save the model with the highest validation F1_{micro} for evaluation against the test partition. See Appendix A.2.1 for implementation details. We consider this model a high-performing non-GNN baseline encoder.[7]

GNN Encoder: We use 2-layer Graph Convolution Networks (GCN) (Kipf and Welling, 2017) as a representative GNN encoder for experiments investigating GNN domain knowledge encoding. Choi et al. (2020) demonstrates the correspondence between normalized adjacency matrix calculations in GCN and the attention equation in the Transformer (Vaswani et al., 2017) architecture. Similar to how LAAT utilizes attention mechanism to focus on relevant parts of the input data (represented

[4]Other types of corpus-based embeddings have been proposed to represent concepts in the UMLS, notably Cui2Vec (Beam et al., 2020) and Med2Vec (Choi et al., 2016). However, Chang et al. (2020) observe that these approaches have limitations due to data inaccessibility, high computational requirements, and low coverage, which make their usability for downstream tasks limited.

[5]The link to the data files is published through the SNOMED CT Knowledge Graph Embeddings Git repository: https://github.com/dchang56/snomed_kge

[6]See Appendix A.2.2 for KGE training hyperparameters.

[7]Higher performing encoders have since been proposed and our study can be extrapolated to them; however, for simplicity and discussion, we designate LAAT as a strong non-GNN baseline for this task.

Encoder	Embedding	Precision		Recall		F1		AUC		P@5
		macro	micro	macro	micro	macro	micro	macro	micro	
LAAT (50)	W2V	59.11	64.90	48.92	55.03	53.53	59.56	86.07	89.41	58.06
	KGE	**64.11**	**68.46**	**54.55**	**59.02**	**58.94**	**63.39**	**88.22**	**91.14**	**60.69**
	Text	72.04	75.60	61.84	66.95	66.55	71.01	92.79	94.60	67.28
LAAT (Full)	W2V	7.26	65.78	4.70	35.44	5.70	46.07	84.92	97.77	73.31
	KGE	**7.86**	64.78	**5.47**	**37.80**	**6.45**	**47.74**	**86.62**	**98.05**	**74.41**
	Text	10.65	65.70	9.19	50.64	9.87	57.20	89.84	98.56	80.91
GCN_{EHR} (50)	W2V	54.81	65.04	34.75	44.15	42.53	52.60	83.96	87.02	54.49
	KGE	**58.75**	**65.24**	**41.61**	**48.41**	**48.71**	**55.58**	**84.72**	**87.72**	**56.23**
GCN_{EHR} (Full)	W2V	3.53	60.19	1.55	18.17	2.16	27.92	75.31	96.28	58.61
	KGE	**3.89**	**60.69**	**1.56**	**18.91**	**2.23**	**28.84**	**76.10**	**96.40**	**59.32**

Table 3: Results from experiments on the LAAT and GCN models with the MIMIC-III Top-50 and Full test sets comparing KGE and W2V CUI embedding types. Text input results are included as a reference as it is the input type in Vu et al. (2020). Underlined scores are highest across input types; **bold** ones are the highest within CUI input.

Version	Model	Precision		Recall		F1		AUC		P@5
		macro	micro	macro	micro	macro	micro	macro	micro	
Top-50	GCN_{BASE}	**62.12**	**67.81**	38.22	45.02	47.33	54.11	84.54	87.40	56.00
	GCN_{EHR}	58.76	65.24	**41.61**	**48.41**	**48.72**	**55.58**	**84.72**	**87.72**	**56.23**
Full	GCN_{BASE}	2.86	55.53	1.31	17.81	1.80	26.97	**77.19**	96.07	55.60
	GCN_{EHR}	**3.89**	**60.69**	**1.56**	**18.91**	**2.23**	**28.84**	76.10	**96.40**	**59.32**

Table 4: Results from GCN experiment comparing different edge connection approaches; all models use KGE node embeddings to represent CUIs.

as an output of an LSTM encoder), GCN encoder and the readout function output a graph-level representation of the input document that focuses on relevant concept nodes in the graph.

Each input document that has been processed into a sequence of CUIs is represented as a graph $\mathcal{G} = \{\mathcal{V}, \mathcal{E}\}$, where $\mathcal{V}$ and $\mathcal{E}$ are nodes and edges. Each node in $\mathcal{V}$ represents a unique CUI in a document. An edge in $\mathcal{E}$ represents a connection or relation between CUIs (nodes) as determined by different graph construction methods. To obtain a document-level representation for classification, we specify a sum pooling readout function as it has been shown to be optimal for graph classification tasks (Xu et al., 2018). A readout function can be a simple sum, mean, or max pooling function or more complex (Xu et al., 2018; Ying et al., 2018; Zheng et al., 2020); however, this is beyond the focus of this work.

3.4 Experiment Settings

Implicit Graph Structures with KGE: We compare performance between KGE and W2V embeddings on the LAAT model for the CUI-represented input and on the GCN encoder model. We investigate if KGE pre-training and the implicit relational information from the external UMLS knowledge base improve ICD-9 classification.

Explicit Graph Structures with GNN: We compare a graph edge construction method that explicitly follows clinical reasoning steps as reflected in CUIs co-occurrences against a baseline approach guided by relations in the UMLS KG. As observed in Choi et al. (2020) and our manual annotation (see Appendix A.3), there is a relationship between diagnostic information and treatments that is also reflected in EHR structural features as shown in Table 2. In this work, we refer to the process of relating treatments or procedures to diagnostic information as clinical reasoning. Since ICD codes encompass health-related phenomena (e.g. signs and symptoms, findings, complaints, social factors etc.) and treatment concepts, we investigate if the explicit relational information encoding following a domain-knowledge guided approach improves ICD-9 classification.

1. **Baseline** (GCN_{BASE}) Nodes representing CUIs in a document have edges between them if both nodes (CUIs) are related in the UMLS KG used in pre-training KGE.

2. **Domain-Knowledge Guided** (GCN_{EHR})

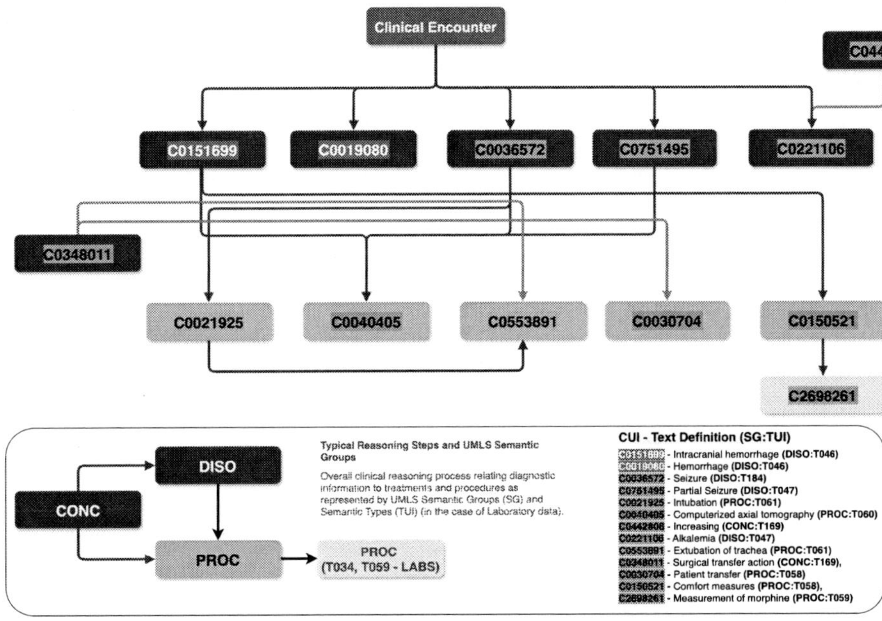

Figure 2: The clinical reasoning steps relating distantly mentioned CUIs in the manual annotation example shown in Figure 5 of Appendix A.3 are demonstrated in this flow chart. The CUIs are color-coded by their UMLS Semantic Group (SG) and are organized into EHR structural features described in Table 2. The arrows demonstrate how Diagnostic (DISO) CUIs are related to Procedural (PROC) and Lab (CHEM, T034, T059) CUIs and how Concept (CONC) CUIs are associated with both Diagnostic and Procedural CUIs.

From manual annotation of 5 randomly selected samples in the Top-50 version of the training dataset[8], we observe co-occurrences between CUIs that also follow typical clinical presentations. For instance, CUIs describing diagnoses are present along with CUIs for certain procedures. As shown in Figure 2, it is possible to group CUIs corresponding to EHR feature types such as diagnoses, procedures, concepts, and lab data based on the UMLS semantic information. While a domain expert with clinical experience can easily relate diagnostic concepts and commonly associated treatment procedures, conditional probabilities between CUIs of different semantic groups can provide a useful edge connection guidance that follows clinical reasoning as proposed in Choi et al. (2020). The steps are summarized as follows:

(a) CUIs are grouped by their UMLS Semantic Group (SG) and EHR feature type described in Table 2.

(b) Conditional probabilities of the co-occurrences of CUIs across these groups are calculated from the training partition as in Choi et al. (2020).

(c) Edges are present between CUIs if their conditional probability exceeds a specified threshold: 0.3, 0.5, 0.7, 0.8.

[8]See Appendix A.3 for an annotated example.

3.5 Attention-based Reasoning Evaluation

To evaluate the attention-based reasoning interpretability, we analyze input text and concept tokens from the Top-50 LAAT experiments. After filtering out test partition samples with no predicted labels, we randomly select 10 samples that contain predictions of the most commonly occurring labels in the test partition. We extract tokens with normalized activation weights from LAAT Attention Layer **A** (Eq. 2) of at least 0.5 of the maximum attention weight (for each predicted label) and compare them to tokens annotated by an intensive care clinician[9] as relevant. We choose 0.5 as results in Teng et al. (2020) comparing interpretability evaluation of text segments extracted from higher attention weights (0.8 threshold) show lower accuracy

[9]We use the definition of clinician as explained in Institute of Medicine (US) Committee on the Future of Primary Care (1994).

than those from lower weights; their findings suggest lower weight ranges may identify potentially informative tokens.

4 Results

Results in Table 3 demonstrate the benefits of implicit graph-representation in the form of KGE on both LAAT and GCN encoders over corpus-based CUI embeddings. KGE shows improvement over W2V CUI embeddings across all metrics on the LAAT model in the Top-50 and Full versions, with an exception of the Precision_{micro} where W2V performance is higher. On GCN_{EHR} model, KGE shows slightly higher performance across all metrics over W2V embeddings. Our findings support observations noted in Chang et al. (2020) and Teng et al. (2020) that KGEs improve domain knowledge representation on the input document space in leveraging relational information. However, with the exception of $\text{Precision}_{\text{micro}}$ and $\text{AUC}_{\text{micro}}$ metrics in the Full version where CUI results are comparable to text-input baseline, concept features result in lower performance than text features. For critical-domain applications, the interpretability advantage of concept-based features over text-based input type as demonstrated in Section 4.1 may justify some performance trade-offs.

Table 4 shows the impact of graph edge construction approaches on GCN performance. Across most of the metrics, a graph construction method that incorporates clinical reasoning and EHR structure offers some benefits over baseline, where edges are connected based on KG relations. An exception is observed in the Top-50 Precision, where the baseline KG-guided construction outperforms the EHR-guided approach. The more noticeable difference in the Full version can be attributed to a larger code base exceeding KG coverage, thus, contributing to a lower Recall in the GCN_{BASE} approach. While GCN as a standalone encoder provides an ability to explicitly encode relational information that reflects clinical reasoning and EHR structural features in the graph construction methods, possibly improving model's interpretability by domain experts, this contribution is limited due to much lower performance across all metrics in comparison to LAAT model.

EHR Conditional Probability Threshold: Among the GCN_{EHR} approaches, performance varies according to minimum co-occurrence conditional probability threshold between EHR structural feature groups. As shown in Figure 3, this variability is more noticeable in the Top-50 than in the Full version. Based on fine-tuning for the highest F1_{micro} among GCN_{EHR} experiments over different thresholds, the optimal minimum probabilities for the GCN_{EHR} are 0.7 and 0.5 for the Top-50 and Full version respectively. GCN_{EHR} results reported in Table 4 are based on these thresholds for their respective version.

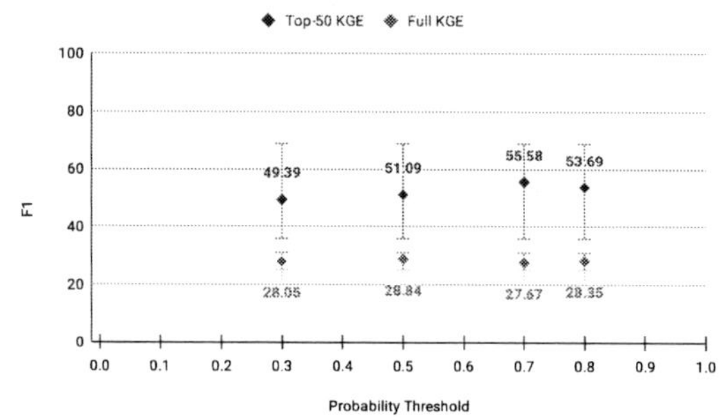

Figure 3: F1_{micro} score in relation to minimum conditional probability threshold in the Top-50 & Full versions of GCN_{EHR} model. Error bars indicate the standard deviation from the mean F1 scores of each group; boundaries are shown at 6 times the standard deviation for clearer visualization.

4.1 Attention-based Reasoning Interpretability

Examples in Table 5 demonstrate the impact of different input feature types on the model's attention mechanism. Clinician-annotated text and CUI tokens are shown as a reference. Our goal is to verify that label predictions are made following clinically informative attention-based reasoning. A false positive example ("401.9") is included to illustrate if erroneous predictions are avoidable, i.e. given the available information (in the form of document text or CUI tokens), would a clinician make similarly incorrect label predictions?

In the example where the ICD label, its CUI, and description match with the input CUI or their text description, KGE and W2V concept features are equally informative as in the example of "427.31:Atrial Fibrillation". Both concept embedding types are more precise than the highlighted text tokens ("fib" and "fibrillation"), possibly due to exact CUI matching. Dropping "a" from "a fib" suggests that the attention mechanism may potentially associate the same text token for both "a fib", "v fib" (ventricular fibrillation), or other terms that are partially similar in the text-input model.

ICD-9:Description (CUI)	Feature Type	Attention Weight ≥ 0.5 % of Max
427.31:Atrial Fibrillation (C0004238)	Text	fib, **fibrillation**
	KGE	C0004238 - Atrial fibrillation
	W2V	C0004238 - Atrial Fibrillation C0344434 - ECG: atrial fibrillation
	$Text_{human}$	a fib, atrial fibrillation
	CUI_{human}	C0004238-Atrial fibrillation
038.9:Septicemia (C0036690)	Text	septic
	KGE	C0349410 - Single organ dysfunction (2:0.9-1.0) C0026766 - Multiple organ failure (5:0.6-0.9) C0277524 - Infectious colitis C1457868 - Worse
	W2V	C0349410 - Single organ dysfunction C0004030 - Aspergillosis
	$Text_{human}$	drop in blood pressure, iv fluids, pressors, hyperdynamic left ventricle presumed to be septic, samples grew mold
	CUI_{human}	C0020649 - Low blood pressure C0349410 - Single organ dysfunction C0948268 - Hemodynamic instability C0009450 - Disorder due to infection
995.92:Severe Sepsis (C1719672)	Text	**septic**, pressors, central
	KGE	C0026766 - Multiple organ failure (4:0.5-1.0) C0349410 - Single organ dysfunction (2:0.8) C1457868 - Worse C0004030 - Aspergillosis
	W2V	C0349410 - Single organ dysfunction C0004030 - Aspergillosis
	$Text_{human}$	drop in blood pressure, iv fluids, pressors, hyperdynamic left ventricle presumed to be septic, multisystem organ failure worsened, hemodynamic status worsened
	CUI_{human}	C0020649 - Low blood pressure C0026766 - Multiple organ failure C0948268 - Hemodynamic instability C0009450 - Disorder due to infection C0443343 - Unstable status
96.72:Continuous invasive mechanical ventilation for 96 consecutive hours or more (C2349745)	Text	Intubated, mold, **which**, aspergillis
	KGE	C0553891 - Extubation of trachea C0011065 - Death (2:0.65-0.9) C0425043 - Death of relative C0205463 - Physiologic
	W2V	C0011065 - Death C0278060 - Mental state
	$Text_{human}$	Intubation, remained intubated, over the next several days, extubation
	CUI_{human}	C0021925 - Intubation C0553891 - Extubation of trachea
401.9:Essential Hypertension (C0085580)*	Text	hypertension
	KGE	C0020538 - Hypertensive disorder (4:0.6-1.0) C0020473 - Hyperlipidemia C0221155 - Systolic hypertension (3:0.5-0.7) C0235222 - Diastolic hypertension (3:0.5-0.6)
	W2V	C0428465 - Serum lipids high C0221155 - Systolic hypertension (3:0.7-0.8) C0235222 - Diastolic hypertension (4:0.6-0.7) C1696708 - Prehypertension (2:0.7) C0019099 - Congo-Crimean hemorrhagic fever C0020538 - Hypertensive disorder C0020473 - Hyperlipidemia
	$Text_{human}$	no† prior history of htn, hypertension, due to pain† post procedure or undiagnosed† htn
	CUI_{human}	C0030193 - Pain† C0262534 - Labile hypertension due to being in a clinical environment†

Table 5: Comparison of tokens with attention weights ≥ 0.5 of the highest attention weight across feature types. ⋆ indicates a false positive label example. **Bold** font indicates text tokens with highest attention weights. †indicates tokens are crucial to preventing false predictions. CUI tokens are ordered from highest to lowest weights with number of occurrences and attention weight % range in parentheses.

When the label CUIs are not present in the input document, as in "038.9:Septicemia", "995.92:Severe Sepsis", and "96.72:Continuous invasive mechanical ventilation for 96 consecutive hours or more" examples, the model's attention mechanism identifies more clinically informative CUIs in the KGE model than in the W2V model. Slightly different KGE CUIs and attention weight distributions are associated with "038.9" and "995.92" labels. In contrast, the exact same W2V CUIs and almost identical attention distributions are associated with both labels. In the case of label "96.72", KGE model does identify one of the relevant tokens (C0553891 - Extubation of trachea, which implies prior intubation and continuous invasive mechanical ventilation), while W2V model does not identify either of them. While both models predict equally correct labels, the external knowledge implicitly represented in KGE helps facilitate more clinically intuitive attention-based reasoning compared to W2V embeddings.

Both KGE and W2V attentions include neighboring tokens and their synonyms, e.g. C0011065, C0425043, C0278060, C0019099 for "96.72" and "401.9". The presence of extraneous CUIs that are similar concept-wise to relevant collocate CUIs such as "C0019099 - Congo-Crimean hemorrhagic fever" and "C0425043 - Death of relative" highlights the importance of optimizing the concept extraction accuracy in concept-based models. While the extraneous CUI tokens can be clinically associated with the relevant tokens or the predicted label concept-wise, the text-input attention mechanism can identify tokens that have no clinical importance as being most associated with a correctly predicted label, e.g. "which" has the highest attention weight for the label "96.72". Making correct predictions based on unjustifiable reasoning is undesirable as it raises concerns over the model's trustworthiness.

Regardless of feature type, the attention mechanism ignores negation. Negated mentions are common in EHR as clinicians document their assessments, noting findings as absent as opposed to not mentioning them at all; the latter may lead to the undesirable assumption of not having made an assessment. As seen in the "401.9" example, "no" or "undiagnosed" are not considered relevant, as indicated by the tokens being omitted by attention weights, leading to a false prediction. In contrast, the clinician-annotated example shows these negation tokens are relevant for excluding the false positive label. As there are no CUIs indicating negation or a diagnostic absence in the input document, it appears that negation in the text input is filtered out during the concepts extraction step. Despite the absence of negation-like CUIs in the input documents, clinician-annotated CUIs include concepts that can prevent the false "401.9" prediction: "C0262534 - hypertension due to being in a clinical environment" in conjunction with "C0030193 - pain". This observation regarding negation-related errors aligns with findings in Hossain et al. (2020) (despite their analysis being with respect to machine translation systems), indicating that the presence of negation can significantly lower downstream output quality. The presence of CUIs that can lead to excluding negation-related false positive labels without needing to encode negation as a concept suggests a potential alternative for future works in addressing this challenge.

4.2 Limitations & Future Works

UMLS KG covers broad medical concepts and relations that may not overlap with rules in the ICD-9 coding guidelines that are periodically updated. While our results suggest that GCN performance is impacted by graph construction approaches, heuristics based on clinical reasoning may not be as useful for ICD coding, particularly if the intended purpose is non-clinical. Future works on ICD-9 coding on this dataset should explore KG construction from concepts and relations according to rules in the dataset's edition of ICD coding guidelines.

Our qualitative analysis is based on a small sample size and one clinician's annotation; future works with more resources should expand the sample size and include analysis by multiple experts from the intended application domain. To maintain a defined scope of our study with respect to existing reference models results, our experiments are conducted only on one dataset and one version of ICD-9 codes, excluding ICD-10. A more recent dataset, MIMIC-IV (Johnson et al., 2023), has been released since the time of our experiments. Additionally, a recent study by Edin et al. (2023) comparing benchmark models on both MIMIC-III (Johnson et al., 2016) and MIMIC-IV (Johnson et al., 2023) datasets with results on both ICD-9 and ICD-10 codes should facilitate the extrapolation of our approach to broader datasets.

As shown in Table 1, documents represented as concept-based (CUI) tokens are 1/3 in length of those represented as text-based tokens. The shorter input documents enable future experiments on larger models previously deemed incompatible. Since text-based models still lead in performance, utilizing CUI descriptions instead of the CUI themselves as features is worth exploring. CUI and ICD codes have meanings through their corresponding descriptions. Considering KGE's low concept coverage and recent works involving domain-knowledge-augmented (UMLS) BERT (Michalopoulos et al., 2021), future research directions may include leveraging generative models in KG expansion and using concept-based KGE or GCN encoded relational information to augment text-based features.

Standard MLC evaluation metrics, which consider all label classes to be independent (Kosmopoulos et al., 2015), can be problematic as a model predicting more generalized labels, e.g. parent labels encompassing the ground truths, or sibling labels in the ICD code structure, would be considered as low-performing as a model predicting completely unrelated labels. Depending on downstream applications, hierarchical evaluation metrics that are more suitable for MLC of dependent label classes should also be considered for automatic ICD coding evaluation.

5 Conclusion

Our investigation into implicit graph representation in the input space highlights the benefits of KGE over corpus-based concept-feature embeddings in improving the model's attention-based reasoning interpretability. The experiments involving explicit relational information representation through graph construction approaches demonstrate the limitations of GCN as a standalone encoder in ICD coding task. The qualitative analysis of the attention-based reasoning identifies challenges that contribute to erroneous predictions and provides insight into how KG construction may be improved in future works. Our contributions underscore the potential for graph concept-based features while addressing the difficulties associated with medical codes classification as an MLC problem from long input documents, domain knowledge requirements, and interpretability.

Acknowledgements

We thank the anonymous reviewers, Josef van Genabith, and Tanja Bäumel for their constructive feedback. The work was partially funded by the European Union (EU) through the project PERKS (ID: 101120323) under the "Digital, Industry, and Space" funding program and the German Federal Ministry of Education and Research (BMBF) through the project XAINES (ID: 01IW20005).

References

Dzmitry Bahdanau, Kyunghyun Cho, and Yoshua Bengio. 2015. Neural Machine Translation by Jointly Learning to Align and Translate. In *3rd International Conference on Learning Representations, ICLR 2015, San Diego, CA, USA, May 7-9, 2015, Conference Track Proceedings*.

Andrew L. Beam, Benjamin Kompa, Allen Schmaltz, Inbar Fried, Griffin Weber, Nathan Palmer, Xu Shi, Tianxi Cai, and Isaac S. Kohane. 2020. Clinical Concept Embeddings Learned from Massive Sources of Multimodal Medical Data. *Pacific Symposium on Biocomputing. Pacific Symposium on Biocomputing*, 25:295–306.

Olivier Bodenreider. 2004. The Unified Medical Language System (UMLS): Integrating Biomedical Terminology. *Nucleic Acids Research*, 32(Database issue):D267–D270.

Antoine Bordes, Nicolas Usunier, Alberto Garcia-Duran, Jason Weston, and Oksana Yakhnenko. 2013. Translating Embeddings for Modeling Multi-relational Data. In *Advances in Neural Information Processing Systems*, volume 26. Curran Associates, Inc.

Pengfei Cao, Yubo Chen, Kang Liu, Jun Zhao, Shengping Liu, and Weifeng Chong. 2020. HyperCore: Hyperbolic and Co-graph Representation for Automatic ICD Coding. In *Proceedings of the 58th Annual Meeting of the Association for Computational Linguistics*, pages 3105–3114, Online. Association for Computational Linguistics.

David Chang, Ivana Balažević, Carl Allen, Daniel Chawla, Cynthia Brandt, and Andrew Taylor. 2020. Benchmark and Best Practices for Biomedical Knowledge Graph Embeddings. In *Proceedings of the 19th SIGBioMed Workshop on Biomedical Language Processing*, pages 167–176, Online. Association for Computational Linguistics.

Edward Choi, Mohammad Taha Bahadori, Elizabeth Searles, Catherine Coffey, Michael Thompson, James Bost, Javier Tejedor-Sojo, and Jimeng Sun. 2016. Multi-layer Representation Learning for Medical Concepts. In *Proceedings of the 22nd ACM SIGKDD International Conference on Knowledge Discovery and Data Mining*, pages 1495–1504, San Francisco California USA. ACM.

Edward Choi, Zhen Xu, Yujia Li, Michael Dusenberry, Gerardo Flores, Emily Xue, and Andrew Dai. 2020. Learning the Graphical Structure of Electronic Health Records with Graph Convolutional Transformer. *Proceedings of the AAAI Conference on Artificial Intelligence*, 34(01):606–613.

Jacob Devlin, Ming-Wei Chang, Kenton Lee, and Kristina Toutanova. 2019. BERT: Pre-training of Deep Bidirectional Transformers for Language Understanding. In *Proceedings of the 2019 Conference of the North American Chapter of the Association for Computational Linguistics: Human Language Technologies, Volume 1 (Long and Short Papers)*, pages 4171–4186, Minneapolis, Minnesota. Association for Computational Linguistics.

Joakim Edin, Alexander Junge, Jakob D. Havtorn, Lasse Borgholt, Maria Maistro, Tuukka Ruotsalo, and Lars Maaløe. 2023. Automated Medical Coding on MIMIC-III and MIMIC-IV: A Critical Review and Replicability Study. In *Proceedings of the 46th International ACM SIGIR Conference on Research and Development in Information Retrieval*, SIGIR '23, pages 2572–2582. Association for Computing Machinery.

Md Mosharaf Hossain, Antonios Anastasopoulos, Eduardo Blanco, and Alexis Palmer. 2020. It's not a Non-Issue: Negation as a Source of Error in Machine Translation. In *Findings of the Association for Computational Linguistics: EMNLP 2020*, pages 3869–3885. Association for Computational Linguistics.

Institute of Medicine (US) Committee on the Future of Primary Care. 1994. *Defining Primary Care: An Interim Report*. National Academies Press (US).

Alistair E. W. Johnson, Lucas Bulgarelli, Lu Shen, Alvin Gayles, Ayad Shammout, Steven Horng, Tom J. Pollard, Sicheng Hao, Benjamin Moody, Brian Gow, Li-wei H. Lehman, Leo A. Celi, and Roger G. Mark. 2023. MIMIC-IV, a Freely Accessible Electronic Health Record Dataset. 10(1):1. Publisher: Nature Publishing Group.

Alistair E.W. Johnson, Tom J. Pollard, Lu Shen, Li-wei H. Lehman, Mengling Feng, Mohammad Ghassemi, Benjamin Moody, Peter Szolovits, Leo Anthony Celi, and Roger G. Mark. 2016. MIMIC-III, a Freely Accessible Critical Care Database. *Scientific Data*, 3:160035.

Rajvir Kaur, Jeewani Anupama Ginige, and Oliver Obst. 2021. A Systematic Literature Review of Automated ICD Coding and Classification Systems using Discharge Summaries. *arXiv:2107.10652 [cs]*.

Thomas N. Kipf and Max Welling. 2017. Semi-Supervised Classification with Graph Convolutional Networks. In *Proceedings of the 5th International Conference on Learning Representations*, ICLR '17, Palais des Congrès Neptune, Toulon, France.

Aris Kosmopoulos, Ioannis Partalas, Eric Gaussier, Georgios Paliouras, and Ion Androutsopoulos. 2015. Evaluation Measures for Hierarchical Classification: A Unified View and Novel Approaches. *Data Mining and Knowledge Discovery*, 29(3):820–865.

Siting Liang, Mareike Hartmann, and Daniel Sonntag. 2023. Cross-domain German medical named entity recognition using a pre-trained language model and unified medical semantic types. In *Proceedings of the 5th Clinical Natural Language Processing Workshop*, pages 259–271, Toronto, Canada. Association for Computational Linguistics.

Ilya Loshchilov and Frank Hutter. 2018. Decoupled Weight Decay Regularization. In *International Conference on Learning Representations*.

Thang Luong, Hieu Pham, and Christopher D. Manning. 2015. Effective Approaches to Attention-based Neural Machine Translation. In *Proceedings of the 2015 Conference on Empirical Methods in Natural Language Processing*, pages 1412–1421, Lisbon, Portugal. Association for Computational Linguistics.

Hehuan Ma, Yu Rong, and Junzhou Huang. 2022. Graph Neural Networks: Scalability. In Lingfei Wu, Peng Cui, Jian Pei, and Liang Zhao, editors, *Graph Neural Networks: Foundations, Frontiers, and Applications*, pages 99–119. Springer Nature Singapore, Singapore.

Takuma Matsubara, Makoto Miwa, and Yutaka Sasaki. 2023. Distantly Supervised Document-Level Biomedical Relation Extraction with Neighborhood Knowledge Graphs. In *The 22nd Workshop on Biomedical Natural Language Processing and BioNLP Shared Tasks*, pages 363–368, Toronto, Canada. Association for Computational Linguistics.

George Michalopoulos, Yuanxin Wang, Hussam Kaka, Helen Chen, and Alexander Wong. 2021. Umls-BERT: Clinical Domain Knowledge Augmentation of Contextual Embeddings Using the Unified Medical Language System Metathesaurus. In *Proceedings of the 2021 Conference of the North American Chapter of the Association for Computational Linguistics: Human Language Technologies*, pages 1744–1753, Online. Association for Computational Linguistics.

Tomas Mikolov, Kai Chen, Greg Corrado, and Jeffrey Dean. 2013. Efficient Estimation of Word Representations in Vector Space. *CoRR*, abs/1301.3781.

Elias Moons, Aditya Khanna, Abbas Akkasi, and Marie-Francine Moens. 2020. A Comparison of Deep Learning Methods for ICD Coding of Clinical Records. *Applied Sciences*, 10(15):5262.

James Mullenbach, Sarah Wiegreffe, Jon Duke, Jimeng Sun, and Jacob Eisenstein. 2018. Explainable Prediction of Medical Codes from Clinical Text. In *Proceedings of the 2018 Conference of the North American Chapter of the Association for Computational Linguistics: Human Language Technologies, Volume 1 (Long Papers)*, arXiv:1802.05695, pages 1101–1111, New Orleans, Louisiana. Association for Computational Linguistics.

Mark Neumann, Daniel King, Iz Beltagy, and Waleed Ammar. 2019. ScispaCy: Fast and Robust Models for Biomedical Natural Language Processing. *Proceedings of the 18th BioNLP Workshop and Shared Task*, pages 319–327.

Adam Paszke, Sam Gross, Soumith Chintala, Gregory Chanan, Edward Yang, Zachary DeVito, Zeming Lin, Alban Desmaison, Luca Antiga, and Adam Lerer. 2017. Automatic differentiation in PyTorch. *NIPS-W*.

Lin Qiu, Yunxuan Xiao, Yanru Qu, Hao Zhou, Lei Li, Weinan Zhang, and Yong Yu. 2019. Dynamically Fused Graph Network for Multi-hop Reasoning. In *Proceedings of the 57th Annual Meeting of the Association for Computational Linguistics*, pages 6140–6150, Florence, Italy. Association for Computational Linguistics.

Radim Řehůřek and Petr Sojka. 2010. Software Framework for Topic Modelling with Large Corpora. In *Proceedings of the LREC 2010 Workshop on New Challenges for NLP Frameworks*, pages 45–50, Valletta, Malta. ELRA.

Deepak Saini, Arnav Kumar Jain, Kushal Dave, Jian Jiao, Amit Singh, Ruofei Zhang, and Manik Varma. 2021. GalaXC: Graph Neural Networks with Labelwise Attention for Extreme Classification. In *Proceedings of the Web Conference 2021*, pages 3733–3744, Ljubljana Slovenia. ACM.

Zhiqing Sun, Zhi-Hong Deng, Jian-Yun Nie, and Jian Tang. 2018. RotatE: Knowledge Graph Embedding by Relational Rotation in Complex Space. In *International Conference on Learning Representations*.

Fei Teng, Wei Yang, Li Chen, LuFei Huang, and Qiang Xu. 2020. Explainable Prediction of Medical Codes With Knowledge Graphs. *Frontiers in Bioengineering and Biotechnology*, 8.

Ashish Vaswani, Noam Shazeer, Niki Parmar, Jakob Uszkoreit, Llion Jones, Aidan N Gomez, Łukasz Kaiser, and Illia Polosukhin. 2017. Attention is All you Need. In *Advances in Neural Information Processing Systems*, volume 30. Curran Associates, Inc.

Thanh Vu, Dat Quoc Nguyen, and Anthony Nguyen. 2020. A Label Attention Model for ICD Coding from Clinical Text. In *Twenty-Ninth International Joint Conference on Artificial Intelligence*, volume 4, pages 3335–3341.

Minjie Wang, Da Zheng, Zihao Ye, Quan Gan, Mufei Li, Xiang Song, Jinjing Zhou, Chao Ma, Lingfan Yu, Yu Gai, Tianjun Xiao, Tong He, George Karypis, Jinyang Li, and Zheng Zhang. 2020. Deep Graph Library: A Graph-Centric, Highly-Performant Package for Graph Neural Networks.

Keyulu Xu, Weihua Hu, Jure Leskovec, and Stefanie Jegelka. 2018. How Powerful are Graph Neural Networks? *CoRR*, abs/1810.00826.

Zhitao Ying, Jiaxuan You, Christopher Morris, Xiang Ren, Will Hamilton, and Jure Leskovec. 2018. Hierarchical Graph Representation Learning with Differentiable Pooling. In *Advances in Neural Information Processing Systems*, volume 31. Curran Associates, Inc.

Zheng Yuan, Chuanqi Tan, and Songfang Huang. 2022. Code Synonyms Do Matter: Multiple Synonyms Matching Network for Automatic ICD Coding. In *Proceedings of the 60th Annual Meeting of the Association for Computational Linguistics (Volume 2:*

Short Papers), pages 808–814, Dublin, Ireland. Association for Computational Linguistics.

Da Zheng, Xiang Song, Chao Ma, Zeyuan Tan, Zihao Ye, Jin Dong, Hao Xiong, Zheng Zhang, and George Karypis. 2020. DGL-KE: Training Knowledge Graph Embeddings at Scale. In *Proceedings of the 43rd International ACM SIGIR Conference on Research and Development in Information Retrieval*, SIGIR '20, pages 739–748, New York, NY, USA. Association for Computing Machinery.

Daoming Zong and Shiliang Sun. 2020. GNN-XML: Graph Neural Networks for Extreme Multi-label Text Classification. *arXiv:2012.05860 [cs]*.

A Supplementary Material

Additional information regarding the UMLS and ICD-9 codes are explained in the following sections. Implementation details including hyper-parameters specified in our experiments are provided for reproducibility. Our Git repository[10] also contains further implementation details and code to reproduce our experiments. Additional experiment results not part of the main contributions are also included.

A.1 ICD-9 Code Structure

Moons et al. (2020) describes the structure of ICD-9 codes as consisting of at most five numbers: the first three represent a disease category, a fourth number narrows down to specific diseases, and a fifth number differentiates between specific disease variants. This structure creates a hierarchical taxonomy with up to 4 layers (L1 - L4) from the root level as shown in Figure 4.

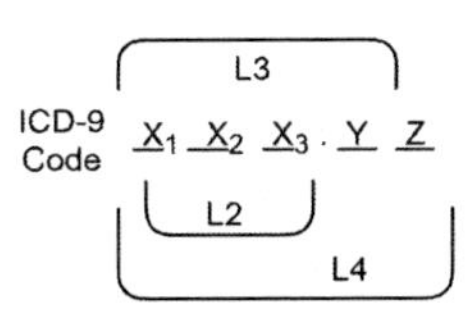

240-279:	Endocrine, nutritional and metabolic diseases	(L1)
250:	Diabetes mellitus	(L2)
250.2:	Diabetes with hyperosmolarity	(L3)
250.21:	Diabetes with hyperosmolarity of type 1	(L4)

Figure 4: An example of ICD-9 codes with code descriptions illustrating the hierarchical layers. The example here shows how diabetes mellitus and its specific variants are represented in the ICD-9 code taxonomy. Illustration is reproduced from Moons et al. (2020).

Being a subset of the UMLS Knowledge Bases (Bodenreider, 2004), ICD-9 codes have corresponding Concept Unique Identifiers (CUIs) in the UMLS, which also contains Semantic Type Information (TUI); examples from the Top-50 ICD-9 codes of the MIMIC-III dataset and their UMLS information are shown in Table 6. Within the UMLS, high-level grouping based on TUI is noted among the codes in Table 6; both C0176511 and C0189898 share the same TUI as they both describe diagnostic procedures. The grouping in the UMLS does not always correspond to the same hierarchy in the ICD-9 taxonomy as noted by the mentioned codes being under two distinct L2-level numbers.

[10]https://github.com/pokarats/CoDER

ICD-9	CUI	TUI	Description
33.24	C0176511	T060	Closed [endoscopic] biopsy of bronchus
37.23	C0189898	T060	Catheterization of both left and right heart
38.91	C0007431	T061	Arterial catheterization
38.93	C0162203	T058	Venous catheterization, not elsewhere classified

Table 6: Examples of ICD-9 codes and their corresponding UMLS CUI, TUI, and descriptions from the Top-50 ICD-9 code labels of the MIMIC-III dataset (Johnson et al., 2016).

A.2 Implementation Details

The following sections describe hyper-parameters used in our experiments. We do not fine-tune hyper-parameters for our specific dataset training; we prioritize keeping hyper-parameters as close as possible to those reported as optimal by Vu et al. (2020) for the LAAT model.

A.2.1 LAAT

As in Vu et al. (2020), we train for 50 epochs, using a batch size of 8, with AdamW (Loshchilov and Hutter, 2018) optimizer and learning rate of 0.001. We also use a learning rate scheduler to reduce the learning rate by 10% if there is no improvement in F1_{micro} on the validation set for 5 epochs. We apply a drop-out probability of 0.3. We specify the LSTM hidden size $u = 256$ and projection size $d_a = 256$ for the Top-50 version and $u = 512$, $d_a = 512$ for the Full version as these are the optimal hyper-parameters reported in Vu et al. (2020). The text input results in Table 8 verify that our re-implementation of the LAAT model reproduces comparable performance on the same dataset as reported in Vu et al. (2020) following the same pre-processing steps and hyper-parameters.

A.2.2 KGE

We obtain KGE for CUI entities following training steps described in Chang et al. (2020) using DGL-KE (Zheng et al., 2020) implementation of TransE (Bordes et al., 2013). The *case4* train, dev,

Version	Model	Precision		Recall		F1		AUC		P@5
		macro	micro	macro	micro	macro	micro	macro	micro	
Top-50	$GCN_{0.7}$	**62.12**	**67.81**	38.22	45.02	47.33	**54.11**	**84.54**	**87.40**	**56.00**
	$GCN_{0.83}$	56.44	63.22	**41.61**	**47.05**	**47.98**	53.95	83.75	86.22	54.23

Table 7: Results from GCN_{BASE} experiments on the MIMIC-III Top-50 with CUI input type, comparing entity linking threshold of 0.7 and 0.83. All GCN models use KGE as node embeddings to represent each CUI node in a graph.

Encoder	Implementation	F1		AUC		P@5
		macro	micro	macro	micro	
LAAT (50)	Vu et al. (2020)	66.60	71.50	92.50	94.60	67.50
	Ours	66.55	71.01	92.79	94.60	67.28
LAAT (Full)	Vu et al. (2020)	8.70	58.10	92.60	98.80	81.80
	Ours	9.87	57.20	89.84	98.56	80.91

Table 8: Text input results on the MIMIC-III Top-50 and Full test sets from our implementation of the LAAT model in comparison to the results reported in Vu et al. (2020).

and test files are downloaded from SNOMED CT Knowledge Graph Embeddings Git repository[11]. We use the following key configuration parameters for training:

```
model_name: TransE_l2, max_step: 60000,
batch_size: 1024, batch_size_eval: 1000,
neg_sample_size: 64,
neg_sample_size_eval: 90000,
hidden_dim: 100, lr: 0.1,
gamma: 10.0,
adversarial_temperature: 1.0,
regularization_coef: 1e-07,
pairwise: false, loss_genre: Logsigmoid
```

A.2.3 GCN

Our 2-layer GCN classification is implemented using DGL (Wang et al., 2020) with PyTorch (Paszke et al., 2017) backend. We control the hyper-parameters to be as similar to the LAAT specifications as possible. For the GCN layers, we specify the hidden size $u = 256$ and projection size $d_a = 256$ for the Top-50 and $u = 512$, $d_a = 512$ for the Full versions analogous to the hyper-parameters for the LSTM encoder in the LAAT experiments. We train for 50 epochs, using a batch size of 8, and learning rate of 0.001, and AdamW (Loshchilov and Hutter, 2018). We also use the same learning rate scheduler and dropout probability.

[11]https://github.com/dchang56/snomed_kge

A.3 From EHR to GCN Graph Construction

To demonstrate the relational characteristics in EHR structural features and clinical reasoning, we manually annotate 5 randomly selected discharge summaries from the Top-50 version of the MIMIC-III (Johnson et al., 2016) training dataset. The annotations in Figure 5 illustrate that extracted concepts representing parts of a note provide sufficient information for a clinical domain expert to relate the assigned ICD codes to relevant parts of the document. Despite having only clinical domain knowledge without ICD coding training, we are able to identify relevant spans of text and CUIs that relate to the assigned ICD codes.

A.4 CUI Extraction Entity Linking Threshold Comparison

We notice many CUIs in the randomly selected samples do not seem relevant to the clinical presentation described in the note nor assigned ICD codes. We verify if a more selective (higher) threshold has an impact on performance by experimenting with the Top-50 GCN_{BASE} and setting the EL threshold to 0.83. Results in Table 7 show performance scores of the GCN_{BASE} model with EL thresholds of 0.7 and 0.83. Evaluation scores are higher in most metrics with the 0.7 threshold. $Recall_{macro,micro}$ and $F1_{macro}$ are the only metrics where the 0.83 threshold shows higher performance. Considering the evaluation scores between the two EL thresholds are within a few % points of each other, it does not seem computationally worthwhile to repeat all experiments with the 0.83 threshold.

A.5 Runtime Comparison

LAAT experiments are run on NVIDIA GeForce RTX 3090 and GCN on NVIDIA RTX A6000. Table 9 illustrates training runtime and mean input document lengths in number of text or CUI tokens for the LAAT model. CUI input models (W2V and KGE) show training runtimes that are multitudes less than the text input model. The shorter

Note id: 16525_134157

Text Input Type

name known lastname known firstname unit no numeric identifier admission date discharge date date of birth sex f service addendum this is an addendum to the previous **MICU** green discharge summary l hospital course the patient was admitted on after **being found down** l at that time she was noted to have **multiple intracranial bleeds** l the patient then had a **seizure** and was **intubated on [SIC - TEMPORAL]** l **ct scan** on showed **increasing midline shift** and at that time the decision was made to make the patient comfort measures only per the family l the patient was then **extubated on** [SIC - TEMPORAL] and **transferred to the medicine floor for comfort measures** where she was under the care of dr first name4 namepattern1 last name namepattern1lin conjunction with the palliative care consult service the patient was made comfortable utilizing **morphine drip** and discharge status the patient expired l final diagnosis l **subarachnoid hemorrhage with intraparenchymal hemorrhage** lname6 md name8 md m dlmd number dictated by last name l namepattern1 medquist36 d t job job number

MIMIC-III ICD Codes (Top-50 Version)

276.1:Hyposmolality and/or hyponatremia (C0020645)

401.9:Essential Hypertension (C0085580)

285.9:Anemia (C0002871)

96.04:Intubation, Intratracheal (C0021932)

96.72:Continuous invasive mechanical ventilation for 96 consecutive hours or more (C2349745)

38.93:Venous catheterization, not elsewhere classified (C0162203)

38.91:Arterial catheterization (C0007431)

CUI Input Type

C0151699 C0019080 C0036572 C0751495 C0270844 C0021925 C0040405 C3472245 C1699633 C0034606 C0442808 C0221106 C0178415 C0020459 C0455769 C0423908 C1879489 C0242485 C0553891 C0348011 C0030704 C0150521 C0184573 C0150192 C0009763 C0030231 C2698261 C1260880 C0586514 C0011900 C0002928 C0019080 C0029163 C0426747 C0475072 C3698285 C2937358 C0026850, C0242271 C0242271

Highlighted Input Document CUI - Text Definition (SG:TUI)

C0151699 - Intracranial hemorrhage **(DISO:T046)**
C0019080 - Hemorrhage **(DISO:T046)**
C0036572 - Seizure **(DISO:T184)**
C0751495 - Partial Seizure **(DISO:T047)**
C0270844 - Tonic seizure **(DISO:T047)**
C0021925 - Intubation **(PROC:T061)**
C0040405 - Computerized axial tomography **(PROC:T060)**
C0442808 - Increasing **(CONC:T169)**
C0221106 - Alkalemia **(DISO:T047)**
C0553891 - Extubation of trachea **(PROC:T061)**
C0348011 - Surgical transfer action **(CONC:T169),**
C0030704 - Patient transfer **(PROC:T058)**
C0150521 - Comfort measures **(PROC:T058),**
C2698261 - Measurement of morphine **(PROC:T059)**
C0475072 - Cerebral hemorrhage following injury **(DISO:T037),**
C3698285 - Nontraumatic intraparenchymal cerebral hemorrhage **(DISO:T046)**
C2937358 - Cerebral hemorrhage **(DISO:T046)**

Annotation Color References:

ICD Codes CUI - Semantic Group (SG) - Semantic Type (TUI)

C0020645 DISO - T033
C0085580 DISO - T047
C0002871 DISO - T047
C0154298 DISO - T047
C0021932 PROC - T061
C2349745 PROC - T061
C0162203 PROC - T058
C0007431 PROC - T061

SG - TUI - Description

DISO T033 - Finding
DISO T037 - Injury or Poisoning
DISO T046 - Pathologic Function
DISO T047 - Disease or Syndrome
DISO T184 - Sign or Symptom
CONC T169 - Functional Concept
PROC T060 - Diagnostic Procedure
PROC T061 - Therapeutic or Preventive Procedure
PROC T058 - Health Care Activity
PROC T059 - Laboratory Procedure

Figure 5: Spans of text and extracted CUIs in the input document are highlighted with colors that correspond to the assigned ICD codes. Red-highlighting designates codes that we cannot definitively infer from the input document. Additional information provided by the UMLS such as Semantic Type Information (TUI), Semantic Group (SG), and corresponding CUI to each ICD code demonstrate correspondence between the input document and output label space. The additional highlight colors in the annotation references group CUIs by their SG: DISO, CONC, and PROC.

Version	Model	Training Runtime (hh:mm:ss)	Mean Training Input Length (tokens)
Top-50	LAAT_{text}	04:53:10	1783
	LAAT_{W2V}	00:41:13	396
	LAAT_{KGE}	00:40:31	396
Full	LAAT_{text}	21:35:34	1731
	LAAT_{W2V}	05:40:58	385
	LAAT_{KGE}	05:36:59	385

Table 9: Training runtime comparison between text and CUI input types for the Top-50 and Full versions of the MIMIC-III dataset. Mean number of tokens for the training partition is provided. Runtime is only for training the model and is exclusive of time required for concepts extraction and pre-processing.

Version	Model	Training Runtime (hh:mm:ss)	Mean # Nodes	Mean # Edges	Mean # Sub-graphs
Top-50	GCN_{BASE}	00:17:48	246	419	167
	GCN_{EHR}	00:09:44	246	513	145
	GCN_{COMBO}	00:14:11	246	684	90
Full	GCN_{BASE}	01:04:40	241	408	165
	GCN_{EHR}	00:49:25	241	1024	50
	GCN_{COMBO}	01:08:22	241	1189	28

Table 10: Training runtime comparison between GCN graph construction approaches for the Top-50 and Full versions of the MIMIC-III dataset. Mean node, edge, and sub-graphs (connected components) numbers for the training partition are provided. Runtime is for training the GCN model and is exclusive of time spent on pre-processing or building graph datasets.

runtime appears to correlate with shorter average input lengths. Table 10 compares training runtime across GCN graph construction approaches. Contrary to LAAT models, there does not seem to be a notable relationship between runtime and graph nodes, edges, or sub-graphs numbers. As noticeable in the table, graph construction heuristic affects the number of sub-graphs on average; more edges result in fewer sub-graphs. Due to the multiple steps involved in our proposed pipeline, from concepts extraction to graph construction heuristics, application to other datasets requires additional data preparation and pre-processing time.

The LAAT model suffers from time and memory complexity issues associated with the LSTM encoder and attention mechanism. The GCN models are also limited by the memory requirement to store a completed adjacency matrix; additional sampling algorithms and alternative models are required for scalability to larger datasets (Ma et al., 2022).

Leveraging Graph Structures to Detect Hallucinations in Large Language Models

Noa Nonkes*, **Sergei Agaronian***, **Evangelos Kanoulas**, **Roxana Petcu**

University of Amsterdam

noanonkes@gmail.com, r.m.petcu@uva.nl

Abstract

Large language models are extensively applied across a wide range of tasks, such as customer support, content creation, educational tutoring, and providing financial guidance. However, a well-known drawback is their predisposition to generate hallucinations. This damages the trustworthiness of the information these models provide, impacting decision-making and user confidence. We propose a method to detect hallucinations by looking at the structure of the latent space and finding associations within hallucinated and non-hallucinated generations. We create a graph structure that connects generations that lie closely in the embedding space. Moreover, we employ a Graph Attention Network which utilizes message passing to aggregate information from neighboring nodes and assigns varying degrees of importance to each neighbor based on their relevance. Our findings show that 1) there exists a structure in the latent space that differentiates between hallucinated and non-hallucinated generations, 2) Graph Attention Networks can learn this structure and generalize it to unseen generations, and 3) the robustness of our method is enhanced when incorporating contrastive learning. When evaluated against evidence-based benchmarks, our model performs similarly without access to search-based methods.[1]

1 Introduction

Large Language Models (LLMs) have recently surged in popularity, notably due to the emergence of agents and models such as ChatGPT, Bard, Vicuna, and LLaMA (Brown et al., 2020a; Pichai, 2023; Ji, 2023; Touvron et al., 2023). Despite their increased capabilities for complex reasoning (Brown et al., 2020a), substantial challenges persist in grounding LLM generations to verified real-world knowledge. Ensuring that LLM generations are not only plausible but also factually correct poses a complex problem (Xu et al., 2024), which can be minimized (Liang et al., 2024) but so far not eliminated. Needless to say, even though LLMs possess an unparalleled ability to produce fast, credible, and human-like output, they are prone to hallucination (Ji et al., 2023a; Kasneci et al., 2023). This challenge expresses the non-trivial need for robust methods that detect and mitigate the spread of LLM-generated hallucinations.

Motivation The first underlying premise of this study is that LLM hallucinations are not unstructured, i.e., hallucinations share characteristics in the latent space. While extensive work has been done to mitigate LLM hallucinations (Ji et al., 2023b; Feldman et al., 2023; Martino et al., 2023), identifying these by their structural properties remains largely unexplored. Manakul et al. (2023) make a first step into identifying model-agnostic hallucinations through their SelfCheckGPT method, reliant solely on black-box access to the model to infer new generations. This method aligns with the idea that, given the same query, non-hallucinated samples exhibit a higher degree of similarity with each other than with hallucinated samples. We aim to extend this exploration by analyzing if, **independent** of the query, hallucinations share a higher degree of similarity with each other than with non-hallucinated generations. While SelfCheckGPT employs an implicit approach to model consistencies, we aim to do it explicitly by exploring semantic correspondences between hallucinations in the latent space. The second premise relies on the principle of homophily, which expresses that entities that share similar characteristics are more likely to form connections with each other (Zhang et al., 2016). In the context of hallucinations and text representations, homophily suggests that samples that share text-level characteristics tend to lie closer in the embedding space. We study if the degree of hallucination is such a characteristic.

*Equal contribution.

[1]The full code can be found on our GitHub repository.

Proceedings of TextGraphs-17: Graph-based Methods for Natural Language Processing, pages 93–104
August 15, 2024 ©2024 Association for Computational Linguistics

Based on the outlined premises and assumptions, we propose leveraging graph structures and message passing to reveal underlying patterns in the data. Comparing sentences in the embedding space involves assessing pairwise similarities between any pair of sentences. This results in $N(N-1)/2$ computations for N sentences, which is not computationally expensive for a one-time calculation, however, applying a neural network on top of this structure does not scale computationally, even with a simple single-layer feed-forward network. However, by leveraging the principle of homophily, we can form a graph where only similar nodes will have a direct connection between them, significantly reducing computational costs.

Objectives This study proposes two hypotheses: 1) LLM hallucinations arise from a pattern, which reflects in shared characteristics in the embedding space, and 2) we can efficiently leverage these characteristics using graph structures. We can formulate the following research questions:

1. Do LLM-generated hallucinations share characteristics?

2. Can we leverage graph structures to identify and learn these characteristics?

3. If learned, can we use this knowledge to identify hallucinations among new incoming LLM generations through label recovery?

Contributions We introduce a hallucination detection framework for LLM-generated content. Given an existing dataset of hallucinations and true statements, we 1) leverage semantically rich sentence embeddings, 2) construct a graph structure where semantically similar sentences are connected, 3) train a Graph Attention Network (GAT) model that facilitates message passing, neighborhood attention attribution and selection, and 4) employ the GAT model to categorize new sentences as hallucinated or non-hallucinated statements.

According to our findings, 1) using semantic information to form connections between entities in the latent space helps to uncover links within hallucinated and non-hallucinated statements, 2) non-local aggregation enhances these links, 3) contrastive learning helps in distinguishing embeddings and leads to better performance, and 4) our method can accurately classify new unseen sentences as hallucinations or true statements.

The focus of this study is not getting on par performance with SOTA. Instead, we bring new hypotheses on the characteristics of LLM hallucinations. We implement and experiment with our method on multiple datasets: 1) we generate our own dataset by prompting an LLM to generate both true and misleading statements given a query and a context, and 2) we apply our framework to existing benchmark datasets to evaluate its performance on non-controlled data. Comparisons with benchmarks such as (Manakul et al., 2023; Thorne et al., 2018a) show that our method achieves close performance. Notably, we do not need access to external knowledge, LLM logits, or additional inference passes to the LLM, while keeping computational costs minimal.

We hypothesize that the latent space holds rich information beyond features such as contextualized, syntactic, and semantic information, for which the embeddings have been previously trained to capture. We also hypothesize that this information can be discovered and leveraged using geometric information. We propose a method that can be extended beyond the hallucination problem, and which can be generalized, applied to, and experimented with using any categorical label.

2 Related Work

LLMs The field of Natural Language Processing (NLP) has seen a significant evolution, from early probabilistic approaches such as Naive Bayes (Kim et al., 2006) to transformer models (Wolf et al., 2020) with attention mechanisms (Vaswani et al., 2017). This evolution also leads to LLMs which play a significant role in NLP tasks and applications (Alec et al., 2019; Brown et al., 2020b), yet they face a significant challenge known as *hallucination generation* that has been thoroughly studied.

Prompt verification SelfCheckGPT (Manakul et al., 2023) mitigates hallucinations using a sampling-based approach that facilitates fact-checking in a zero-resource fashion. The authors leverage the idea that if an LLM has knowledge on a certain subject, true generations from the same query are likely to be similar and factually consistent. They compare multiple query-dependent generated responses to identify fact inconsistencies indicative of hallucinations. Instead of only retrieving the most likely generated sequence of the model, they draw N further stochastic LLM responses and query the model itself to ascertain whether each sample supports the hallucination.

In essence, SelfCheckGPT does not need external knowledge but utilizes its internal knowledge to self-detect structural aspects of hallucinations. This approach, called prompt verification, achieves a notable 67% AUC-PR score in factual knowledge classification, showing potential for zero-shot fact-checking. However, it involves computational overhead as sampling LLM generations requires multiple forward passes to classify each single statement. Outside of SelfCheckGPT, multiple other approaches leverage prompt verification (Dhuliawala et al., 2023; Varshney et al., 2023).

Retrieval-based The Fact Extraction and Verification (FEVER) Shared Task (Thorne et al., 2018a) brings together several other approaches to hallucination detection. The task participants were challenged to classify whether human-written facts can be supported or refuted while having access to documents retrieved from Wikipedia. The task is mostly split into three parts. For document selection, many teams adopt a multi-step approach, which typically involves techniques such as Named Entity Recognition (Shaalan, 2014), Noun Phrases (Zhang et al., 2007), and Capitalized Expression Identification. The results are then used as inputs for querying a search API such as Wikipedia. The next step involves extracting relevant sentences through methods such as keyword matching, supervised classification, and sentence similarity scoring. Finally, for natural language inference, the extracted evidence sentences are often concatenated with the claim and passed through models such as a simple multilayer perceptron (MLP), Enhanced LSTMs (Chen et al., 2017), or encoder models to synthesize and evaluate the relationships between them. One notable difference between FEVER models and previously described work (Manakul et al., 2023) is that they have access to external sources.

Benchmark datasets TruthfulQA (Lin et al., 2022) proposes a benchmark for analyzing how accurate a language model is in generating answers given a question. The benchmark includes 817 questions spanning over 38 categories, which require a wide range of reasoning capabilities, such as questions in health, law, finance, and politics. Moreover, the questions are crafted in a manner that could lead humans to provide incorrect answers due to false beliefs or misconceptions. In this work, the authors analyze the performance of models such as GPT-3, GPT-Neo, GPT-J, GPT-2 and T-5 (Brown et al., 2020b; Black et al., 2022; Alec et al., 2019; Raffel et al., 2020), identifying that the best model was truthful on only 56% of the generations, while human performance reaches 94%. Compared with the other hallucination benchmarks, the correctness of an answer in TruthfulQA can only be assessed in association with its query. Therefore, we do not consider these answers as hallucinations on their own. While we could model this dataset by merging all answers with their associated queries, that would induce a major bias in the semantic similarity calculations when forming our method's graph structure. As a result, we do not evaluate our method on TruthfulQA but focus on datasets where hallucinations can be detected on the answer level only.

Other hallucination detection methods There are numerous alternative approaches. Luo et al. (2023) tests the familiarity of the LLM with the query prior to generation. The model withholds generation if the familiarity is low. Other studies look into Bayesian estimation in retrieval-augmented generation. Wang et al. (2023) achieves an AUC-PR of around 62% for factual knowledge, but introduces additional time and compute due to reliance on a search engine for external evidence retrieval. Another approach (Chen et al., 2023) aims to detect hallucinations through training a discriminator on the RelQA LLM-generated question-answering dialogue dataset. Their method achieves 85.5% accuracy on automatic labels and 82.6% AUC-PR on human labels, although reliance on human annotations introduces ambiguity.

In comparison to previous work, our method does not require access to external knowledge, nor to the LLM used for generating data, avoids biases associated with additional prompting, and eliminates costs associated with further inference.

3 Methodology

Assume a dataset $D = \{(x_i, y_i)\}_{i=1}^{n}$ consisting of n samples, where x_i denotes a sentence and y_i represents an ordinal categorical label indicating the degree of hallucination of x_i.

3.1 Graph Construction

Consider a model $\phi(x) = e$, where $e \in \mathbb{R}^{768}$, which maps x_i to its sentence-level embedding representation e_i. We construct a graph $\mathcal{G} = (\mathcal{V}, \mathcal{E})$ as follows:

- $\mathcal{V}$ is the set of nodes. Each node $v \in \mathcal{V}$ corresponds to a single data point x_i from dataset D. More precisely, the features of a node consist of the sentence-level embedding $\phi(x_i)$. We employ BERT (Devlin et al., 2019) as the model ϕ to transform textual representations into embeddings.

- Two utterances $\{u, v\} \in \mathcal{V}$ are connected with an edge $(u, v) \in \mathcal{E}$ if and only if the semantic similarity between nodes u and v exceeds a threshold τ. The semantic similarity between two utterances is calculated using cosine similarity.

The choice of τ must ensure a balance in graph connectivity. Ideally, the node degree distribution should be relatively uniform, with a limited number of both highly connected and disconnected nodes. Additionally, we aim to avoid spikes in node degrees, as they may indicate the formation of hubs. The value of τ is dependent on the D.

3.2 Graph Attention Network

We employ a GAT model (Veličković et al., 2018) on our semantically-driven graph structure $\mathcal{G}$. Computing attention scores over sentence embeddings involves significant computational costs due to their high-dimensional representation. Consequently, we first reduce the dimensionality of node features by training a basic MLP. Then, we apply GAT on the reduced node features. The model will learn to map the sentence embeddings to a label indicating its degree of hallucination. We choose to model this problem with graph structures for two primary reasons: 1) to aggregate information via message passing, driven by our intuition that sentences that exhibit similar degrees of factuality share common structural components, and 2) to leverage edge weights, such that the level of similarity influences the information shared through message passing is expected to influence the message passing mechanism. We formalize the problem as an ordinal regression task as follows:

- **Label Encoding**: If a data point x_i has associated label L, then it is classified into all lower labels. Let L be an ordinal label and encode(L) be the corresponding encoding. Then, we can define encode(L) as:

$$\text{encode}(L)_i = \begin{cases} 1 & \text{if } i \leq L \\ 0 & \text{otherwise} \end{cases} \tag{1}$$

where encode$(L)_i$ represents the ith element of the encoding vector.

By employing a graph-based model, we aim to validate our assumptions that hallucinations exhibit shared characteristics within the embedding space. We add connections between sentences that show a high degree of similarity and, during training, we exchange information between nodes and their local neighborhood.

3.3 Label Recovery Task

Assume a new evaluation dataset D'. We first append D' to the existing graph $\mathcal{G} = (\mathcal{V}, \mathcal{E})$, and then perform one forward pass to the trained GAT using the new graph $\mathcal{G}' = (\mathcal{V} \cup \mathcal{V}', \mathcal{E} \cup \mathcal{E}' \cup \mathcal{A})$ to solve a label recovery task. $\mathcal{A}$ represents the edges formed between the nodes V and V'. We define the label recovery task as follows:

- **Label recovery**: Consider a graph $\mathcal{G} = (\mathcal{V}, \mathcal{E})$, where $\mathcal{V}$ is the set of vertices and $\mathcal{E}$ the set of edges. The label recovery task involves inferring missing labels for a subset of nodes $\mathcal{U} \subseteq \mathcal{V}$ based on available information of the known labels of nodes $\mathcal{V} \setminus \mathcal{U}$.

3.4 Data Generation

We first apply our method to our own hallucination-generated dataset. Creating our own dataset allows for more control over the modeling choices and requirements of our methodology, such as degree of connectivity, homophily, and encoding techniques, ensuring a more targeted evaluation. However, we recognize the importance of generalizability, and therefore we also validate our approach on existing datasets to assess its performance across diverse contexts and benchmarks.

Prompt During the process of LLM-driven hallucination generation, we design a prompt that guides the model to create statements for a multiple-choice exam, as shown in Appendix A. In our prompt, we refer to *hallucinations* as *misleading statements*. This is a modeling choice we took because *hallucinations* and *misleading statements* are conceptually similar, however, by labeling them as *misleading* we guide the model to generate statements intended to deceive the reader into believing they are true. This approach ensures the generation of hard in-context hallucinations instead of general hallucinations.

Retrieval-based generation We construct our data using retrieval-augmented generation on a representative question-answer (QA) dataset. We first sample queries along with their corresponding answer and associated context. We then instruct the LLM to generate a multiple-choice exam, where queries act as exam questions. This technique orients the LLM to generate misleading statements alongside true statements for each prompting stage, as a form of conditional generation. The evaluation of the generated data is conducted solely through human assessment. Although the exam-instruction format facilitates the generation of misleading statements, we acknowledge that LLMs are susceptible to bias and hallucinations, which can be reflected in our generated dataset. Existing biases in the model might skew the types of hallucinations in an unintended way, however, we assume that the effects of LLM hallucinations when intentionally induced have minimal impact on our study. We use two prompting techniques for instructing the LLM to generate both true and misleading answers, given either 1) the query, or 2) the query with its associated context, both part of the QA dataset. The latter is aimed at obtaining context-aware true statements from the LLM.

We thus generate a dataset that contains, for each query, 11 statements: 1 true *extracted* from the QA dataset, 1 true without context *generated*, 1 true with context *generated*, and 8 hallucinated *generated* statements. The overview of this process is illustrated in Figure 1. We provide the prompts in Appendix A. Each statement is assigned a label $y_i \in [0, 1, 2, 3]$ representing hallucinated, true w/o context, true w/ context, and true statement. We solve a categorical regression task, and as such, the labels are ordinal one-hot encoded as presented in Section 3.2.

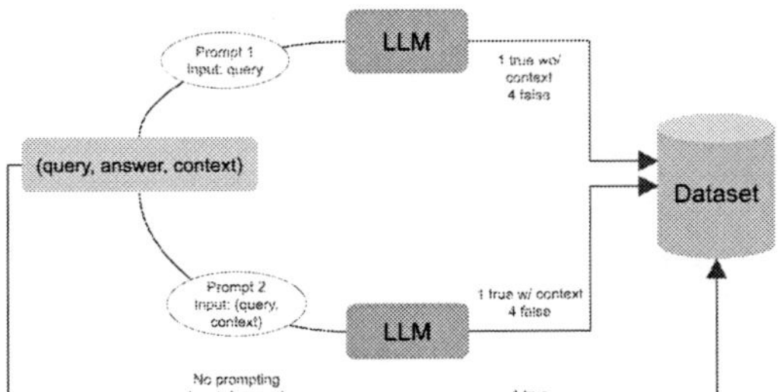

Figure 1: Data generation process.

4 Experimental Setup

4.1 Dataset

We used data from MSMARCO-QA (Nguyen et al., 2016), selecting 2000 questions within the biomedical domain (Xu et al., 2020) with answers consisting of a minimum of five words, to avoid sentences with explicit meaning only when paired with their corresponding question (examples are: "*Yes*", "*No*", "*Non-surgical*", or "*Virus infection*"). As mentioned in Section 3.4, each entry in the MSMARCO-QA dataset consists of the query, answer, and context. We use the queries and context to generate true w/ context, true w/o context, and hallucinated statements by prompting Meta's instruction-tuned Llama2 (Touvron et al., 2023) $13B$ model[2]. The dataset is randomly divided into three segments: training, validation, and test, with partitions of 70%, 15%, and 15%, respectively. The random division is done on the sentence level, therefore same query generations are not necessarily in the same data partition.

4.2 Graph

We use the English uncased version of BERT (Devlin et al., 2019)[3] for sentence embeddings. The graph is constructed over the entire dataset, with designated masks for the training, validation, and test sets. Edges are formed between nodes with cosine similarity above a threshold $\tau = 0.85$, which was selected empirically to strike a balance, ensuring a reasonable level of graph connectivity. The resulting undirected graph has approximately $26M$ out of a potential of $240M$ edges (fully-connected). Additionally, we use the cosine similarity values as edge attributes.

4.3 Graph Attention Network

The embeddings are reduced to a dimensionality of 32 features using a trained single-layer MLP. The GAT model incorporates a single graph attention convolutional layer, transitioning from 32 to 3 dimensions, with 2 attention heads. The GAT model explores and aggregates information from the immediate neighborhood based on the attention mechanism.

[2]https://huggingface.co/OpenAssistant/llama2-13b-orca-8k-3319

[3]https://huggingface.co/bert-base-uncased

4.4 Baselines

We employ a three-layer MLP with ReLU activations, using the same BERT model for sentence embeddings, but with concatenated query-answer as inputs. As a second baseline, we employ a larger pre-trained language model DeBERTa (He et al., 2021)[4], processing query-answer pairs in a unified encoder for improved contextual understanding and predictions. The MLP offers a simple yet powerful method for analyzing relationships between the generations and respective queries and has been shown to be efficient in sentence-level analysis (Ramdhani et al., 2022; Akhtar et al., 2017). Meanwhile, DeBERTa is a complex transformer model that facilitates deeper comparisons of attention effects and structural differences between transformers and lightly connected graphs. Unlike our graph-based model, which relies solely on answer embeddings, the baselines utilize embeddings from both queries and answers, enhancing semantic expressiveness for better differentiation among classes.

4.5 Training

The model selection process is based on optimal macro-recall performance on the validation split, offering a comprehensive evaluation of the model's ability to identify instances across all classes, crucial in the context of highly imbalanced data. Training spans over 500 epochs utilizing the Adam optimizer (Kingma and Ba, 2017) with fixed learning rate 1×10^{-3}. The model is trained to solve a categorical regression task using Binary Cross Entropy (BCE) loss (Good, 1952). This choice reflects the need for nuanced penalization of misclassifications, where the model applies a lower penalty for misclassifying adjacent, compared to further-apart labels. Efforts are made to prevent data leakage between the data partitions. During training, weights corresponding to edges that connect nodes with either validation or test nodes are nullified, ensuring no information exchange (Equation 2). Backpropagation happens exclusively over the training nodes. Similarly, during validation, we modify edges connecting to test nodes (Equation 3). Recall is calculated exclusively on validation nodes. The full graph is used to assess performance on the test set (Equation 4).

[4]https://huggingface.co/MoritzLaurer/DeBERTa-v3-base-mnli-fever-anli

$$\mathcal{N}(i) = \{j|(i,j) \in \mathcal{E}, i \in \mathcal{N}_{train} \text{ and } j \in \mathcal{N}\backslash\{\mathcal{N}_{val} \cup \mathcal{N}_{test}\}\} \quad (2)$$

$$\mathcal{N}(i) = \{j|(i,j) \in \mathcal{E}, i \in \mathcal{N}_{val} \text{ and } j \in \mathcal{N}\backslash\mathcal{N}_{test}\} \quad (3)$$

$$\mathcal{N}(i) = \{j|(i,j) \in \mathcal{E}, i \in \mathcal{N}_{test}\} \quad (4)$$

4.6 Evaluation Metrics

We calculate three metrics to evaluate the performance of our approach. Macro-recall assesses the model's accuracy in identifying individual classes, while macro-precision evaluates prediction accuracy per class. AUC-PR calculates the area under the precision-recall curve, providing a measure for binary classification performance. Additionally, these metrics are robust against class imbalance, making them suitable for evaluating our model on our imbalanced dataset.

4.7 Benchmark Datasets

In our study, we utilize two human-generated and annotated benchmarking datasets, namely FEVER (Thorne et al., 2018a) and SelfCheck-GPT (Manakul et al., 2023). Our method can be generalized across other domains. To apply our method to another dataset, we re-construct the graph with the respective data partitions and redefine the labeling accordingly. These datasets are used for evaluating the performance of our models under conditions that mimic real-world scenarios. The specific methodologies employed for their use are discussed in Section 2.

The FEVER dataset (Thorne et al., 2018a) contains 185445 claims which are divided into three types of claims, namely *Supports*, *Refutes*, and *Not Enough Info*, each paired with evidence sentences. To apply our method to the FEVER dataset, we re-define the label as $y_i \in [0, 1, 2]$ and generate the graph based on the train/val/test partitions of FEVER. The participating models (Thorne et al., 2018a) formulate careful data processing approaches and make use of external sources to verify the factuality of the claims. If search-based evidence is found for a claim, it is classified as *Supports* or *Refutes*. Similarly, if no evidence is found, it is labeled as *Not Enough Info*.

The SelfCheckGPT dataset (Manakul et al., 2023) consists of 1908 sentences categorized as *Accurate*, *Minor inaccurate*, and *Major inaccurate*. To apply our method to SelfCheckGPT, we again redefine the labels as $y_i \in [0, 1, 2]$ and generate the graph by randomly splitting the data into train/val/test sets.

5 Results

5.1 Non-local Aggregation

To address our first research question, more specifically *1. Do LLM-generated hallucinations share characteristics?*, we analyze if our framework identifies an underlying structure of the embedding space. As shown in Table 1, GAT exhibits better performance compared to DeBERTa-QA and MLP-QA on all metrics. GAT has approximately 17% higher recall than both baseline models on the validation set. This suggests its superior ability to identify positive instances, reduce false positives, and effectively differentiate between true and hallucinated statements.

Table 1: Comparing performance between GAT, 3-layer MLP, and DeBERTa using query answer (QA). The best results for each metric and dataset split are highlighted in bold.

Split	Model	Recall	Precision	AUC-PR
Train	GAT	**0.5069**	**0.5844**	**0.4153**
	DeBERTa-QA	0.3882	0.5404	0.3517
	MLP-QA	0.3214	0.3880	0.2718
Val	GAT	**0.4972**	**0.5717**	**0.4096**
	DeBERTa-QA	0.3206	0.5059	0.3357
	MLP-QA	0.3150	0.3622	0.2953

5.2 Contrastive Learning

Initial experiments revealed that BERT embeddings are not discriminative enough for our task. This is intuitively to be expected: we hypothesize that hallucinations share features in the latent space. However, this does not imply that these features are inherently discriminative within BERT embeddings, as BERT is trained to capture contextual, syntactic, and semantic information, rather than "validity" or "truthfulness".

To acquire enriched embeddings, we train a Contrastive Learning (CL) (Khosla et al., 2020) MLP on the train set. This choice aims to strengthen the model's ability to differentiate between classes. In CL, larger batch sizes often enhance performance by allowing more comparisons with negative examples, smoothing loss gradients. We found that a batch size of 256 suffices for good results. Extended training periods notably benefit CL. We train for 1000 epochs using a decoupled weight decay optimizer (Loshchilov and Hutter, 2019). Parameter group learning rates are set with a cosine annealing schedule (Loshchilov and Hutter, 2017). Our contrastive learned MLP (CL + MLP) consists of two linear layers: input size 768, sequentially transitioning to 768, and then to 128 with ReLU activation. After contrastive learning, the 32-dimensionality reduction MLP is applied.

5.3 Ablation Study

To assess the impact of incorporating CL, we compare the metrics of GAT with and without CL, alongside the MLP baseline. We train the MLP with CL to differentiate between answers only, leading to a new baseline MLP-A. This MLP is a two-layer model with hidden sizes 64 and 32, and ReLU activation. This comparison is excluded for the DeBERTa model, as MLP-A is trained solely on answers, and DeBERTa uses different embeddings, potentially leading to a distribution shift.

To further address our first research question, we evaluate the model's performance both with and without contrastive learning (CL). Table 2 reveals significant improvements in GAT's performance with CL, particularly a remarkable 32% increase in recall on the train set. While the validation set also shows overall improvements, there is a slight 3% dip in precision, countered by an approximate 3% increase in recall. Without CL, MLP's performance appears random. After using CL, there is an apparent improvement across all metrics. In particular, there is a 20% improvement in both precision and recall for the train set. Validation recall sees an approximate 10% increase, while precision increases by around 20%.

Table 2: Comparing performance between GAT, MLP, and kNN using contrastive learning (CL) versus without, with only answer (A) embeddings. For kNN we only show validation results. The best results for each metric and data split are highlighted in bold.

Split	Model	Recall	Precision	AUC-PR
Train	GAT	0.5069	0.5844	0.4153
	CL + GAT	**0.8244**	**0.8281**	**0.7118**
	MLP-A	0.2512	0.3123	0.2014
	CL + MLP-A	0.4286	0.5892	0.3987
Val	GAT	0.4972	**0.5717**	0.4096
	CL + GAT	**0.5305**	0.5438	**0.4212**
	MLP-A	0.2256	0.3110	0.2057
	CL + MLP-A	0.3589	0.4956	0.3278
	kNN	0.2434	0.1895	0.2494

Despite CL significantly improving the results, the ablation study reveals it is not the only factor in improving performance. To answer our next research question 2. *Can we leverage graph structures to identify and learn these characteristics?*, we employ k-Nearest Neighbour (kNN) with CL-learned embeddings. We assess the independent expressiveness of these embeddings, anticipating that sufficiently robust embeddings would enable a reliable majority-voting mechanism. However, with $k = 5$, kNN shows consistent underperformance (detailed in Table 2). Further exploration involved training the same MLP as introduced in Section 5.2, which showed improved performance compared to MLP without CL-learned embeddings. However, the MLP still trailed the performance of GAT, with approximately a 20% decrease in validation recall, highlighting the significance of the graph structure. The attention mechanism of GAT is crucial in accurately identifying important neighbors. This refined approach which is solely reliant on spatial similarity outperformed the kNN method, highlighting the advantages of graph structures for efficient information propagation. Furthermore, edge masking ensures robustness by preventing information exchange between training and validation/test nodes during training. This method acts as a regularizer, enhancing the model's generalization capabilities (Rong et al., 2020).

5.4 Test Set Performance

Finally, to address the research question 3. *If learned, can we use this knowledge to identify hallucinations among new incoming LLM generations through label recovery?*, we analyze the best-performing models by validation recall. The models that showcase the highest performance are GAT with and without contrastive learning. To ensure a fair comparison, we also consider the performance of the third-best model on the test set. The results are shown in Table 3. Performance on the test set reveals that GAT with CL outperforms the other models on every metric except precision. The GAT structure proves crucial for higher recall.

Table 3: Comparing performance on the test set between the best performing models: GAT, MLP with CL, and GAT without CL. The best results for each metric and data split are highlighted in bold.

	Recall	Precision	AUC-PR
CL + GAT	**0.5142**	0.5430	**0.4057**
GAT	0.4830	**0.5603**	0.3887
CL + MLP-A	0.3727	0.5122	0.3419

5.5 Generalizability on Other Benchmarks

We assess the generalizability of our method on two real-world datasets, namely FEVER (Thorne et al., 2018a) and SelfCheckGPT (Manakul et al., 2023). Section 2 discusses their original applications, while Section 4.7 details how we modify the labels for our model.

To benchmark our model's performance, we compare the results against the best performance of the first FEVER Shared Task challenge (Thorne et al., 2018b), shown in Table 4 as UNC-NLP. Our model outperforms UNC-NLP in precision, with accuracy being 4% lower. However, it is important to stress that, in comparison, we solve a closed-book problem, avoiding the computational overload and necessity of any external data or search-based model.

Table 4: For FEVER(Thorne et al., 2018a): Performance metrics on the FEVER dataset. The best results are highlighted in bold.

Method	Recall	Precision	Label Accuracy
CL + GAT	0.7079	**0.4712**	0.6471
UNC-NLP	**0.7091**	0.4227	**0.6821**

Following the methodology in SelfCheckGPT (Manakul et al., 2023), we use DeBERTa-large for sentence embeddings. Our model falls short of the pairwise consistency metrics computed using DeBERTa-large embeddings (with BERTScore), as demonstrated in Table 5. A plausible explanation is the dataset's small size. The method with BERTScore needs multiple LLM-generated statements, while our method, trained on a small set, requires more examples for effective learning.

Table 5: For SelfCheckGPT(Manakul et al., 2023): Factual sentences are labelled as *Accurate*, NonFactual sentences are labelled as *Major-* and *Minor-inaccurate*. AUC-PR scores for Random and w/ BERTScore are computed on the entire dataset; our method's scores are calculated on the test set. The best results are highlighted in bold.

Method	Sentence-level (AUC-PR)	
	NonFactual	Factual
Random	0.7296	0.2704
LLM + BERT Scores	**0.8196**	**0.4423**
CL + GAT	0.7799	0.4002

6 Conclusion

This study shows the potential of GAT in LLM hallucination detection. Its adaptability and capabilities to find underlying graphical structures provide a significant advantage in discriminating between real and hallucinated generations. In the realm of hallucination detection, where information interconnects in complex ways, GATs' proficiency in navigating these connections proves invaluable.

Overall, this research reveals the pivotal role of structural information within graphs in discriminating between true and hallucinated statements. The incorporation of non-local aggregation serves to fortify these connections. The integration of a contrastive learned embedder enhances the discernment between true and hallucinated statements. Furthermore, this framework exhibits the capacity to extend beyond initial data, enabling generalization to real hallucinations.

Limitations and Future Work Several limitations to our approach should be considered: 1) it requires effort to model the data, create ordinal categorical labels, and construct the graph structure; 2) it does not allow for transparency at all; 3) the method is difficult to scale, as adding nodes involves an exponential number of embedding comparisons for adding edges in the graph. Moreover, GATs face a limitation when adding new nodes to the graph, hindering real-time classification. Addressing these limitations could be a focus for future work, with the exploration of dynamic graph attention networks (Shi et al., 2021) offering potential solutions. Dynamic GATs may facilitate the addition of new nodes, enabling real-time adaptation to evolving graph structures and addressing the current impracticality of real-time classification. Moreover, while the idea of this research was to model semantic relationships between individual utterances without explicitly assuming any connection between retrieval-based true statements and generations, it would be interesting to also simulate the query-answer baseline setting with the attention mechanism and analyze how the performance of our model changes.

References

Md Shad Akhtar, Abhishek Kumar, Deepanway Ghosal, Asif Ekbal, and Pushpak Bhattacharyya. 2017. A multilayer perceptron based ensemble technique for fine-grained financial sentiment analysis. In *Proceedings of the 2017 conference on empirical methods in natural language processing*, pages 540–546.

Radford Alec, Wu Jeffrey, Child Rewon, Luan David, Amodei Dario, and Sutskever Ilya. 2019. Language Models are Unsupervised Multitask Learners. *OpenAI Blog*, 1(8):9.

Sid Black, Stella Biderman, Eric Hallahan, Quentin Anthony, Leo Gao, Laurence Golding, Horace He, Connor Leahy, Kyle McDonell, Jason Phang, Michael Pieler, USVSN Sai Prashanth, Shivanshu Purohit, Laria Reynolds, Jonathan Tow, Ben Wang, and Samuel Weinbach. 2022. Gpt-neox-20b: An open-source autoregressive language model. *CoRR*, abs/2204.06745.

Tom B. Brown, Benjamin Mann, Nick Ryder, Melanie Subbiah, Jared Kaplan, Prafulla Dhariwal, Neelakantan Arvind, Shyam Pranav, Sastry Girish, Amanda Askell, Sandhini Agarwal, Ariel Herbert-Voss, Gretchen Krueger, Tom Henighan, Rewon Child, Aditya Ramesh, Daniel M. Ziegler, Jeffrey Wu, Clemens Winter, Christopher Hesse, Mark Chen, Eric Sigler, Mateusz Litwin, Scott Gray, Benjamin Chess, Jack Clark, Christopher Berner, Sam McCandlish, Alec Radford, Ilya Sutskever, and Dario Amodei. 2020a. Language models are few-shot learners. In *Advances in Neural Information Processing Systems 33: Annual Conference on Neural Information Processing Systems 2020, NeurIPS 2020, December 6-12, 2020, virtual*.

Tom B. Brown, Benjamin Mann, et al. 2020b. Language models are few-shot learners. In *Advances in Neural Information Processing Systems*, volume 2020-Decem. Neural information processing systems foundation.

Qian Chen, Xiaodan Zhu, Zhen-Hua Ling, Si Wei, Hui Jiang, and Diana Inkpen. 2017. Enhanced LSTM for natural language inference. In *Proceedings of the 55th Annual Meeting of the Association for Computational Linguistics, ACL 2017, Vancouver, Canada, July 30 - August 4, Volume 1: Long Papers*, pages 1657–1668. Association for Computational Linguistics.

Yuyan Chen, Qiang Fu, Yichen Yuan, Zhihao Wen, Ge Fan, Dayiheng Liu, Dongmei Zhang, Zhixu Li, and Yanghua Xiao. 2023. Hallucination detection: Robustly discerning reliable answers in large language models. In *Proceedings of the 32nd ACM International Conference on Information and Knowledge Management*, CIKM '23, page 245–255, New York, NY, USA. Association for Computing Machinery.

Jacob Devlin, Ming Wei Chang, Kenton Lee, and Kristina Toutanova. 2019. BERT: Pre-training of Deep Bidirectional Transformers for Language Understanding. In *NAACL HLT 2019 - 2019 Conference of the North American Chapter of the Association for Computational Linguistics: Human Language Technologies - Proceedings of the Conference*, volume 1, pages 4171–4186. Association for Computational Linguistics (ACL).

Shehzaad Dhuliawala, Mojtaba Komeili, Jing Xu, Roberta Raileanu, Xian Li, Asli Celikyilmaz, and Jason Weston. 2023. Chain-of-verification reduces hallucination in large language models. *CoRR*, abs/2309.11495.

Philip Feldman, James R. Foulds, and Shimei Pan. 2023. Trapping LLM hallucinations using tagged context prompts. *CoRR*, abs/2306.06085.

Irving John Good. 1952. Rational decisions. *Journal of the Royal Statistical Society: Series B (Methodological)*, 14(1):107–114.

Pengcheng He, Xiaodong Liu, Jianfeng Gao, and Weizhu Chen. 2021. DEBERTA: DECODING-ENHANCED BERT WITH DISENTANGLED ATTENTION. In *ICLR 2021 - 9th International Conference on Learning Representations*. International Conference on Learning Representations, ICLR.

Bin Ji. 2023. Vicunaner: Zero/few-shot named entity recognition using vicuna. *CoRR*, abs/2305.03253.

Ziwei Ji, Nayeon Lee, Rita Frieske, Tiezheng Yu, Dan Su, Yan Xu, Etsuko Ishii, Ye Jin Bang, Andrea Madotto, and Pascale Fung. 2023a. Survey of Hallucination in Natural Language Generation. *ACM Comput. Surv.*, 55(12):1–38.

Ziwei Ji, Tiezheng Yu, Yan Xu, Nayeon Lee, Etsuko Ishii, and Pascale Fung. 2023b. Towards mitigating LLM hallucination via self reflection. In *Findings of the Association for Computational Linguistics: EMNLP 2023, Singapore, December 6-10, 2023*, pages 1827–1843. Association for Computational Linguistics.

Enkelejda Kasneci, Kathrin Sessler, et al. 2023. ChatGPT for good? On opportunities and challenges of large language models for education. *Learning and Individual Differences*, 103:102274.

Prannay Khosla, Piotr Teterwak, Chen Wang, Aaron Sarna, Yonglong Tian, Phillip Isola, Aaron Maschinot, Ce Liu, and Dilip Krishnan. 2020. Supervised Contrastive Learning. In *Advances in Neural Information Processing Systems*, volume 2020-December.

Sang-Bum Kim, Kyoung-Soo Han, Hae-Chang Rim, and Sung-Hyon Myaeng. 2006. Some effective techniques for naive bayes text classification. *IEEE Trans. Knowl. Data Eng.*, 18(11):1457–1466.

Diederik P. Kingma and Jimmy Ba. 2017. Adam: A method for stochastic optimization. *Preprint*, arXiv:1412.6980.

Yuxin Liang, Zhuoyang Song, Hao Wang, and Jiaxing Zhang. 2024. Learning to trust your feelings: Leveraging self-awareness in llms for hallucination mitigation. *CoRR*, abs/2401.15449.

Stephanie Lin, Jacob Hilton, and Owain Evans. 2022. TruthfulQA: Measuring How Models Mimic Human Falsehoods. In *Proceedings of the Annual Meeting of the Association for Computational Linguistics*, volume 1, pages 3214–3252. Association for Computational Linguistics (ACL).

Ilya Loshchilov and Frank Hutter. 2017. SGDR: Stochastic Gradient Descent with Warm Restarts. In *5th International Conference on Learning Representations, ICLR 2017 - Conference Track Proceedings*. International Conference on Learning Representations, ICLR.

Ilya Loshchilov and Frank Hutter. 2019. Decoupled Weight Decay Regularization. In *7th International Conference on Learning Representations, ICLR 2019*. International Conference on Learning Representations, ICLR.

Junyu Luo, Cao Xiao, and Fenglong Ma. 2023. Zero-resource hallucination prevention for large language models. *CoRR*, abs/2309.02654.

Potsawee Manakul, Adian Liusie, and Mark JF Gales. 2023. SelfCheckGPT: Zero-Resource Black-Box Hallucination Detection for Generative Large Language Models. *Preprint*, arXiv:2303.08896.

Ariana Martino, Michael Iannelli, and Coleen Truong. 2023. Knowledge injection to counter large language model (LLM) hallucination. In *The Semantic Web: ESWC 2023 Satellite Events - Hersonissos, Crete, Greece, May 28 - June 1, 2023, Proceedings*, volume 13998 of *Lecture Notes in Computer Science*, pages 182–185. Springer.

Tri Nguyen, Mir Rosenberg, Xia Song, Jianfeng Gao, Saurabh Tiwary, Rangan Majumder, and Li Deng. 2016. MS MARCO: A Human Generated MAchine Reading COmprehension Dataset. In *CEUR Workshop Proceedings*, volume 1773. CEUR-WS.

Sundar Pichai. 2023. An important next step on our ai journey.

Colin Raffel, Noam Shazeer, Adam Roberts, Katherine Lee, Sharan Narang, Michael Matena, Yanqi Zhou, Wei Li, and Peter J. Liu. 2020. Exploring the limits of transfer learning with a unified text-to-text transformer. *J. Mach. Learn. Res.*, 21:140:1–140:67.

Yudi Ramdhani, Hanii Mustofa, Salman Topiq, Doni Purnama Alamsyah, Sandy Setiawan, and Leni Susanti. 2022. Sentiment analysis twitter based lexicon and multilayer perceptron algorithm. In *2022 10th International Conference on Cyber and IT Service Management (CITSM)*, pages 1–6. IEEE.

Yu Rong, Wenbing Huang, Tingyang Xu, and Junzhou Huang. 2020. Dropedge: Towards deep graph convolutional networks on node classification. *Preprint*, arXiv:1907.10903.

Khaled Shaalan. 2014. A survey of arabic named entity recognition and classification. *Comput. Linguistics*, 40(2):469–510.

Min Shi, Yu Huang, Xingquan Zhu, Yufei Tang, Yuan Zhuang, and Jianxun Liu. 2021. GAEN: Graph Attention Evolving Networks. In *IJCAI International Joint Conference on Artificial Intelligence*, pages 1541–1547.

James Thorne, Andreas Vlachos, Christos Christodoulopoulos, and Arpit Mittal. 2018a. FEVER: a large-scale dataset for fact extraction and VERification. In *NAACL-HLT*.

James Thorne, Andreas Vlachos, Oana Cocarascu, Christos Christodoulopoulos, and Arpit Mittal. 2018b. The fact extraction and verification (fever) shared task. *arXiv preprint arXiv:1811.10971*.

Hugo Touvron, Louis Martin, et al. 2023. Llama 2: Open Foundation and Fine-Tuned Chat Models. *Preprint*, arXiv:2307.09288.

Neeraj Varshney, Wenlin Yao, Hongming Zhang, Jianshu Chen, and Dong Yu. 2023. A stitch in time saves nine: Detecting and mitigating hallucinations of llms by validating low-confidence generation. *CoRR*, abs/2307.03987.

Ashish Vaswani, Noam Shazeer, Niki Parmar, Jakob Uszkoreit, Llion Jones, Aidan N. Gomez, Łukasz Kaiser, and Illia Polosukhin. 2017. Attention is all you need. In *Advances in Neural Information Processing Systems*, volume 2017-Decem, pages 5999–6009. Neural information processing systems foundation.

Petar Veličković, Arantxa Casanova, Pietro Liò, Guillem Cucurull, Adriana Romero, and Yoshua Bengio. 2018. Graph Attention Networks. In *6th International Conference on Learning Representations, ICLR 2018 - Conference Track Proceedings*. International Conference on Learning Representations, ICLR.

Xiaohua Wang, Yuliang Yan, Longtao Huang, Xiaoqing Zheng, and Xuanjing Huang. 2023. Hallucination detection for generative large language models by bayesian sequential estimation. In *Proceedings of the 2023 Conference on Empirical Methods in Natural Language Processing, EMNLP 2023, Singapore, December 6-10, 2023*, pages 15361–15371. Association for Computational Linguistics.

Thomas Wolf, Lysandre Debut, Victor Sanh, Julien Chaumond, Clement Delangue, Anthony Moi, Pierric Cistac, Tim Rault, Rémi Louf, Morgan Funtowicz, Joe Davison, Sam Shleifer, Patrick von Platen, Clara Ma, Yacine Jernite, Julien Plu, Canwen Xu, Teven Le Scao, Sylvain Gugger, Mariama Drame, Quentin Lhoest, and Alexander M. Rush. 2020. Transformers: State-of-the-art natural language processing. In *Proceedings of the 2020 Conference on Empirical Methods in Natural Language Processing: System Demonstrations, EMNLP 2020 - Demos, Online, November 16-20, 2020*, pages 38–45. Association for Computational Linguistics.

Ying Xu, Xu Zhong, Antonio Jose Jimeno Yepes, and Jey Han Lau. 2020. Forget Me Not: Reducing Catastrophic Forgetting for Domain Adaptation in Reading Comprehension. In *Proceedings of the International Joint Conference on Neural Networks*. Institute of Electrical and Electronics Engineers Inc.

Ziwei Xu, Sanjay Jain, and Mohan S. Kankanhalli. 2024. Hallucination is inevitable: An innate limitation of large language models. *CoRR*, abs/2401.11817.

Daokun Zhang, Jie Yin, Xingquan Zhu, and Chengqi Zhang. 2016. Homophily, structure, and content augmented network representation learning. In *IEEE 16th International Conference on Data Mining, ICDM 2016, December 12-15, 2016, Barcelona, Spain*, pages 609–618. IEEE Computer Society.

Wei Zhang, Shuang Liu, Clement T. Yu, Chaojing Sun, Fang Liu, and Weiyi Meng. 2007. Recognition and classification of noun phrases in queries for effective retrieval. In *Proceedings of the Sixteenth ACM Conference on Information and Knowledge Management, CIKM 2007, Lisbon, Portugal, November 6-10, 2007*, pages 711–720. ACM.

A Appendix

Figure 2: Prompt 1: Without provided Context

Task: {*Imagine you are crafting a multiple-choice exam in the field of biomedical studies.*}

{*Your task is to generate a set of statements related to a given question.*}

{*Provide one accurate statement as the correct answer (Answer 1) and four misleading statements that should appear as plausible distractors (Answers 2 to 5).*}

{*Ensure that the incorrect answers are not easily mistaken for accurate information related to the question.*}

Question: {*What is the role of the BRCA1 gene in breast cancer?*}

Context: { }

Figure 3: Prompt 2: With provided Context

. . . .

Task: {*Imagine you are crafting a multiple-choice exam in the field of biomedical studies.*}

{*Your task is to generate a set of statements related to a given question.*}

{*Provide one accurate statement as the correct answer (Answer 1) and four misleading statements that should appear as plausible distractors (Answers 2 to 5).*}

{*Ensure that the incorrect answers are not easily mistaken for accurate information related to the question.*}

Question: {*What is the role of the BRCA1 gene in breast cancer?*}

Context: {*The BRCA1 gene is a gene on chromosome 17 that produces a protein responsible for repairing DNA. Mutations in this gene can lead to reduced protein functionality, impairing DNA repair processes. This impairment increases the risk of mutations in other genes, which can result in uncontrolled cell growth and potentially lead to the development of breast cancer. The presence of mutated BRCA1 is a significant marker for an increased risk of breast and ovarian cancers in women, making genetic testing a key preventive measure for those with a family history of these cancers.*}

. . . .

Semantic Graphs for Syntactic Simplification: A Revisit from the Age of LLM

Peiran Yao and **Kostyantyn Guzhva** and **Denilson Barbosa**
Department of Computing Science
University of Alberta
{peiran, denilson}@ualberta.ca

Abstract

Symbolic sentence meaning representations, such as AMR (Abstract Meaning Representation) provide expressive and structured semantic graphs that act as intermediates that simplify downstream NLP tasks. However, the instruction-following capability of large language models (LLMs) offers a shortcut to effectively solve NLP tasks, questioning the utility of semantic graphs. Meanwhile, recent work has also shown the difficulty of using meaning representations merely as a helpful auxiliary for LLMs. We revisit the position of semantic graphs in syntactic simplification, the task of simplifying sentence structures while preserving their meaning, which requires semantic understanding, and evaluate it on a new complex and natural dataset. The AMR-based method that we propose, AMRS[3], demonstrates that state-of-the-art meaning representations can lead to easy-to-implement simplification methods with competitive performance and unique advantages in cost, interpretability, and generalization. With AMRS[3] as an anchor, we discover that syntactic simplification is a task where semantic graphs are helpful in LLM prompting. We propose AMRCoC prompting that guides LLMs to emulate graph algorithms for explicit symbolic reasoning on AMR graphs, and show its potential for improving LLM on semantic-centered tasks like syntactic simplification.

1 Introduction

Frameworks for symbolic sentence meaning representations, exemplified by UCCA (Abend and Rappoport, 2013), Abstract Meaning Representation (AMR) (Banarescu et al., 2013), and UMR (Gysel et al., 2021), provide varying levels of abstraction away from the lexical and syntactical structures of natural language sentences, commonly in the form of *semantic graphs* (Oepen et al., 2020). Compared to dense representations such as semantically meaningful embeddings (Reimers and Gurevych, 2019), representing the meaning of a sentence as a graph allows for the use of classical (and explainable) algorithms (e.g. traversal and partition) to ease the development of more controllable and interpretable methods for semantic-focused NLP applications, including but not limited to text simplification (Sulem et al., 2018), question answering from knowledge bases (Kapanipathi et al., 2021), and text-style transfer (Shi et al., 2023).

Meanwhile, large language models (LLMs), representatively the ChatGPT (Ouyang et al., 2022; OpenAI, 2023) and Llama (AI@Meta, 2024) families, have demonstrated prevailing performance in the aforementioned applications. Their instruction following capability (Ouyang et al., 2022) enables training-free adaptation to specific tasks, which, in terms of the burden for implementation, is at a similar level to that of writing graph algorithms on top of semantic graphs. This prompts researchers to rethink the role of symbolic meaning representations in the era of LLMs, and to explore the potential of combining the two paradigms, with the negative findings that directly appending AMR to the input of LLMs is not beneficial, if not harmful, in many tasks (Jin et al., 2024).

Along these lines, we study the task of syntactic simplification and aim to answer two research questions: **RQ1** (§4): Can state-of-the-art meaning representing semantic graphs provide a light-weight, easy-to-implement, and interpretable alternative to LLMs for this task? **RQ2** (§5): Can it be helpful to supply semantic graphs as auxiliaries to LLMs to improve their performance on this task?

Syntactic simplification, including variants like Split and Rephrase (Narayan et al., 2017), sentence splitting (Niklaus et al., 2019) and Gao et al. (2021), is a type of text simplification task that aims to rewrite sentences to reduce the syntactic complexity while preserving its meaning, typically operationalized by converting a complex text into a

Code, models, and data are available at https://github.com/U-Alberta/AMRS3.

Proceedings of TextGraphs-17: Graph-based Methods for Natural Language Processing, pages 105–115
August 15, 2024

set of atomic sentences with simpler structures. It has practical applications in improving text accessibility for less-proficient readers (Watanabe et al., 2009), improving weaker NLP pipelines (Niklaus et al., 2023), and detecting hallucination in complex statements (Hou et al., 2024). Despite modifying syntactic structures as the outcome, the task is inherently semantic-focused, as sentences are expected to be atomic in meaning and semantically equivalent to the original complex sentence, making semantic graphs a natural choice as an intermediate.

To answer RQ1, we propose AMRS^3 (shorthand for **A**bstract **M**eaning **R**epresentation for **S**yntactic **S**entence **S**implification), a simple yet effective graph-based algorithm that breaks down the AMR graph of a complex sentence into a set of subgraphs, each corresponding to a semantic unit. The subgraphs then guide the generation of simpler sentences which form the final output. AMR is chosen as it is the meaning representation that receives more attention in recent developments of treebanks (Knight et al., 2020), parsing (Xu et al., 2023), text generation (Bai et al., 2022), and cross-lingual adaptation (Wein and Schneider, 2024), and it reflects the state-of-the-art of graph-based meaning representation. We demonstrate that with a well-developed semantic graph like AMR, a syntactic simplification system can be derived from simple rules as a lightweight alternative to LLMs. Evaluations on the synthetic WebSplit (Narayan et al., 2017) dataset and real-world complex sentences from a Humanities corpus (Brown et al., 2022) show that AMRS^3 yields simplifications that are comparable to those of complex existing systems and LLMs in terms of both syntactic simplicity and meaning preservation, while enjoying, in principle, the merits of simplicity, interpretability, and language-neutrality.

It is unsurprising that LLM outperforms symbolic methods in syntactic simplification (Ponce et al., 2023). We aim to answer RQ2 and see whether AMR still has merits as an auxiliary to LLMs (namely GPT-3.5 and Llama-3-8B) in this task. Contrary to Jin et al.'s (2024) report that directly adding AMR to the input is harmful in many tasks, we find syntactic simplification slightly benefits from the auxiliary AMR inputs. We investigate what elements of AMR are helpful to LLMs in our case, and find that prompting in Chain-of-Code (Li et al., 2023) style allows LLMs to emulate the execution process of AMRS^3 and perform reasoning over AMR graphs, providing insights on how AMR can be made a useful auxiliary for LLMs in this and other semantic-centered tasks.

We contribute a LLM-era's perspective on graphical approaches toward the long-standing task of syntactic simplification: the task is benchmarked on a hard and natural complex sentence dataset that we construct; we offer a reference point of the latest developments in symbolic meaning representations for the task; and finally, we provide insights on the role of symbolic meaning representations in the era of LLMs that complement recent work.

2 Related Work

Text Simplification. Syntactic simplification is a subtask of automated text simplification, the problem of improving text readability and understandability while retaining information, that has a wide spectrum of forms (Al-Thanyyan and Azmi, 2022): complementing syntactic simplification, lexical simplification focuses on replacing complex words with simpler synonyms (Paetzold and Specia, 2017). Meanwhile, summarization is another form of simplification that removes superfluous information or unnecessary details (Nenkova et al., 2011). Given the difference in focuses, general text simplification benchmarks and evaluations such as those of Maddela et al. (2023) and Alva-Manchego et al. (2021) do not directly apply to syntactic simplification in isolation.

Syntactic Simplification. Prior to LLMs, syntactic simplification was commonly modeled as a sequence-to-sequence task where systems are trained on parallel corpora synthesized from knowledge graphs (Narayan et al., 2017), mined from Wikipedia (Botha et al., 2018) and translations (Kim et al., 2021), or crowd-sourced (Gao et al., 2021). These specialized models struggle to generalize to unseen data, which our work demonstrates is solvable with simple rule-based methods combined with a powerful semantic representation (AMR). This combination is admittedly not a new idea: DisSim (Niklaus et al., 2023) is a performative simplification system, yet it relies on a larger set of expert-crafted lexical rules that is not as simple and transferrable as our approach. DSS (Sulem et al., 2018) uses UCCA as the semantic representation, and we inherit its idea and build on AMR which is more powerful. Ponce et al. (2023) evaluates fine-tuning LLMs on a split-and-rephrase dataset, while our analysis on LLM focuses on the zero-shot instruction-following setting.

Symbolic Reasoning for LLM. Jin et al. (2024) suggest that adding serialized AMR graphs to the input of LLM in a direct manner is not effective in prompting LLM to perform implicit reasoning over the AMR graph. This is consistent with the observation that LLM needs guidance on task decomposition to perform complex reasoning (Wei et al., 2022) such as manipulating AMR. However, symbolic data, such as code and AMR, likely has the potential to benefit LLM (Yang et al., 2024). Our work investigates whether methods prompting LLM to perform explicit symbolic reasoning, such as Chain-of-Code (Li et al., 2023), can be more helpful than direct prompting as in Jin et al. (2024). An alternative to prompting, which is beyond the scope of this work, is to fine-tune the LLM across symbolic reasoning tasks including AMR to improve its reasoning ability Xu et al. (2023).

3 Task Setting

In our studies, we consider only the hard cases of syntactic simplification (Niklaus et al., 2019) where a complex sentence needs to be simplified into multiple ones (typically more than two). To the best of our knowledge, there is a lack of high-quality benchmarking datasets for this task. Synthetic and mined datasets such as WikiSplit (Botha et al., 2018) and BiSECT (Kim et al., 2021) come with reference simplifications, but they only focus on binary splits, with WebSplit (Narayan et al., 2017) being an exception. The manually labeled DeSSE dataset (Gao et al., 2021) is in the domain of student essays where the sentences are relatively simple. The usefulness of the provided reference simplifications is limited, as they are often not of high quality and the granularity of the splits is predefined by the dataset generation process. This motivates us to use reference-less evaluation metrics to assess the quality of the generated splits from the aspects of simplicity and meaning preservation separately (Cripwell et al., 2024), and create a natural and realistic dataset of complex sentences.

Datasets. As an instance of traditionally used benchmark datasets, we use WebSplit's test set (WEBSPLIT), with the caveat that it is unnatural. Meanwhile, we mine for sentences with high word and entity mention counts from the Orlando bibliography corpus (Brown et al., 2022), which results in a set of structurally-complex realistic sentences expressing rich relations, written by digital humanists (ORLANDO). Table 1 provides a summary of the size and nature of the two datasets.

Assessing Simplicity. We measure the opposite of simplicity, the syntactic complexity of sentences, by L2SCA (Lu, 2010), a widely adopted set of features that highly correlate with human judgments of syntactic complexity. It measures 14 features from five syntactic aspects. For the clarity of presentation, from each aspect, we choose one feature with the highest correlation with human judgments.

Assessing Meaning Preservation. Following recent work (Ponce et al., 2023; Cripwell et al., 2024), we use BERTScore Recall (Zhang et al., 2020) computed with DeBERTa-NLI[1] (He et al., 2021) to assess whether the meaning of the original sentence is preserved in the simplification. We do not follow previous work relying on BLEU as its lack of semantic understanding is criticized for being particularly unsuitable for simplification tasks (Sulem et al., 2018; Alva-Manchego et al., 2021).

4 AMR for Rule-based Simplification

We argue that Abstract Meaning Representation (AMR) is suitable for syntactic simplification, as its abstraction away from surface strings and syntactic structures (Oepen et al., 2020) allows us to define concise and interpretable rules for simplification, and its well-developed resources for parsing and generation provide a guarantee for high-quality conversions between text and graphs. This leads to the development of AMRS[3] , an AMR-based system for syntactic simplification that is driven by a handful of simple and interpretable rules.

4.1 Rule Set

As illustrated in Figure 1, AMRS[3] at a high-level projects a complex sentence to the space of AMR graphs using a semantic parser, and then breaks down the AMR graph of a complex sentence into a set of subgraphs, each corresponding to a semantic unit, which are then realized into simpler sentences using an AMR-to-text model.

An AMR graph (as in Fig. 1) is a rooted directed acyclic graph where nodes represent *concepts* and edges represent *relations* between concepts (Banarescu et al., 2013). Non-leaf nodes in AMR are usually *core concepts* (highlighted nodes in Fig. 1)

[1] `microsoft/deberta-xlarge-mnli` as suggested by latest BERTScore guidelines.

Dataset	Size	Example
WEBSPLIT	938	*Addiction journal is about addiction and is published by Wiley-Blackwell which has John Wiley & Sons as the parent company .*
ORLANDO	1,104	*She covers several British trials on sexual matters and on what might be described as trumped-up evidence: the prosecution of Penguin Books for publishing Lawrence's Lady Chatterley's Lover, 1960, the trial of ex- Liberal Party leader Jeremy Thorpe for conspiracy to murder, and the trial of Stephen Ward (described by the Oxford Dictionary of National Biography both as osteopath and scapegoat and as the British Dreyfus) for living on immoral earnings in the wake of the resignation of Minister John Profumo on 4 June 1963.*

Table 1: Summary the two datasets of complex sentences, where WEBSPLIT is synthesized and unnatural while ORLANDO contains natural sentences of *absurd* complexity similar to the examples.

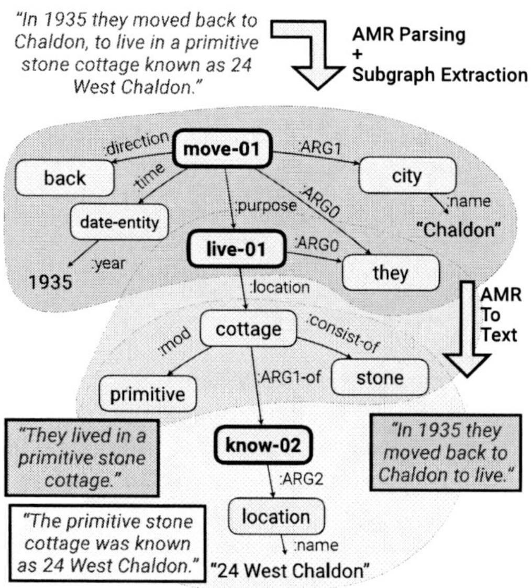

Figure 1: Three stages of AMRS[3] : (1) Complex input sentence (top) is parsed into an AMR graph. In the AMR graph, core concepts are highlighted. (2) Subgraphs (three encircled graphs) that correspond to simpler sentences are identified using the subgraph extraction algorithm. (3) The subgraphs are realized into text (three boxes at the bottom) using an AMR-to-text model.

Algorithm 1 Extract subgraphs from an AMR graph G by performing DFS and applying the rules defined in §4.1.

procedure SUBGRAPHS(G)
  $r \leftarrow \varnothing; q \leftarrow \{G.root\}$
  for all $e \in G.edges$, e is inverse **do**
    $q \leftarrow q \cup \{e.from\}$ ▷ Rule 3
    $e.from, e.to \leftarrow e.to, e.from$
  while $|q| > 0$ **do** ▷ Extract from roots
    $g' \leftarrow$ DFSCOPY($q.pop(), q$)
    $r \leftarrow r \cup \{g'\}$
  return r
procedure DFSCOPY(n, q)
  if n is leaf **return** n
  if n is core concept, $|n.edges| > \sigma$ **then**
    $q \leftarrow q \cup \{n\}$ ▷ Rule 1
    return n
  if n was visited **then** ▷ Rule 2
    for all $e \in n.edges$, e is non-core **do**
      $n.addEdge$(DFSCOPY($e.to, q$))
  else for all $e \in n.edges$ **do**
    $n.addEdge$(DFSCOPY($e.to, q$))
  return n

that map to predicates in OntoNotes (Pradhan et al., 2007) semantic roles, and the remaining nodes are arguments of the core concepts such as (named) entities. AMR concepts are not anchored to words, and a core concept captures an event even if the word that realizes it is a noun, adjective, or is of another part-of-speech. This allows us to simplify the sentence by focusing on and only on the core concepts and their arguments:

Rule 1 (Core Concept): If a node is a core concept and has more than σ arguments, it is considered a semantic unit, and the subgraph rooted at this node is extracted as a subgraph.

A single concept (e.g. *they* in Fig. 1) can be the argument of multiple core concepts. To avoid redundancy, we only extract all relations of a concept on the first occurrence and only keep non-core relations (names, values, etc. as opposed to subjects and objects) on subsequent occurrences.

Rule 2 (Revisit): If a node has been visited before, only extract non-core relations.

AMR by default is rooted at a single predicate (e.g. *move-01*) as its focus. Non-focused predicates, except for the arguments of the focused predicate, are connected by inverse relations (e.g. *know-02* `:ARG1-of` *cottage* in Fig. 1) that are often realized as relative clauses. Depending on the granularity of simplification, we may choose to extract unfocused concepts as their own subgraphs as well by reversing the direction of the inverse relations and creating a new root.

Rule 3 (Inverse Relations): (Optional) If a node is connected by an inverse relation, reverse the direction of the inverse relation and extract the subgraph rooted at the node.

4.2 Implementation

Using depth-first search (DFS) with the rules above, we extract a set of subgraphs from the AMR graph (Algorithm 1), where σ is heuristically set at 2. We use AMRBART[2] (Bai et al., 2022), a unified model with strong performance in both AMR parsing and AMR-to-text, to parse the complex sentence into AMR graphs and realize the subgraphs into text. During AMR-to-text generation, we adopt the common practice of anonymizing named entities (Konstas et al., 2017).

As suggested by Bai et al. (2022), text-AMR pairs generated by semantic parsers (silver data) can benefit the training of AMR-to-text models. To adapt AMRBART to simple sentences, we leverage this property and finetune AMRBART on silver text-AMR pairs by parsing sentences from Simple English Wikipedia[3] using AMRBART. After finetuning, AMRBART realizations on the held-out set achieve a BLEU of 46.23, compared to the base model's BLEU of 39.53.

4.3 Baselines

We perform a comparison between AMRS³ and the following existing systems for syntactic simplification using the evaluation methods outlined in §3. The results are reported in Table 2.

DisSim. DisSim (Niklaus et al., 2023) performs a recursive transformation of a sentence based on a set of 35 hand-crafted syntactic and lexical rules related to the sentence's phrase structure.

ABCD. ABCD (Gao et al., 2021) represents a sentence as a graph where edges are dependency and neighboring relations, and trains a neural network to predict actions on the edges. We use its MinWiki-MLP release.

DSS. DSS (Sulem et al., 2018) uses UCCA as the semantic representation, splits the UCCA graph based on parallel and elaborator scenes, and converts the subgraphs into text using a neural model.

LLM. We directly instruct GPT-3.5 (turbo-0125; Ouyang et al., 2022) and Llama-3 (8B-Instruct; AI@Meta, 2024) with Prompt 1.

Prompt 1: Direct Prompting

`[System]` You are a helpful assistant that simplifies syntactic structures.
`[User]` Rewrite the following paragraph using simple sentence structures and no clauses or conjunctions: `{complex sentence}`

4.4 Discussion

AMRS³ achieves competitive performance without specialized supervised training. Overall, simplifications generated by AMRS³ are on par with or better than the baselines in terms of meaning preservation on both datasets, as shown by the comparisons in Table 2, despite not being trained on task-specific supervised data. The performance is close to Llama-3, a state-of-the-art LLM. The syntactic simplicity of the generated sentences, measured by L2SCA, is at the same level as the best-performing baselines on WEBSPLIT and better on ORLANDO, suggesting that the good performance of meaning preservation is not achieved by sacrificing syntactic simplicity. The interpretable rule set of AMRS³ makes the method easily customizable. The comparison between AMRS³ with and without Rule 3 exemplifies how a compromise between simplicity and meaning preservation can be made by simple adjustments of the rules.

AMRS³ enjoys unique merits beyond empirical performance. Specially trained models such as ABCD suffer from the lack of generalizability to new domains, as seen in its drastic performance drop on ORLANDO texts. In contrast, AMR models that AMRS³ relies on are trained on a diverse set of data and can be easily improved for new domains by finetuning on silver data. LLMs are powerful and training-free, while AMRS³ is lightweight and performs similarly well to open-weight LLMs. Admittedly, rule-based DisSim is lightweight and is performant in the evaluation. Compared to models based on semantic representation, DisSim requires a complex set of 35 lexical and syntactic rules,

[2] `AMRBART-large-v2 (AMR3.0)`

[3] Sentences extracted from `simplewiki-20230101` dump, with 5,000 held out as test set.

Method	BERTScore ↑		L2SCA ↓				
	Mean	Median	MLT	C/S	C/T	T/S	CN/T
			on ORLANDO				
AMRS[3]	0.73	0.72	12.00	1.02	1.07	0.96	1.22
AMRS[3] (w/o Rule 3)	0.79	0.79	18.17	1.30	1.32	0.98	1.89
ABCD	0.50	0.51	14.99	0.94	1.19	0.80	1.98
DisSim	0.74	0.74	11.15	1.18	1.16	1.02	1.24
DSS†	-	-	-	-	-	-	-
GPT-3.5	0.80	0.82	12.65	1.14	1.13	1.01	1.26
Llama-3-8B	0.74	0.74	7.89	1.07	1.07	1.00	0.70
Exact Copy	1.00	1.00	157.25	2.66	2.18	1.22	4.69
			on WEBSPLIT				
AMRS[3]	0.81	0.81	8.92	1.00	1.02	0.99	0.68
AMRS[3] (w/o Rule 3)	0.86	0.86	12.26	1.16	1.16	1.00	1.16
ABCD	0.90	0.91	9.53	1.00	1.10	0.91	0.94
DisSim	0.87	0.87	8.54	1.05	1.05	0.99	0.67
DSS†	0.74	0.74	10.69	0.97	1.19	0.81	1.05
GPT-3.5	0.90	0.90	7.79	1.02	1.02	1.00	0.52
Llama-3-8B	0.84	0.85	6.69	1.01	1.01	1.00	0.38
Exact Copy	1.00	1.00	16.57	1.64	1.50	1.10	1.72

Table 2: Evaluation results of AMRS[3] and baselines on ORLANDO and WEBSPLIT. BERTScore measures meaning preservation (↑ the higher the better), and L2SCA measures syntactic complexity (↓ the lower the better). † We use the output provided by Sulem et al. (2018) on WebSplit only, as no code is available. Five L2SCA metrics correspond to production unit length, overall complexity, subordination, coordination, and phrasal complexity. See Lu (2010) for the exact definition of L2SCA metrics.

while AMRS[3] only needs three simple rules. The rules of DisSim are crafted for English only and are hard to transfer to other languages, while despite AMR not being an interlingua (Banarescu et al., 2013) the rules of AMRS[3] are language-agnostic and can be easily adapted to other languages with AMR parsers. Methods based on other semantic representations, such as UCCA-based DSS, perform worse despite having a similar workflow to AMRS[3] , showcasing the *"free upgrades"* that advances in semantic representation tools can bring.

Takeaways. As AMRS[3] demonstrates, semantic graphs like AMR are mature enough to support the easy development of lightweight and interpretable systems, that still have certain advantages in LLM's age, for tasks like syntactic simplification.

5 AMR for LLM-based Simplification

Given the position of AMR as an expressive and suitable intermediate for syntactic simplification and LLM's strong performance in the task, a natural question arises as to whether AMR can be used as an auxiliary to LLMs to improve their performance in syntactic simplification in the scenario of zero-shot prompting. We investigate this question by designing a set of controlled prompting strategies to examine how the elements of AMR affect LLM. This is an addition to Jin et al. (2024) which tested directly appending AMR to the prompt in a variety of tasks, while syntactic simplification was not included in their study. Extending their work, we explore a new prompting strategy (named AMR Chain-of-Code or AMRCoC) that guides LLMs to perform explicit symbolic reasoning over AMR graphs instead of making implicit inferences as in Jin et al. (2024).

Prompt 2: Direct Full AMR Prompting (Jin et al., 2024)

`[User]` You are given a paragraph and its abstract meaning representation (AMR).
Paragraph
`{complex sentence}`
AMR
`{amr}`
Rewrite the paragraph using simple sentence structures and no clauses or conjunctions. You can refer to the provided AMR if it helps you in the rewriting.
The rewritten paragraph:

	Prompting	BERTScore ↑ Mean	Median	MLT ↓		Prompting	BERTScore ↑ Mean	Median	MLT ↓
				on ORLANDO					
GPT-3.5	*vanilla*	0.80	0.82	12.65	Llama-3	*vanilla*	0.74	0.74	7.89
	direct AMR	0.81	0.82	12.79		*direct AMR*	0.78	0.78	11.74
	subgraphs	0.80	0.81	11.65		*subgraphs*	0.78	0.78	12.45
	entities	0.79	0.80	10.99		*entities*	0.70	0.71	7.75
	predicates	0.73	0.74	7.34		*predicates*	0.70	0.70	7.55
	AMRCoC	0.79	0.81	17.29		*AMRCoC*	0.76	0.77	14.03
				on WEBSPLIT					
GPT-3.5	*vanilla*	0.90	0.90	7.79	Llama-3	*vanilla*	0.84	0.85	6.69
	direct AMR	0.88	0.89	8.59		*direct AMR*	0.83	0.85	8.15
	subgraphs	0.87	0.88	8.35		*subgraphs*	0.82	0.84	7.41
						entities	0.78	0.79	6.63
						predicates	0.76	0.77	7.12
	AMRCoC	0.89	0.90	9.15		*AMRCoC*	0.84	0.85	8.27

Table 3: Evaluation results of GPT-3.5 and Llama-3 on ORLANDO and WEBSPLIT with different prompting strategies. Notations are consistent with Table 2. Due to space limit, we only show one L2SCA metric, MLT, that has the highest variance across prompts.

5.1 Direct AMR Prompting

Jin et al.'s (2024) evaluation framework simply supplies linearized AMR in PENMAN format (Matthiessen and Bateman, 1991) in parallel with text, providing only vague instructions to the LLM on how to use the AMR, and requiring the LLM to directly produce the output *without* [4] explicitly producing reasoning steps. To add to their tests, we adapt their framework to the syntactic simplification task as in Prompt 2.

Performance. Interestingly, our evaluations (Table 3) show that the direct AMR prompting does not harm the performance of LLMs in syntactic simplification, and in some cases, it provides improvements especially for more complex inputs. This adds syntactic simplification as a counterexample to the findings of Jin et al. (2024).

Effect of Elements. To isolate the effects of different elements (subgraphs, entities, and predicates) of AMR, we further design a set of controlled prompts following the same format of Prompt 2, where the linearization of complete AMR is replaced by specific parts of the AMR:
(1) Instead of the sole AMR corresponding to the whole complex sentence, we provide a list of AMR graphs extracted with Algorithm 1 for each semantic unit in the sentence (**subgrpahs**);
(2) We provide only a list of predicates in the AMR (**predicates**), e.g. *"move, live, know"* as in Figure 1;
(3) We provide only a list of entities as reflected by the non-core concepts in the AMR (**entities**), e.g. *"date (1935), they, city (Chaldon), location (24 West Chaldon)"* as in Figure 1.

Both predicates and entities provide incomplete information about the events of a sentence, while not requiring LLM's capability to reason over a symbolic graph. However, we find that for the tasks and LLMs in question, LLMs are capable of directly and implicitly using information in the AMR as appropriate, while trading information completeness for the ease of symbolic graph processing offers more harms than benefits (Table 3).

Takeaways. Directly supplying AMR to LLMs is not monochromatically harmful across tasks. Growing the list of tasks benefited and harmed by direct AMR prompting is needed to draw conclusions on the role of meaning representations in the LLM era.

5.2 AMRCoC Prompting

Despite the evidence that LLMs can benefit from direct AMR prompting, it is widely accepted (Wei et al., 2022; Saparov and He, 2023, *inter alia*) that LLM's reasoning capability over complex tasks (e.g. processing AMR) can be improved by explicitly decomposing them into reasoning steps. To remedy the lack of explicit reasoning, we build on Chain-of-Code (CoC) prompting (Li et al., 2023), where pseudocode execution is shown helpful for the LLM to perform explicit algorithmic reasoning in general tasks, and design AMRCoC prompting

[4] Despite having an imprecise name "AMR for Chain-of-Thought" prompting in the original paper.

Prompt 3: AMR-Chain-of-Code Prompting (with simplification and an example)

```
[User]
You are given a paragraph and its abstract meaning representation (AMR). AMR captures "who is doing what to whom" in a sentence. Begin your steps with # Steps.
# Functions to process AMR
EXTRACT_SUBGRAPH(root: Node) -> AMR
extracts the subgraph rooted at 'root'.
AMR_TO_TEXT(graph: AMR) -> str
converts an AMR graph back to text.
# Example program
for predicate in amr:
g = EXTRACT_SUBGRAPH(predicate)
print(AMR_TO_TEXT(g))

[Assistant]
# Steps
g = EXTRACT_SUBGRAPH(flow-01) => (z1 / flow-01
:ARG1(...) ...)
print(AMR_TO_TEXT(g))
=> It flows through the town of Yeovil.
g = EXTRACT_SUBGRAPH(join-01) => (z5 / join-01
:ARG1 (z2 / it) ...)
...
# Output
It flows through the town of Yeovil. It joins River Parrett.
```

(Prompt 3): LLM is guided to produce explicit reasoning steps over AMR graphs by using functions to process AMR, and an example program that demonstrates the use of these functions. The functions and programs are not formally defined but in the form of function signatures or pseudocode, as we expect LLM to emulate the execution (Li et al., 2023; Chae et al., 2024).

Performance. AMRCoC offers the same level of meaning preservation (last rows of Table 3) compared to direct AMR prompting, although the simplicity of generations degrades to the level of AMRS[3] , which is perhaps unsurprising as we prompt the LLM to follow a similar algorithm. The example program in the prompt may not be optimal, but it is possible to synthesize or improve the program using LLM (Chae et al., 2024).

Emulated Execution. More importantly, the breakdown of AMRCoC execution (Table 4) verifies that LLMs can be prompted to perform explicit algorithmic reasoning over AMR graphs, which is a promising direction for future research. LLM almost always emulates the execution of the example pseudocode program ("Following algorithm" in Table 4). The extracted AMR graphs, although not always grammatically correct especially for complex inputs ("Grammatical AMR"), are not hallucinated and are based on existing nodes and edges

Property	Orlando	Websplit
Following algorithm	99.8%	92.8%
Grammatical AMR	31.3%	67.8%
Node and edge existence	98.6%	99.7%
Node coverage	72.3%	90.0%
Matching algorithm output	52.1%	66.0%

Table 4: Success rates of Llama-3's Chain-of-Code execution at different stages. Numbers are macro-averaged across all input complex sentences. For the first four rows, higher values are always favored.

in the input AMR ("Node and edge existence"), and mostly match the real execution results of Algorithm 1 ("Matching algorithm output"). When combined, AMR graphs extracted by LLM cover most of the semantic information in the input AMR ("Node coverage"), providing a guarantee for meaning preservation.

Takeaways. Chain-of-Code prompting provides a way for LLM to perform symbolic reasoning over semantic graphs via algorithm emulation. This provides a way to bring algorithmic graph processing to LLMs for semantic-centered NLP applications, to enjoy the benefits of both worlds.

6 Conclusion

In light of recent developments in semantic representations and LLMs, we presented a retrospective view of using semantic representation graphs for syntactic simplification, with refreshed datasets and up-to-date semantic representation models. In prospect, we added to the case studies of the beneficial and harmful effects of using AMR for LLM, and proposed a new AMRCoC prompting strategy with the potential of bridging symbolic and graphical algorithms to LLMs.

Limitations

The proposed AMRS[3] is not the best performing syntactic simplification system in terms of having the highest absolute numbers of BERTScore and L2SCA metrics across the datasets, as is particularly overshadowed by LLMs. The main conclusion is more about the current state of semantic representations: they are still handy in building solutions for semantic tasks, and that solution can have merits that make it a good fit in certain scenarios. Despite that, the design of AMR has some disadvantages that make it less effective to be used out-of-the-box for text simplification, namely the absence of inflectional morphology for tense and number. Banarescu et al. (2013) suggested that this can be remedied by adding these notions to AMR as an extension, which is a direction for future work.

Our evaluation of syntactic simplification is limited to automated methods. Although previous work has shown high correlations between the metrics we use and human judgments on meaning preservation, syntactic complexity, and reading difficulty, we acknowledge that those conclusions might not hold for domains out of their respective evaluations. A systematic evaluation method, tailored to the specific task of syntactic simplification and aligned with human judgments, similar to Alva-Manchego et al. (2021); Maddela et al. (2023), would be beneficial for similar studies but is out of the scope of this work.

Finally, the applicability of AMRCoC prompting is only tested on the single task of syntactic simplification. Although the properties it demonstrates are promising, we have yet to test it on other tasks such as the ones in Jin et al. (2024).

Acknowledgements

We acknowledge the support of the Natural Sciences and Engineering Research Council of Canada (NSERC). This work is also supported in part by a gift from Scotiabank. We thank Natalie Hervieux and Dr. Susan Brown for preparing the ORLANDO dataset. We also thank the anonymous reviewers for their valuable feedback.

References

Omri Abend and Ari Rappoport. 2013. UCCA: A semantics-based grammatical annotation scheme. In *Proceedings of the 10th International Conference on Computational Semantics (IWCS 2013) – Long Papers*, pages 1–12, Potsdam, Germany. Association for Computational Linguistics.

AI@Meta. 2024. Llama 3 model card.

Suha Al-Thanyyan and Aqil M. Azmi. 2022. Automated text simplification: A survey. *ACM Comput. Surv.*, 54(2):43:1–43:36.

Fernando Alva-Manchego, Carolina Scarton, and Lucia Specia. 2021. The (Un)Suitability of Automatic Evaluation Metrics for Text Simplification. *Computational Linguistics*, 47(4):861–889.

Xuefeng Bai, Yulong Chen, and Yue Zhang. 2022. Graph pre-training for AMR parsing and generation. In *Proceedings of the 60th Annual Meeting of the Association for Computational Linguistics (Volume 1: Long Papers)*, pages 6001–6015, Dublin, Ireland. Association for Computational Linguistics.

Laura Banarescu, Claire Bonial, Shu Cai, Madalina Georgescu, Kira Griffitt, Ulf Hermjakob, Kevin Knight, Philipp Koehn, Martha Palmer, and Nathan Schneider. 2013. Abstract Meaning Representation for sembanking. In *Proceedings of the 7th Linguistic Annotation Workshop and Interoperability with Discourse*, pages 178–186, Sofia, Bulgaria. Association for Computational Linguistics.

Jan A. Botha, Manaal Faruqui, John Alex, Jason Baldridge, and Dipanjan Das. 2018. Learning to split and rephrase from Wikipedia edit history. In *Proceedings of the 2018 Conference on Empirical Methods in Natural Language Processing*, pages 732–737, Brussels, Belgium. Association for Computational Linguistics.

Susan Brown, Patricia Clements, and Isobel Grundy. 2022. Orlando: Women's writing in the british isles from the beginnings to the present. `https://orlando.cambridge.org`. Accessed September 27, 2023.

Hyungjoo Chae, Yeonghyeon Kim, Seungone Kim, Kai Tzu-iunn Ong, Beong-woo Kwak, Moohyeon Kim, Seonghwan Kim, Taeyoon Kwon, Jiwan Chung, Youngjae Yu, and Jinyoung Yeo. 2024. Language models as compilers: Simulating pseudocode execution improves algorithmic reasoning in language models. *CoRR*, abs/2404.02575.

Liam Cripwell, Joël Legrand, and Claire Gardent. 2024. Evaluating document simplification: On the importance of separately assessing simplicity and meaning preservation. In *Proceedings of the 3rd Workshop on Tools and Resources for People with REAding DIfficulties (READI) @ LREC-COLING 2024*, pages 1–14, Torino, Italia. ELRA and ICCL.

Yanjun Gao, Ting-Hao Huang, and Rebecca J. Passonneau. 2021. ABCD: A graph framework to convert complex sentences to a covering set of simple sentences. In *Proceedings of the 59th Annual Meeting of the Association for Computational Linguistics and the 11th International Joint Conference on Natural Language Processing (Volume 1: Long Papers)*, pages 3919–3931, Online. Association for Computational Linguistics.

Jens E. L. Van Gysel, Meagan Vigus, Jayeol Chun, Kenneth Lai, Sarah R. Moeller, Jiarui Yao, Tim O'Gorman, Andrew Cowell, William Croft, Chu-Ren Huang, Jan Hajic, James H. Martin, Stephan Oepen, Martha Palmer, James Pustejovsky, Rosa Vallejos, and Nianwen Xue. 2021. Designing a uniform meaning representation for natural language processing. *Künstliche Intell.*, 35(3):343–360.

Pengcheng He, Xiaodong Liu, Jianfeng Gao, and Weizhu Chen. 2021. Deberta: Decoding-enhanced bert with disentangled attention. In *International Conference on Learning Representations*.

Bairu Hou, Yang Zhang, Jacob Andreas, and Shiyu Chang. 2024. A probabilistic framework for llm hallucination detection via belief tree propagation. *Preprint*, arXiv:2406.06950.

Zhijing Jin, Yuen Chen, Fernando Gonzalez Adauto, Jiarui Liu, Jiayi Zhang, Julian Michael, Bernhard Schölkopf, and Mona Diab. 2024. Analyzing the role of semantic representations in the era of large language models. In *Proceedings of the 2024 Conference of the North American Chapter of the Association for Computational Linguistics: Human Language Technologies (Volume 1: Long Papers)*, pages 3781–3798, Mexico City, Mexico. Association for Computational Linguistics.

Pavan Kapanipathi, Ibrahim Abdelaziz, Srinivas Ravishankar, Salim Roukos, Alexander Gray, Ramón Fernandez Astudillo, Maria Chang, Cristina Cornelio, Saswati Dana, Achille Fokoue, Dinesh Garg, Alfio Gliozzo, Sairam Gurajada, Hima Karanam, Naweed Khan, Dinesh Khandelwal, Young-Suk Lee, Yunyao Li, Francois Luus, Ndivhuwo Makondo, Nandana Mihindukulasooriya, Tahira Naseem, Sumit Neelam, Lucian Popa, Revanth Gangi Reddy, Ryan Riegel, Gaetano Rossiello, Udit Sharma, G P Shrivatsa Bhargav, and Mo Yu. 2021. Leveraging Abstract Meaning Representation for knowledge base question answering. In *Findings of the Association for Computational Linguistics: ACL-IJCNLP 2021*, pages 3884–3894, Online. Association for Computational Linguistics.

Joongwon Kim, Mounica Maddela, Reno Kriz, Wei Xu, and Chris Callison-Burch. 2021. BiSECT: Learning to split and rephrase sentences with bitexts. In *Proceedings of the 2021 Conference on Empirical Methods in Natural Language Processing*, pages 6193–6209, Online and Punta Cana, Dominican Republic. Association for Computational Linguistics.

Kevin Knight, Bianca Badarau, Laura Baranescu, Claire Bonial, Madalina Bardocz, Kira Griffitt, Ulf Hermjakob, Daniel Marcu, Martha Palmer, Tim O'Gorman, and Nathan Schneider. 2020. Abstract meaning representation (amr) annotation release 3.0. In *Linguistic Data Consortium*.

Ioannis Konstas, Srinivasan Iyer, Mark Yatskar, Yejin Choi, and Luke Zettlemoyer. 2017. Neural AMR: Sequence-to-sequence models for parsing and generation. In *Proceedings of the 55th Annual Meeting of the Association for Computational Linguistics (Volume 1: Long Papers)*, pages 146–157, Vancouver, Canada. Association for Computational Linguistics.

Chengshu Li, Jacky Liang, Fei Xia, Andy Zeng, Sergey Levine, Dorsa Sadigh, Karol Hausman, Xinyun Chen, Li Fei-Fei, and brian ichter. 2023. Chain of code: Reasoning with a language model-augmented code interpreter. In *NeurIPS 2023 Foundation Models for Decision Making Workshop*.

Xiaofei Lu. 2010. Automatic analysis of syntactic complexity in second language writing. *International journal of corpus linguistics*, 15(4):474–496.

Mounica Maddela, Yao Dou, David Heineman, and Wei Xu. 2023. LENS: A learnable evaluation metric for text simplification. In *Proceedings of the 61st Annual Meeting of the Association for Computational Linguistics (Volume 1: Long Papers)*, pages 16383–16408, Toronto, Canada. Association for Computational Linguistics.

Christian M.I.M. Matthiessen and John A. Bateman. 1991. Text generation and systemic-functional linguistics: Experiences from english and japanese. In *Communication in Artificial Intelligence Series*, pages xxii + 348. Pinter Publisher.

Shashi Narayan, Claire Gardent, Shay B. Cohen, and Anastasia Shimorina. 2017. Split and rephrase. In *Proceedings of the 2017 Conference on Empirical Methods in Natural Language Processing*, pages 606–616, Copenhagen, Denmark. Association for Computational Linguistics.

Ani Nenkova, Kathleen McKeown, et al. 2011. Automatic summarization. *Foundations and Trends® in Information Retrieval*, 5(2–3):103–233.

Christina Niklaus, Matthias Cetto, André Freitas, and Siegfried Handschuh. 2023. Discourse-aware text simplification: From complex sentences to linked propositions. *CoRR*, abs/2308.00425.

Christina Niklaus, André Freitas, and Siegfried Handschuh. 2019. MinWikiSplit: A sentence splitting corpus with minimal propositions. In *Proceedings of the 12th International Conference on Natural Language Generation*, pages 118–123, Tokyo, Japan. Association for Computational Linguistics.

Stephan Oepen, Omri Abend, Lasha Abzianidze, Johan Bos, Jan Hajic, Daniel Hershcovich, Bin Li, Tim O'Gorman, Nianwen Xue, and Daniel Zeman. 2020. MRP 2020: The second shared task on cross-framework and cross-lingual meaning representation parsing. In *Proceedings of the CoNLL 2020 Shared Task: Cross-Framework Meaning Representation Parsing*, pages 1–22, Online. Association for Computational Linguistics.

OpenAI. 2023. Gpt-4 technical report. *Computing Research Repository*, arXiv:2303.08774.

Long Ouyang, Jeffrey Wu, Xu Jiang, Diogo Almeida, Carroll L. Wainwright, Pamela Mishkin, Chong Zhang, Sandhini Agarwal, Katarina Slama, Alex Ray, John Schulman, Jacob Hilton, Fraser Kelton, Luke Miller, Maddie Simens, Amanda Askell, Peter Welinder, Paul F. Christiano, Jan Leike, and Ryan Lowe. 2022. Training language models to follow instructions with human feedback. In *Advances in Neural Information Processing Systems 35: Annual Conference on Neural Information Processing Systems 2022, NeurIPS 2022, New Orleans, LA, USA, November 28 - December 9, 2022*.

Gustavo H Paetzold and Lucia Specia. 2017. A survey on lexical simplification. *Journal of Artificial Intelligence Research*, 60:549–593.

David Ponce, Thierry Etchegoyhen, Jesús Calleja-Perez, and Harritxu Gete. 2023. Split and rephrase with large language models. *CoRR*, abs/2312.11075.

Sameer S. Pradhan, Eduard Hovy, Mitch Marcus, Martha Palmer, Lance Ramshaw, and Ralph Weischedel. 2007. Ontonotes: A unified relational semantic representation. In *International Conference on Semantic Computing (ICSC 2007)*, pages 517–526.

Nils Reimers and Iryna Gurevych. 2019. Sentence-BERT: Sentence embeddings using Siamese BERT-networks. In *Proceedings of the 2019 Conference on Empirical Methods in Natural Language Processing and the 9th International Joint Conference on Natural Language Processing (EMNLP-IJCNLP)*, pages 3982–3992, Hong Kong, China. Association for Computational Linguistics.

Abulhair Saparov and He He. 2023. Language models are greedy reasoners: A systematic formal analysis of chain-of-thought. In *The Eleventh International Conference on Learning Representations, ICLR 2023, Kigali, Rwanda, May 1-5, 2023*. OpenReview.net.

Kaize Shi, Xueyao Sun, Li He, Dingxian Wang, Qing Li, and Guandong Xu. 2023. AMR-TST: Abstract Meaning Representation-based text style transfer. In *Findings of the Association for Computational Linguistics: ACL 2023*, pages 4231–4243, Toronto, Canada. Association for Computational Linguistics.

Elior Sulem, Omri Abend, and Ari Rappoport. 2018. Simple and effective text simplification using semantic and neural methods. In *Proceedings of the 56th Annual Meeting of the Association for Computational Linguistics (Volume 1: Long Papers)*, pages 162–173, Melbourne, Australia. Association for Computational Linguistics.

Willian Massami Watanabe, Arnaldo Cândido Júnior, Vinícius Rodrigues de Uzêda, Renata Pontin de Mattos Fortes, Thiago Alexandre Salgueiro Pardo, and Sandra M. Aluísio. 2009. Facilita: reading assistance for low-literacy readers. In *Proceedings of the 27th Annual International Conference on Design of Communication, SIGDOC 2009, Bloomington, Indiana, USA, October 5-7, 2009*, pages 29–36. ACM.

Jason Wei, Xuezhi Wang, Dale Schuurmans, Maarten Bosma, Brian Ichter, Fei Xia, Ed H. Chi, Quoc V. Le, and Denny Zhou. 2022. Chain-of-thought prompting elicits reasoning in large language models. In *Advances in Neural Information Processing Systems 35: Annual Conference on Neural Information Processing Systems 2022, NeurIPS 2022, New Orleans, LA, USA, November 28 - December 9, 2022*.

Shira Wein and Nathan Schneider. 2024. Assessing the Cross-linguistic Utility of Abstract Meaning Representation. *Computational Linguistics*, pages 1–55.

Fangzhi Xu, Zhiyong Wu, Qiushi Sun, Siyu Ren, Fei Yuan, Shuai Yuan, Qika Lin, Yu Qiao, and Jun Liu. 2023. Symbol-llm: Towards foundational symbol-centric interface for large language models. *CoRR*, abs/2311.09278.

Ke Yang, Jiateng Liu, John Wu, Chaoqi Yang, Yi Fung, Sha Li, Zixuan Huang, Xu Cao, Xingyao Wang, Heng Ji, and ChengXiang Zhai. 2024. If LLM is the wizard, then code is the wand: A survey on how code empowers large language models to serve as intelligent agents. In *ICLR 2024 Workshop on Large Language Model (LLM) Agents*.

Tianyi Zhang, Varsha Kishore, Felix Wu, Kilian Q. Weinberger, and Yoav Artzi. 2020. Bertscore: Evaluating text generation with BERT. In *8th International Conference on Learning Representations, ICLR 2020, Addis Ababa, Ethiopia, April 26-30, 2020*. OpenReview.net.

TextGraphs 2024 Shared Task on Text-Graph Representations for Knowledge Graph Question Answering

Andrey Sakhovskiy[1,2 ◇] **Mikhail Salnikov**[2,3 ◇] **Irina Nikishina**[4] **Aida Usmanova**[5]
Angelie Kraft[4] **Cedric Möller**[4] **Debayan Banerjee**[4] **Junbo Huang**[4]
Longquan Jiang[4] **Rana Abdullah**[4] **Xi Yan**[4] **Dmitry Ustalov**[6]
Elena Tutubalina[1,3,7] **Ricardo Usbeck**[4,5] **Alexander Panchenko**[2,3]
[1]Kazan Federal University [2]Skoltech [3]AIRI [4]Universität Hamburg
[5]Leuphana University Lüneburg [6]JetBrains [7]HSE University
{andrei.sakhovskii, m.salnikov}skol.tech firstname.lastname@uni-hamburg.de
aida.usmanova@stud.leuphana.de lastname@airi.net dmitry.ustalov@jetbrains.com

Abstract

This paper describes the results of the Knowledge Graph Question Answering (KGQA) shared task that was co-located with the TextGraphs 2024 workshop.[1] In this task, given a textual question and a list of entities with the corresponding KG subgraphs, the participating system should choose the entity that correctly answers the question. Our competition attracted thirty teams, four of which outperformed our strong ChatGPT-based zero-shot baseline. In this paper, we overview the participating systems and analyze their performance according to a large-scale automatic evaluation. To the best of our knowledge, this is the first competition aimed at the KGQA problem using the interaction between large language models (LLMs) and knowledge graphs.

1 Introduction

Recent years have witnessed remarkable advances in natural language processing (NLP) and network science domains that mostly develop independently with rare intersections. We believe that a proper utilization of graph-based methods for reasoning over a knowledge graph (KG) is a prospective way to overcome critical limitations of the existing large language models (LLMs) which lack interpretability and factual knowledge and are prone to the hallucination problem. In order to encourage novel research efforts that aim to explore the hot topic of LLM prompting from the unique perspective of graph theory, we organized a shared task focused on Knowledge Graph Question Answering (KGQA) as a part of the TextGraphs 2024 workshop on graph-based methods for natural language processing, which was co-located with the ACL 2024 conference hosted on August 15 in Bangkok, Thailand.[2]

The goal of our KGQA shared task was to investigate *how the output of LLMs can be enhanced with KGs*, push the boundaries of current methodologies, and to foster innovative solutions that leverage the strengths of both LLMs and KGs. We formulate the problem as follows. Given an entity from a KG that corresponds to a given textual question, the participating teams have to build a system that classifies whether the entity constitutes the correct answer to this question, or not. The distinctive feature of our task is that it does not only provide pairs of textual question and answer, but provides every pair with a graph representation of the shortest path in KG from entities in the query to the candidate entity generated by an LLM. This setup allows the participants to experiment with different strategies for text and graph information fusion.

The KGQA setup with textual passages anchored to relevant KG subgraphs has been addressed previously. Yasunaga et al. (2022) proposed to pretrain and fine-tune with joint intermodal text-graph interaction on arbitrary text passages linked to ConceptNet (Speer et al., 2017). In LC-QuaD dataset (Trivedi et al., 2017), questions are paired with SPARQL queries for the DBPedia (Lehmann et al., 2015) database. LC-QuaD 2.0 (Dubey et al., 2019) extends LC-QuaD to cover both DBPedia and Wikidata[3] with broader question type coverage.

[1] https://codalab.lisn.upsaclay.fr/competitions/18214

◇ Equal contribution

[2] https://sites.google.com/view/textgraphs2024

[3] https://www.wikidata.org

Proceedings of TextGraphs-17: Graph-based Methods for Natural Language Processing, pages 116–125
August 15, 2024 ©2024 Association for Computational Linguistics

While LC-QuaD's SPARQL queries are inferred from manually curated question-specific SPARQL templates, we stick to the algorithmic approach of Salnikov et al. (2023) to find relevant subgraphs as shortest path KG subgraphs. Thus, we present the first KGQA dataset with a graph construction procedure unified across all questions and Wikidata as reference KG. Previous approaches tried to combine LLMs and KGs by using linearized graphs for fine-tuning (Salnikov et al., 2023; Nikishina et al., 2023) or by fusing encoded representations from a pre-trained Transformer encoder and a graph neural network (Zhang et al., 2022).

The work, as described in this paper, has the following contribution:

- We released a novel dataset for the KGQA binary classification task: given a question, an answer candidate, and a KG subgraph, the goal is to identify whether the provided candidate is a correct answer for the given question using factual information from the graph.
- We organized the open-call shared task and built a public leaderboard to evaluate reasoning-over-graph approaches in a unified controllable set-up by providing questions paired with shortest question-answer paths retrieved from the Wikidata knowledge graph.

Unlike the existing datasets for end-to-end KGQA, our dataset eliminates the potential effect of erroneous entity retrieval, linking, and subgraph retrieval by focusing solely on the fusion phase for textual questions and provided KG subgraph. Thus, it encourages future research focused on cross-modal text and graph interaction.

2 TextGraphs 2024 KGQA Dataset

We constructed a novel dataset for KGQA that was inferred from Mintaka (Sen et al., 2022). Mintaka is a dataset for end-to-end knowledge graph question answering, where each question q is annotated with a set of Wikidata entities $\mathcal{E}_q$ mentioned in the question and ground truth answers A_q for q. Entities from $\mathcal{E}_q$ can serve as anchors for further KG subgraph retrieval and reasoning over the retrieved relevant entities. Although the Mintaka dataset contains the correct answers, we decided to focus on the reasoning part only in our shared task to offer a more controllable environment. In our case, a participating system has to choose the correct answer from a list of possible answer options and the corresponding KG subgraphs.

For our shared task, we followed the KG subgraph construction pipeline proposed by Salnikov et al. (2023). We find the shortest paths between $\mathcal{E}_q$ and the answer candidate entities A_q generated by a language model, such as T5 (Raffel et al., 2020), further linked to the Wikidata KG. The summary of our dataset is presented in Table 1.

Dataset Format. Each instance of the dataset in our shared task was a tuple $s = (q, \mathcal{E}_q, c, \mathcal{G}(\mathcal{E}_q, c), y)$ of the following elements:

- q: question text
- $\mathcal{E}_q$: set of Wikidata entities mentioned in q
- c: candidate answer for q. Unlike Mintaka, we ensure each candidate to be a valid Wikidata entity
- $\mathcal{G}(Q, C)$: a node- and edge-labeled oriented graph obtained as a union of shortest path graphs from each $e \in \mathcal{E}_q$ to candidate c
- y: a binary label describing whether c is a correct answer for q: $y = 1$ if $c \in A_q$ and $y = 0$ otherwise

Data Split. Our dataset was split into two parts:

- The **train set** set consists of 3,535 unique questions inferred solely from Mintaka. We make all ground truth question-candidate binary labels publicly available during the competition.
- The **test set** set covers 1,000 unique questions. 357 of the questions are absent in Mintaka and are manually created and labeled with ground truth answer entities from scratch. The test set consists of two subparts: (i) public and (ii) private with 700 and 300. The private part (300 unique questions) includes newly created questions exclusively.

2.1 Wikidata Knowledge Graph

Wikidata is a collaborative knowledge graph that contains nearly two billion facts, covering a diverse range of topics including geography, history, famous people, and events.[4] It serves as a centralized

[4]https://www.wikidata.org/wiki/Wikidata:Statistics

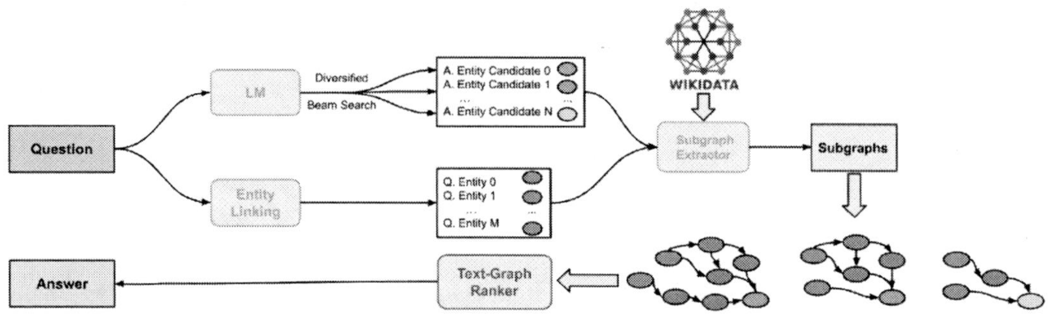

Figure 1: Overview of the pipeline for TextGraphs 2024 shared task workflow. We link entities mentioned in question and answer candidates generated by an LM to Wikidata KG. Then, we extract shortest path subgraphs between question and candidates. Question and candidate graph can be further passed to a ranking network to obtain a confidence score of a candidate being the correct answer to the given question.

repository for structured data and supports various Wikimedia projects and external applications. The data in Wikidata can be accessed through a public SPARQL endpoint.[5] However, due to the large volume of information, the endpoint is limited to shorter queries. Nevertheless, Wikidata is fully downloadable, allowing users to locate all the data on local servers and bypass public endpoint restrictions by using SPARQL query engines or graph databases such as iGraph, which we have used to manage our local Wikidata dump.

2.2 Answer Candidate Generation

To generate an initial set of answers, we use the T5-large language model (Raffel et al., 2020), which has been trained on the Mintaka training dataset (Sen et al., 2022). To increase the diversity of the generated responses, we employ Diverse Beam Search (Vijayakumar et al., 2016), a generalized framework for producing a list of varied sequences, which may be used instead of the traditional beam search approach.

Partition	# Questions	# Candidates
Train	3,535	36,762
Test (Total)	1,000	10,961
Public Test	700	7,694
Private Test	300	3,267

Table 1: Summary of the dataset used in the shared task.

2.3 Candidate Entity Linking

Entity linking with Wikidata involves identifying and linking entities to their corresponding entries in the Wikidata knowledge graph using generated strings. This process can be challenging due to the large number of entities in Wikidata, variations in their names, and the high ambiguity of entity mentions. To address these challenges, modern neural network-based approaches require extensive processing (Cao et al., 2022). For our shared task, we used the public Wikimedia APIs[6] that use search engines to retrieve entities based on their labels and aliases. By indexing Wikidata entities and their associated textual data in a search engine like Elasticsearch, which is used by the public Wikimedia API, we can efficiently retrieve candidate entities through queries based on their profiles generated from contextual mentions.

2.4 Answer Candidate Filtering

While our answer candidate generation and linking pipeline could produce an arbitrary number of negative samples, we aimed at mining a small subset of only the hardest ones. We assumed that a harder negative candidate entity should be semantically similar to the ground truth answer. For example, for a question "In Greek mythology, who stole fire from Olympian gods to give it to humanity?" with the correct answer "Prometheus" (Titan, culture hero, and trickster figure in Greek mythology), a more challenging negative sample would be "Hermes" (Olympian god in Greek religion and

[5] https://query.wikidata.org

[6] https://www.wikidata.org/w/api.php

mythology) rather than "Pythia" (priestess of the Temple of Apollo at Delphi). For a given question q and ground truth answers set A_q, we sampled a random true answer $a \in A_q$. Next, we ranked each negative candidate c with respect to the semantic similarity of its description $\mathrm{desc}(c)$ to the description $\mathrm{desc}(a)$ of a. As a similarity measure, we adopted the mutual implication score[7] (MIS), a RoBERTa$_{large}$-based (Liu et al., 2019) similarity metric designed for paraphrase detection (Babakov et al., 2022). For each question, we truncated its negative candidate count to 9 having the highest MIS score and removed questions with less than five negative candidates.

2.5 Subgraph Construction

We associated each question-answer pair with the corresponding induced subgraph from the Wikidata KG. This subgraph was generated by extracting the shortest paths between an entity derived from the question and a candidate answer entity, and then by identifying all distinct nodes along these paths. The extraction process also preserves all edges between these nodes, ensuring that relationships between the entities in the question and answer are maintained. The goal of this approach was to create a comprehensive representation of relevant information from the KG for each question-answer pair, accurately reflecting the connections between entities present in the original graph. Figure 2 shows simple examples of the obtained shortest path graphs.

3 Shared Task Description

Typically, an end-to-end KGQA pipeline includes multiple subtasks, such as named entity recognition and entity linking of entities mentioned in a question; construction of a KG subgraph for reasoning. It is challenging in multi-step KGQA pipelines to determine whether a prediction error comes from inaccurate entity retrieval and linking, or the model failed to perform reasoning over a fine-grained and informative graph. In our shared task, we used a simplified setup with fixed question-candidate subgraphs to enable more accessible evaluation of knowledge graph reasoning systems.

3.1 Baselines

As baselines, we adopted three supervised approaches built upon a BERT-based encoder (Devlin et al., 2019) and ChatGPT[8] model as a zero-shot LLM-based baseline. Additionally, we reported the quality for constant baseline. For non-LLM baselines, the task was formulated as a binary classification task: each question-candidate pair is labeled with either 1 or 0 independently of other candidates.

For three encoder-based supervised baselines, we adopt encoder-only MPNet[9] model (Song et al., 2020) as a base model and perform a 9:1 train/validation split. Each model is trained for five epochs with a batch size of 64 using Adam optimizer (Kingma and Ba, 2015) and cross-entropy loss. For prediction, we load each model's parameters from the best epoch in terms of validation F_1 score. The classification threshold of 0.5 remains constant for all three baselines.

Graph Linearization. For shortest path graphs representation, we adopt the graph linearization format from Salnikov et al. (2023) to represent each candidate graph as a textual string. We traverse graph edges starting from question entities $\mathcal{E}_q$ moving to candidate answer entities $\mathcal{E}_c$. Each labeled edge (h, r, t) of type r starting in h leading to t is linearized as "h, r, t". If either $h = c$ or $t = c$, they were additionally emphasized with BERT model's `[SEP]` tokens: e.g., "`[SEP]` h `[SEP]` r `[SEP]` t" if $h = c$. A linearized graph $\mathcal{L}(\mathcal{G}(\mathcal{E}_q, c))$ for question q and candidate c was obtained as a concatenation of all its linearized edges.

Text-Only Baseline. This baseline completely ignored the presence of question-candidate graphs and learned to classify textual question-candidate pairs. Specifically, we pass concatenated question and candidate string "q `[SEP]` c" to a binary classifier, where `[SEP]` was a special separator token of a BERT-based model.

Graph-Only Baseline. This baseline aimed to explore what quality a model would demonstrate seeing only linearized graph $\mathcal{L}(\mathcal{G}(\mathcal{E}_q, c))$ without even knowing what question q produced graph $\mathcal{G}(\mathcal{E}_q, c)$.

Text+Graph Baseline. As a simple joint text-and-graph reasoning baseline, we adopted a binary classifier over the concatenation of question and linearized candidate graph following (Salnikov et al., 2023): "q `[SEP]` $\mathcal{L}(\mathcal{G}(\mathcal{E}_q, c))$".

[7] `https://huggingface.co/s-nlp/Mutual_Implication_Score`

[8] `https://chat.openai.com`

[9] `https://huggingface.co/sentence-transformers/all-mpnet-base-v2`

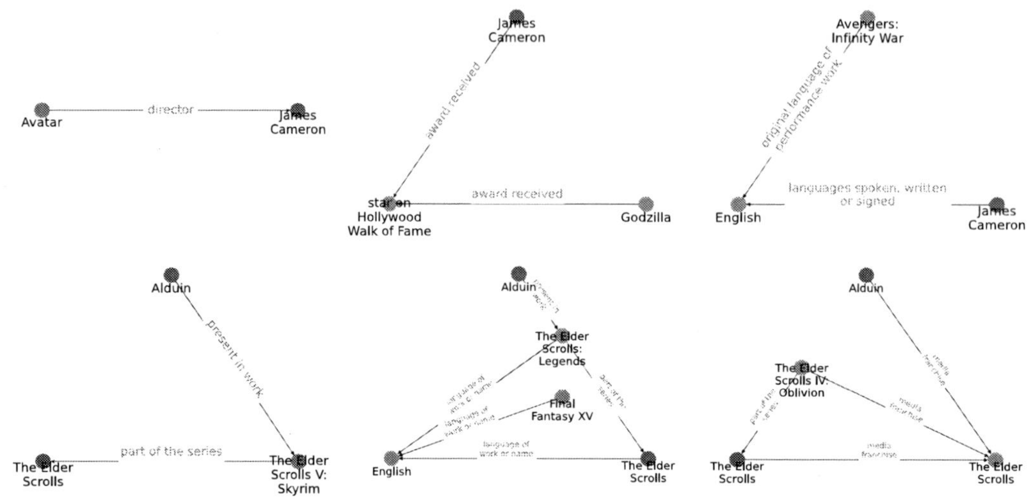

Figure 2: Question-candidate graph visualizations. **First row:** question "Which film directed by James Cameron became the highest-grossing movie of all time?" and three answer candidates: (i) Titanic (true answer), (ii) Godzilla, and (iii) Avengers: Infinity War. **Second row:** question "Which game is in The Elder Scrolls series and has Alduin as the main villain?" Entities mentioned in question (e.g., "James Cameron") are colored blue, intermediate nodes on the path from question entities to a candidate are colored grey. Correct and incorrect answer candidates are colored in green and red, respectively

ChatGPT Baseline. As an LLM baseline, we adopted ChatGPT version *gpt-4-0613*. To let the model differentiate between candidate answers with matching textual names but different underlying Wikidata entities, we modified ambiguous answer choices by adding the type of graph edge leading to the candidate node in the question-candidate graph. For instance, for the question "Which film directed by James Cameron became the highest-grossing movie of all time?" there are two candidate answers named "Titanic": (i) 1997 film by James Cameron and (ii) 1953 film by Jean Negulesco. The types of edges leading to these two candidate answers are "director" and "original language of performance work". Table 2 shows an example of the prompt.

Constant Baseline. This baseline assigned label 1 to all samples, i.e., marked all candidate answers as being correct.

3.2 Evaluation

Our shared task was deployed on the Codalab competition platform.[10] All submitted systems were evaluated on precision, recall, and F_1-score for positive class as well as classification accuracy. We performed the ranking of submitted systems based on F_1 score. Overall, the task consisted of three phases: development, evaluation, and post-evaluation.

Development Phase. This phase started with the release of the labeled train set on March 10, 2024. The participants were invited to get acquainted with the data format and to start their preliminary experiments. The phase can be considered closed with the release of the test set on March 25, 2024.

Evaluation Phase. On March 25, 2024, we released the test set with no ground truth labels provided. The set consisted of both public and private subsets, but the participants were not informed of what subset each test sample belongs to. At this stage, the participants were encouraged to submit test set prediction to the **public** leader board which provided evaluation results for the public test subset. By the end of the evaluation phase on May 6, 2024, participants were allowed to make their final submission to obtain evaluation scores on both **private** and **public** subsets. Private evaluation results were made publicly available after May 6, 2024.

Post-Evaluation Phase. After the end of Shared Task's official evaluation part on May 6, 2024, all participants can make submissions on the test data.

[10] https://codalab.lisn.upsaclay.fr/competitions/18214

Baseline	Input Examples
Text-Only	- Which film directed by James Cameron became the highest-grossing movie of all time? </s> Avatar - Which film directed by James Cameron became the highest-grossing movie of all time? </s> Titanic
Graph-Only	- </s> Titanic </s>, director, James Cameron - </s> Godzilla </s>, award received, star on Hollywood Walk of Fame James Cameron, award received, star on Hollywood Walk of Fame
Text+Graph	- Which film directed by James Cameron became the highest-grossing movie of all time? </s> </s> Titanic </s>, director, James Cameron - Which film directed by James Cameron became the highest-grossing movie of all time? </s> </s> Godzilla </s>, award received, star on Hollywood Walk of Fame James Cameron, award received, star on Hollywood Walk of Fame
ChatGPT	**Please answer the following question.** **provide one or more comma-separated option ids as an answer.** Which film directed by James Cameron became the highest-grossing movie of all time? 0. Avatar 1. Avengers: Infinity War 2. Godzilla 3. Home Alone 4. Home Alone: The Holiday Heist 5. Spectasia 6. Terminator 2: Judgment Day 7. Terminator II 8. The Terminator 9. Titanic (director) 10. Titanic (original language of performance work)

Table 2: Input examples for baseline models; </s> is a separator token of the MPNet encoder used for baselines.

These submissions have a separate leaderboard and are not considered for the official public evaluation summary.

4 Official Results

In total, we have received submissions from 30 teams, including both public and private leaderboards. After the end of the evaluation phase, we asked the participants to describe their systems.

4.1 Shared Task Submissions

Team NLPeople applied the Chain-of-Thought (CoT, Wei et al. (2022)) technique to decompose the target question into a series of sub-questions and attempted to use question-specific prompts based on question types (Moses et al., 2024). The final prediction is an ensemble of three LLM-based solutions: (1) Llama3-70B-Instruct[11] with CoT, (2) GPT-3.5 with CoT, and (3) Llama3-70b-instruct with Question-Specific prompts. In cases when the ensemble failed to make a prediction, a zero shot GPT-4's prediction was reported.

Team HW-TSC implemented an LLM prompt design based on self-ranking and emotional incentives (Tang et al., 2024). Self-ranking implied that the `gpt-4-1015-preview` base model is asked to score its answer choices with confidence levels. Emotional prompts were aimed at encouraging the model to carefully examine a question.

Team Skoltech adopted question-candidate graph sizes and Wikidata entity description as additional features to enhance the initial GPT-4 pre-

[11] `https://huggingface.co/meta-llama/Meta-Llama-3-70B-Instruct`

Team Name	Private Evaluation					Public Evaluation				
	Rank	P	R	F_1	Acc	Rank	P	R	F_1	Acc
NLPeople	1	**86.67**	85.14	**85.90**	**97.39**	1	**86.54**	85.45	**86.00**	**97.41**
HW-TSC	2	84.34	82.11	83.21	96.91	2	83.95	81.96	82.94	96.87
Skoltech	3	81.78	84.26	83.00	96.78	3	81.05	84.34	82.66	96.71
POSTECH	4	82.50	80.65	81.56	96.60	4	82.14	80.42	81.27	96.56
Baseline: ChatGPT	5	59.91	78.59	67.99	93.09	5	58.11	78.18	66.67	92.73
Team <blank>	6	60.54	72.73	66.07	93.03	6	58.20	71.47	64.16	92.58
BpHigh	7	55.99	75.86	64.43	92.18	—	—	—	—	—
tigformer	8	40.39	80.35	53.76	87.10	7	39.93	79.02	53.05	87.00
CUFE	9	51.92	55.52	53.66	91.05	—	—	—	—	—
Team_87	10	65.13	42.72	51.59	92.52	8	63.71	43.22	51.50	92.44
Iron Autobots	11	73.15	35.68	47.96	92.77	9	77.05	32.87	46.08	92.85
nlp_enjoyers	12	40.90	39.98	40.43	89.01	10	39.29	38.46	38.87	88.76
NLPunks	13	40.61	37.83	39.17	89.03	12	41.23	32.87	36.58	89.41
KseniiaPetrushina	14	34.90	44.18	39.00	87.10	11	33.96	40.28	36.85	87.17
Transformers-Spring24	15	29.19	44.48	35.24	84.75	16	28.56	40.70	33.56	85.03
Cordyceps	16	35.60	34.80	35.20	88.04	15	34.43	33.71	34.06	87.87
YAR	17	40.99	30.69	35.10	89.41	17	42.70	26.99	33.08	89.85
Transformers-Spring24	18	34.27	34.70	34.48	87.69	—	—	—	—	—
Fancy Transformers	19	39.31	30.01	34.04	89.14	19	38.64	27.83	32.36	89.19
xren	20	48.40	22.19	30.43	90.53	22	51.16	21.68	30.45	90.80
ThangDLU	21	18.56	67.55	29.12	69.31	20	22.29	58.04	32.21	77.29
adugeen	22	50.14	17.89	26.37	90.68	18	46.63	25.17	32.70	90.37
Baseline: Text+Graph	23	64.88	15.35	24.82	91.32	28	72.41	11.75	20.22	91.38
IRRRR	24	15.27	57.77	24.16	66.14	25	16.03	59.16	25.22	67.40
YAR	25	65.61	14.17	23.31	91.30	—	—	—	—	—
Baseline: Text-Only	26	15.04	38.32	21.60	74.04	27	14.57	38.88	21.20	73.13
mathamateur (–)	27	10.01	86.51	17.95	26.17	21	35.49	26.85	30.57	88.67
Baseline: Constant	28	9.33	**100.00**	17.07	09.33	29	9.29	**100.00**	17.01	9.2
Baseline: Graph-Only	29	62.16	6.74	12.17	90.91	30	66.67	06.99	12.66	91.03
hawkeoni	30	23.86	2.05	3.78	90.25	13	24.68	68.11	36.24	77.72
Hijli_JU_NLP	31	17.65	1.47	2.71	90.17	31	22.64	1.68	3.12	90.33
a063mg	—	—	—	—	—	14	42.71	28.67	34.31	89.80
russabiswas	—	—	—	—	—	23	28.47	29.23	28.85	86.60
__Team1()__	—	—	—	—	—	24	43.37	18.74	26.17	90.17
GrahamSquad	—	—	—	—	—	26	70.78	15.24	25.09	91.54

Table 3: Official evaluation results of the TextGraphs 2024 Shared Task for the public and private evaluation phases. **P**, **R**, $\mathbf{F_1}$, and **Acc** stand for positive class precision, recall, F_1-score, and accuracy, respectively. The best values for each metric are highlighted in **bold**. Official baselines are highlighted in cyan.

dictions (Lysyuk and Braslavski, 2024). They rephrased the given questions to further question rephrasing technique, we further strengthen their prediction.

Team <Blank> used `gpt-3.5-turbo` enhanced with CoT and XML tags prompting techniques.

Team tigformer implemented a late interaction for exchanging information between text and graph representations via an attention-pooling layer (Rakesh et al., 2024). They employed Graphformer (Ying et al., 2021) to encode question-candidate graphs and a T5 model (Raffel et al., 2020) to obtain textual representations.

Team nlp_enjoyers fine-tuned an MPNet encoder (Song et al., 2020) using LoRA (Hu et al., 2022). For a given question q and candidate c, they modified the input format for Text+Graph baseline as: "$\mathcal{E}_q$: q `[SEP]` $\mathcal{L}(\mathcal{G}(\mathcal{E}_q, c))$" and separated each edge in the linearized graph with a semicolon (Kurdiukov et al., 2024). They assumed only a single candidate for each question to be correct and reformulated the task from binary classification to

[11] `https://huggingface.co/sentence-transformers/all-mpnet-base-v2`

ranking: given a question, they select the most probable answer based on model scores for all candidate answers.

Team Fancy Transformers experimented with different graph characteristics including length, density, degree centrality, eigenvector centrality, closeness centrality and PageRank. They adopted the encoder-only all-MiniLM-L12-v2[12] and all-MiniLM-L6-v2[13] models for encoding textual information. They reported that the latter model achieved higher performance.

Team JellyBell applied Retrieval-Augmented Generation (RAG) (Lewis et al., 2020) approach to answering questions (Belikova et al., 2024). They retrieved relevant to question documents from internet by DuckDuckGo API[14] and generated answer by prompting LLM with fetched documnets.

5 Discussion

Table 3 presents the evaluation results for both public and private phases of the TextGraphs 2024 shared task on knowledge graph question answering. Three teams have managed to outperform a strong ChatGPT baseline with their LLM-based systems showing that large models are good at memorizing factual knowledge during pre-training.

Since one of the primary goals of our shared task was to evaluate the ability of LMs to reason over given KG subgraphs, we highlight the teams that submitted non-LLM solutions. **Team tigformer** has gained rank 8 of 31 with 53.76% F_1-score using two separate encoders for textual and graph information with late intermodal interaction. It is worth noting that while **Team nlp_enjoyers** only achieved the 12th place on the private leaderboard, they managed to surpass the initial Text+Graph baseline by 15.6% F_1-score with light-weighted modifications only. Their results indicate that while resource-demanding and computationally expensive LLM dominate the task in general, there might be some room for improving light-weighted task-specific solutions. **Team Fancy Transformers** has achieved 34.04% F_1-score using *all-MiniLM-L6-v2* encoder having 22.7M parameters only enhanced with classical non-neural graph features.

[12]https://huggingface.co/sentence-transformers/all-MiniLM-L12-v2

[13]https://huggingface.co/sentence-transformers/all-MiniLM-L6-v2

[14]https://duckduckgo.com

6 Conclusion

We presented an overview of the TextGraphs 2024 shared task on knowledge graph questions answering (KGQA) with pre-calculated shortest path graphs for Wikidata entities mentioned in the question and a candidate answer. Analysis of the results has revealed that large language models (LLMs) currently show superior performance even in a very simplified binary classification task formulation when a model is asked to find the right answer among the pre-defined set of answer candidates. While LLMs are extremely resource-demanding, the exploration of effective light-weighted systems for question-oriented graph representation and reasoning still remains a challenge

We hope that our competition will encourage further research on developing effective reasoning methods over retrieved KG subgraphs, exploring novel subgraph representation techniques, and improving the interpretability and explainability of the resulting question answering models.

Acknowledgements

Participants affiliated with Universität Hamburg extend their gratitude to NFDI4DS (National Research Data Infrastructure for Data Science) for their gracious support and endorsement of this shared task. We acknowledge the computational resources of HPC facilities at the HSE University. We would like to thank all the participating teams who contributed to the success of the shared task through their interesting approaches and experiments.

References

Nikolay Babakov, David Dale, Varvara Logacheva, and Alexander Panchenko. 2022. A large-scale computational study of content preservation measures for text style transfer and paraphrase generation. In *Proceedings of the 60th Annual Meeting of the Association for Computational Linguistics: Student Research Workshop*, pages 300–321, Dublin, Ireland. Association for Computational Linguistics.

Julia Belikova, Evegeniy Beliakin, and Vasily Konovalov. 2024. Jellybell at textgraphs-17 shared task: Fusing large language models with external knowledge for enhanced question answering. In *Proceedings of the TextGraphs-17: Graph-based Methods for Natural Language Processing*, Bangkok, Thailand. Association for Computational Linguistics.

Nicola De Cao, Ledell Wu, Kashyap Popat, Mikel Artetxe, Naman Goyal, Mikhail Plekhanov, Luke

Zettlemoyer, Nicola Cancedda, Sebastian Riedel, and Fabio Petroni. 2022. Multilingual autoregressive entity linking. *Trans. Assoc. Comput. Linguistics*, 10:274–290.

Jacob Devlin, Ming-Wei Chang, Kenton Lee, and Kristina Toutanova. 2019. BERT: Pre-training of deep bidirectional transformers for language understanding. In *Proceedings of the 2019 Conference of the North American Chapter of the Association for Computational Linguistics: Human Language Technologies, Volume 1 (Long and Short Papers)*, pages 4171–4186, Minneapolis, Minnesota. Association for Computational Linguistics.

Mohnish Dubey, Debayan Banerjee, Abdelrahman Abdelkawi, and Jens Lehmann. 2019. Lc-quad 2.0: A large dataset for complex question answering over wikidata and dbpedia. In *The Semantic Web - ISWC 2019 - 18th International Semantic Web Conference, Auckland, New Zealand, October 26-30, 2019, Proceedings, Part II*, volume 11779 of *Lecture Notes in Computer Science*, pages 69–78. Springer.

Edward J. Hu, Yelong Shen, Phillip Wallis, Zeyuan Allen-Zhu, Yuanzhi Li, Shean Wang, Lu Wang, and Weizhu Chen. 2022. Lora: Low-rank adaptation of large language models. In *The Tenth International Conference on Learning Representations, ICLR 2022, Virtual Event, April 25-29, 2022*. OpenReview.net.

Diederik P. Kingma and Jimmy Ba. 2015. Adam: A method for stochastic optimization. In *3rd International Conference on Learning Representations, ICLR 2015, San Diego, CA, USA, May 7-9, 2015, Conference Track Proceedings*.

Nikita Kurdiukov, Pavel Tikhomirov, Viktoriia Zinkovich, and Sergey Karpukhin. 2024. nlp_enjoyers at textgraphs-17 shared task: Text-graph representations for knowledge graph question answering using all-mpnet. In *Proceedings of the TextGraphs-17: Graph-based Methods for Natural Language Processing*, Bangkok, Thailand. Association for Computational Linguistics.

Jens Lehmann, Robert Isele, Max Jakob, Anja Jentzsch, Dimitris Kontokostas, Pablo N. Mendes, Sebastian Hellmann, Mohamed Morsey, Patrick van Kleef, Sören Auer, and Christian Bizer. 2015. Dbpedia - A large-scale, multilingual knowledge base extracted from wikipedia. *Semantic Web*, 6(2):167–195.

Patrick S. H. Lewis, Ethan Perez, Aleksandra Piktus, Fabio Petroni, Vladimir Karpukhin, Naman Goyal, Heinrich Küttler, Mike Lewis, Wen-tau Yih, Tim Rocktäschel, Sebastian Riedel, and Douwe Kiela. 2020. Retrieval-augmented generation for knowledge-intensive NLP tasks. In *Advances in Neural Information Processing Systems 33: Annual Conference on Neural Information Processing Systems 2020, NeurIPS 2020, December 6-12, 2020, virtual*.

Yinhan Liu, Myle Ott, Naman Goyal, Jingfei Du, Mandar Joshi, Danqi Chen, Omer Levy, Mike Lewis, Luke Zettlemoyer, and Veselin Stoyanov. 2019. Roberta: A robustly optimized BERT pretraining approach. *CoRR*, abs/1907.11692.

Maria Lysyuk and Pavel Braslavski. 2024. Skoltech at textgraphs-17 shared task: Finding gpt-4 prompting strategies for multiple choice questions. In *Proceedings of the TextGraphs-17: Graph-based Methods for Natural Language Processing*, Bangkok, Thailand. Association for Computational Linguistics.

Movina Moses, Vishnudev Kuruvanthodi, Mohab Elkaref, Shinnosuke Tanaka, James Barry, Geeth De Mel, and Campbell D Watson. 2024. Nlpeople at textgraphs-17 shared task: Chain of thought questioning to elicit decompositional reasoning. In *Proceedings of the TextGraphs-17: Graph-based Methods for Natural Language Processing*, Bangkok, Thailand. Association for Computational Linguistics.

Irina Nikishina, Polina Chernomorchenko, Anastasiia Demidova, Alexander Panchenko, and Chris Biemann. 2023. Predicting terms in IS-a relations with pre-trained transformers. In *Findings of the Association for Computational Linguistics: IJCNLP-AACL 2023 (Findings)*, pages 134–148, Nusa Dua, Bali. Association for Computational Linguistics.

Colin Raffel, Noam Shazeer, Adam Roberts, Katherine Lee, Sharan Narang, Michael Matena, Yanqi Zhou, Wei Li, and Peter J. Liu. 2020. Exploring the limits of transfer learning with a unified text-to-text transformer. *J. Mach. Learn. Res.*, 21:140:1–140:67.

Mayank Rakesh, Parikshit Saikia, and Saket Kumar Shrivastava. 2024. Tigformer at textgraphs-17 shared task: A late interaction method for text and graph representations in kbqa classification task. In *Proceedings of the TextGraphs-17: Graph-based Methods for Natural Language Processing*, Bangkok, Thailand. Association for Computational Linguistics.

Mikhail Salnikov, Hai Le, Prateek Rajput, Irina Nikishina, Pavel Braslavski, Valentin Malykh, and Alexander Panchenko. 2023. Large language models meet knowledge graphs to answer factoid questions. In *Proceedings of the 37th Pacific Asia Conference on Language, Information and Computation*, pages 635–644, Hong Kong, China. Association for Computational Linguistics.

Priyanka Sen, Alham Fikri Aji, and Amir Saffari. 2022. Mintaka: A complex, natural, and multilingual dataset for end-to-end question answering. In *Proceedings of the 29th International Conference on Computational Linguistics*, pages 1604–1619, Gyeongju, Republic of Korea. International Committee on Computational Linguistics.

Kaitao Song, Xu Tan, Tao Qin, Jianfeng Lu, and Tie-Yan Liu. 2020. Mpnet: Masked and permuted pre-training for language understanding. In *Advances in Neural Information Processing Systems 33: Annual Conference on Neural Information Processing Systems 2020, NeurIPS 2020, December 6-12, 2020, virtual*.

Robyn Speer, Joshua Chin, and Catherine Havasi. 2017. Conceptnet 5.5: An open multilingual graph of general knowledge. In *Proceedings of the Thirty-First AAAI Conference on Artificial Intelligence, February 4-9, 2017, San Francisco, California, USA*, pages 4444–4451. AAAI Press.

Wei Tang, Xiaosong Qiao, Xiaofeng Zhao, Min Zhang, Chang Su, Yuang Li, Yinglu Li, Yilun Liu, Feiyu Yao, Shimin Tao, Hao Yang, and He Xianghui. 2024. Hw-tsc at textgraphs-17 shared task: Enhancing inference capabilities of llms with knowledge graphs. In *Proceedings of the TextGraphs-17: Graph-based Methods for Natural Language Processing*, Bangkok, Thailand. Association for Computational Linguistics.

Priyansh Trivedi, Gaurav Maheshwari, Mohnish Dubey, and Jens Lehmann. 2017. Lc-quad: A corpus for complex question answering over knowledge graphs. In *The Semantic Web - ISWC 2017 - 16th International Semantic Web Conference, Vienna, Austria, October 21-25, 2017, Proceedings, Part II*, volume 10588 of *Lecture Notes in Computer Science*, pages 210–218. Springer.

Ashwin K. Vijayakumar, Michael Cogswell, Ramprasaath R. Selvaraju, Qing Sun, Stefan Lee, David J. Crandall, and Dhruv Batra. 2016. Diverse beam search: Decoding diverse solutions from neural sequence models. *CoRR*, abs/1610.02424.

Jason Wei, Xuezhi Wang, Dale Schuurmans, Maarten Bosma, Brian Ichter, Fei Xia, Ed H. Chi, Quoc V. Le, and Denny Zhou. 2022. Chain-of-thought prompting elicits reasoning in large language models. In *Advances in Neural Information Processing Systems 35: Annual Conference on Neural Information Processing Systems 2022, NeurIPS 2022, New Orleans, LA, USA, November 28 - December 9, 2022*.

Michihiro Yasunaga, Antoine Bosselut, Hongyu Ren, Xikun Zhang, Christopher D. Manning, Percy Liang, and Jure Leskovec. 2022. Deep bidirectional language-knowledge graph pretraining. In *Advances in Neural Information Processing Systems 35: Annual Conference on Neural Information Processing Systems 2022, NeurIPS 2022, New Orleans, LA, USA, November 28 - December 9, 2022*.

Chengxuan Ying, Tianle Cai, Shengjie Luo, Shuxin Zheng, Guolin Ke, Di He, Yanming Shen, and Tie-Yan Liu. 2021. Do transformers really perform badly for graph representation? In *Advances in Neural Information Processing Systems 34: Annual Conference on Neural Information Processing Systems 2021, NeurIPS 2021, December 6-14, 2021, virtual*, pages 28877–28888.

Xikun Zhang, Antoine Bosselut, Michihiro Yasunaga, Hongyu Ren, Percy Liang, Christopher D. Manning, and Jure Leskovec. 2022. Greaselm: Graph reasoning enhanced language models. In *The Tenth International Conference on Learning Representations, ICLR 2022, Virtual Event, April 25-29, 2022*. OpenReview.net.

nlp_enjoyers at TextGraphs-17 Shared Task: Text-Graph Representations for Knowledge Graph Question Answering using all-MPNet

Nikita Kurdiukov*, **Viktoriia Zinkovich***, **Sergey Karpukhin*** and **Pavel Tikhomirov**
The Skolkovo Institute of Science and Technology, Moscow, Russia
{nikita.kurdiukov, viktoriia.zinkovich, sergey.karpukhin, pavel.tikhomirov}@skoltech.ru

Abstract

This paper presents a model for solving the Multiple Choice Question Answering (MCQA) problem, focusing on the impact of subgraph extraction from a Knowledge Graph on model performance. The proposed method combines textual and graph information by adding linearized subgraphs directly into the main question prompt with separate tokens, enhancing the performance of models working with each modality separately. The study also includes an examination of Large Language Model (LLM) backbones and the benefits of linearized subgraphs and sequence length, with efficient training achieved through fine-tuning with LoRA. The top benchmark, using subgraphs and MPNet, achieved an F1 score of 0.3887. The main limitation of the experiments is the reliance on pre-generated subgraphs/triplets from the graph, and the lack of exploration of in-context learning and prompting strategies with decoder-based architectures.

1 Introduction

With the exponential growth of digital information, developing tools for prompt and efficient data retrieval has become a top priority in Natural Language Processing (NLP). Many state-of-the-art approaches have been proposed to solve such problems, especially encoder-only models, including BERT (Devlin et al., 2019) and its variants, such as RoBERTa (Liu et al., 2019) and ALBERT (Lan et al., 2020), which show good performance in retrieval tasks.

However, one important area of research focuses on solving Multiple Choice Question Answering problems (MCQA), where the model needs to select one correct answer among several options autonomously, without external context (Huang et al., 2022; Sakhovskiy et al., 2024). This task remains quite challenging in NLP, as in order to answer a quiz question, the developed model should not only have a large knowledge base (Talmor et al., 2019), but also be able to make logical inferences (Li et al., 2022).

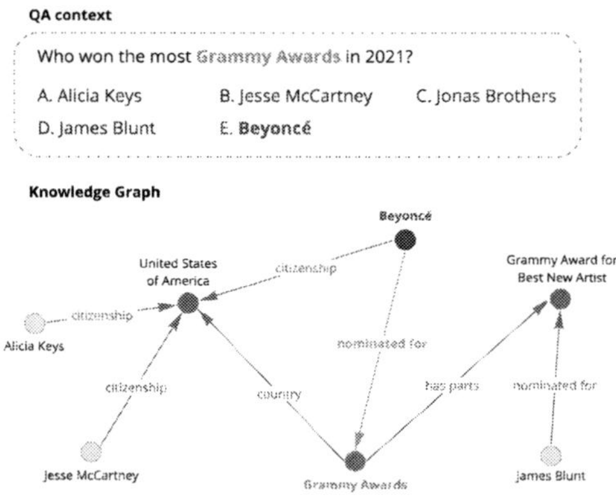

Figure 1: Example of a knowledge graph instance for a sample in a text dataset: the graph incorporates information about relations between the concept in question ("Grammy Awards") and candidate answer concepts

To solve such tasks, different LLMs can be applied, e.g., T5 (Raffel et al., 2020) and BART (Lewis et al., 2020), which are encoder-decoder models for natural language generation (NLG). However, even such SOTA models can generally fall short on MCQA. One common reason is that models try to predict the most likely answer in terms of grammatical construction without considering the logical coherence of the text (Robinson et al., 2023).

To enhance the performance of LLMs, in the following work, we incorporate structured knowledge graphs into the model training process (Fig.1), as this method has been noted many times in earlier works (Salnikov et al., 2023). The graph is obtained by taking the shortest paths from all mentioned concepts in the corresponding questions to a candidate answer entity in the knowledge graph of Wikidata.

* Equal contribution

Proceedings of TextGraphs-17: Graph-based Methods for Natural Language Processing, pages 126–130
August 15, 2024

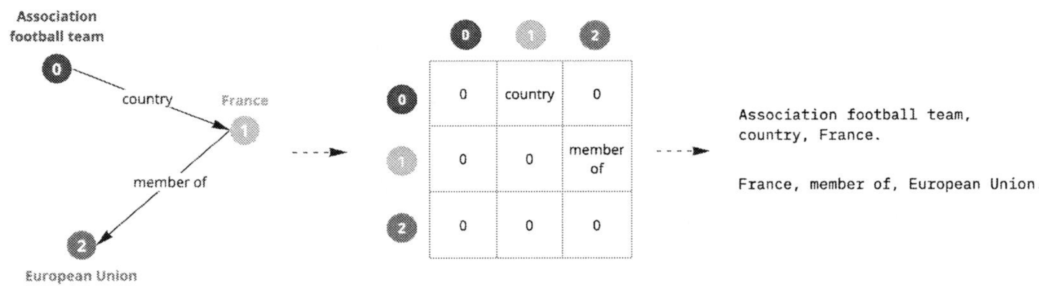

Figure 2: Example of the process of a subgraph linearization into text

Thus, the **main contributions of the following work** are as follows:

- We propose a method of combining textual and graph information. Adding linearized subgraphs directly into the main question prompt with additional separate tokens allows for improved performance of models working with each modality separately.
- We conducted a thorough study of LLM backbones and performed a wide hyper-parameter search. For efficient training, we applied fine-tuning with LoRA.

2 Method

We propose implementing the MPNet (Song et al., 2020) model and training it on question-answer pairs with incorporated linearized knowledge graphs. Additionally, we utilize the LoRA implementation from the `peft` library and apply an oversampling technique to address imbalance in the training dataset.

Our approach ultimately relies on tuning of LLM for binary classification task while also including information from the Wikidata graph domain in the LLM pipeline. The representations for target prediction on the question-answer pair are acquired by accessing the last hidden layer representation of the `[CLS]` token of the model.

Given the nature of the task, it is obvious that only one of the candidate answers is correct; however the number of candidate answers for a single question is not known beforehand. During inference, we utilize the knowledge that only one candidate answer is correct and select the most probable answer based on model scores. This naturally allows the use of a model trained for a classification target to rank the top-1 candidate answer.

2.1 Dataset

For our research, we utilized the TextGraphs17-shared-task dataset, which consists of 37,672 question-answer pairs annotated with Wikidata entities. This dataset includes 10 different types of data, notably entities from Wikidata mentioned in both the answer and the corresponding question, as well as a shortest-path graph for each <`question`, `candidate` answer> pair.

2.2 Evaluation metrics

During training and evaluation of our models, we use the same metrics as those present in the workshop leaderboard, which include **accuracy, precision, recall** and **F1-score**. It is important to note that accuracy is quite uninformative here due to the dataset's imbalance, with incorrect answers constituting 90% of the data.

2.3 Input preprocessing

Since the subgraphs from the knowledge graph are already provided, we only need to preprocess them for the model. To incorporate information from the subgraphs, they are linearized into text according to Salnikov et al. (2023). The process is nearly identical, except that distinct triplets are separated with a semicolon. Specifically, subgraphs are converted to a binary adjacency matrix. If nodes indexed i and j are connected, their edge label is stored in the corresponding [i, j] matrix element. The matrix is then unraveled row by row to generate linearized sentences from corresponding triples (`node_from`, edge, `node_to`) in the adjacency matrix (Fig.2).

The resulting input text for the model has the following form: `Question entities + ' : ' + Question + ' [SEP] ' + Linearized graph`. Details of various backbones, processing pipelines and scores are reported in Sections 3 and 4.

3 Experiments

All fine-tuning experiments were conducted using the LoRA implementation from the `peft` library (Hu et al., 2021). The default LoRA parameters are as follows: a LoRA rank of 16, a LoRA alpha of 32, and a LoRA dropout of 0.1. The target modules of LoRA are the query and value weight matrices.

Our default model training is conducted for 50 epochs with best checkpoint saving, Binary Cross-entropy loss, a batch size of 64, a sequence length of 256, the AdamW optimizer, a learning rate of $3 \cdot 10^{-4}$, and a default weight decay of 10^{-2}. Additionally, we apply oversampling during training by using a weighted sampler with probabilities inversely proportional to the labels in dataset.

We split the data into training and validation subsets by grouping samples with distinct questions in an 80:20 proportions, respectively.

3.1 MiniLM experiments

The MiniLM employed is `all-MiniLM`[1], a fine-tuned and diminished version of `MiniLM` by Wang et al. (2020). The training procedure is default.

3.2 T5 experiments

We fine-tuned `T5-Small`[2] by Chepurova et al. (2023), which was trained on tail and entity prediction in a knowledge graph using the graph's context represented by the node's neighborhood. The result on the public test is presented in Table 1.

The classifier head utilizes the last hidden representation of the `[EOS]` token due to the encoder-decoder architecture. The model was fine-tuned for 30 epochs with the Adafactor optimizer, a learning rate of $8 \cdot 10^{-5}$, and a batch size of 32. LoRA alpha was set to 64 for this model.

The input format for this model was adjusted to match the original format the model was trained on. The resulting input format: `'predict [SEP] ' + Question + '[SEP]' + Linearized graph + '[SEP]' + Answer Entity`

3.3 MPNet experiments

Another BERT-like model we used is `all-MPNet-base`[3]. The model was trained for 20 epochs with a batch size of 32, a sequence length of 200, the Adam optimizer, and a learning rate of $1 \cdot 10^{-4}$.

[1]https://huggingface.co/sentence-transformers/all-MiniLM-L6-v2

[2]https://huggingface.co/DeepPavlov/t5-wikidata5M-with-neighbors

[3]https://huggingface.co/sentence-transformers/all-mpnet-base-v2

4 Additional Experiments

4.1 Ablation study of sequence length and linearized graph usage

The impact of sequence length and linearized graph usage on performance was examined using the all-MiniLM model, see Table 2. We report the F1 score on the public test subset achieved by our best model checkpoints.

SL	Linearized Graph	F1 Score
256	No	0.2276
256	Yes	0.3279
512	**Yes**	**0.3463**

Table 2: Ablation of the Sequence Length (SL) and usage of linearized graph on all-MiniLM performance. Public test scores achieved by best model checkpoints.

4.2 Usage of different backbones

Additionally, we experimented with Phrase-BERT. In brief, this model was pretrained with a contrastive objective to predict similarity between texts separated by the `[SEP]` token hidden state. In our pipeline, we attempted to predict the correct answer from the candidates as the 'closest' to the question. We fine-tuned this model with LoRA parametrization, as described in Section 3, structuring the input as `Question entities + ' ' + Question + ' [SEP] + Answer entities`. Information from the graph was not used during experiments with this model. In our experiments this approach didn't provide significant quality improvements.

5 Conclusion

The encoder transformer architecture showed the best results in text comprehension tasks. The size of the model once again proved to have a positive influence on its performance, with the MPNet architecture outperforming MiniLM.

Despite the popularity of the T5 model for answer candidates generation, it underperformed in our experiments. Perhaps it is worth utilizing only the encoder part of the model or using a different training procedure.

Another valuable aspect that was confirmed is the benefit of incorporating graph knowledge into the model. The linearized graph indeed provided the model with valuable information, improving

Model	F1 Score
T5-Small-wikidata5M (Chepurova et al., 2023)	0.3180
all-MiniLM	0.3463
all-MPNet	**0.3887**

Table 1: Public test F1 scores. Best checkpoints' scores are reported.

its ability to answer questions. More advanced subgraph/triplet sampling or generation strategies could further improve the model's performance, making this a promising direction for future research.

Limitations

The biggest constraint of our experiments is the reliance on pre-existing subgraphs or triplets derived from the graph. There remains a wide array of potential experiments to be conducted in this area.

Furthermore, we have not investigated the application of in-context learning and prompting techniques with decoder architectures, which could be of even more significant interest due to their current popularity and proven effectiveness.

Acknowledgements

The authors gratefully acknowledge Professor Alexander Panchenko of Skoltech for his guidance during the "Deep Learning for Natural Language Processing" course, during which this work was conducted.

References

Alla Chepurova, Aydar Bulatov, Yuri Kuratov, and Mikhail Burtsev. 2023. Better together: Enhancing generative knowledge graph completion with language models and neighborhood information. In *Findings of the Association for Computational Linguistics: EMNLP 2023*, pages 5306–5316, Singapore. Association for Computational Linguistics.

Jacob Devlin, Ming-Wei Chang, Kenton Lee, and Kristina Toutanova. 2019. BERT: Pre-training of deep bidirectional transformers for language understanding. In *Proceedings of the 2019 Conference of the North American Chapter of the Association for Computational Linguistics: Human Language Technologies, Volume 1 (Long and Short Papers)*, pages 4171–4186, Minneapolis, Minnesota. Association for Computational Linguistics.

Edward J. Hu, Yelong Shen, Phillip Wallis, Zeyuan Allen-Zhu, Yuanzhi Li, Shean Wang, Lu Wang, and Weizhu Chen. 2021. Lora: Low-rank adaptation of large language models.

Zixian Huang, Ao Wu, Jiaying Zhou, Yu Gu, Yue Zhao, and Gong Cheng. 2022. Clues before answers: Generation-enhanced multiple-choice qa.

Zhenzhong Lan, Mingda Chen, Sebastian Goodman, Kevin Gimpel, Piyush Sharma, and Radu Soricut. 2020. Albert: A lite bert for self-supervised learning of language representations. In *International Conference on Learning Representations*.

Mike Lewis, Yinhan Liu, Naman Goyal, Marjan Ghazvininejad, Abdelrahman Mohamed, Omer Levy, Veselin Stoyanov, and Luke Zettlemoyer. 2020. BART: Denoising sequence-to-sequence pre-training for natural language generation, translation, and comprehension. In *Proceedings of the 58th Annual Meeting of the Association for Computational Linguistics*, pages 7871–7880, Online. Association for Computational Linguistics.

Xiao Li, Gong Cheng, Ziheng Chen, Yawei Sun, and Yuzhong Qu. 2022. Adalogn: Adaptive logic graph network for reasoning-based machine reading comprehension.

Yinhan Liu, Myle Ott, Naman Goyal, Jingfei Du, Mandar Joshi, Danqi Chen, Omer Levy, Mike Lewis, Luke Zettlemoyer, and Veselin Stoyanov. 2019. Roberta: A robustly optimized bert pretraining approach.

Colin Raffel, Noam Shazeer, Adam Roberts, Katherine Lee, Sharan Narang, Michael Matena, Yanqi Zhou, Wei Li, and Peter J. Liu. 2020. Exploring the limits of transfer learning with a unified text-to-text transformer. *Journal of Machine Learning Research*, 21(140):1–67.

Joshua Robinson, Christopher Michael Rytting, and David Wingate. 2023. Leveraging large language models for multiple choice question answering.

Andrey Sakhovskiy, Mikhail Salnikov, Irina Nikishina, Aida Usmanova, Angelie Kraft, Cedric Möller, Debayan Banerjee, Junbo Huang, Longquan Jiang, Rana Abdullah, Xi Yan, Elena Tutubalina, Ricardo Usbeck, and Alexander Panchenko. 2024. TextGraphs 2024 shared task on text-graph representations for knowledge graph question answering. In *Proceedings of the Seventeen Workshop on Graph-Based Methods for Natural Language Processing (TextGraphs-17)*, Bangkok, Thailand. Association for Computational Linguistics.

Mikhail Salnikov, Hai Le, Prateek Rajput, Irina Nikishina, Pavel Braslavski, Valentin Malykh, and

Alexander Panchenko. 2023. Large language models meet knowledge graphs to answer factoid questions.

Kaitao Song, Xu Tan, Tao Qin, Jianfeng Lu, and Tie-Yan Liu. 2020. Mpnet: Masked and permuted pre-training for language understanding.

Alon Talmor, Jonathan Herzig, Nicholas Lourie, and Jonathan Berant. 2019. CommonsenseQA: A question answering challenge targeting commonsense knowledge. In *Proceedings of the 2019 Conference of the North American Chapter of the Association for Computational Linguistics: Human Language Technologies, Volume 1 (Long and Short Papers)*, pages 4149–4158, Minneapolis, Minnesota. Association for Computational Linguistics.

Wenhui Wang, Furu Wei, Li Dong, Hangbo Bao, Nan Yang, and Ming Zhou. 2020. Minilm: Deep self-attention distillation for task-agnostic compression of pre-trained transformers.

HW-TSC at TextGraphs-17 Shared Task: Enhancing Inference Capabilities of LLMs with Knowledge Graphs

Wei Tang, Xiaosong Qiao, Xiaofeng Zhao, Min Zhang, Chang Su,
Yuang Li, Yinglu Li, Yilun Liu, Feiyu Yao, Shimin Tao, Hao Yang, Xianghui He
Huawei Translation Services Center, Beijing, China
{tangwei133, qiaoxiaosong, zhaoxiaofeng14, zhangmin186, suchang8, liyuang3
liyinglu, liuyilun3, yaofeiyu1, taoshimin, yanghao30, hexianghui}@huawei.com

Abstract

In this paper, we present an effective method for TextGraphs-17 Shared Task. This task requires selecting an entity from the candidate entities that is relevant to the given question and answer. The selection process is aided by utilizing the shortest path graph in the knowledge graph, connecting entities in the query to the candidate entity. This task aims to explore how to enhance LLMs output with KGs, although current LLMs have certain logical reasoning capabilities, they may not be certain about their own outputs, and the answers they produce may be correct by chance through incorrect paths. In this case, we have introduced a LLM prompt design strategy based on self-ranking and emotion. Specifically, we let the large model score its own answer choices to reflect its confidence in the answer. Additionally, we add emotional incentives to the prompts to encourage the model to carefully examine the questions. Our submissions was conducted under zero-resource setting, and we achieved the second place in the task with an F1-score of 0.8321.

1 Introduction

In 2023, the widespread adoption of ChatGPT and the introduction of GPT-4 (OpenAI, 2023) marked a significant milestone in artificial intelligence (AI). GPT-4 achieved remarkable progress in the MMLU benchmark test (Hendrycks et al., 2021), demonstrating exceptional performance on various question answering (QA) and natural language inference (NLI) datasets. This breakthrough led to the emergence of large-scale language models (LLMs) like LLaMa-2 (Touvron et al., 2023), Falcon (Almazrouei et al., 2023), Gemini (Anil et al., 2023), Baichuan-2 (Yang et al., 2023), ChatGLM (Du et al., 2022), and others.

Despite the success of existing LLMs, even advanced LLMs struggle to accurately answer factual questions without a knowledge graph (KG). The answers often involve fictional or hypothetical statements or brief/trivial information. While language models can provide answers (Sen et al., 2022; Dubey et al., 2019), their quality may not meet desired standards. Addressing this challenge relies on structured knowledge sources like DBPedia (Auer et al., 2007), Wikidata (Vrandečić and Krötzsch, 2014), or NELL (Mitchell et al., 2018). This paper aims to explore and bridge this research gap.

2 Task Description

The objective of the shared task[1] (Sakhovskiy et al., 2024) is a Knowledge-based Question Answering (KBQA) problem, which aims to address the challenge of selecting the most appropriate knowledge graph (KG) entity, given a textual question and a set of candidate entities. Notably, this task incorporates a unique feature whereby each question-answer (Q-A) pair is accompanied by a graph representation consisting of shortest paths in the KG, connecting the entities mentioned in the query to the LLM-generated candidate entity, including the intermediate nodes. This provision enables participants to systematically explore and evaluate diverse text-graph fusion strategies for enhancing the performance of language model outputs in a controlled manner.

The primary goal of this task is to investigate methods for augmenting the capabilities of language models (LLMs) through the integration of KGs. To facilitate comprehensive experimentation, participants are provided with a pre-extracted graph, as there exist multiple approaches for extracting and fragmenting the text-graph modality fusion experiments. Specifically, participants are presented with the following resources:

- **Text1**: A query accompanied by a list of men-

[1]The related data for the task is publicly available at https://github.com/uhh-lt/TextGraphs17-shared-task/

Proceedings of TextGraphs-17: Graph-based Methods for Natural Language Processing, pages 131–136
August 15, 2024 ©2024 Association for Computational Linguistics

Query: Who was formerly an actor and now a Republican senator?		
Entitie Candidates	**Sub-graphs**	**Answer**
Arnold Schwarzenegger	<Arnold Schwarzenegger, member of political party, Republican Party>, <Arnold Schwarzenegger, occupation, actor>	True
Bob Dole	<United States, described by source, Small Brockhaus and Efron Encyclopedic Dictionary>, <United States, country, United States>, <Republican Party, country, United States> <actor, described by source, Small Brockhaus and Efron Encyclopedic Dictionary>, <Bob Dole, country of citizenship, United States>, <Bob Dole, member of political party, Republican Party>	**False**
John McCain	<television presenter, subclass of, actor> , <John McCain, occupation, television presenter> <John McCain, member of political party, Republican Party>	**False**
...	...	...

Figure 1: An example of data: query, answer candidates, and respective sub-graphs. Answers are provided in the training set, but not in the testing set.

tioned Wikidata entities.

- **Text2**: 5-10 answer candidates presented as Wikidata entities.
- **Graph**: A Wikidata sub-graph comprising the shortest paths connecting the entities in the question to the candidate entities.

Among the provided candidates, one is the correct answer, while the others are incorrect. The task entails identifying the correct answer, thus entailing a binary classification objective. Furthermore, for the same query, there may be multiple entities with the same name among the provided candidate entities, while they represent different entities. Therefore, it is not feasible to solely rely on the entity names to determine the correctness of the answer. This necessitates the model to rely on the knowledge subgraph to make judgments about the correctness of the answer. A concrete data example is given in Figure 1. The evaluation metric employed for this task is the F1 score, given that the task involves binary classification.

3 Method

In this section, we will provide a detailed explanation of the proposed LLM prompt design strategy, which is based on self-rank and emotion. Additionally, we will outline the process of summarizing the outputs of LLM and generating the final submission result. Additionally, the competition task is a binary classification problem, and we employ a trick to transform it into a single-choice question, thereby avoiding the issue of the model selecting multiple correct answers for the same query. The whole process can be found in Figure 2.

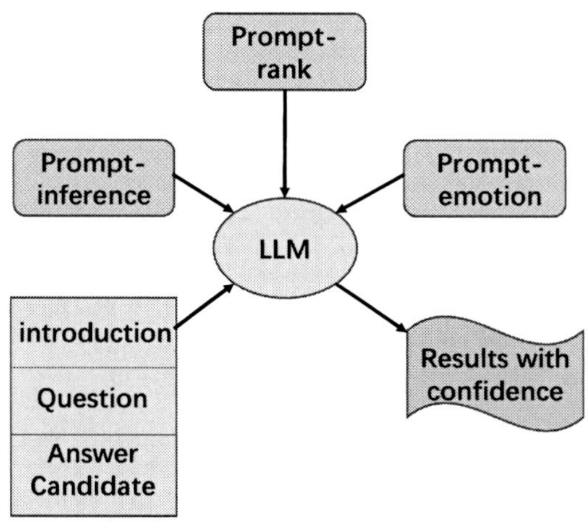

Figure 2: The whole process of our method, where yellow part denotes basic inputs, green parts denote various prompts and pink part denotes the output results.

3.1 Basic prompt-inference

Our basic prompt for inference took the following form: *"I have a new NLP reasoning task. As a smart assistant, you can help me decide which answer is correct. I will provide a question, a few answers and a few reasoning paths associated with the answers. Only one of these answers is correct. Please determine which answer is correct based on the corresponding reasoning path. Even if you believe there is no correct answer, please still choose the answer option that you think is the most*

Error types	Example	Solution
Output inconsistency	Correct: "Bob-8", Wrong: ["Bob-ID 8", "id 8", "Bob"]	regular expression
Unreasonability	"Unable to determine based on the provided reasoning paths."	random choice
Ambiguity	"Answer-1 and Answer-2 are both correct."	random choice from the two options

Table 1: Some error types of LLM-outputs, including output inconsistency, unreasonability and ambiguity with corresponding examples and solutions.

Emotion-based prompt
1. This is very import to my career.
2. You'd be better be sure about the answer.
3. Are sure that's your final answer ? It might be worth taking another look.
Ranking-based prompt
1. Give me a confidence score between 0-5 for your answer.

Table 2: Some examples of emotion-based prompts and ranking-based prompts.

plausible. The output format is: correct answer: answer-id, confidence: score:". In this prompt, we have assigned the role of Claude 3 (Anthropic, 2024) intelligent assistant and provided it with an understanding of the task's input and output. Additionally, we have imposed two constraints: (1) The answer must be inferred from the reasoning path, and (2) The answer must be unique and selected. These constraints are set based on the following considerations: (1) In some question-answering data for this task, there may be multiple candidate answers with the same entity name but different reasoning paths. Therefore, we require the model to consider the reasoning path when providing an answer. Furthermore, this is why our model answer format is "answer-id", which clearly indicate which candidate answer is chosen. (2) The second constraint ensures that the model does not give multiple answers, and when the model believes there is no correct answer, it can utilize its own knowledge to provide an approximate answer.

3.2 Prompt-rank and prompt-emotion

Although the basic prompt is enough for the LLM to output the answers. However, recent researchers (Li et al., 2023; Wang et al., 2024) have found that it can be effective to improve the response of LLM by emotional push and self-ranking push without extra model training. Inspired by these discoveries, we add prompt-rank and prompt-emotion based on the basic prompt, which now reads: *"I have a new NLP reasoning task. This task is very important to me. As a smart assistant, you can help me decide which answer is correct. I will provide a question, a few answers and a few reasoning paths associated with the answers. Only one of these answers is correct. Please determine which answer is correct based on the corresponding reasoning path. Even if you believe there is no correct answer, please still choose the answer option that you think is the most plausible. Please provide a confidence rank [A, B, C, D, E] for the larger model's answer, where A=highest confidence, E=lowest confidence. The output format is: correct answer: answer-id, confidence: score:"*, where green part and red part are emotion-based prompt and ranking-based prompt, respectively. In fact, the formats of emotion-based prompts and ranking-based prompts are very flexible. For instance, they can also be designed in the form shown in Table 2.

3.3 Refining final results

It is worth noting that our base model is Claude 3. However, considering the high cost of using Claude 3, we initially validate the effectiveness of our strategy on the open-source Mistral 7B model (Jiang et al., 2023) before migrating it to Claude 3. Another issue is that even though we have strictly define the answer out format of LLM, it is inevitably to observe LLM does not output the answer following the answer format. For example, it may directly output the answer without id, then we use regular expressions to extract the answer numbers from the non-standardized output. For clarity, we list common abnormal types of answers with corresponding examples and solutions in Table 1.

4 Results and Analysis

4.1 Overview

Table 3 presents the results of Mistrial 7B using different strategies on the test set for this task. The evaluation metrics include accuracy, precision, recall, and F1 score, with the F1 score being the primary determinant of the final ranking. As depicted in Table 3, Claude 3 employing both prompt-rank

Model	Accuracy	Precision	Recall	F1 score
Mistral 7B	0.9245	0.6650	0.3776	0.4817
Mistral 7B + Prompt-rank	0.9277	0.6819	0.4168	0.5174
Mistral 7B + Prompt-emotion	0.9268	0.6704	0.4182	0.5151
Mistral 7B + Prompt-rank + Prompt-emotion	0.9285	0.6888	0.4210	0.5226
Claude 3 + Prompt-rank + Prompt-emotion	**0.9691**	**0.8434**	**0.8211**	**0.8321**

Table 3: Results of different models with various strategies for test.

and prompt-emotion strategies achieves the highest scores across all metrics. Specifically, the prompt-rank and prompt-emotion strategies enhance the inference capabilities of the basic Mistral 7B model. The prompt-rank strategy increases the F1 score by an absolute margin of 3.57%, while the prompt-emotion strategy improves it by 3.34%. By combining these two strategies, Mistrial 7B demonstrates a 4.09% improvement. This clearly demonstrates the effectiveness of these two strategies. Additionally, the high scores obtained by Claude 3 equipped with these strategies serve as evidence of the transferability of our prompts. In terms of format, the prompt-rank strategy is designed to prompt the language models (LLMs) to rank the candidate answers, encouraging them to compare and jointly consider these answers. This approach promotes deeper inference by facilitating joint thinking. On the other hand, the prompt-emotion strategy is intended to evoke human-like emotions and encourage more cautious inference. Exploring ways to emotionally influence LLMs for better responses is an interesting direction to pursue.

Query: *Which The Lunar Chronicles books was not published in year 2015?*
Response: *"The question asks which book from The Lunar Chronicles was not published in 2015. To determine the correct answer, we need to identify which of the provided answers are actually books from The Lunar Chronicles, and then use the publication year to narrow down the answer. The reasoning paths provided offer insights into the relationship between the answers and The Lunar Chronicles, but none of them directly address the publication year. Therefore, we must rely on external knowledge about The Lunar Chronicles series by Marissa Meyer· · ·"*

Table 4: The response of Claude 3 to a specific query. The highlighted section indicates areas where Language Models (LLMs) believe external knowledge is necessary.

4.2 Case study

Although we specify in the inference prompt that LLM should derive the answer based on reasoning paths, it is highly possible that these paths alone are inadequate for inferring the correct answer. Consequently, LLMs need to rely on their intrinsic external knowledge to enhance their inference capabilities. Figure 4 presents a similar scenario that illustrates this point. In this case, Claude 3 determines that the provided reasoning path is insufficient to find the correct answer. Therefore, it combines its intrinsic knowledge with the reasoning path to arrive at the answer. The insight from this example is that the knowledge extracted from a knowledge graph based on key entities may not be useful. Although the model can access its external knowledge, this external knowledge is outdated. In the future, we can explore whether the model can independently access APIs to find the desired knowledge, as the model's knowledge may be outdated.knowledge

5 Conclusion

In this article, we propose an effective method for the TextGraphs-17 Shared Task in Knowledge-based Question Answering (KBQA). We explore the use of Claude 3 and prompt learning to enhance causal reasoning capabilities. Our research shows that incorporating ranking prompts and emotional prompts significantly improves performance. We provide reproducible experiments with extractable results using regular expressions. Due to limitations, we conducted an ablation study on Mistrial 7B instead of Claude 3 and have unresolved questions about reducing output errors in the Language Model (LLM), including inconsistencies, unreasonability, and ambiguity. These challenges require further investigation and development in future research.

References

Ebtesam Almazrouei, Hamza Alobeidli, Abdulaziz Alshamsi, Alessandro Cappelli, Ruxandra Cojocaru, Merouane Debbah, Etienne Goffinet, Daniel Heslow, Julien Launay, Quentin Malartic, Badreddine Noune, Baptiste Pannier, and Guilherme Penedo. 2023. Falcon-40B: an open large language model with state-of-the-art performance.

Rohan Anil, Sebastian Borgeaud, Yonghui Wu, Jean-Baptiste Alayrac, Jiahui Yu, Radu Soricut, Johan Schalkwyk, Andrew M. Dai, Anja Hauth, Katie Millican, David Silver, Slav Petrov, Melvin Johnson, Ioannis Antonoglou, Julian Schrittwieser, Amelia Glaese, Jilin Chen, Emily Pitler, Timothy P. Lillicrap, Angeliki Lazaridou, Orhan Firat, James Molloy, Michael Isard, Paul Ronald Barham, Tom Hennigan, Benjamin Lee, Fabio Viola, Malcolm Reynolds, Yuanzhong Xu, Ryan Doherty, Eli Collins, Clemens Meyer, Eliza Rutherford, Erica Moreira, Kareem Ayoub, Megha Goel, George Tucker, Enrique Piqueras, Maxim Krikun, Iain Barr, Nikolay Savinov, Ivo Danihelka, Becca Roelofs, Anaïs White, Anders Andreassen, Tamara von Glehn, Lakshman Yagati, Mehran Kazemi, Lucas Gonzalez, Misha Khalman, Jakub Sygnowski, and et al. 2023. Gemini: A family of highly capable multimodal models. *CoRR*, abs/2312.11805.

Anthropic. 2024. Claude 3 haiku: our fastest model yet.

Sören Auer, Christian Bizer, Georgi Kobilarov, Jens Lehmann, Richard Cyganiak, and Zachary G. Ives. 2007. Dbpedia: A nucleus for a web of open data. In *The Semantic Web, 6th International Semantic Web Conference, 2nd Asian Semantic Web Conference, ISWC 2007 + ASWC 2007, Busan, Korea, November 11-15, 2007*, volume 4825 of *Lecture Notes in Computer Science*, pages 722–735. Springer.

Zhengxiao Du, Yujie Qian, Xiao Liu, Ming Ding, Jiezhong Qiu, Zhilin Yang, and Jie Tang. 2022. GLM: general language model pretraining with autoregressive blank infilling. In *Proceedings of the 60th Annual Meeting of the Association for Computational Linguistics (Volume 1: Long Papers), ACL 2022, Dublin, Ireland, May 22-27, 2022*, pages 320–335. Association for Computational Linguistics.

Mohnish Dubey, Debayan Banerjee, Abdelrahman Abdelkawi, and Jens Lehmann. 2019. Lc-quad 2.0: A large dataset for complex question answering over wikidata and dbpedia. In *The Semantic Web - ISWC 2019 - 18th International Semantic Web Conference, Auckland, New Zealand, October 26-30, 2019, Proceedings, Part II*, volume 11779 of *Lecture Notes in Computer Science*, pages 69–78. Springer.

Dan Hendrycks, Collin Burns, Steven Basart, Andy Zou, Mantas Mazeika, Dawn Song, and Jacob Steinhardt. 2021. Measuring massive multitask language understanding. In *9th International Conference on Learning Representations, ICLR 2021, Virtual Event, Austria, May 3-7, 2021*. OpenReview.net.

Albert Q. Jiang, Alexandre Sablayrolles, Arthur Mensch, Chris Bamford, Devendra Singh Chaplot, Diego de las Casas, Florian Bressand, Gianna Lengyel, Guillaume Lample, Lucile Saulnier, Lélio Renard Lavaud, Marie-Anne Lachaux, Pierre Stock, Teven Le Scao, Thibaut Lavril, Thomas Wang, Timothée Lacroix, and William El Sayed. 2023. Mistral 7b. *Preprint*, arXiv:2310.06825.

Cheng Li, Jindong Wang, Yixuan Zhang, Kaijie Zhu, Wenxin Hou, Jianxun Lian, Fang Luo, Qiang Yang, and Xing Xie. 2023. Large language models understand and can be enhanced by emotional stimuli. *Preprint*, arXiv:2307.11760.

Tom M. Mitchell, William W. Cohen, Estevam R. Hruschka Jr., Partha P. Talukdar, Bo Yang, Justin Betteridge, Andrew Carlson, Bhavana Dalvi Mishra, Matt Gardner, Bryan Kisiel, Jayant Krishnamurthy, Ni Lao, Kathryn Mazaitis, Thahir Mohamed, Ndapandula Nakashole, Emmanouil A. Platanios, Alan Ritter, Mehdi Samadi, Burr Settles, Richard C. Wang, Derry Wijaya, Abhinav Gupta, Xinlei Chen, Abulhair Saparov, Malcolm Greaves, and Joel Welling. 2018. Never-ending learning. *Commun. ACM*, 61(5):103–115.

OpenAI. 2023. GPT-4 technical report. *CoRR*, abs/2303.08774.

Andrey Sakhovskiy, Mikhail Salnikov, Irina Nikishina, Aida Usmanova, Angelie Kraft, Cedric Möller, Debayan Banerjee, Junbo Huang, Longquan Jiang, Rana Abdullah, Xi Yan, Dmitry Ustalov, Elena Tutubalina, Ricardo Usbeck, and Alexander Panchenko. 2024. TextGraphs 2024 shared task on text-graph representations for knowledge graph question answering. In *Proceedings of the TextGraphs-17: Graph-based Methods for Natural Language Processing*, Bangkok, Thailand. Association for Computational Linguistics.

Priyanka Sen, Alham Fikri Aji, and Amir Saffari. 2022. Mintaka: A complex, natural, and multilingual dataset for end-to-end question answering. In *Proceedings of the 29th International Conference on Computational Linguistics, COLING 2022, Gyeongju, Republic of Korea, October 12-17, 2022*, pages 1604–1619. International Committee on Computational Linguistics.

Hugo Touvron, Louis Martin, Kevin Stone, Peter Albert, Amjad Almahairi, Yasmine Babaei, Nikolay Bashlykov, Soumya Batra, Prajjwal Bhargava, Shruti Bhosale, Dan Bikel, Lukas Blecher, Cristian Canton-Ferrer, Moya Chen, Guillem Cucurull, David Esiobu, Jude Fernandes, Jeremy Fu, Wenyin Fu, Brian Fuller, Cynthia Gao, Vedanuj Goswami, Naman Goyal, Anthony Hartshorn, Saghar Hosseini, Rui Hou, Hakan Inan, Marcin Kardas, Viktor Kerkez, Madian Khabsa, Isabel Kloumann, Artem Korenev, Punit Singh Koura, Marie-Anne Lachaux, Thibaut Lavril, Jenya Lee, Diana Liskovich, Yinghai Lu, Yuning Mao, Xavier Martinet, Todor Mihaylov, Pushkar Mishra, Igor Molybog, Yixin Nie, Andrew Poulton, Jeremy Reizenstein, Rashi Rungta, Kalyan Saladi, Alan Schelten,

Ruan Silva, Eric Michael Smith, Ranjan Subramanian, Xiaoqing Ellen Tan, Binh Tang, Ross Taylor, Adina Williams, Jian Xiang Kuan, Puxin Xu, Zheng Yan, Iliyan Zarov, Yuchen Zhang, Angela Fan, Melanie Kambadur, Sharan Narang, Aurélien Rodriguez, Robert Stojnic, Sergey Edunov, and Thomas Scialom. 2023. Llama 2: Open foundation and fine-tuned chat models. *CoRR*, abs/2307.09288.

Denny Vrandečić and Markus Krötzsch. 2014. Wikidata: a free collaborative knowledgebase. *Commun. ACM*, 57(10):78–85.

Yikun Wang, Rui Zheng, Haoming Li, Qi Zhang, Tao Gui, and Fei Liu. 2024. Rescue: Ranking llm responses with partial ordering to improve response generation. *Preprint*, arXiv:2311.09136.

Aiyuan Yang, Bin Xiao, Bingning Wang, Borong Zhang, Ce Bian, Chao Yin, Chenxu Lv, Da Pan, Dian Wang, Dong Yan, Fan Yang, Fei Deng, Feng Wang, Feng Liu, Guangwei Ai, Guosheng Dong, Haizhou Zhao, Hang Xu, Haoze Sun, Hongda Zhang, Hui Liu, Jiaming Ji, Jian Xie, Juntao Dai, Kun Fang, Lei Su, Liang Song, Lifeng Liu, Liyun Ru, Luyao Ma, Mang Wang, Mickel Liu, MingAn Lin, Nuolan Nie, Peidong Guo, Ruiyang Sun, Tao Zhang, Tianpeng Li, Tianyu Li, Wei Cheng, Weipeng Chen, Xiangrong Zeng, Xiaochuan Wang, Xiaoxi Chen, Xin Men, Xin Yu, Xuehai Pan, Yanjun Shen, Yiding Wang, Yiyu Li, Youxin Jiang, Yuchen Gao, Yupeng Zhang, Zenan Zhou, and Zhiying Wu. 2023. Baichuan 2: Open large-scale language models. *CoRR*, abs/2309.10305.

TIGFORMER at TextGraphs-17 Shared Task: A Late Interaction Method for text and Graph Representations in KBQA Classification Task

Mayank Rakesh[1], **Parikshit Saikia**[2] and **Saket Kumar Shrivastava**[3]
[1]StatusNeo Technology Consulting Pvt Ltd
[2]Greyb Research Pvt Ltd
[3]SLB Pvt Ltd
[1]mayank.rakesh@statusneo.com, [2]parikshit.saikia@greyb.com and [3]Sshrivastava9@slb.com

Abstract

This paper introduces a novel late interaction mechanism for knowledge base question answering (KBQA) systems, combining Graphormer and transformer representations. We conducted extensive experiments, comparing various pooling mechanisms and configurations. Our results demonstrate significant improvements in F1-score compared to traditional baselines. Specifically, we found that attention pooling, in conjunction with linearized graph and question features alongside sub-graph representations, yields the best performance. Our study highlights the importance of advanced interaction mechanisms and the integration of diverse modalities in KBQA systems.

1 Introduction

Transformer models have dramatically reshaped the field of Natural Language Processing (NLP), exemplified by their robust ability to capture intricate textual semantics. Pioneering models such as BERT have revolutionized various NLP tasks, particularly in the domain of question-answering (QA) systems (Devlin et al., 2019). However, despite these advancements, the challenge of accurately answering factoid questions, which often demand precise, context-specific information, continues to pose unique hurdles for language models (Dubey et al., 2019; Sen et al., 2022). While BERT and its successors excel in text processing, their application is sometimes limited without the integration of structured, contextual data from external sources. These challenges often require not just an understanding of the text but also the effective navigation and interpretation of structured knowledge embedded within knowledge graphs. Recent advancements in the field have seen a shift towards leveraging such graphs, which encapsulate rich, interlinked data that can enhance the contextual grounding of answers (Z. Zhang et al., 2020). Knowledge Graphs has been increasingly utilized for solving complex tasks to enrich language models' responses, making them more accurate and contextually aware (Saxena et al., 2020). One notable approach proposes an innovative method of integrating Large Language Models (LLMs) with Knowledge Graphs to enhance QA systems (Salnikov et al., 2023). This method significantly boosts the accuracy of LLMs by using sub-graph extraction based on question entities and re-ranking answer candidates through the linearization of these sub-graphs.

Building upon these foundational insights, this paper aims to further enhance the integration of Language models with Knowledge Graphs. We propose a novel solution that utilizes both transformer-based text embeddings and knowledge graph embeddings more efficiently[1].

2 Related Work

The ability of transformers to capture textual semantics has led towards a lot of research in knowledge and domain adaptation of transformers for question answering tasks (Blom & Pereira, 2023; Cao et al., 2020; Nassiri & Akhloufi, 2023; Yue et al., 2021).

Proceedings of TextGraphs-17: Graph-based Methods for Natural Language Processing, pages 137–141
August 15, 2024 ©2024 Association for Computational Linguistics

For instance, recent studies have explored the integration and text representations and transformers for KGQA tasks (Lan et al., 2021; Pereira et al., 2022).

The current work is an extension of retrieval-based methods for knowledge base question answering systems. Previous works have analyzed kg-entity-embedding to question embedding comparison and ranking for fetching answer candidates (Razzhigaev et al., 2023; Saxena et al., 2020) or reranking extracted subgraphs using importance prediction (Sun et al., 2019). All these methods are limited to using text features (entities) from these graphs. Thus, treating it as a single modality Natural Language Processing (NLP) problem. (Salnikov et al., 2023) generates candidates using LLMs and uses graph linearization to integrate graph data into t5-transformers for ranking. (Wang et al., 2022) studied the use of convolution neural networks for scoring answer entities in relation to question and graph paths features. (X. Zhang et al., 2022) developed a multi-modal approach fusing text and graph representations. QA-GNN (Yasunaga et al., 2021) explored suggested using message forwarding to update the LM and GNN embeddings simultaneously. Contrasting to all these approaches, the current approach explores the use of transformers and graph transformers representation using multiple late-interaction heads and binary classifying the candidates generated by LLMs using (Salnikov et al., 2023) for correct answer candidates.

3 Methodology

Figure 1 depicts the overview of our late interaction mechanism for Graphormer and transformer representations. The text and graph interactions after pooling are passed through multiple interaction heads. Finally, these fully interacted representations are used to binary classify; question, answer-entity and sub-graph set for correct and incorrect answers.

3.1 Dataset

The dataset[2] (Sakhovskiy et al., 2024) consists of questions with a list of Wikidata entities mentioned in them. For each question, there are 5-10 answer candidates provided, all in the form of Wikidata entities. Additionally, a Wikidata sub-graph is given, which includes the shortest paths between the entities mentioned in the question and the entities listed as answer candidates.

3.2 Text Module

To extract textual information, we embed text representations into a language model encoder. Here we are using a t5-transformer encoder with multi head attention for encoding our representations. The text embedding is represented in Eq. 1.

$$\left\{\widetilde{h_{int}^{(l)}}, \widetilde{h_1^{(l)}}, \cdots, \widetilde{h_T^{(l)}}\right\} = LM\left(\left\{h_{int}^{(l-1)}, h_1^{(l-1)}, \cdots, h_T^{(l-1)}\right\}\right), \tag{1}$$

where $\widetilde{h_{int}^{(l)}}$, denotes representation of text before late interaction.

3.3 Graph Module

We employed Graphormer to depict sub-graph paths and structures (Ying et al., 2021). The native NetworkX encoding of our sub-graphs' structural information includes edge encoding in the attention, spatial (shortest path between node matrices), and centrality (in/out degrees). The graph embeddings are represented with Eq. 2.

$$\left\{\widetilde{g_{int}^{(l)}}, \widetilde{g_1^{(l)}}, \cdots, \widetilde{g_J^{(l)}}\right\} = Graphormer\left(\left\{g_{int}^{(l-1)}, g_1^{(l-1)}, \cdots, g_J^{(l-1)}\right\}\right). \tag{2}$$

Where $\widetilde{g_{int}^{(l)}}$ denotes representation of graph before late interaction.

3.4 Interaction Module

Pooled text and graph representations are calculated by passing them through a pooling layer. Mean Pooling, CLS pooling, and attention pooling are used as candidates for our experiments. To interact with and exchange information between text and graph representations, a text-graph interaction module (Eq. 3) is utilized, drawing inspiration from (Lei et al., 2022).

$$\left(g_{int}^{(l)}, h_{int}^{(l)}\right) = inter\left(\widetilde{g_{int}^{(l)}}, \widetilde{h_{int}^{(l)}}\right). \tag{3}$$

The above equation utilizes a inter function. The function first calculates the self and cross modality similarity coefficients between pooled text and graph embeddings:

$$
\begin{aligned}
w_{hh} &= \tilde{h}_{int}^{(l)} \otimes \left(\theta_1 \cdot \tilde{h}_{int}^{(l)}\right), \\
w_{hg} &= \tilde{h}_{int}^{(l)} \otimes \left(\theta_2 \cdot \tilde{g}_{int}^{(l)}\right), \\
w_{gg} &= \tilde{g}_{int}^{(l)} \otimes \left(\theta_2 \cdot \tilde{g}_{int}^{(l)}\right), \\
w_{gh} &= \tilde{g}_{int}^{(l)} \otimes \left(\theta_1 \cdot \tilde{h}_{int}^{(l)}\right),
\end{aligned} \tag{4}
$$

where "⊗" indicates the dot product and θ_1 and θ_2 are hyper-parameters that convert the modality representations into the interaction-sensitive space. The final similarity weights are then obtained using a softmax function:

$$
\begin{aligned}
\widetilde{w}_{hh}, \widetilde{w}_{hg} &= \text{softmax}\left(w_{hh}, w_{hg}\right), \\
\widetilde{w}_{gg}, \widetilde{w}_{gh} &= \text{softmax}\left(w_{gg}, w_{gh}\right).
\end{aligned} \tag{5}
$$

In the end, the interaction modules use the computed similarity weights to enable interaction between the two representations:

$$
\begin{aligned}
h_{int}^{(l)} &= \widetilde{w}_{hh}\tilde{h}_{int}^{(l)} + \widetilde{w}_{hg}\tilde{g}_{int}^{(l)}, \\
g_{int}^{(l)} &= \widetilde{w}_{gg}\tilde{g}_{int}^{(l)} + \widetilde{w}_{gh}\tilde{h}_{int}^{(l)}.
\end{aligned} \tag{6}
$$

3.5 Classification Module

The post interaction graph and text representation are passed through a concatenation layer and finally through a classification head to classify if the set of question, answer entity and sub-graph is factually correct or not.

4 Results and Discussion

The outcomes of the proposed approach are shown in this section, along with comparisons to several baselines. The number of interaction heads for all the experiments were taken as 10 with a learning rate 3e-5. A learning scheduler was using for avoiding overfitting and training was conducted for a total of 10 epochs. F1-score was considered as the evaluation metric. The results are summarized in Table 1. It is demonstrated that, our late interaction framework outperforms the baselines of baseline-text -only, baseline-graph-only and baseline-text-graph. Different pooling mechanisms were compared for the study (Table 1). Attention pooling mechanism outperformed CLS and mean pooling. Attention Pooling layer with linearized graph and question as text features and sub-graph as graph feature representation inter-action provided best results. We also compared out interaction function with other interaction function such as:

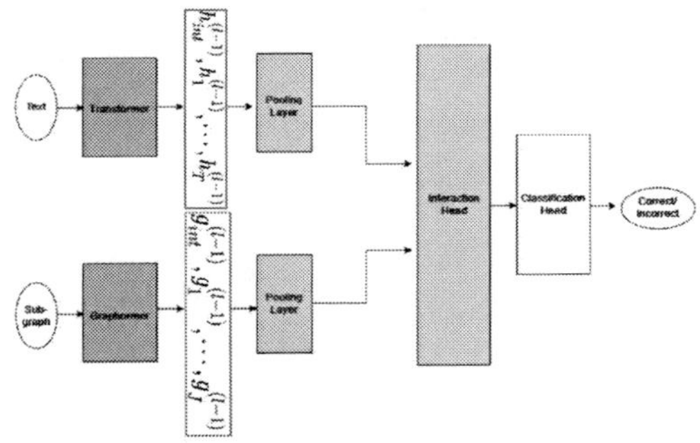

Figure 1: The framework for the proposed interaction method between text and graph representations.

- **Average** Function calculates the average of text and graph representation.
- **Soft** function calculates new representation using two learnable parameters as weights for interaction.

Our proposed method outperforms both interaction mechanism in terms of F1-score.

5 Conclusion

For knowledge base question answering (KBQA) systems, our work presents a novel late interaction method that combines transformer and Graphormer representations. Compared to conventional baselines, this method performs significantly better, showing gains in F1-scores.

We discovered that attention pooling leads to the best classification performance, particularly when combined with question features and linearized graphs with sub-graph representations.

To improve KBQA systems, our research emphasizes the significance of combining various modalities and using cutting-edge interaction methods. By enhancing model robustness and performance through efficient integration of textual and graph-based data, this research paves a path for further improvements in factoid-based question answering.

[1] https://github.com/mayank-rakesh-mck/TextGraphs17-shared-task

[2] https://github.com/uhh-lt/TextGraphs17-shared-task/tree/main

Approach	Pooling Layer	F1-score	Precision	Recall	Accuracy
Baseline-graph-only		0.1266	0.6667	0.0699	0.9103
Baseline-text-graph		0.2022	0.7241	0.1175	0.9138
Baseline-text-only		0.2120	0.1457	0.3888	0.7313
Answer-question-text-subgraph-interaction	Mean Pooling	0.2708	0.2613	0.2811	0.8593
linearized-graph-question-subgraph-interaction	Mean Pooling	0.2996	0.3028	0.2965	0.8711
linearized-graph-question-subgraph-interaction	CLS pooling	0.3054	0.2307	0.4517	0.8090
linearized-graph-question-subgraph-interaction	Attention Pooling	**0.5305**	0.3992	**0.7902**	0.8700

Table 1: A comparison of proposed late interaction method with the baselines

References

Blom, B., & Pereira, J. L. M. (2023). *Domain Adaptation in Transformer Models: Question Answering of Dutch Government Policies* (pp. 196–208). https://doi.org/10.1007/978-3-031-48232-8_19

Cao, Q., Trivedi, H., Balasubramanian, A., & Balasubramanian, N. (2020). *DeFormer: Decomposing Pre-trained Transformers for Faster Question Answering.*

Devlin, J., Chang, M.-W., Lee, K., & Toutanova, K. (2019). BERT: Pre-training of Deep Bidirectional Transformers for Language Understanding. *Proceedings of the 2019 Conference of the North,* 4171–4186. https://doi.org/10.18653/v1/N19-1423

Dubey, M., Banerjee, D., Abdelkawi, A., & Lehmann, J. (2019). *LC-QuAD 2.0: A Large Dataset for Complex Question Answering over Wikidata and DBpedia* (pp. 69–78). https://doi.org/10.1007/978-3-030-30796-7_5

Lan, Y., He, G., Jiang, J., Jiang, J., Zhao, W. X., & Wen, J.-R. (2021). A Survey on Complex Knowledge Base Question Answering: Methods, Challenges and Solutions. *Proceedings of the Thirtieth International Joint Conference on Artificial Intelligence,* 4483–4491. https://doi.org/10.24963/ijcai.2021/611

Lei, Z., Wan, H., Zhang, W., Feng, S., Chen, Z., Li, J., Zheng, Q., & Luo, M. (2022). *BIC: Twitter Bot Detection with Text-Graph Interaction and Semantic Consistency.*

Nassiri, K., & Akhloufi, M. (2023). Transformer models used for text-based question answering systems. *Applied Intelligence, 53*(9), 10602–10635. https://doi.org/10.1007/s10489-022-04052-8

Pereira, A., Trifan, A., Lopes, R. P., & Oliveira, J. L. (2022). Systematic review of question answering over knowledge bases. *IET Software, 16*(1), 1–13. https://doi.org/10.1049/sfw2.12028

Razzhigaev, A., Salnikov, M., Malykh, V., Braslavski, P., & Panchenko, A. (2023). A System for Answering Simple Questions in Multiple Languages. *Proceedings of the 61st Annual Meeting of the Association for Computational Linguistics (Volume 3: System Demonstrations),* 524–537. https://doi.org/10.18653/v1/2023.acl-demo.51

Sakhovskiy, A., Salnikov, M., Nikishina, I., Usmanova, A., Kraft, A., Möller, C., Banerjee, D., Huang, J., Jiang, L., Abdullah, R., Yan, X., Ustalov, D., Tutubalina, E., Usbeck, R., & Panchenko, A. (2024, August). TextGraphs 2024 Shared Task on Text-Graph Representations for Knowledge Graph Question Answering. *Proceedings of the TextGraphs-17: Graph-Based Methods for Natural Language Processing.*

Salnikov, M., Le, H., Rajput, P., Nikishina, I., Braslavski, P., Malykh, V., & Panchenko, A. (2023). *Large Language Models Meet Knowledge Graphs to Answer Factoid Questions.*

Saxena, A., Tripathi, A., & Talukdar, P. (2020). Improving Multi-hop Question Answering over Knowledge Graphs using Knowledge Base Embeddings. *Proceedings of the 58th Annual Meeting of the Association for Computational Linguistics,* 4498–4507.

https://doi.org/10.18653/v1/2020.acl-main.412

Sen, P., Aji, A. F., & Saffari, A. (2022). Mintaka: A Complex, Natural, and Multilingual Dataset for End-to-End Question Answering. *Proceedings of the 29th International Conference on Computational Linguistics*, 1604–1619.

Sun, H., Bedrax-Weiss, T., & Cohen, W. (2019). PullNet: Open Domain Question Answering with Iterative Retrieval on Knowledge Bases and Text. *Proceedings of the 2019 Conference on Empirical Methods in Natural Language Processing and the 9th International Joint Conference on Natural Language Processing (EMNLP-IJCNLP)*, 2380–2390. https://doi.org/10.18653/v1/D19-1242

Wang, J., Li, W., Guo, Y., & Zhou, X. (2022). Path-aware Multi-hop Question Answering Over Knowledge Graph Embedding. *2022 IEEE 34th International Conference on Tools with Artificial Intelligence (ICTAI)*, 459–466. https://doi.org/10.1109/ICTAI56018.2022.00074

Yasunaga, M., Ren, H., Bosselut, A., Liang, P., & Leskovec, J. (2021). *QA-GNN: Reasoning with Language Models and Knowledge Graphs for Question Answering.*

Ying, C., Cai, T., Luo, S., Zheng, S., Ke, G., He, D., Shen, Y., & Liu, T.-Y. (2021). *Do Transformers Really Perform Bad for Graph Representation?*

Yue, Z., Kratzwald, B., & Feuerriegel, S. (2021). Contrastive Domain Adaptation for Question Answering using Limited Text Corpora. *CoRR*, *abs/2108.13854*. https://arxiv.org/abs/2108.13854

Zhang, X., Bosselut, A., Yasunaga, M., Ren, H., Liang, P., Manning, C. D., & Leskovec, J. (2022). *GreaseLM: Graph REASoning Enhanced Language Models for Question Answering.*

Zhang, Z., Liu, X., Zhang, Y., Su, Q., Sun, X., & He, B. (2020). Pretrain-KGE: Learning Knowledge Representation from Pretrained Language Models. *Findings of the Association for Computational Linguistics: EMNLP 2020*, 259–266. https://doi.org/10.18653/v1/2020.findings-emnlp.25

NLPeople at TextGraphs-17 Shared Task: Chain of Thought Questioning to Elicit Decompositional Reasoning

Movina Moses[1] **and Vishnudev Kuruvanthodi**[2] **and Mohab Elkaref**[2] **and**
Shinnosuke Tanaka[2] and **James Barry**[2] and **Geeth De Mel**[2] and **Campbell D Watson**[1]
IBM Research[1] and IBM Research Europe[2]
{movina.moses, vishnudev.k, mohab.elkaref, shinnosuke.tanaka
james.barry}@ibm.com, geeth.demel@uk.ibm.com, cwatson@us.ibm.com

Abstract

This paper presents the approach of the NLPeople team for the Text-Graph Representations for KGQA Shared Task at TextGraphs-17 (Sakhovskiy et al., 2024). The task involved selecting an answer for a given question from a list of candidate entities. We show that prompting Large Language models (LLMs) to break down a natural language question into a series of sub-questions, allows models to understand complex questions. The LLMs arrive at the final answer by answering the intermediate questions using their internal knowledge without needing additional context. Our approach to the task uses an ensemble of prompting strategies to guide how LLMs interpret various types of questions. Our submission achieves an F1 score of 85.90, ranking 1st among the other participants in the task.

1 Introduction

This paper outlines the NLPeople submission to the Text-Graph Representations for KGQA Shared Task at TextGraphs-17. The task involved selecting the correct answer from a list of candidate answers for a given question. Knowledge Graph Question Answering (KGQA) involves using the structured knowledge and relations present in a Knowledge Graph (KG) to answer a natural language question. Previous KGQA methods focused on two approaches: knowledge retrieval and semantic parsing. Knowledge retrieval attempts to extract entities, relations, or triples from the KG that are relevant to the question and can be used to deduce the answer (Sun et al., 2019). On the other hand, semantic parsing transforms the question from unstructured natural language into a structured logical form (Yih et al., 2016). This form can be converted into a query and executed over a KG to obtain relevant answers. However, these methods still struggle to perform the complex reasoning required to answer natural language questions.

To deal with these challenges, recent KGQA research leverages the reasoning and language comprehension capabilities of large language models (LLMs) (Gu et al., 2023; Sen et al., 2023). These methods try to incorporate the structural knowledge present in KGs to address the factual hallucination generated by LLMs during its reasoning process (Baek et al., 2023; Guan et al., 2023).

We propose a chain-of-thought based prompting mechanism, which allows an LLM to deduce the answer by breaking down the initial question into sub-questions, which when answered, lead to the final answer. Furthermore, we present our results using question-type-specific prompting strategies to address the difficulties models face while reasoning over complex question types. We present results for these methods using Llama3-8b-instruct, Llama3-70b-instruct, Mixtral 8x7B, and GPT 3.5. Overall, our results rank 1st with an F1 score of 85.90 improving the baseline GPT 3.5 results by approximately 18%.

2 Methodology

2.1 Problem Formulation

For a given question and a list of candidate entities, the task is to choose the candidate entity that correctly answers the question. Each candidate is associated with a graph of the shortest paths from the entities mentioned in the question to the candidate entity including links of the intermediate nodes.

The dataset is annotated with Wikidata entities and includes seven types of complex questions: generic, ordinal, intersection, superlative, difference, multihop, and comparative. The questions used in this dataset originate from the Mintaka dataset (Sen et al., 2022), which is a large-scale, complex, and natural language dataset. In this section, we detail the elements of our final submission.

Proceedings of TextGraphs-17: Graph-based Methods for Natural Language Processing, pages 142–148
August 15, 2024 ©2024 Association for Computational Linguistics

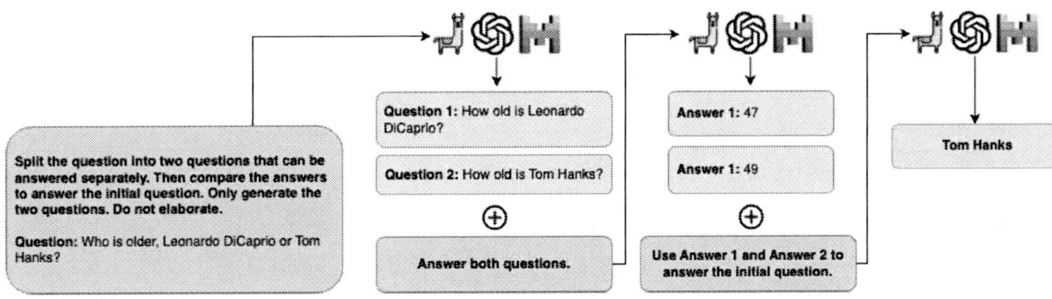

Figure 1: An example of Chain of Thought Questioning

2.2 Chain of Thought Questioning

LLMs can perform closed-book question-answering tasks using the knowledge stored in their parameters (Petroni et al., 2019; Roberts et al., 2020). However, generating a chain-of-thought (CoT) improves the ability of LLMs to perform the complex reasoning required to answer natural language questions. Wei et al. (2023) show how these reasoning abilities emerge when a model is shown examples of intermediate reasoning steps. We propose a variant of CoT prompting called CoT-questioning, where LLMs are instructed to decompose questions into a series of sub-questions that can be answered independently or in sequence to arrive at the final answer. The model is provided with one example suggesting how the model should approach its instructions (Brown et al., 2020) as shown in Figure 1. This style of prompting simplifies the reasoning the model has to do to understand a complex question by mimicking the thought process a human would use and guiding its reasoning path.

Entity Selection The above method provides a list of one or more possible candidate entities. The dataset maps candidate entities to their corresponding Wikidata entity IDs. A candidate entity could map to more than one entity ID since each entity could be different but have the same name. For example, the entity named Beyoncé corresponds to Q15303590: 2013 studio album by Beyoncé and Q36153: American singer (born 1981). While the sub-graphs provide the links and relations between the question and candidate entities, these links do not always provide the information required to reason out the answer. To disambiguate between entities, we prompt the model to select the correct entity by providing the entity name, ID, and WikiData description for the candidate entities using the prompt in Table 7. If the above method does not produce a list of candidates, the model is prompted with all the candidate entities.

2.3 Question Specific Prompts

The dataset comprises questions of different complexity types. Each type would benefit from different intermediate steps and reasoning to arrive at the answer. We propose a prompting methodology that uses different few-shot prompts for each type of question. These types are identified using the question complexity types from the Mintaka dataset. Specifically, we target questions of type ordinal, difference, intersection, and superlative since they are difficult to decompose due to their complexity.

Superlative and Ordinal Type Questions Such questions involve a comparison over possible answers. For superlative questions the task is to select the answer with the maximum or minimum value for a certain property. For ordinal questions the task is to select an answer at a certain position when all answers are ordered with respect to a certain property. Our strategy for both types is to decompose these questions into their constituent factoid questions, followed by a comparative operation to choose the final answer. For example, for the question "Who is the youngest movie director?" can be decomposed into "How old is `[candidate]`?", where `[candidate]` is replaced with each candidate answer, and the answer is decided by the `[candidate]` that returns the minimum answer.

Zero-Shot Reasoning Prompt Some questions demand abstract reasoning across multiple paths. For instance, to answer the question "Who was not an original Spice Girl?" the model must identify the original Spice Girls and determine who was replaced. However, the question could also be interpreted as selecting someone who is not a Spice Girl at all. To address difference questions, we utilize the zero-shot prompt listed in Table 9. It

Prompt Method	Model	Precision	Recall	F1	Accuracy
CoT-Questioning	llama3-8b-instruct	67.46	63.64	65.50	93.67
	llama3-70b-instruct	**82.10**	**78.50**	**80.26**	**96.35**
	mixtral-8x7b-instruct-v01	70.18	68.59	69.38	94.29
	gpt-3.5	75.55	76.94	76.24	95.47
Question-Specific Prompts	llama3-8b-instruct	71.26	69.44	70.34	94.47
	llama3-70b-instruct	**84.61**	**80.90**	**82.71**	**96.81**
	mixtral-8x7b-instruct-v01	68.72	75.53	71.97	94.45
	gpt-3.5	77.99	78.21	78.11	95.86
MCQ Prompts with Additional Context	llama3-8b-instruct	80.17	80.06	80.11	96.25
	llama3-70b-instruct	**81.42**	**81.19**	**81.30**	**96.48**
	mixtral-8x7b-instruct-v01	76.10	76.09	76.10	95.49
	gpt-3.5	79.35	79.35	79.35	96.11

Table 1: Development results using the methods detailed in Section 2.

explicitly asks the model to apply reasoning when answering the question. However, when the model does not produce an answer listed in the candidate entities, we perform entity selection with the top five candidate entities ranked based on the score produced by the cross-encoder[1] when we perform retrieval over the wikipedia page mapped to the entity ID using the query and linearised graph string. This prompt can be used for all types of questions.

2.4 MCQ Prompts with Additional Context

In this approach, context is prepared from multiple sources. In the end, the context, question and filtered answer options are provided to an LLM for it to pick the correct answer.

First, the LLM is prompted to answer a given question and provide an explanation. We then verify that the answer is present in the list of candidate entities. If present, the answer with the explanation is added to the main context along with the question entities and their first paragraphs from Wikipedia, for the answer entities, descriptions, and entity types are fetched from Wikidata. For example, for an answer entity named Nile, the context would look like: A. The Nile (Q110044631): (type watercolour painting) and B. Nile (Q3392): (type river) major river in northeastern Africa. The type and description provide additional context for the LLM to disambiguate and pick the correct option. The context and candidate entities are used to re-rank the entities based on their sentence embeddings. The lowest-ranking options which likely contain the wrong candidates are removed. Finally, using the constructed context and filtered options, the LLM is prompted to select the correct option.

[1]huggingface.co/cross-encoder/ms-marco-MiniLM-L-6-v2

3 Results and Discussion

3.1 Experimental Setup

We evaluate our prompting methods on a 20% split of the train set containing 7497 samples and 707 questions using Llama 3-8b-Instruct, Llama 3-70b-Instruct (AI@Meta, 2024), Mixtral 8x7B[2] and GPT-3.5[3]. The prompts for each model were amended using their prompt formats and special tokens. Wikidata entity descriptions were fetched using the Wikidata client library[4]. We report the results of our methods in Table 1. All models are decoded using greedy sampling.

3.2 Development Results

CoT-Questioning In our CoT-questioning experiments, we used the few-shot prompt outlined in Appendix Table 6. This example was hand-crafted using a question from the training data chosen after examining the scores with multiple few-shot examples. The results show that Llama3-70b-Instruct performed the best, achieving an F1 score of 80.26, followed by GPT-3.5 with a score of 76.24. The smaller Llama and Mistral models yield significantly lower F1 scores.

As shown in Table 2, using entity selection with Wikidata entity descriptions produces much higher scores than using the linearized graph strings from the graphs provided by the dataset. This may be because the shortest path from the question entity to the candidate entity does not always contain the information necessary for the model to select the correct entity. Additionally, some larger graphs with repeated words could mislead the model to select the wrong entity.

[2]huggingface.co/mistralai/Mixtral-8x7B-Instruct-v0.1
[3]platform.openai.com/docs/models/gpt-3-5-turbo
[4]wikidata.readthedocs.io/

	Precision	Recall	F1	Accuracy
Linearized Graph String	79.66	74.25	76.86	95.78
Description	**82.10**	**78.50**	**80.26**	**96.35**

Table 2: Llama3-70b-instruct results using entity selection with Wikidata descriptions vs. linear graph string.

Question-Specific Prompting The results from our zero-shot reasoning prompt is presented in Table 3. We infer that when explicitly asked to reason before they answer, the LLM tends to reason out the correct answer. We notice the biggest difference in F1 among superlative and ordinal type questions here. While difference questions score lower in the development split, they eventually score better on the public test set as shown in Table 4.

Question Type	Count	CoT Questioning	Question-Specific Prompts
difference	95	**71.79**	69.23
intersection	157	89.38	**90.96**
ordinal	95	75.28	**83.87**
superlative	126	64.13	**71.90**
Overall F1	707	80.20	**82.71**

Table 3: F1 scores using question-specific prompts with Llama3-70b-instruct.

MCQ Prompts with Additional Context The naive approach with zero-shot prompts of questions and options without any additional context led to poor results. The presence of similar but different options made it difficult to pick the right answer. The additional context from the Wikidata improved the score. This approach performed well on intersection, ordinal and comparative-type questions. However, the F1 scores were lower for the superlative type of questions. Table 11 details the F1 scores by question type.

3.3 Official Results

Final Submission As stated previously, we observed that models produce varying answers for different question types. We ensemble the outputs of the best-performing models - Llama3-70b-instruct and GPT 3.5 using CoT-questioning, to get the best results. We found that when one model gives an incorrect answer, the other often provides the correct one. For a question, if the predicted answers differ, we perform entity selection using GPT 3.5 between the predictions of both models to choose the correct answer. For unanswered questions, we prompted GPT-4 to answer the question and performed entity selection to select the correct answer. Finally, we used outputs from question-type specific prompts with Llama3-70b-Instruct. In each case, we compared the model's output to the previous outputs that produced a high F1 score. Table 4 details the individual results at each step of the ensemble.

Ensembled Method	F1
llama3-70b-instruct with CoT-Questioning	80.29
+ gpt-3.5 with CoT-Questioning	82.81
+ gpt-4 with Zero-Shot Answer	85.19
+ llama3-70b-instruct with Question-Specific Prompt	85.99
Final Ensemble	**85.99**

Table 4: Ensembled system results on public test set.

Results on Private Test Set The official results are presented in Table 5. Our best submission achieves an F1 score of 85.90 on the private test set outperforming the other teams.

Team	F1	Rank
zlatamaria	83.00	2
daeheekim	81.26	3
baseline_chatgpt	67.99	4
mmoses	**85.90**	**1**

Table 5: Top results on the official private test set.

4 Limitations

The effectiveness of CoT-Questioning depends on the model used. As observed from the results, larger models excel at simplifying questions. Additionally, the accuracy of the final answers depends on the data the model has been trained with, so it can produce outdated answers. Better methods to incorporate the information present in KGs could help address this problem.

5 Conclusion

In this paper, we described the NLPeople submission to the TextGraphs-17 Shared Task. We present three different prompting techniques: (1) chain of thought questioning (2), question-type specific prompts, and (3) MCQ prompts with additional context. We demonstrated that by decomposing a question into a series of sub-questions, LLMs can reason over complex questions effectively. Additionally, using question-type specific prompts and demonstrations yields positive results for superlative, ordinal, and difference-type questions. These techniques only require a single demonstration and need no additional context. Our final submission using an ensemble of the above techniques achieves a score of 85.90, which ranks 1st among the other participants.

References

AI@Meta. 2024. Llama 3 model card.

Jinheon Baek, Alham Fikri Aji, and Amir Saffari. 2023. Knowledge-augmented language model prompting for zero-shot knowledge graph question answering. In *Proceedings of the 1st Workshop on Natural Language Reasoning and Structured Explanations (NLRSE)*, pages 78–106, Toronto, Canada. Association for Computational Linguistics.

Tom Brown, Benjamin Mann, Nick Ryder, Melanie Subbiah, Jared D Kaplan, Prafulla Dhariwal, Arvind Neelakantan, Pranav Shyam, Girish Sastry, Amanda Askell, Sandhini Agarwal, Ariel Herbert-Voss, Gretchen Krueger, Tom Henighan, Rewon Child, Aditya Ramesh, Daniel Ziegler, Jeffrey Wu, Clemens Winter, Chris Hesse, Mark Chen, Eric Sigler, Mateusz Litwin, Scott Gray, Benjamin Chess, Jack Clark, Christopher Berner, Sam McCandlish, Alec Radford, Ilya Sutskever, and Dario Amodei. 2020. Language models are few-shot learners. In *Advances in Neural Information Processing Systems*, volume 33, pages 1877–1901. Curran Associates, Inc.

Yu Gu, Xiang Deng, and Yu Su. 2023. Don't generate, discriminate: A proposal for grounding language models to real-world environments. In *Proceedings of the 61st Annual Meeting of the Association for Computational Linguistics (Volume 1: Long Papers)*, pages 4928–4949, Toronto, Canada. Association for Computational Linguistics.

Xinyan Guan, Yanjiang Liu, Hongyu Lin, Yaojie Lu, Ben He, Xianpei Han, and Le Sun. 2023. Mitigating large language model hallucinations via autonomous knowledge graph-based retrofitting. *Preprint*, arXiv:2311.13314.

Fabio Petroni, Tim Rocktäschel, Sebastian Riedel, Patrick Lewis, Anton Bakhtin, Yuxiang Wu, and Alexander Miller. 2019. Language models as knowledge bases? In *Proceedings of the 2019 Conference on Empirical Methods in Natural Language Processing and the 9th International Joint Conference on Natural Language Processing (EMNLP-IJCNLP)*, pages 2463–2473, Hong Kong, China. Association for Computational Linguistics.

Adam Roberts, Colin Raffel, and Noam Shazeer. 2020. How much knowledge can you pack into the parameters of a language model? In *Proceedings of the 2020 Conference on Empirical Methods in Natural Language Processing (EMNLP)*, pages 5418–5426, Online. Association for Computational Linguistics.

Andrey Sakhovskiy, Mikhail Salnikov, Irina Nikishina, Aida Usmanova, Angelie Kraft, Cedric Möller, Debayan Banerjee, Junbo Huang, Longquan Jiang, Rana Abdullah, Xi Yan, Dmitry Ustalov, Elena Tutubalina, Ricardo Usbeck, and Alexander Panchenko. 2024. TextGraphs 2024 shared task on text-graph representations for knowledge graph question answering. In *Proceedings of the TextGraphs-17: Graph-based Methods for Natural Language Processing*, Bangkok, Thailand. Association for Computational Linguistics.

Priyanka Sen, Alham Fikri Aji, and Amir Saffari. 2022. Mintaka: A complex, natural, and multilingual dataset for end-to-end question answering. In *Proceedings of the 29th International Conference on Computational Linguistics*, pages 1604–1619, Gyeongju, Republic of Korea. International Committee on Computational Linguistics.

Priyanka Sen, Sandeep Mavadia, and Amir Saffari. 2023. Knowledge graph-augmented language models for complex question answering. In *Proceedings of the 1st Workshop on Natural Language Reasoning and Structured Explanations (NLRSE)*, pages 1–8, Toronto, Canada. Association for Computational Linguistics.

Haitian Sun, Tania Bedrax-Weiss, and William Cohen. 2019. PullNet: Open domain question answering with iterative retrieval on knowledge bases and text. In *Proceedings of the 2019 Conference on Empirical Methods in Natural Language Processing and the 9th International Joint Conference on Natural Language Processing (EMNLP-IJCNLP)*, pages 2380–2390, Hong Kong, China. Association for Computational Linguistics.

Jason Wei, Xuezhi Wang, Dale Schuurmans, Maarten Bosma, Brian Ichter, Fei Xia, Ed Chi, Quoc Le, and Denny Zhou. 2023. Chain-of-thought prompting elicits reasoning in large language models. *Preprint*, arXiv:2201.11903.

Wen-tau Yih, Matthew Richardson, Chris Meek, Ming-Wei Chang, and Jina Suh. 2016. The value of semantic parse labeling for knowledge base question answering. In *Proceedings of the 54th Annual Meeting of the Association for Computational Linguistics (Volume 2: Short Papers)*, pages 201–206, Berlin, Germany. Association for Computational Linguistics.

A Appendix

A.1 Prompts

We show detailed prompts used by our prompting techniques in Table 6, 7, 8, 9 and 10.

A.2 Additional Results

Table 11 presents the F1 scores obtained by the methods detailed in Section 2 for each question type.

```
Split the question into two questions that can be answered separately. Then compare the answers
to answer the initial question. Only generate the two questions. Do not elaborate.
Question: Who is older, Leonardo DiCaprio or Tom Hanks?
Question 1: How old is Leonardo DiCaprio?
Question 2: How old is Tom Hanks?
Answer both questions.
Answer 1: 49
Answer 2: 67
Use Answer 1 and Answer 2 to answer the initial question.
Tom Hanks
```

Table 6: Few-Shot Example used for CoT Questioning in Section 2.2.

```
**Previous Output**
Select the correct ID that references the answer:
[answerEntityId_1]: answerEntity_1 - answerEntity_1_description
[answerEntityId_2]: answerEntity_2 - answerEntity_2_description
```

Table 7: Example of the entity selection prompt used when a predicted answer entity appears multiple times in the candidate entity list. This prompt is added to the previous prompt and generated output in Section 2.2 and Section 2.3.

```
<|begin_of_text|><|start_header_id|>user<|end_header_id|>
Split the question into two questions that can be answered separately. Then compare the answers
to answer the initial question. Only generate the two questions. Do not elaborate.
Question: Who is older, Leonardo DiCaprio or Tom Hanks?<|eot_id|>
<|start_header_id|>assistant<|end_header_id|> Question 1: How old is Leonardo DiCaprio?
Question 2: How old is Tom Hanks?
<|eot_id|><|start_header_id|>user<|end_header_id|>
Answer both questions.<|eot_id|><|start_header_id|>assistant<|end_header_id|>
Answer 1: 49
Answer 2: 67
<|eot_id|><|start_header_id|>user<|end_header_id|>
Use Answer 1 and Answer 2 to answer the initial question. <|eot_id|>
<|start_header_id|>assistant<|end_header_id|>
Tom Hanks<|eot_id|><|start_header_id|>user<|end_header_id|>
Split the question into two questions that can be answered separately. Then compare the answers
to answer the initial question. Only generate the two questions. Do not elaborate.
Question: Who's won more head-to-head tennis matches between each other, Novak Djokovic or
Roger Federer? <|eot_id|>
<|start_header_id|>assistant<|end_header_id|>
Question 1: How many head-to-head tennis matches has Novak Djokovic won against Roger Federer?
Question 2: How many head-to-head tennis matches has Roger Federer won against Novak Djokovic?
Answer both questions.<|eot_id|><|start_header_id|>assistant<|end_header_id|>
Answer 1: 27
Answer 2: 23
<|eot_id|><|start_header_id|>user<|end_header_id|>
Use Answer 1 and Answer 2 to answer the initial question.<|eot_id|>
<|start_header_id|>assistant<|end_header_id|>
Novak Djokovic <|eot_id|><|start_header_id|>user<|end_header_id|>
Select the correct ID that references the answer:
[Q5812]: Novak Djokovic - Serbian tennis player
[Q15073898]: Novak - family name
[Q21146583]: Djokovic - family name
<|eot_id|><|start_header_id|>assistant<|end_header_id|>
[Q5812]: Novak Djokovic - Serbian tennis player
```

Table 8: An example of the intermediate outputs produced by the CoT-questioning method from Section 2.2 and its its prompt format using Llama3-70b-Instruct. This color are the prompts by the user and these are the outputs produced by the model.

```
Answer the question in a clear and concise form after using proper reasoning.
Question: <question>
Model generates answer with reasoning
Extract all possible answers.
Answer_1, Answer_2, ...
```

Table 9: Zero-shot prompt reasoning prompt used for specific question-types as mentioned in Section 2.3.

```
INSTRUCTION: You are a multiple-choice quiz expert. You will be provided with a question
and multiple-choice answers in the format of A, B, C, D, E, F, G, H, I, J. You have to read the
given CONTEXT and select one answer. Say the answer option (A or B or C or D or E or F or G or H or
I or J) in ANSWER section Do not Guess the answer. Say UNANSWERABLE if you don't know the answer.
CONTEXT:
Franz Kafka Prize(Q19362): (is of type literary award) international literary awardThe Franz
Kafka Prize is an international literary award presented in honour of Franz Kafka, the Jewish,
Bohemian, German-language novelist. The prize was first awarded in 2001 and is co-sponsored by
the Franz Kafka Society and the city of Prague, Czech Republic.
...
New York City(Q60): (is of type city in the United States) most populous city in the United States
....
QUESTION:
In what city was the author of the second book to win the Franz Kafka Prize born?
ANSWER OPTION:
A. Prague (Q1085)
B. Kraków (Q31487)
...
...
J. New York City (Q60)
ANSWER:
```

Table 10: Prompt template used for the MCQ Prompts in Section 2.4.

Question Type	Count	CoT-Questioning Questioning	Question-Specific Prompts	MCQ Prompts with Additional Context
comparative	81	**92.68**	**92.68**	85.19
difference	95	71.79	69.23	**77.25**
generic	81	**84.27**	**84.27**	80.25
intersection	157	89.38	**90.96**	88.82
multihop	72	**85.71**	**85.71**	81.94
ordinal	95	75.28	83.87	**85.26**
superlative	126	64.13	**71.90**	69.84
Overall F1	707	80.20	**82.71**	81.30

Table 11: F1 scores per question type on the development split using the three different methods. These were obtained using the Llama3-70b-instruct model.

Skoltech at TextGraphs-17 Shared Task: Finding GPT-4 Prompting Strategies for Multiple Choice Questions

Maria Lysyuk[1, 2], **Pavel Braslavski**[3]
[1]Skoltech, [2]AIRI
[3]School of Engineering and Digital Sciences, Nazarbayev University, Astana, Kazakhstan
maria.lysyuk@skol.tech, pavel.braslavskii@nu.edu.kz

Abstract

In this paper, we present our solution to the TextGraphs-17 Shared Task on Text-Graph Representations for Knowledge Graph Question Answering (KGQA). GPT-4 alone, with chain-of-thought reasoning and a given set of answers, achieves an F1 score of 0.78. By employing subgraph size as a feature, Wikidata answer description as an additional context, and a question rephrasing technique, we further strengthen this result. These tricks help to answer questions that were not initially answered and to eliminate irrelevant, identical answers. We have managed to achieve an F1 score of 0.83 and took 2nd place, improving the score by 0.05 over the baseline. An open implementation of our method is available on GitHub.[1]

1 Introduction

TextGraphs-17 task is to select a correct answer entity for a given question from a list of several Wikidata entities (Sakhovskiy et al., 2024). These lists of candidates are generated by LLMs; each list item is accompanied by a Wikidata subgraph connecting the potential answer entity to the question entities via a shortest path. Data statistics are summarized in Table 1. The task can be cast as a binary classification: each answer candidate is either correct or incorrect; the F1 score is used as the evaluation measure.

There are two main difficulties with this task. First, there are questions that have more than one correct answer. For example, the question `Who were the first two senators to represent the latest state added to the Union?` has two correct answers: `Hiram Fong (Q926441)` and `Oren E. Long (Q715129)`.

The second difficulty is that there is a significant proportion of questions with several answers with identical textual labels – 35% in the train subset and 47% in the test (see Table 1). For example, for the question `Who wrote the Leatherstocking Tales?` the correct answer is `James Fenimore Cooper (Q167856)`. However, there are two more candidate entities with exactly the same labels: `Q102502290` and `Q102502514`.[2] In such cases, the selection of the correct entity could be based on the KG subgraph analysis and/or on accounting for the descriptions of the candidate entities.

	Train	Test
# questions	3,535	1,000
# questions with identical answers	1,222	474
Avg. subgraph size	4.44	4.69
# answers per question	10.66	10.96

Table 1: Dataset statistics.

2 Method

Baseline. The baseline is obtained with GPT-4[3] chain-of-thought (CoT) prompting (Wei et al., 2022) with the provided set of candidate answers for the given question. The baseline prompt is as follows:

Base prompt

Generate the answer using chain-of-thought reasoning. After generation verify that your answer is in the set of possible answers given in the question. If your answer is not there, select the answer from the set. At the end write the short answer after the phrase "So the answer is:".

[1] `https://github.com/marialysyuk/TextGraphs-17`

[2] These two persons appear to be a grandson and great-grandson of the author of the *Leatherstocking Tales*, see Cooper's genealogical tree `https://www.wikitree.com/wiki/Cooper-7320`.

[3] We employed `gpt-4-0125-preview` model, see `https://platform.openai.com/docs/models/gpt-4-and-gpt-4-turbo`.

Proceedings of TextGraphs-17: Graph-based Methods for Natural Language Processing, pages 149–153
August 15, 2024 ©2024 Association for Computational Linguistics

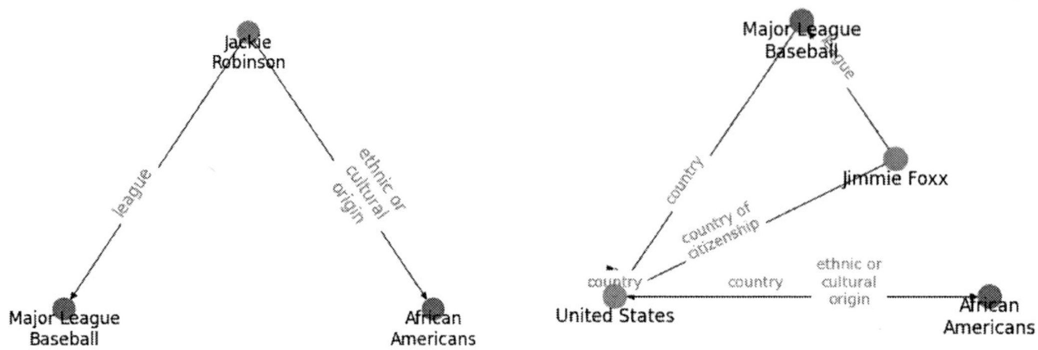

(a) A subgraph for the correct answer

(b) A subgraph for an incorrect answer

Figure 1: Examples of subgraphs corresponding to correct and incorrect answers for the question `Who was the first African American baseball player to play in the American major leagues?` Color codes: correct, **incorrect**, **question**, **intermediate** entities.

An example of the input question with candidate answers:

Q&A example

Q: After publishing A Time to Kill, which book did its author begin working on immediately?

Possible answers: A Clash of Kings, A Feast for Crows, Fear and Loathing in Las Vegas, In Cold Blood, Into the Woods, Kongenes kamp, No Country for Old Men, Slaughterhouse-Five, The Firm, The Last Days of Disco.

The phrase *So the answer is:* is used as a marker to extract the final answer. The extracted answer is compared with the provided candidates after lowercasing and punctuation removed. If there is an exact match between the extracted answer and the provided candidate, this candidate is returned as the final answer.

Post-processing: fuzzy answer matching. The surface form of the baseline answer could be slightly different from the provided candidate answers, for example `Jerry Rice` vs. `Jerry Rice, Jr` or `Mongol Empire` vs. `The Mongol Empire`. To solve these cases, we applied fuzzy string matching with a threshold of 80.[4] In some cases GPT-4 failed to return a short answer from the list of provided candidates. For example, for the question `Who launched the third Roman invasion of Britain?` the LLM returned: `...So the answer is: The question seems to be based on a misunderstanding or mislabeling of the historical invasions of Britain as none of the options provided are known for a "third" invasion, but Claudius would be the closest in context, despite the mismatch with the question's phrasing.` In such cases, we checked whether one of the answer candidates is mentioned in the 'reasoning part'. If we could find exactly one such answer, it was taken as the correct one. Otherwise, no prediction is made, as the mention of the options could be just a part of the reasoning and thus not related to the prediction.

Post-processing: addressing answers with identical labels. As mentioned earlier, for some questions there are several candidate answer entities with the same textual labels, from which we only have to choose one.

Figure 1a shows the subgraph for the question `Who was the first African American baseball player to play in the American Major Leagues?` for the correct answer. Figure 1b illustrates the subgraph for the same question, but with an incorrect answer.

Let's denote the subgraph size as amount of edges in the subgraph. There is an observation that smaller subgraphs lead to correct answers with a higher probability. Indeed, compare the subgraphs in the Figures 1a and 1b – the shorter path leads to the correct answer.

[4]`https://pypi.org/project/fuzzywuzzy/`

Configuration	Precision	Recall	F1 score	Accuracy
GPT-4 (baseline)	0.722	0.837	0.775	0.955
+ fuzzy answer matching	0.716	0.857	0.780	0.955
+ same-text answer selection	0.816	0.839	0.827	0.967
+ all tricks	**0.823**	**0.843**	**0.835**	**0.969**
Llama-3-8B-Instruct (baseline)	0.649	0.660	0.654	0.935
+ fuzzy answer matching	0.635	0.703	0.667	0.935
+ same-text answer selection	0.677	0.665	0.671	0.939
+ all tricks	**0.697**	**0.710**	**0.704**	**0.944**

Table 2: Experiments evaluated at the post-competition stage. *All tricks* include fuzzy answer matching, same-text answer selection, original question rephrasing, and augmenting candidate answers with their Wikipedia description.

Predicting the correct answer as the one with the smallest subgraph leads to an F1 score of 0.248 on the subset of questions with textually identical answers from the training set, which is quite high for such a simple heuristic.

However, there are still cases where the candidate answers with the same labels also have subgraphs of the same size. In this case, we select the entity with a non-empty Wikidata description. If contenders still remain, we represent the question and its candidate answers' Wikidata descriptions as average fastText (Bojanowski et al., 2017) embeddings and choose the most similar pair in terms of cosine similarity. fastText model was trained on the Wikipedia data. Representing words as a collection of n-grams, fastText can capture the semantic meaning of morphologically related words, even for out-of-vocabulary words or rare words. For instance, consider the question `On which KISS album did Ace Frehley not appear, even though he was on the cover?`; there are two answers with the same label `Creatures of the Night`, but different descriptions: `1982 studio album by Kiss (Q1139397)` and `1983 single by Kiss (Q5183668)`. Both corresponding subgraphs are of size six, and the embedding of the correct answer `1982 studio album by Kiss (Q1139397)` is closer to that of the question.

Post-processing: fixing non-answered questions with prompt tricks. For 24 out of 1,000 questions, the proposed baseline and post-processing still result in undefined answers. We address these cases with two additional tricks. First, we task the LLM with rephrasing the question to provide additional information and make it less ambiguous, following the approach of Deng et al. (2023). The following prompt was used to rephrase the original question: `Given the above question, rephrase and expand it to help you do better answering. Maintain all information in the original question.` In this way, the original question `What fighting game did Goku not appear in?` is transformed into its rephrased version `In which fighting game is the character Goku, from the Dragon Ball series, notably absent?` As you can see, LLM adds extra information to the question about the character from the game and emphasises the "absent" with "notably" to make sense of the question more vivid. This is an example of a question where the prompt with the original question failed to produce a valid answer, while the prompt with a paraphrased question was successful.

The second trick is to augment the candidate answers with their Wikidata descriptions. In some cases, the description already incorporates the information necessary to answer the question. For example, the baseline prompt for the question `What was the Alejandro González Iñárrituto movie distributed by Legendary Pictures?` is extended as follows:

Q&A example with answers description

Below are the facts that might be relevant to answer the question:
(("Flesh and Sand", "2017 film by Alejandro González Iñárritu"), ("I'm Not There", 'soundtrack album to the 2007 film of the same title'),
("In the Name of the King", "2007 film directed by Uwe Boll"), ...)

Q: What was the Alejandro González Iñárrituto movie distributed by Legendary Pictures?
Possible answers: Flesh and Sand, I'm Not There, In the Name of the King ...

Place	Team Name	F1 score	Precision	Recall	Accuracy
1	NLPeople	0.859	0.867	0.851	0.974
2	**Skoltech**	**0.830**	**0.818**	**0.843**	**0.968**
3	POSTECH	0.816	0.825	0.807	0.966
4	baseline_chatgpt	0.680	0.599	0.786	0.931
5	Team <blank>	0.661	0.605	0.727	0.930

Table 3: Top-5 participating teams based on private test, ranked by F1 score.

As one can see from the the example, the description of the film `Flesh and Sand` includes the information of interest for the given question, making it possible to select this variant from the set of possible answers.

Multiple correct answers. Since the ratio of the questions with multiple correct answers wasn't large in the training data (3%), we only addressed multiple answers with identical labels. In other words, after removing answers with identical labels, multiple answers to the question could remain if they have different labels (with the respect to lower-casing and removing punctuation).

3 Discussion of Results

The results of different configurations on the private test set are shown in Table 2. It can be seen that fixing the problem of multiple answer entities with identical labels significantly improved the baseline. All the tricks that fixed unanswered questions with alternative to the baseline prompts helped to increase the final scores even more. In the Appendix 6 we add a description of the ideas that we tried but they didn't work.

The competition was held on Codalab.[5] The results on the private test set are presented in Table 3. Our team took the second place, showing competitive results compared to the winning team. Interestingly, the team rankings based on public vs. private test sets are quite similar, which rules out the hypothesis of overfitting on the training set.

4 Ablation study

Since GPT-4 is a proprietary LLM, we tried an open source LLM in the ablation study to see if the approach and tricks used in the paper were transferable to other LLMs. As a baseline, we tried the `Meta-Llama-3-8B-Instruct` model.[6]. As you can see from the table 2, all the tricks gradually improve the accuracy results for both models. Interestingly, for GPT-4 the biggest challenge was to differentiate identical labels, and the biggest increase in accuracy was achieved by solving this problem. For the Llama, on the other hand, the baseline was not as strong and additional tricks with other prompting techniques (rephrasing questions and adding candidate answers with their Wikidata descriptions) were more useful because of the high number of unanswered questions in the baseline.

5 Conclusion

Although LLMs are praised for their emergent properties and generalisability, they are black box models that often fall short of capturing and accessing factual knowledge (Pan et al., 2024). The TextGraphs17 shared task was an excellent competition that addresses this gap by unifying LLMs and KGs.

In this paper, we have given a description of the method used by our team, Skoltech, who came 2nd in the private test ranking with an F1 score of 0.83. We presented a method based on the GPT-4 model. The approach answers almost all questions by implementing additional prompting tricks. Furthermore, we use subgraph size and Wikidata descriptions as features that help us to distinguish between textually similar but factually different answers.

Acknowledgments

Pavel Braslavski acknowledges funding from the School of Engineering and Digital Sciences, Nazarbayev University.

[5]`https://codalab.lisn.upsaclay.fr/competitions/18214#results`

[6]See `https://huggingface.co/meta-llama/Meta-Llama-3-8B-Instruct`

References

Piotr Bojanowski, Edouard Grave, Armand Joulin, and Tomas Mikolov. 2017. Enriching word vectors with subword information. *Transactions of the association for computational linguistics*, 5:135–146.

Stephen Cook. 2000. The p versus np problem. *Clay Mathematics Institute*, 2:6.

Yihe Deng, Weitong Zhang, Zixiang Chen, and Quanquan Gu. 2023. Rephrase and respond: Let large language models ask better questions for themselves. *arXiv preprint arXiv:2311.04205*.

Maria Lysyuk, Mikhail Salnikov, Pavel Braslavski, and Alexander Panchenko. 2024. *Natural Language Processing and Information Systems: 29th International Conference on Applications of Natural Language to Information Systems, NLDB 2024, Turin, Italy, June 25-27, 2024, Proceedings*. Springer.

Shirui Pan, Linhao Luo, Yufei Wang, Chen Chen, Jiapu Wang, and Xindong Wu. 2024. Unifying large language models and knowledge graphs: A roadmap. *IEEE Transactions on Knowledge and Data Engineering*.

Andrey Sakhovskiy, Mikhail Salnikov, Irina Nikishina, Aida Usmanova, Angelie Kraft, Cedric Möller, Debayan Banerjee, Junbo Huang, Longquan Jiang, Rana Abdullah, Xi Yan, Dmitry Ustalov, Elena Tutubalina, Ricardo Usbeck, and Alexander Panchenko. 2024. TextGraphs 2024 shared task on text-graph representations for knowledge graph question answering. In *Proceedings of the TextGraphs-17: Graph-based Methods for Natural Language Processing*, Bangkok, Thailand. Association for Computational Linguistics.

Priyanka Sen, Alham Fikri Aji, and Amir Saffari. 2022. Mintaka: A complex, natural, and multilingual dataset for end-to-end question answering. *arXiv preprint arXiv:2210.01613*.

Jason Wei, Xuezhi Wang, Dale Schuurmans, Maarten Bosma, Fei Xia, Ed Chi, Quoc V Le, Denny Zhou, et al. 2022. Chain-of-thought prompting elicits reasoning in large language models. *Advances in neural information processing systems*, 35:24824–24837.

6 Appendix

The TextGraphs-17 data relies heavily on the Mintaka dataset (Sen et al., 2022). Each question in the original Mintaka has a type annotation that can potentially be utilized for the answer selection task. There are seven question types in Mintaka: superlative, difference, multi-hop, ordinal, generic, intersection, and comparative. An attempt was made to create a few-shot prompt by providing a CoT for each type of question. Thus, in case of ordinal (`When did Metallica put out their fourth album?`) or superlative (`Which US president has had the most votes?`) questions, the options should be ranked by some parameter and the candidate at the interested position is selected. Whereas multi-hop questions (`How many kids does the lead actress of Pretty Woman have?`) require an intermediate reasoning step. For each of the seven question types, only one example was given and it might explain why this idea failed. However, it could be tried the other way round: for each type of question, a special prompt could be generated with few examples for this type of question. In addition, information about the question type is a good signal about the number of expected answers. Obviously, for comparative and superlative question types, a single answer is expected.

Another idea was inspired by the P vs NP problem (Cook, 2000) in computational complexity theory. Informally, it asks whether every problem whose solution can be quickly verified can also be quickly solved. In the baseline prompt, we provide the model with a set of answers and ask it to select one using CoT. What if we slightly change the task, and ask the model about one candidate at a time by replacing the question word by the answer candidate. For example, to the question `Who won the 1900 Election?` is turned into `Democratic Party won the 1900 Election?`. The hypothesis is that it's easier for the model to check the answer if there are fewer options. The idea didn't work probably because the modified question was not grammatically correct.

Finally, an attempt was made to reduce the number of candidate answers by filtering out wrong paths from question entities. In Konstruktor Lysyuk et al. (2024), simple questions are studied where the answer to the question is in 1-hop from the question entity. Thus, by finding the question entity and the relation (the edge between the question entity and the answer), one can find the answer. Using the ranking relation procedure from Konstruktor, we ranked the relations of the question entities. Then only the paths containing these relations remained. While reducing the number of candidate answers didn't lead to an increase in accuracy, this filtering successfully discriminated between multiple identical answers. In other words, the label of the correct answer is more likely to be on the path with selected relations than on the path with relations not selected by the ranking procedure.

JellyBell at TextGraphs-17 Shared Task: Fusing Large Language Models with External Knowledge for Enhanced Question Answering

Julia Belikova[1], **Evegeniy Beliakin**[1], **Vasily Konovalov**[2,1]
[1]Moscow Institute of Physics and Technology, Russia
[2]AIRI, Moscow, Russia
{belikova.iua, beliakin.eo, vasily.konovalov}@phystech.edu

Abstract

This work describes an approach to develop Knowledge Graph Question Answering (KGQA) system for TextGraphs-17 shared task. The task focuses on the fusion of Large Language Models (LLMs) with Knowledge Graphs (KGs). The goal is to select a KG entity (out of several candidates) which corresponds to an answer given a textual question. Our approach applies LLM to identify the correct answer among the list of possible candidates. We confirm that integrating external information is particularly beneficial when the subject entities are not well-known, and using RAG can negatively impact the performance of LLM on questions related to popular entities, as the retrieved context might be misleading. With our result, we achieved 2nd place in the post-evaluation phase.

1 Introduction

While LLM can provide answers to questions, answering factoid questions without access to a KG can be challenging. It has been shown that incorporation of the KG information into LLM significantly improves the results for various NLP tasks (Zhang et al., 2020).

The TextGraph-17[1] workshop focuses on exploring synergies between text and graph processing techniques, specifically targeting the fusion of LLMs with KGs. The shared task presents a novel challenge in the domain of KGQA, where participants are tasked with selecting the correct KG entity corresponding to a textual question, given a set of candidate entities and a graph of shortest paths in the KG connecting the query entities to the LLM-generated candidates. The shared task aims to investigate effective strategies for fusing text and graph modalities, providing a controlled environment for experimentation. By pre-extracting the graph data, the organizers facilitate a standardized testbed, mitigating variations due to different graph extraction methods and enabling researchers to concentrate on enhancing LLM outputs with KG information. Overall, this shared task contributes to advancing the understanding and practical application of LLM-KG integration for improved QA performance.

Our main contributions are three-fold:

1. We show that LLMs do partially incorporate knowledge about Wikidata.
2. We confirm that the QA capability of LLMs can be enhanced by supplying them with relevant external data.
3. We demonstrate that by leveraging UE techniques, we can efficiently combine multiple LLMs, each integrated with distinct external data sources.

2 Related Work

Early approaches in KGQA primarily focused on simple questions involving node-edge-node triples, but the complexity increases with multi-hop and aggregation queries. Izacard and Grave (2021) achieved state-of-the-art results on benchmarks like Natural Questions (Kwiatkowski et al., 2019) and TriviaQA by integrating Wikipedia as an external knowledge source. Similarly, Talmor and Berant (2018) showed how web-search results could enhance the performance of QA systems on complex queries from the ComplexWebQuestions benchmark.

Hybrid systems combining text and graph-based information have been particularly effective for complex multi-choice question answering (MCQA) tasks. PullNet (Sun et al., 2019) and GraftNet (Sun et al., 2018) employ relational graph convolutional networks to iteratively retrieve relevant information from both text and KGs, improving the handling of multi-hop questions. Additionally, using KG embeddings has been a successful strategy, as demon-

[1]https://sites.google.com/view/textgraphs2024

Proceedings of TextGraphs-17: Graph-based Methods for Natural Language Processing, pages 154–160
August 15, 2024 ©2024 Association for Computational Linguistics

strated by Huang et al. (2019), who enhanced candidate retrieval for answers, and Chekalina et al. (2022), who introduced a memory-efficient representation for KG embeddings, improving link prediction and QA tasks.

The fusion of LLMs with KGs has proven especially beneficial for MCQA. The GETT-QA (Banerjee et al., 2023) uses T5 to convert questions into simplified SPARQL queries, which are then mapped to KG entities and relations through a post-processing step, enhancing accuracy by leveraging both the linguistic capabilities of T5 and the structured information in KGs. Furthermore, UniK-QA (Oguz et al., 2022) creates representations for both structured and unstructured knowledge, facilitating open-domain QA over diverse data sources.

3 Dataset

The KGQA dataset is designed for the task of extracting accurate answers from complex knowledge graphs, specifically using information from Wikidata. Each data instance consists of a textual question that contains a list of referenced Wikidata entities. Along with this, there are several candidate answer options, all presented as distinct Wikidata entities. A key feature of the dataset is the provision of a sub-graph extracted from Wikidata, which comprises the shortest paths connecting the entities mentioned in the question to those found within the answer candidates.

The training set includes a substantial amount of 37,672 samples with 3,535 unique questions. Whereas the test set contains 10,961 samples with 1,000 unique questions. The dataset also ensures a balance in terms of candidate answers, with a minimum of 6 options and a maximum of 20 per question (*"Which Stephen King books have not been made into movies yet?"*), making it a challenging yet versatile resource for developing QA systems. The majority of questions (3,425) in the training set have a single correct answer; however, 110 questions have more than one correct answer. Therefore, the primary objective is to classify the answers into two categories: correct or incorrect.

4 Proposed Approach

We based our solution on Llama 3 series of LLMs in 8 billion (8B) and 70 billion (70B) parameter sizes. These models are specifically designed for dialogue applications and have demonstrated superior performance compared to popular open-source chat models on standard industry benchmarks (AI@Meta, 2024).

4.1 Retrieval-Augmented Generation

Retrieval-Augmented Generation (RAG) combines the strengths of LLMs with information from external databases to boost the precision and reliability of generated content, especially for tasks demanding substantial knowledge base. By facilitating seamless updates and integration of specialized data, RAG effectively fuses the internal knowledge of LLMs with the extensive and ever-evolving external data reservoirs, creating a synergy that enhances performance.

Wikidata ID description As the simplest form of external knowledge augmentation, we incorporated the Wikidata ID and answer candidate description from Wikidata.

Web-search results As external knowledge, we used web-search results from DuckDuckGo (Parsania et al., 2016). DuckDuckGo aims to deliver relevant results while respecting user privacy. In addition, DuckDuckGo doesn't require an API key and doesn't apply any limitations on getting web results (10 search results were returned for each query). The prompt including the web-search results can be found in the Appendix A.

Textualized KG Furthermore, we incorporated the subgraphs provided by the organizers as an external knowledge source. For textualizing the graph, we opt to use Llama 3 70B with the following prompt (Wu et al., 2023):

Prompt

Transform this wiki graph into text. Write only the new string that contains the text representation of the graph.

The prompt with textualized graph can be found in the Appendix A.

4.2 Uncertainty Estimation

Uncertainty Estimation (UE) refers to the process of measuring the level of confidence in the predictions generated by a LLM. Initially, UE was employed to identify hallucinations, which are instances where the model fabricates facts without offering users a clear way to assess the truthfulness of its statements (Maksimov et al., 2024). Typically, UE involves calculating it for an entire sequence, requiring us to aggregate the uncertainties

Model	RAG	Precision	Recall	F1	Accuracy
Llama3 8B	–	48.85	47.61	48.22	90.46
	D	51.77	49.95	<u>50.84</u>	90.98
	G + D	42.54	41.54	42.04	89.31
	W + D	60.38	58.84	**59.60**	92.55
	G + W + D	42.54	41.54	42.03	89.30
Llama3 70B	–	74.80	73.41	74.10	95.21
	D	77.19	75.76	76.47	95.65
	G + D	75.60	74.19	74.89	95.36
	W + D	82.05	79.96	**80.99**	96.50
	G + W + D	79.52	77.42	<u>78.45</u>	96.03

Table 1: Evaluation results for two Llama 3 scales (8B and 70B) are as follows. RAG denotes the knowledge sources, where D refers to the textual description of answer candidates from Wikidata, W represents DuckDuckGo web-search results (with the query being the question), and G signifies the textualized graph representation provided in the dataset. When equipped with knowledge from web-search results and Wikidata answer candidate descriptions, Llama 3 outperforms all other external knowledge sources. F1 score serves as the primary competitive metric.

associated with numerous individual token predictions. This often necessitates the use of sophisticated sampling and pruning strategies, such as beam search. However, in our specific scenario, the number of potential prediction choices is fixed and limited by number of answer candidates. As a result, the uncertainty estimation process becomes significantly more streamlined and straightforward. Specifically, we utilized white-box UE methods, including **maximum probability** (Fadeeva et al., 2023) and **margin probability** (Kuhn et al., 2023), i.e. the difference between the probability of the most likely answer and the probability of the second most likely answer.

5 Results and Discussion

Before providing the main results, we first examine the inherent knowledge of the LLM concerning Wikidata entities.

What LLM knows about Wikidata? To demonstrate the inherent capability of LLMs to link a Wikidata entity with its corresponding Wikidata ID, we carried out two fundamental experiments. These involved prompting Llama 3 70B to generate both entity IDs and entities from IDs. However, it emerged that predicting an entity from its ID often led to inaccuracies, with the model succeeding mainly in associating IDs with the most well-known entities, such as *Barack Obama*, *World War II*, *Washington, D.C.*, *Italy*. Moreover, when prompted about being pretrained on Wikidata, Llama 3 confirms positively.

Does the size of LLM make a difference when utilizing non-parametric knowledge? Table 1 presents a comparison of Llama 3 models with varying sizes. While employing external knowledge, one might anticipate that both Llama 3 scales would exhibit similar performance; however, this is not the case. The larger Llama 3 70B model consistently surpasses the smaller Llama 3 8B model across all scenarios. This suggests that the size of the language model remains crucial even with external knowledge, owing to its extra parametric knowledge or improved reasoning abilities.

Whether all external data are equally helpful? Table 1 showcases a comparison of Llama 3 models with different external knowledge sources. Llama 3 augmented with external knowledge in both scales outperforms Llama 3 without it.

Incorporating descriptions from Wikidata is particularly helpful for distinguishing answer candidates with the same name (*Bob Dylan* – Q392, *Bob Dylan* – Q251309).

The Llama 3 70B model, augmented with web-search results and descriptions, surpasses all other approaches, including the Llama 3 70B model that was provided with descriptions, web-search results, and a textualized knowledge graph. This implies that incorporating more diverse knowledge might potentially confuse the model, leading to a decrease in performance.

Furthermore, we establish a correlation between the external knowledge utilized and the correctness

Model	UE	Precision	Recall	F1	Accuracy
Llama3 70B	max prob	83.83	82.11	82.96	96.85
	margin prob	84.23	82.50	83.35	96.92
$\text{Baseline}_{\text{chatgpt}}$	–	58.11	78.18	66.67	92.73
$\text{Best}_{\text{private test}}$	–	86.67	85.14	**85.90**	97.39

Table 2: The evaluation results compare two strategies for combining outputs from three Llama 3 70B models, each enhanced with distinct knowledge resources (description, web-search, and knowledge graph). The margin probability strategy involves selecting an answer from the LLM where the difference $p(top_1) - p(top_2)$ is maximum for a given sample. This ensemble strategy surpasses all other aggregation methods, demonstrating that different external knowledge sources can be advantageous for various questions. F1 score serves as the primary competitive metric.

of answers based on their popularity[2] measured on the training set. Consequently, Llama 3 70B, which uses solely entity descriptions as input, accurately classifies approximately 37% of entities with a popularity score below the median and 63% of those with a score equal to or above the median. On the other hand, the model incorporating web-search context in addition to entity descriptions correctly classifies around 45% of less popular entities and 55% of more popular entities, respectively.

What is the best way to combine LLMs with different external knowledge sources? As shown in the Table 1, integrating all three external knowledge sources degrades the performance. Nevertheless, each knowledge resource offers unique information that can be beneficial for answering certain questions while hindering performance on others. Table 2 compares two strategies for combining outputs from three Llama 3 70B models, each fortified with different knowledge resources (description, web-search, and knowledge graph). The **margin probability** approach entails choosing an answer from the LLM where the difference $p(top_1) - p(top_2)$ reaches its maximum for a given sample. This ensemble strategy outperforms alternative aggregation techniques, highlighting that diverse external knowledge sources can be advantageous for distinct questions.

Also worth noting is the contribution of the various data sources to the final results. Using both uncertainty estimations, the proportion of predictions by Llama 3 70B enhanced with knowledge graph is about 10%, and the web-search and description are about 44% and 46% respectively, with the margin probability estimation using slightly fewer predictions made by incorporating web-search.

[2]The popularity is estimated by the number of views of the corresponding Wiki page per month for the first half of 2023.

The proposed method significantly outperforms the ChatGPT-based baseline; however, it still lags behind the top-performing system.

6 Conclusion

In this paper, we detailed the system submitted for the TextGraph-17 workshop, focusing on the development of KGQA system. We introduced a straightforward yet efficient Llama-3-based pipeline. Our study investigated how incorporating external knowledge into a LLM can notably enhance KGQA performance. We showed that a marginal probability combination of three Llama 3 70B models employing different external resources outperforms all baselines and attained a score comparable to the 2nd place in the post-evaluation phase.

For future work, we propose testing various LLMs at different scales and exploring different methods for integrating external knowledge. Additionally, we aim to compare open LLMs with proprietary LLMs. Furthermore, we did not examine the multilabel capability of our solution, and a comprehensive error analysis is essential.

The proposed KBQA approach can be employed independently or integrated within a NLP framework (Burtsev et al., 2018).

Acknowledgments

This work was supported by a grant for research centers, provided by the Analytical Center for the Government of the Russian Federation in accordance with the subsidy agreement (agreement identifier 000000D730324P540002) and the agreement with the Moscow Institute of Physics and Technology dated November 1, 2021 No. 70-2021-00138.

References

AI@Meta. 2024. Llama 3 model card.

Debayan Banerjee, Pranav Ajit Nair, Ricardo Usbeck, and Chris Biemann. 2023. GETT-QA: graph embedding based T2T transformer for knowledge graph question answering. In *The Semantic Web - 20th International Conference, ESWC 2023, Hersonissos, Crete, Greece, May 28 - June 1, 2023, Proceedings*, volume 13870 of *Lecture Notes in Computer Science*, pages 279–297. Springer.

Mikhail Burtsev, Alexander Seliverstov, Rafael Airapetyan, Mikhail Arkhipov, Dilyara Baymurzina, Nickolay Bushkov, Olga Gureenkova, Taras Khakhulin, Yuri Kuratov, Denis Kuznetsov, and Vasily Konovalov. 2018. Deeppavlov: An open source library for conversational ai. In *NIPS*.

Viktoria Chekalina, Anton Razzhigaev, Albert Sayapin, and Alexander Panchenko. 2022. MEKER: memory efficient knowledge embedding representation for link prediction and question answering. *CoRR*, abs/2204.10629.

Ekaterina Fadeeva, Roman Vashurin, Akim Tsvigun, Artem Vazhentsev, Sergey Petrakov, Kirill Fedyanin, Daniil Vasilev, Elizaveta Goncharova, Alexander Panchenko, Maxim Panov, Timothy Baldwin, and Artem Shelmanov. 2023. Lm-polygraph: Uncertainty estimation for language models. In *Proceedings of the 2023 Conference on Empirical Methods in Natural Language Processing, EMNLP 2023 - System Demonstrations, Singapore, December 6-10, 2023*, pages 446–461. Association for Computational Linguistics.

Xiao Huang, Jingyuan Zhang, Dingcheng Li, and Ping Li. 2019. Knowledge graph embedding based question answering. In *Proceedings of the Twelfth ACM International Conference on Web Search and Data Mining*, WSDM '19, page 105–113, New York, NY, USA. Association for Computing Machinery.

Gautier Izacard and Edouard Grave. 2021. Leveraging passage retrieval with generative models for open domain question answering. In *Proceedings of the 16th Conference of the European Chapter of the Association for Computational Linguistics: Main Volume, EACL 2021, Online, April 19 - 23, 2021*, pages 874–880. Association for Computational Linguistics.

Lorenz Kuhn, Yarin Gal, and Sebastian Farquhar. 2023. Semantic uncertainty: Linguistic invariances for uncertainty estimation in natural language generation. In *The Eleventh International Conference on Learning Representations, ICLR 2023, Kigali, Rwanda, May 1-5, 2023*. OpenReview.net.

Tom Kwiatkowski, Jennimaria Palomaki, Olivia Redfield, Michael Collins, Ankur P. Parikh, Chris Alberti, Danielle Epstein, Illia Polosukhin, Jacob Devlin, Kenton Lee, Kristina Toutanova, Llion Jones, Matthew Kelcey, Ming-Wei Chang, Andrew M. Dai, Jakob Uszkoreit, Quoc Le, and Slav Petrov. 2019. Natural questions: a benchmark for question answering research. *Trans. Assoc. Comput. Linguistics*, 7:452–466.

Ivan Maksimov, Vasily Konovalov, and Andrei Glinskii. 2024. DeepPavlov at SemEval-2024 task 6: Detection of hallucinations and overgeneration mistakes with an ensemble of transformer-based models. In *Proceedings of the 18th International Workshop on Semantic Evaluation (SemEval-2024)*, pages 274–278, Mexico City, Mexico. Association for Computational Linguistics.

Barlas Oguz, Xilun Chen, Vladimir Karpukhin, Stan Peshterliev, Dmytro Okhonko, Michael Sejr Schlichtkrull, Sonal Gupta, Yashar Mehdad, and Scott Yih. 2022. Unik-qa: Unified representations of structured and unstructured knowledge for open-domain question answering. In *Findings of the Association for Computational Linguistics: NAACL 2022, Seattle, WA, United States, July 10-15, 2022*, pages 1535–1546. Association for Computational Linguistics.

Vaishali S Parsania, Foram Kalyani, and Krunal Kamani. 2016. A comparative analysis: Duckduckgo vs. google search engine. *GRD Journals-Global Research and Development Journal for Engineering*, 2(1):12–17.

Haitian Sun, Tania Bedrax-Weiss, and William Cohen. 2019. PullNet: Open domain question answering with iterative retrieval on knowledge bases and text. In *Proceedings of the 2019 Conference on Empirical Methods in Natural Language Processing and the 9th International Joint Conference on Natural Language Processing (EMNLP-IJCNLP)*, pages 2380–2390, Hong Kong, China. Association for Computational Linguistics.

Haitian Sun, Bhuwan Dhingra, Manzil Zaheer, Kathryn Mazaitis, Ruslan Salakhutdinov, and William Cohen. 2018. Open domain question answering using early fusion of knowledge bases and text. In *Proceedings of the 2018 Conference on Empirical Methods in Natural Language Processing*, pages 4231–4242, Brussels, Belgium. Association for Computational Linguistics.

Alon Talmor and Jonathan Berant. 2018. The web as a knowledge-base for answering complex questions. In *Proceedings of the 2018 Conference of the North American Chapter of the Association for Computational Linguistics: Human Language Technologies, NAACL-HLT 2018, New Orleans, Louisiana, USA, June 1-6, 2018, Volume 1 (Long Papers)*, pages 641–651. Association for Computational Linguistics.

Yike Wu, Nan Hu, Sheng Bi, Guilin Qi, Jie Ren, Anhuan Xie, and Wei Song. 2023. Retrieve-rewrite-answer: A kg-to-text enhanced llms framework for knowledge graph question answering. *CoRR*, abs/2309.11206.

Zhiyuan Zhang, Xiaoqian Liu, Yi Zhang, Qi Su, Xu Sun, and Bin He. 2020. Pretrain-KGE: Learning knowledge representation from pretrained language models. In *Findings of the Association for Computational Linguistics: EMNLP 2020*, pages 259–266, Online. Association for Computational Linguistics.

A Prompts

Prompt with web-search context

You are a helpful assistant. You must follow the rules before answering:
- A question and its answer options will be provided.
- The question has only one correct option.
- The correct answer is always given.
- Write only the number of the correct option.
- If you do not know the answer, write only the number of the most likely one.

Below are the facts that might be relevant to answer the question:
1. Review by Karin Tanabe. October 18, 2023 at 11:00 a.m. John Grisham ...
2. Some of his most famous books include ...
If there is no relevant fact, rely on your knowledge or choose a more likely option.

Question:
"After publishing A Time to Kill, which book did its author begin working on immediately?"
Options:
0. {"answer": "A Feast for Crows", "WikiDataID": "Q1764445"}
1. {"answer": "Fear and Loathing in Las Vegas", "WikiDataID": "Q772435"}...

Prompt with textualized graph

You are a helpful assistant. You must follow the rules before answering:
- A question and its answer options will be provided.
- The question has only one correct option.
- The correct answer is always given.
- Write only the number of the correct option.
- If you do not know the answer, write only the number of the most likely one.

Question:
"In Harry Potter literature series wrote by J.K. Rowling, which follows Harry Potter and the Philosopher's Stone?"
Options:
0. {"answer": "Half-blood Prince", "WikiDataID": "Q10355035", "WikiDataGraph": "Harry Potter and the Half-Blood Prince is a book in the Harry Potter universe, written by J. K. Rowling and part of the Harry Potter series..."}
1. {"answer": "Harry Potter", "WikiDataID": "Q8337", "WikiDataGraph": "J. K. Rowling wrote Harry Potter and Harry Potter and the Sorcerer's Stone..."}...

Author Index

Association for Computational Linguistics
209 N. Eighth Street
Stroudsburg, Pennsylvania 18360

CURRAN ASSOCIATES INC.
proceedings.com

ISBN 979-8-3313-0180-4

9 798331 301804